Fruits Basket™

Volume 9

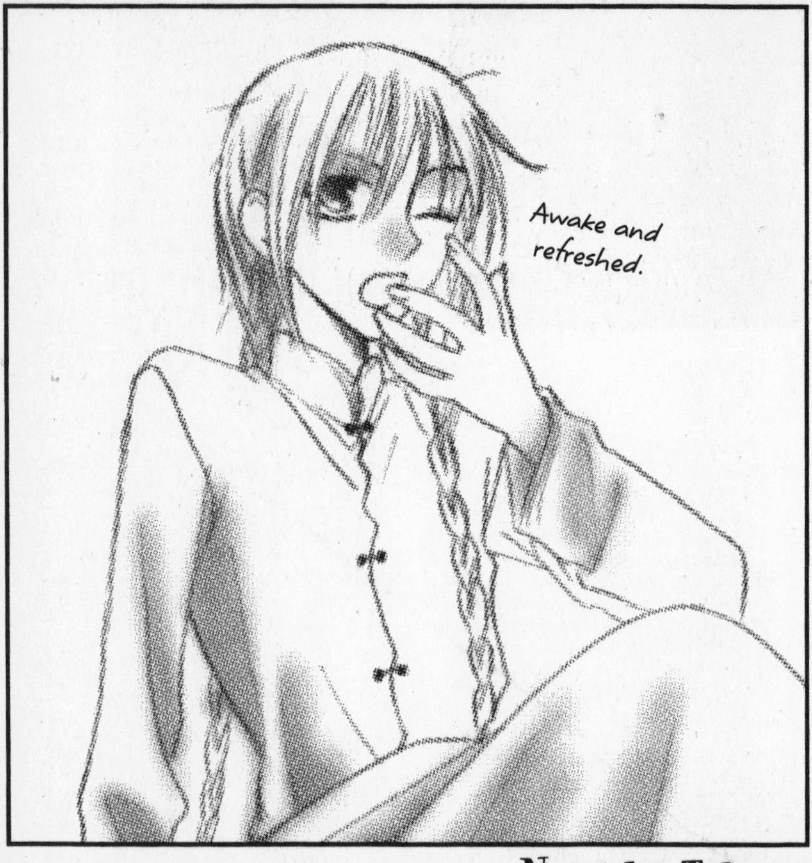
Awake and refreshed.

Natsuki Takaya

Fruits Basket Vol. 9
Created by Natsuki Takaya

Translation - Alethea Nibley and Athena Nibley
English Adaptation - Jake Forbes
Contributing Writer - Adam Arnold
Associate Editor - Peter Ahlstrom
Retouch and Lettering - Deron Bennett
Production Artists - Jose Macasocol, Jr. and Jason Milligan
Cover Design - Gary Shum

r - Paul Morrissey
r - Chris Buford
r - Antonio DePietro
s - Jennifer Miller and Mutsumi Miyazaki
r - Matt Alford
r - Jill Freshney
n - Ron Klamert
f - Mike Kiley
. - John Parker
. - Stuart Levy

 **KYOPOP**® Manga

TOKYOPOP Inc.
5900 Wilshire Blvd. Suite 2000
Los Angeles, CA 90036

E-mail: info@TOKYOPOP.com
Come visit us online at www.TOKYOPOP.com

ISBN: 1-59532-404-6

First TOKYOPOP printing: June 2005
10 9 8 7 6 5 4
Printed in the USA

Fruits Basket

Volume 9

By
Natsuki Takaya

HAMBURG // LONDON // LOS ANGELES // TOKYO

Fruits Basket™

Table of Contents

STORY SO FAR...

Hello, I'm Tohru Honda and I have come to know a terrible secret. After the death of my mother, I was living by myself in a tent, when the Sohma family took me in. I soon learned that the Sohma family lives with a curse! Each family member is possessed by the vengeful spirit of an animal from the Chinese Zodiac. Whenever one of them becomes weak or is hugged by a member of the opposite sex, they change into their Zodiac animal!

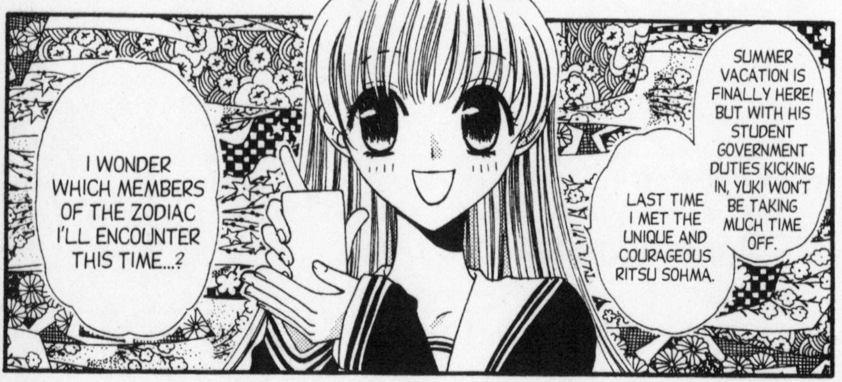
SUMMER VACATION IS FINALLY HERE! BUT WITH HIS STUDENT GOVERNMENT DUTIES KICKING IN, YUKI WON'T BE TAKING MUCH TIME OFF.
LAST TIME I MET THE UNIQUE AND COURAGEOUS RITSU SOHMA.
I WONDER WHICH MEMBERS OF THE ZODIAC I'LL ENCOUNTER THIS TIME...?

Tohru Honda

The ever-optimistic hero of our story. An orphan, she now lives in Shigure's house, along with Yuki and Kyo, and is the only person outside of the family who knows the Sohma family's curse.

Yuki Sohma, the Rat

Soft-spoken. Self-esteem issues. At school he's called "Prince Yuki."

Kyo Sohma, the Cat

The Cat who was left out of the Zodiac. Hates Yuki, leeks and miso. But mostly Yuki.

Kagura Sohma, the Boar

Bashful, yet headstrong. Determined to marry Kyo, even if it kills him.

Fruits Basket Characters

Mabudachi Trio

Shigure Sohma, the Dog

Enigmatic, mischievous and a little perverted. A popular novelist.

Hatori Sohma, the Dragon

Family doctor to the Sohmas. Only thing he can't cure is his broken heart.

Ayame Sohma, the Snake

Yuki's older brother. A proud and playful drama queen…er, king. Runs a costume shop.

Saki Hanajima

"Hana-chan." Can sense people's "waves." Goth demeanor scares her classmates.

Arisa Uotani

"Uo-chan." A tough-talking "Yankee" who looks out for her friends.

Tohru's Best Friends

Momiji Sohma, the Rabbit

Half-German. He's older than he looks.
Mother rejected him because of the Sohma curse.

Hatsuharu Sohma, the Ox

The nicest of guys, except when he goes "Black."
Then you'd better watch out.

Kisa Sohma, the Tiger

Kisa became shy and self-conscious due to constant
teasing by her classmates. Yuki, who has similar
insecurities, feels particularly close to Kisa.

Fruits Basket Characters

Hiro Sohma, the Ram (or sheep)

This caustic tyke is skilled at throwing verbal barbs, but he has a soft spot for Kisa.

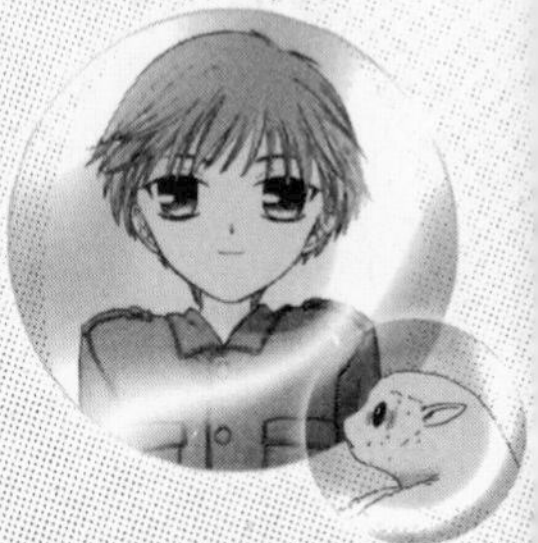

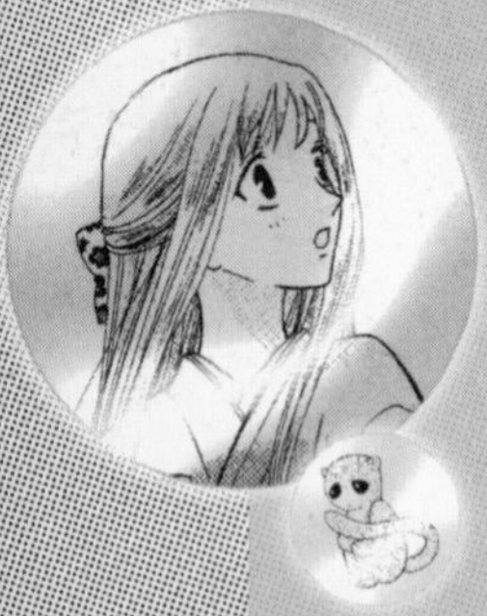

Ritsu Sohma, the Monkey

This shy kimono-wearing memeber of the Sohma family is gorgeous. But this "she" is really a he!! Crossdressing calms his nerves.

Akito Sohma

The head of the Sohma clan. A dark figure of many secrets. Treated with fear and reverence.

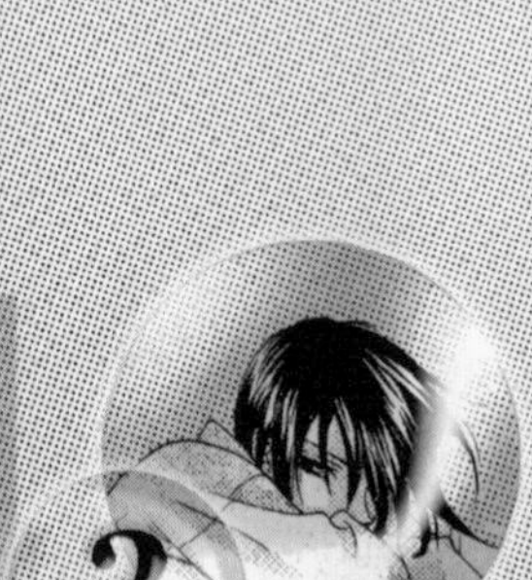
?

Fruits Basket™

Chapter 49

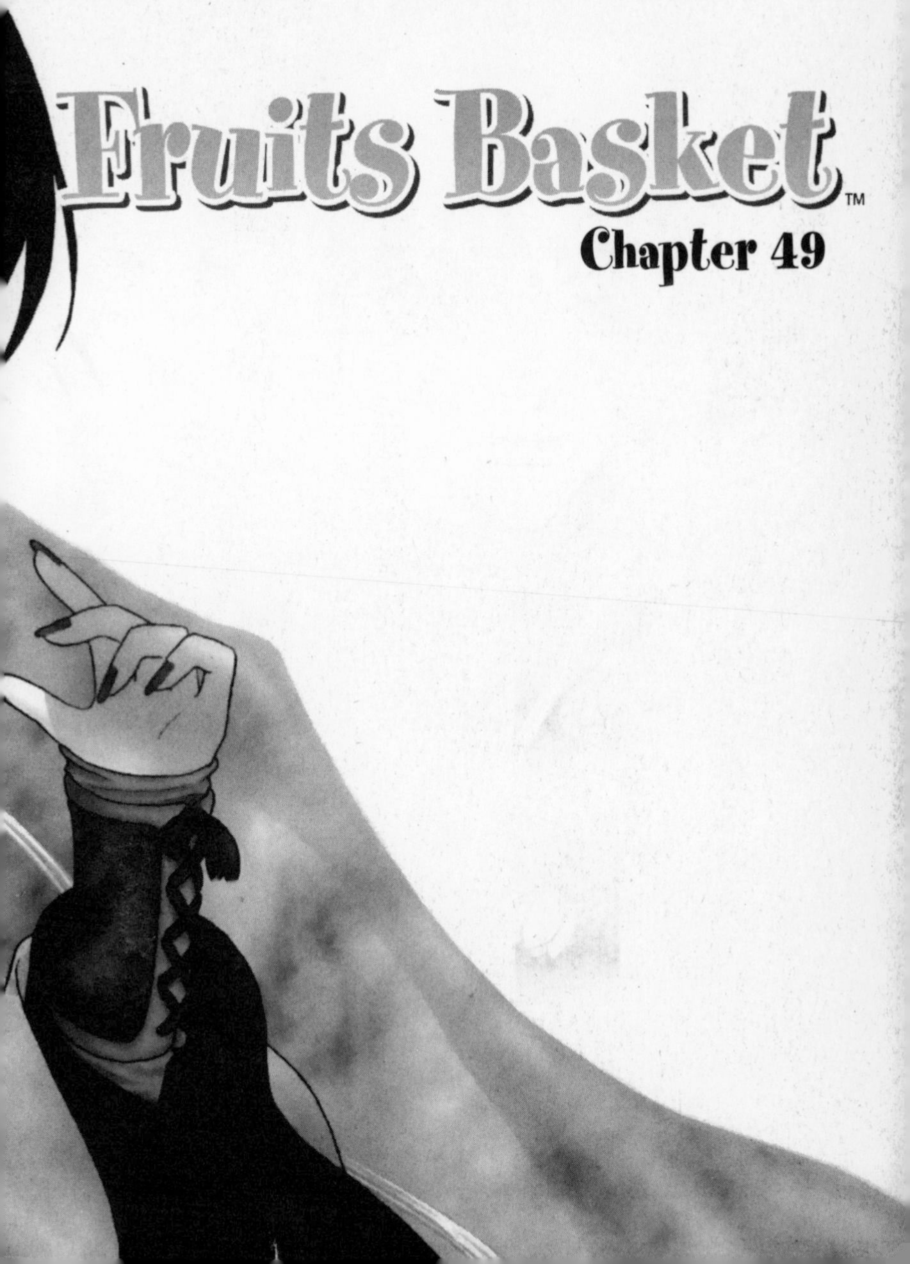

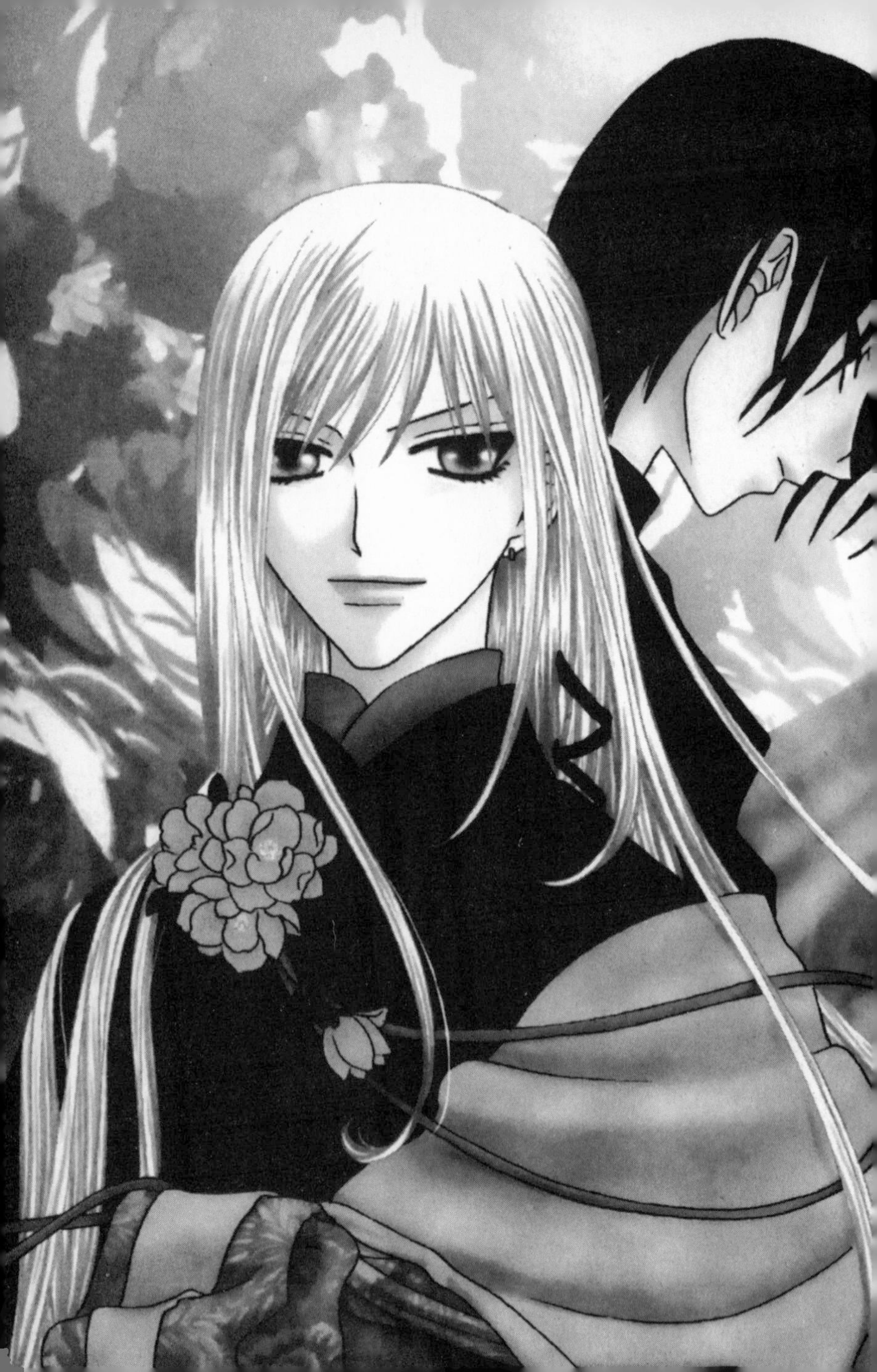

Filler
sketch

Tee
Hee!

His identity will become clear in Chapter 49. Read on...

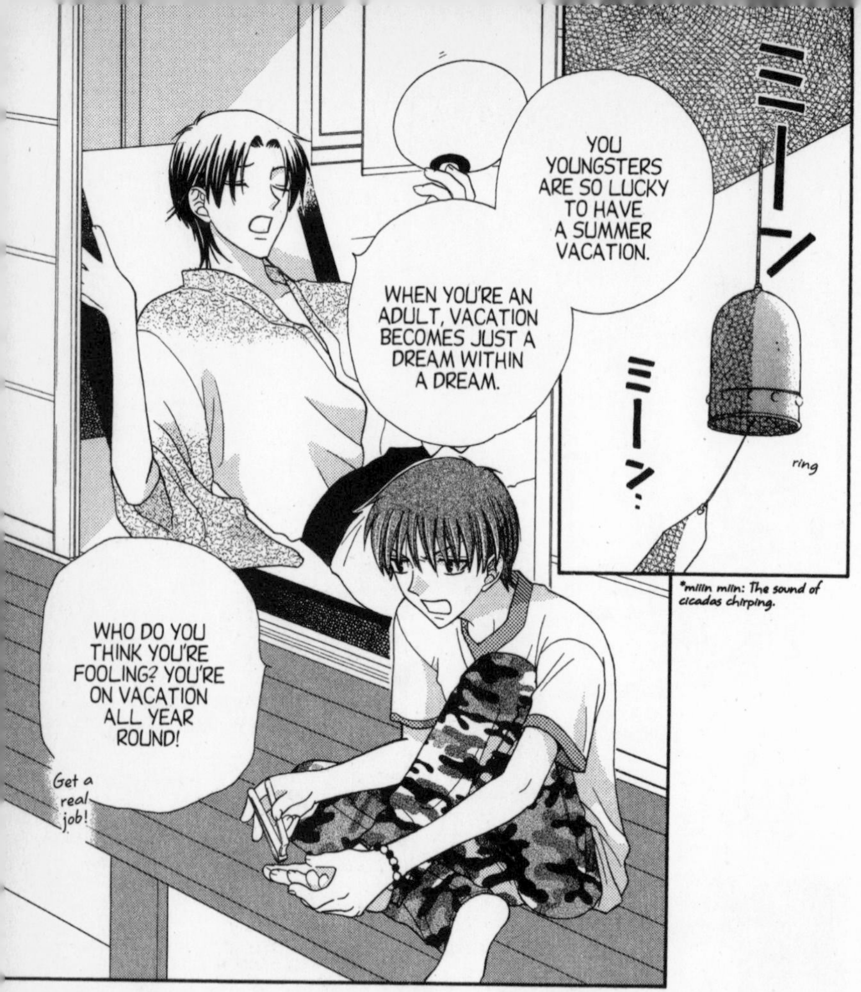
YOU YOUNGSTERS ARE SO LUCKY TO HAVE A SUMMER VACATION.
WHEN YOU'RE AN ADULT, VACATION BECOMES JUST A DREAM WITHIN A DREAM.
ring
WHO DO YOU THINK YOU'RE FOOLING? YOU'RE ON VACATION ALL YEAR ROUND!
Get a real job!

*miin miin: The sound of cicadas chirping.

BLAH, BLAH, BLAH 1

The title keeps getting shorter and shorter. (Pretty soon there won't be any title left at all.) Finally members of the student council (two of them) make an appearance. There won't be any more of them for a while, though.

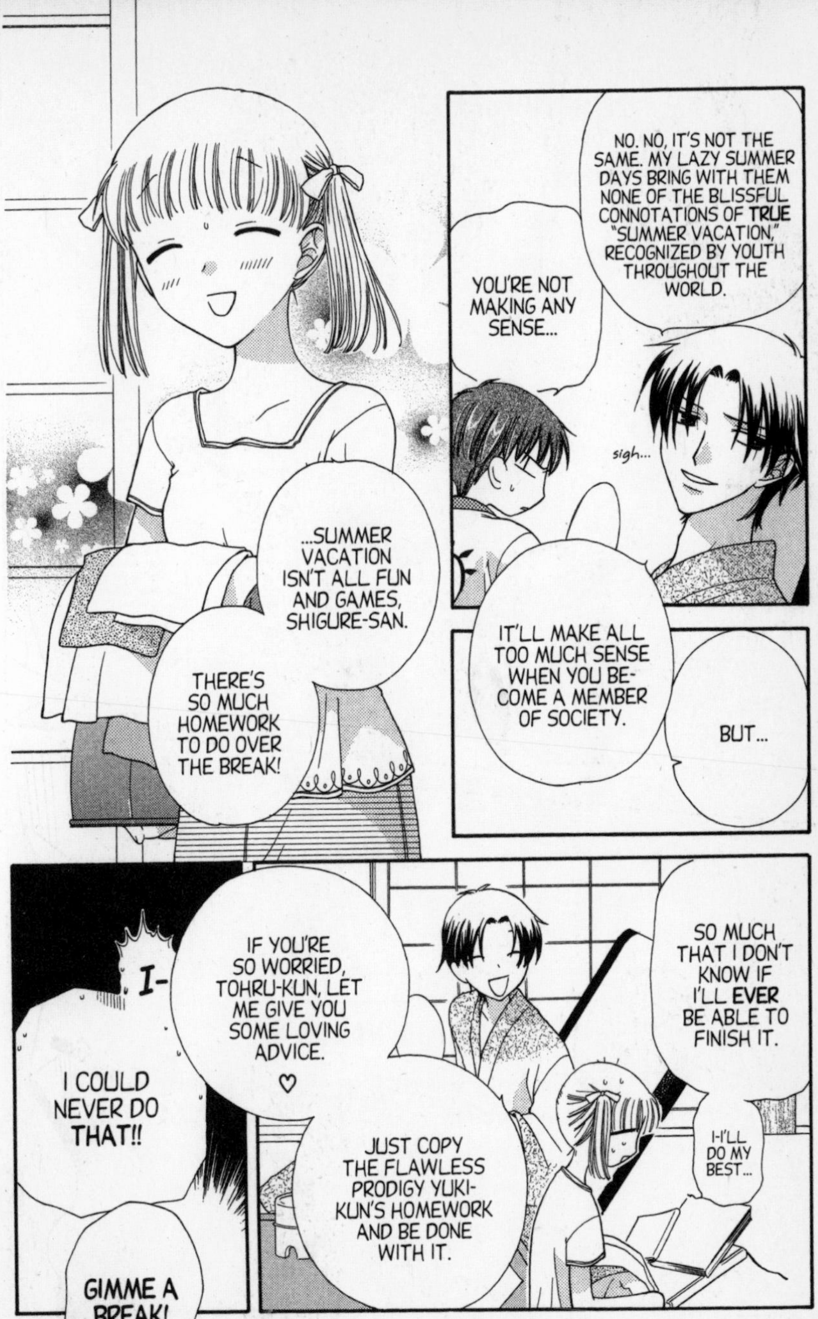
NO. NO, IT'S NOT THE SAME. MY LAZY SUMMER DAYS BRING WITH THEM NONE OF THE BLISSFUL CONNOTATIONS OF TRUE "SUMMER VACATION," RECOGNIZED BY YOUTH THROUGHOUT THE WORLD.
YOU'RE NOT MAKING ANY SENSE...
sigh...
BUT...
IT'LL MAKE ALL TOO MUCH SENSE WHEN YOU BE-COME A MEMBER OF SOCIETY.
...SUMMER VACATION ISN'T ALL FUN AND GAMES, SHIGURE-SAN.
THERE'S SO MUCH HOMEWORK TO DO OVER THE BREAK!
SO MUCH THAT I DON'T KNOW IF I'LL EVER BE ABLE TO FINISH IT.
I-I'LL DO MY BEST...
IF YOU'RE SO WORRIED, TOHRU-KUN, LET ME GIVE YOU SOME LOVING ADVICE. ♡
JUST COPY THE FLAWLESS PRODIGY YUKI-KUN'S HOMEWORK AND BE DONE WITH IT.
I-
I COULD NEVER DO THAT!!
GIMME A BREAK!

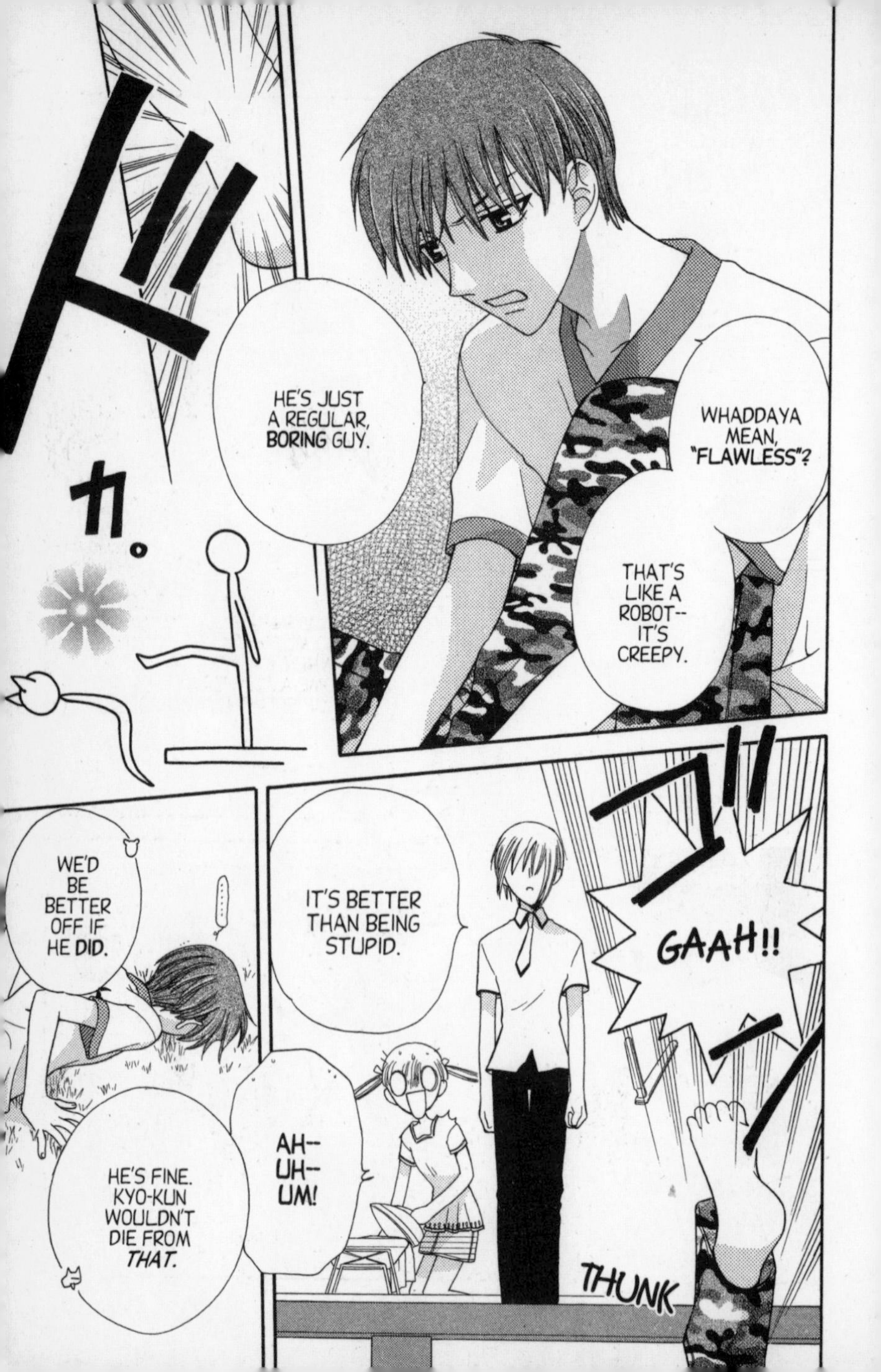
WHADDAYA MEAN, "FLAWLESS"?
THAT'S LIKE A ROBOT-- IT'S CREEPY.
HE'S JUST A REGULAR, BORING GUY.
ド
カ。
ゴ
GAAH!!
IT'S BETTER THAN BEING STUPID.
THUNK
AH-- UH-- UM!
WE'D BE BETTER OFF IF HE DID.
...
HE'S FINE. KYO-KUN WOULDN'T DIE FROM THAT.

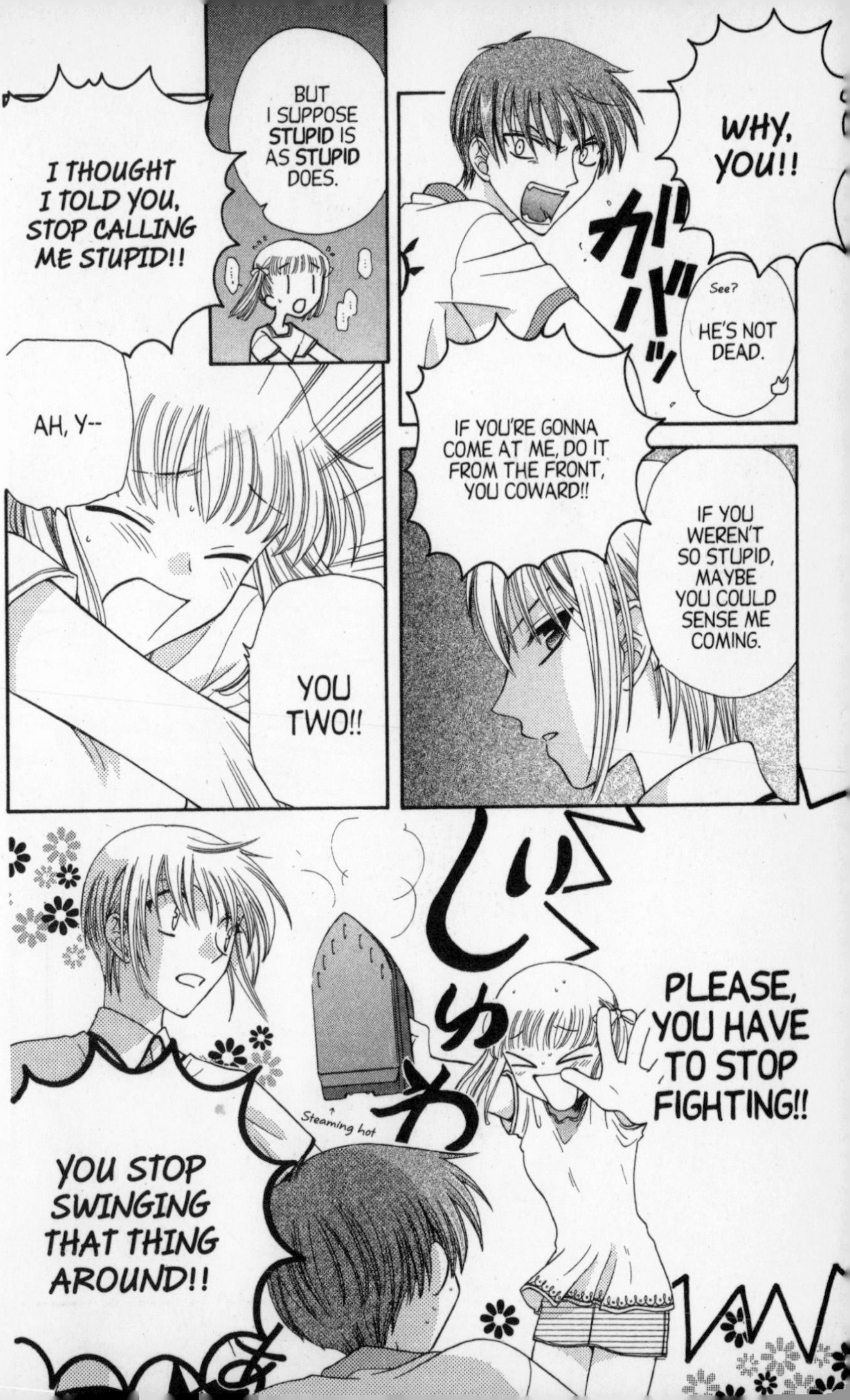
WHY, YOU!!
ガバッ
See?
HE'S NOT DEAD.
I THOUGHT I TOLD YOU, STOP CALLING ME STUPID!!
BUT I SUPPOSE STUPID IS AS STUPID DOES.
IF YOU'RE GONNA COME AT ME, DO IT FROM THE FRONT, YOU COWARD!!
IF YOU WEREN'T SO STUPID, MAYBE YOU COULD SENSE ME COMING.
AH, Y--
YOU TWO!!
じゅわ
PLEASE, YOU HAVE TO STOP FIGHTING!!
Steaming hot
YOU STOP SWINGING THAT THING AROUND!!

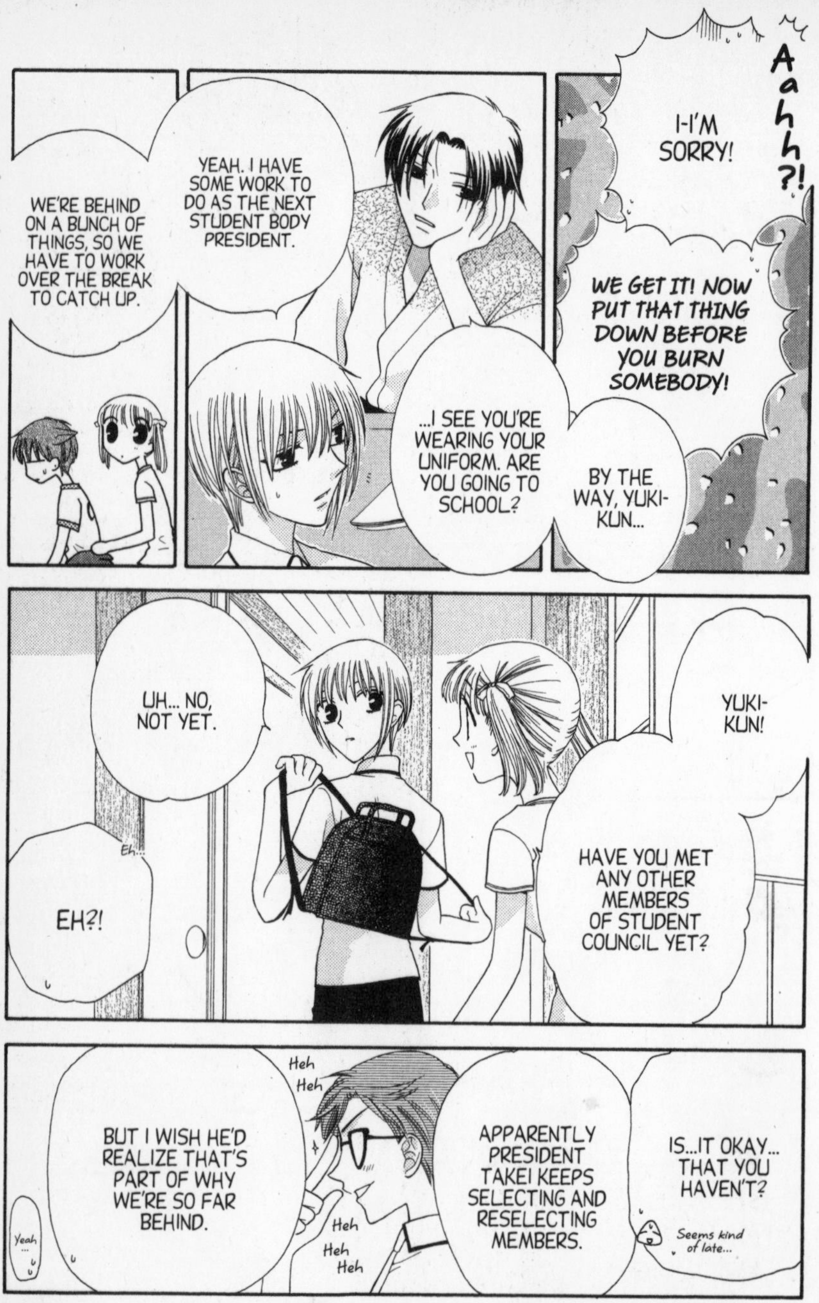
Aahh?!
I-I'M SORRY!
WE GET IT! NOW PUT THAT THING DOWN BEFORE YOU BURN SOMEBODY!
BY THE WAY, YUKI-KUN...
...I SEE YOU'RE WEARING YOUR UNIFORM. ARE YOU GOING TO SCHOOL?
YEAH. I HAVE SOME WORK TO DO AS THE NEXT STUDENT BODY PRESIDENT.
WE'RE BEHIND ON A BUNCH OF THINGS, SO WE HAVE TO WORK OVER THE BREAK TO CATCH UP.
YUKI-KUN!
HAVE YOU MET ANY OTHER MEMBERS OF STUDENT COUNCIL YET?
UH... NO, NOT YET.
Eh...
EH?!
IS...IT OKAY... THAT YOU HAVEN'T?
Seems kind of late...
APPARENTLY PRESIDENT TAKEI KEEPS SELECTING AND RESELECTING MEMBERS.
Heh Heh
Heh Heh Heh
BUT I WISH HE'D REALIZE THAT'S PART OF WHY WE'RE SO FAR BEHIND.
Yeah...

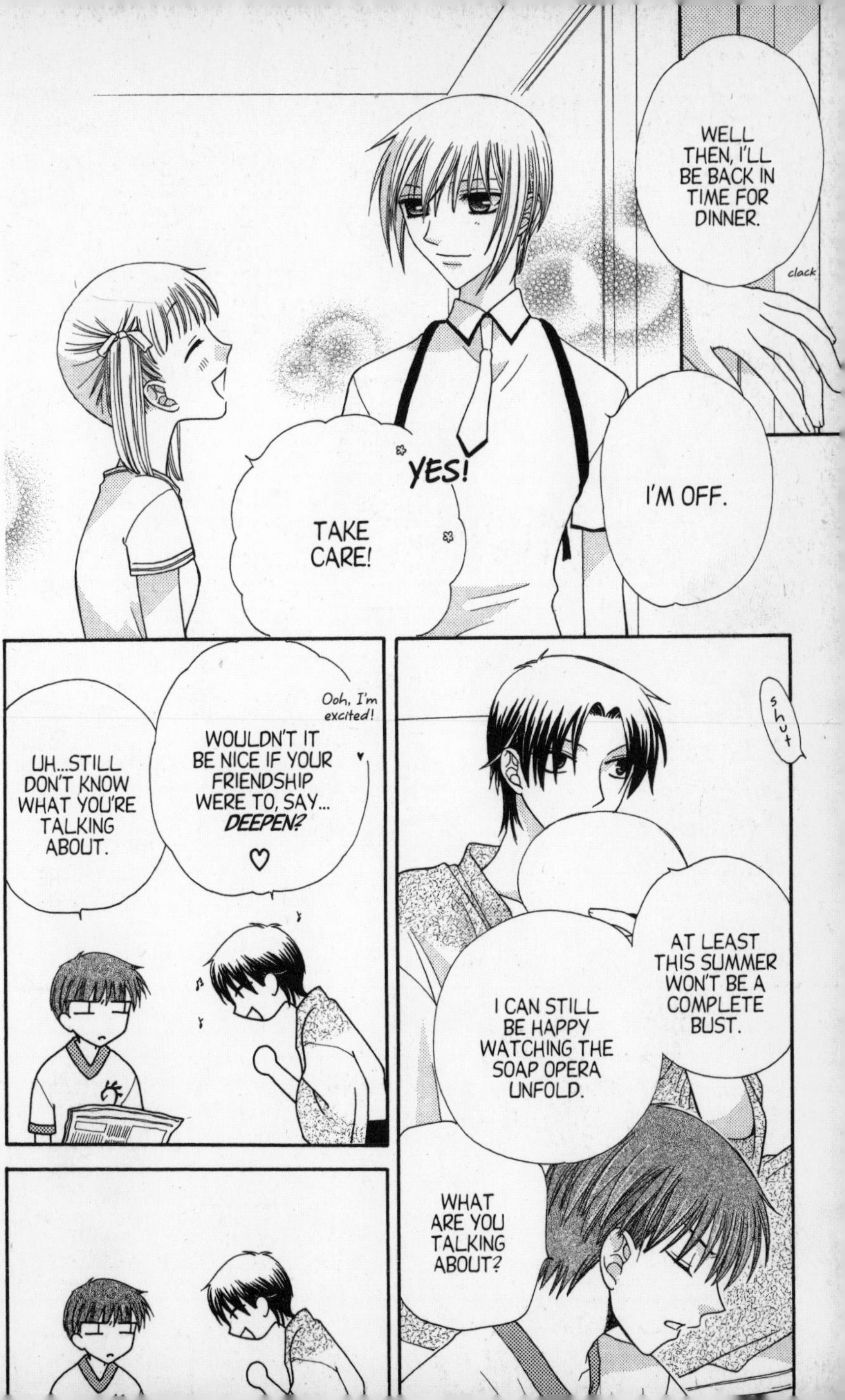
WELL THEN, I'LL BE BACK IN TIME FOR DINNER.
clack
I'M OFF.
YES!
TAKE CARE!
shut
AT LEAST THIS SUMMER WON'T BE A COMPLETE BUST.
I CAN STILL BE HAPPY WATCHING THE SOAP OPERA UNFOLD.
WHAT ARE YOU TALKING ABOUT?
Ooh, I'm excited!
WOULDN'T IT BE NICE IF YOUR FRIENDSHIP WERE TO, SAY... *DEEPEN?* ♡
UH...STILL DON'T KNOW WHAT YOU'RE TALKING ABOUT.

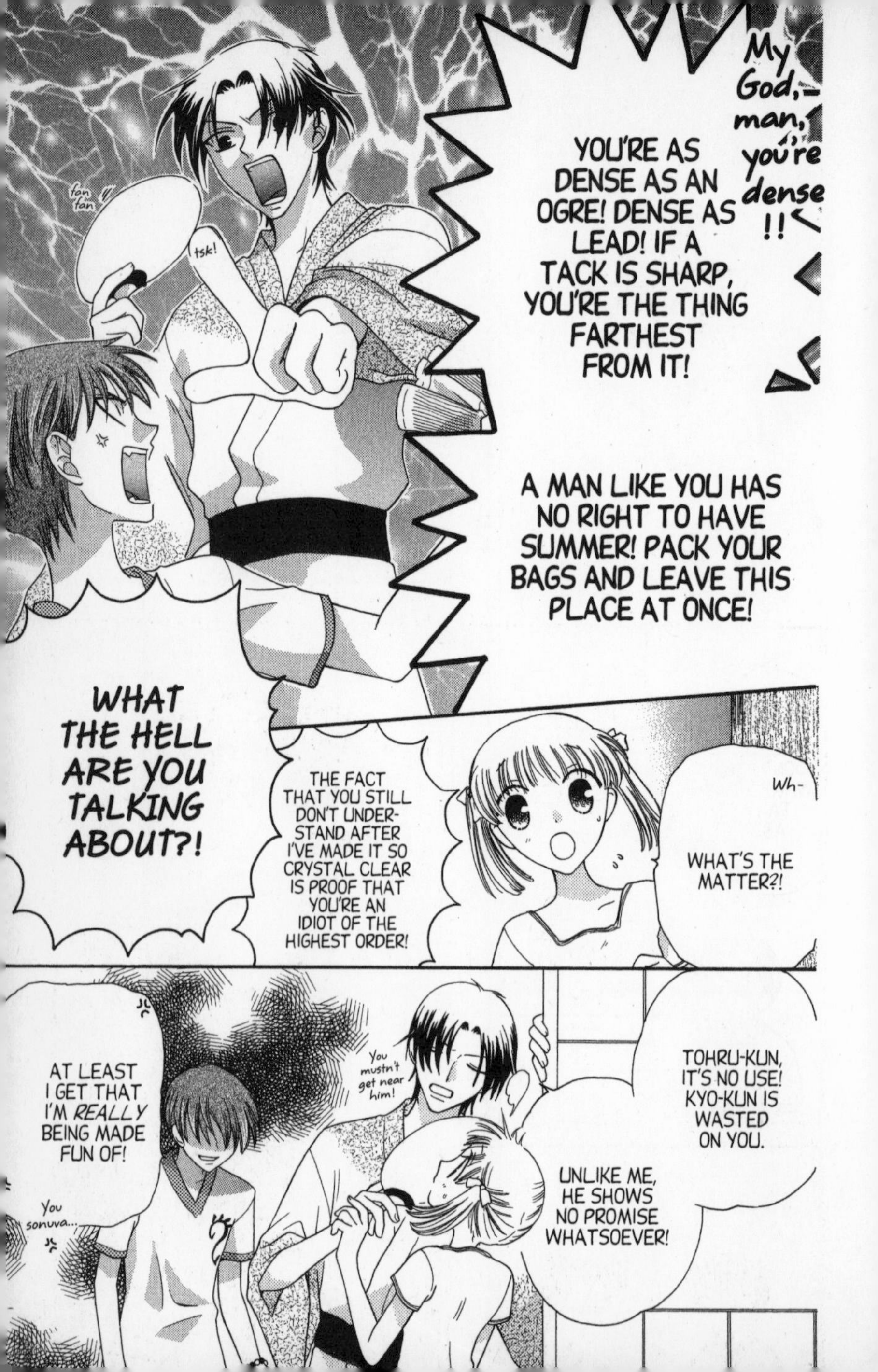
My God,- man, you're dense !!
YOU'RE AS DENSE AS AN OGRE! DENSE AS LEAD! IF A TACK IS SHARP, YOU'RE THE THING FARTHEST FROM IT!
fan fan
tsk!
A MAN LIKE YOU HAS NO RIGHT TO HAVE SUMMER! PACK YOUR BAGS AND LEAVE THIS PLACE AT ONCE!
WHAT THE HELL ARE YOU TALKING ABOUT?!
Wh-
WHAT'S THE MATTER?!
THE FACT THAT YOU STILL DON'T UNDER-STAND AFTER I'VE MADE IT SO CRYSTAL CLEAR IS PROOF THAT YOU'RE AN IDIOT OF THE HIGHEST ORDER!
TOHRU-KUN, IT'S NO USE! KYO-KUN IS WASTED ON YOU.
UNLIKE ME, HE SHOWS NO PROMISE WHATSOEVER!
You mustn't get near him!
AT LEAST I GET THAT I'M *REALLY* BEING MADE FUN OF!
You sonuva...

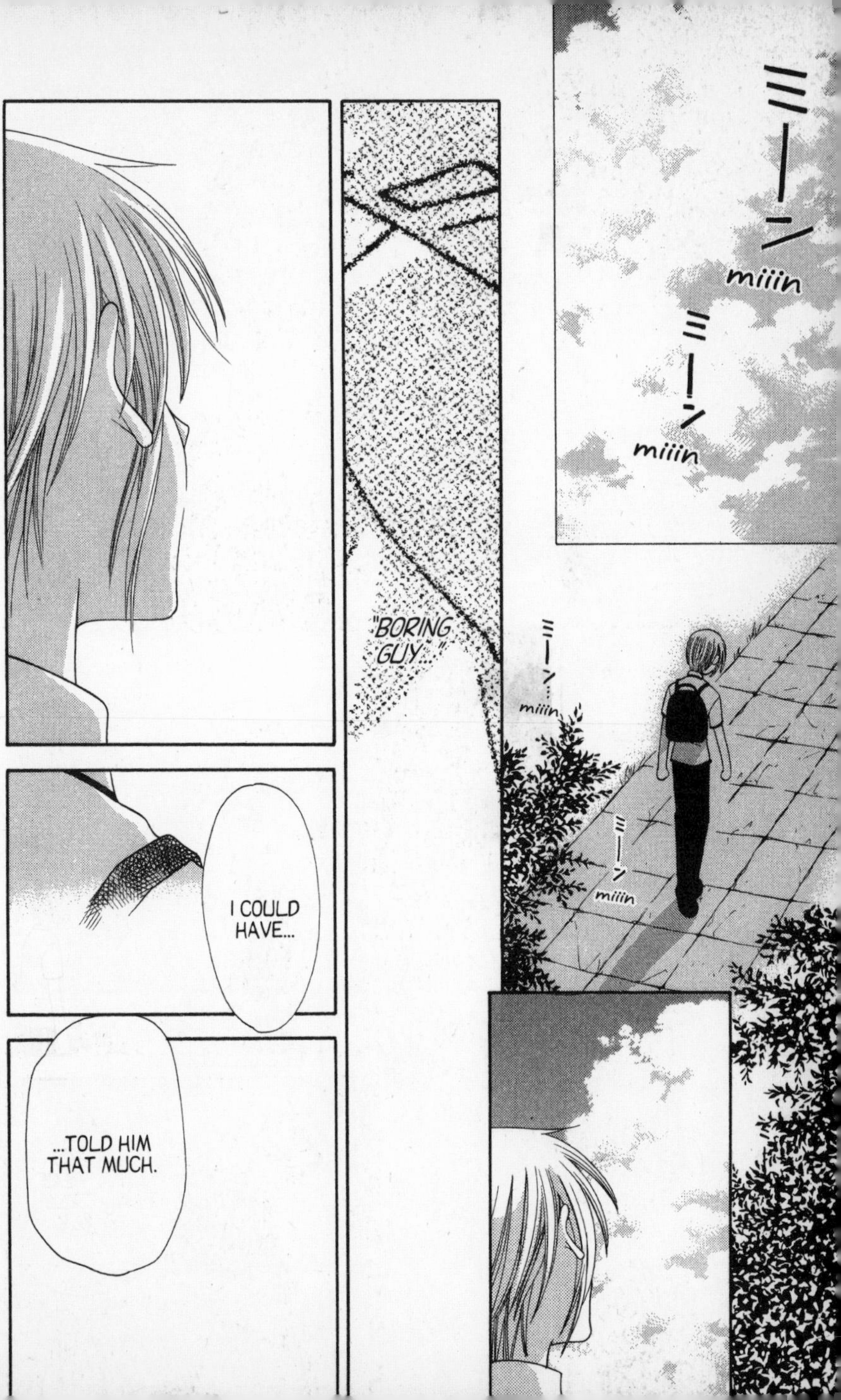
ミーン
miiin
ミーン
miiin
ミーン…
miiin
ミーン
miiin
"BORING GUY..."
I COULD HAVE...
...TOLD HIM THAT MUCH.

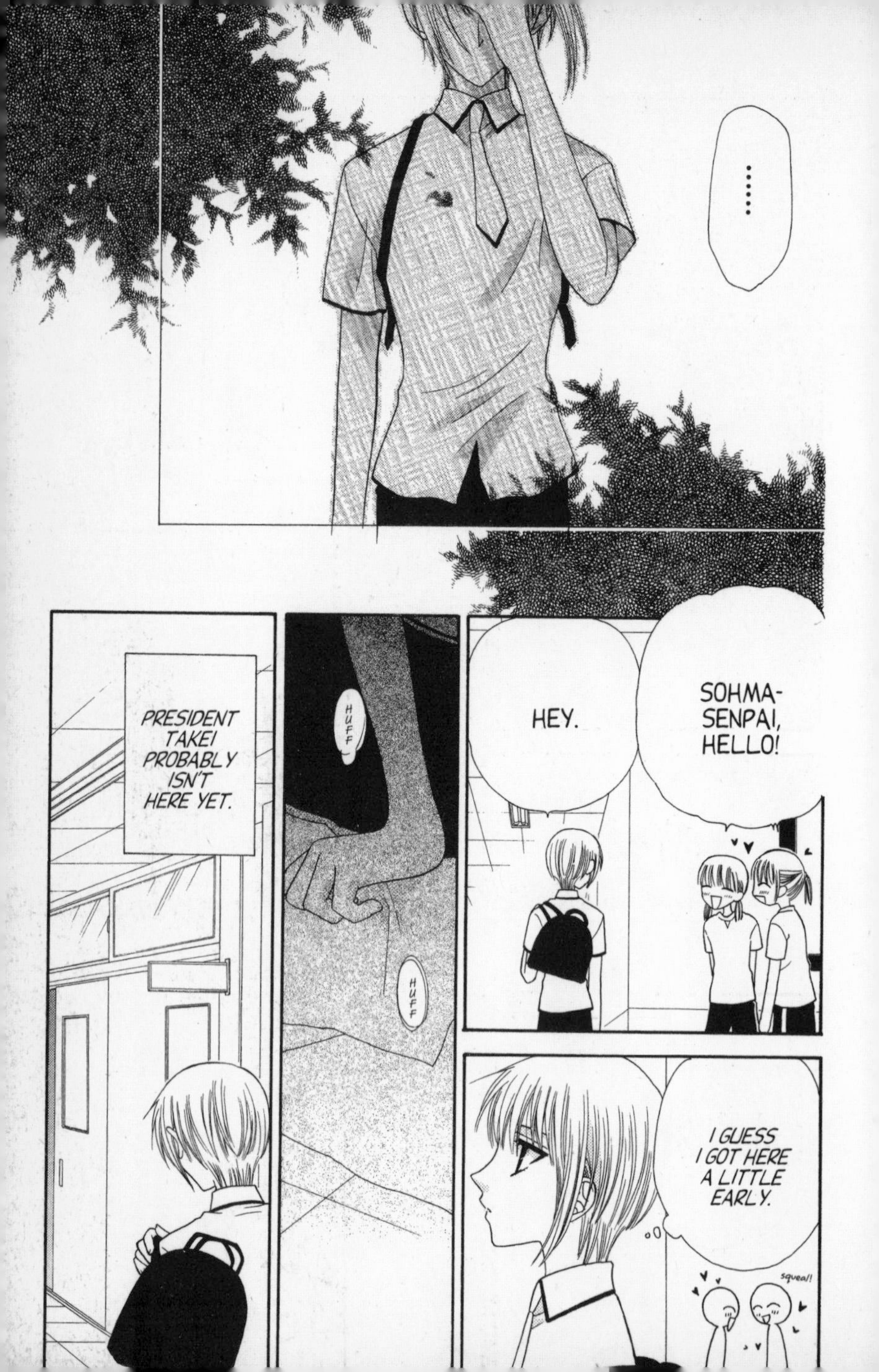
……
SOHMA-SENPAI, HELLO!
HEY.
I GUESS I GOT HERE A LITTLE EARLY.
squeal!
HUFF
HUFF
PRESIDENT TAKEI PROBABLY ISN'T HERE YET.

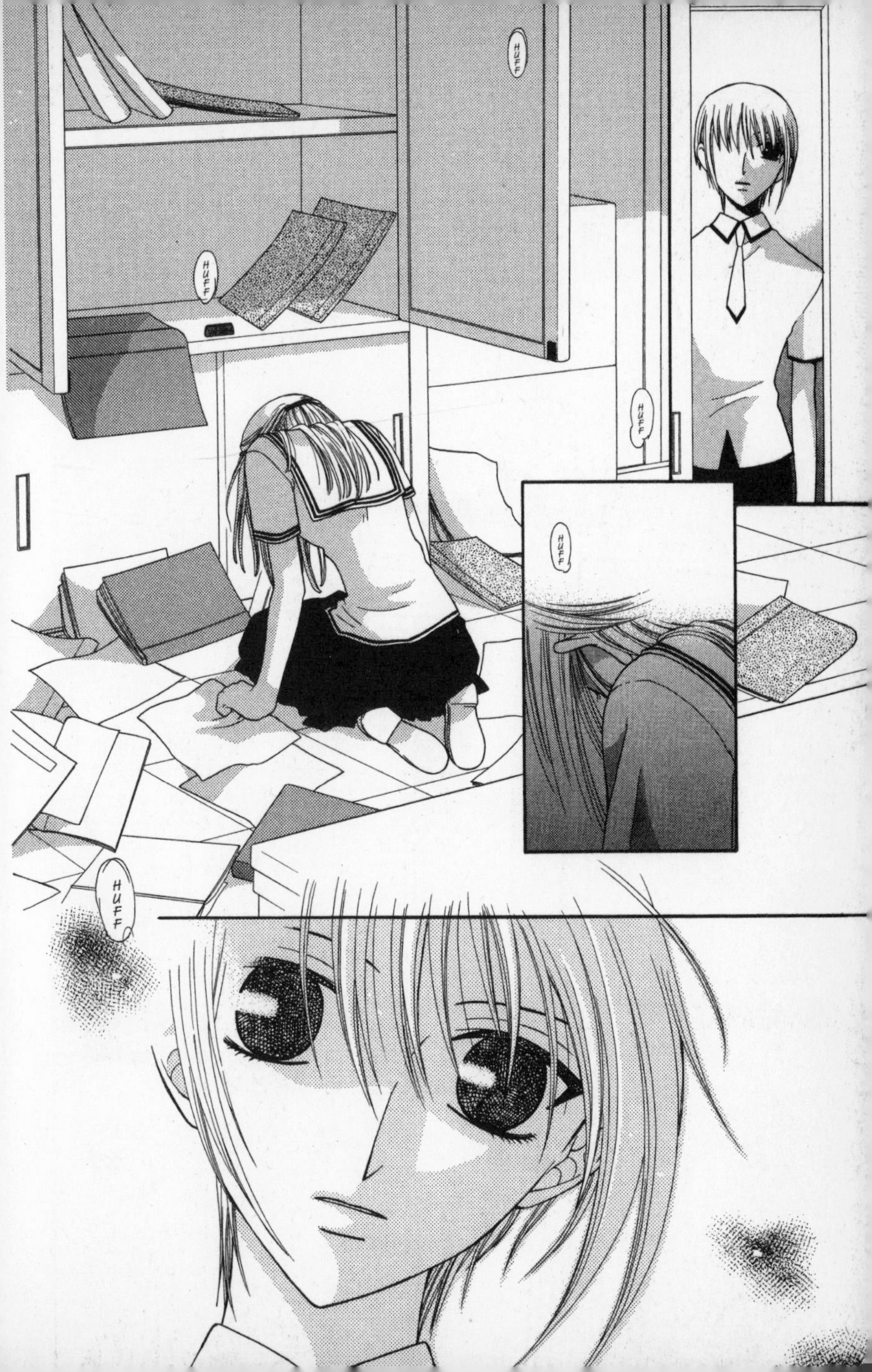
HUFF
HUFF
HUFF
HUFF
HUFF

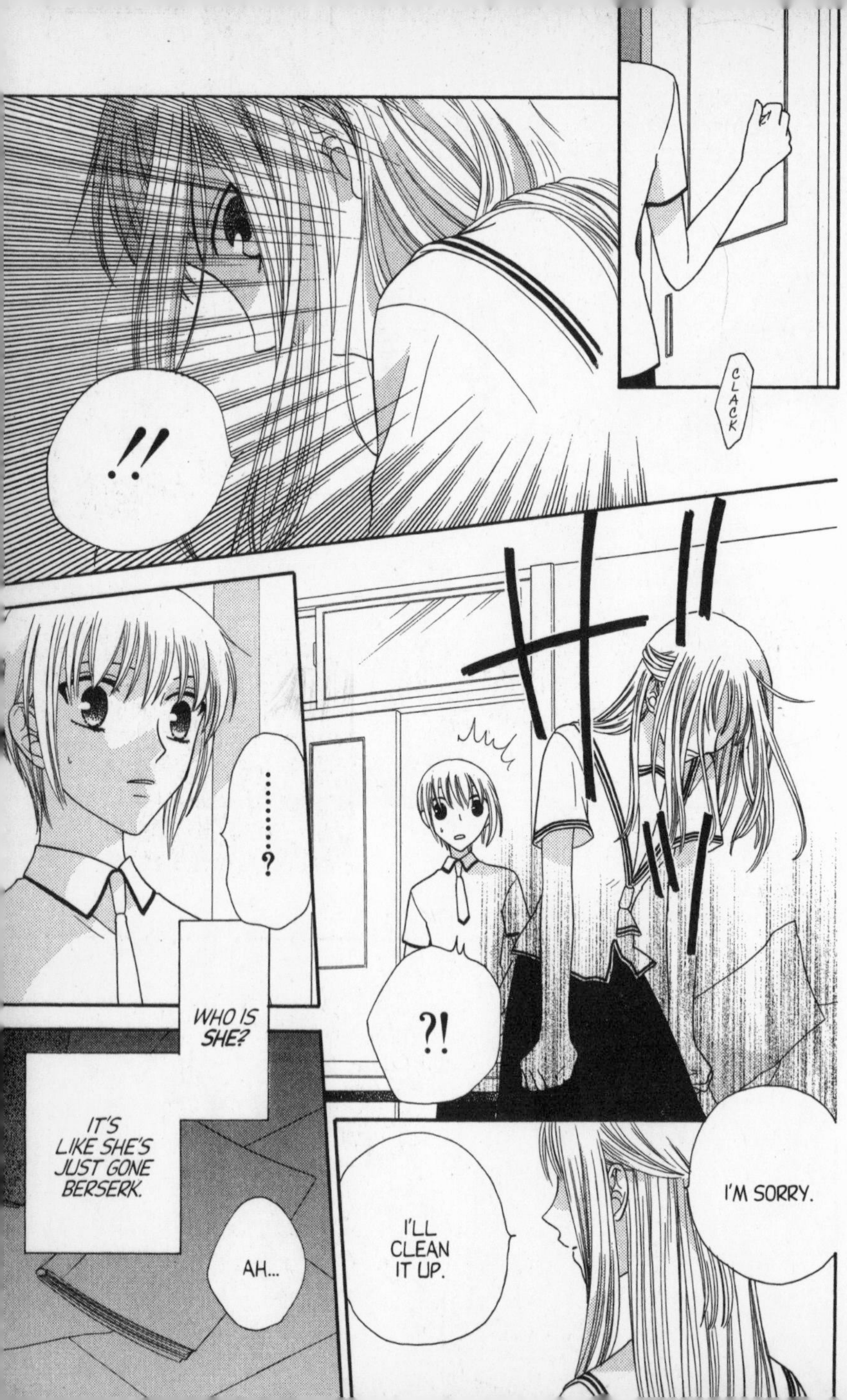
CLACK
!!
?!
......?
WHO IS SHE?
I'M SORRY.
I'LL CLEAN IT UP.
IT'S LIKE SHE'S JUST GONE BERSERK.
AH...

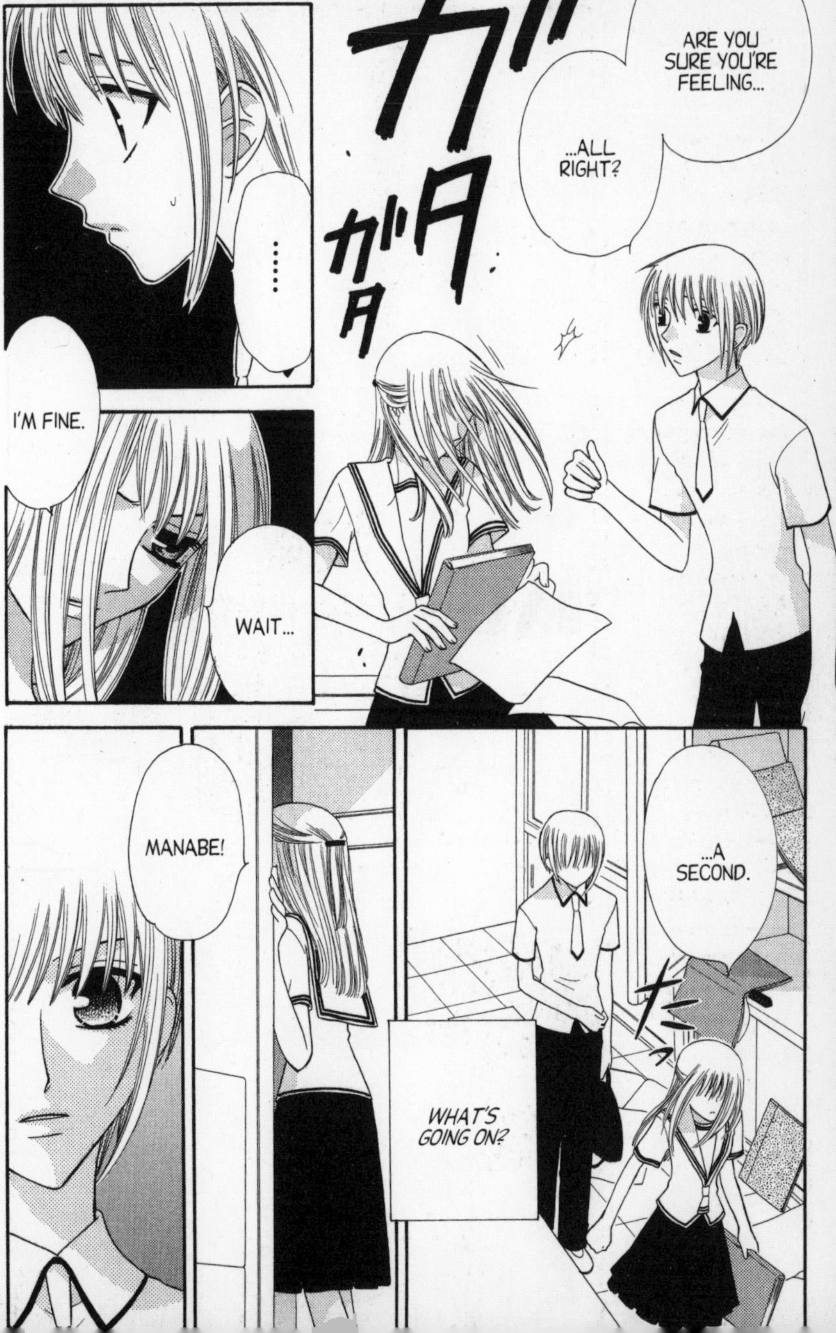
ガタ
ガタ
ARE YOU SURE YOU'RE FEELING...
...ALL RIGHT?
......
I'M FINE.
WAIT...
...A SECOND.
WHAT'S GOING ON?
MANABE!

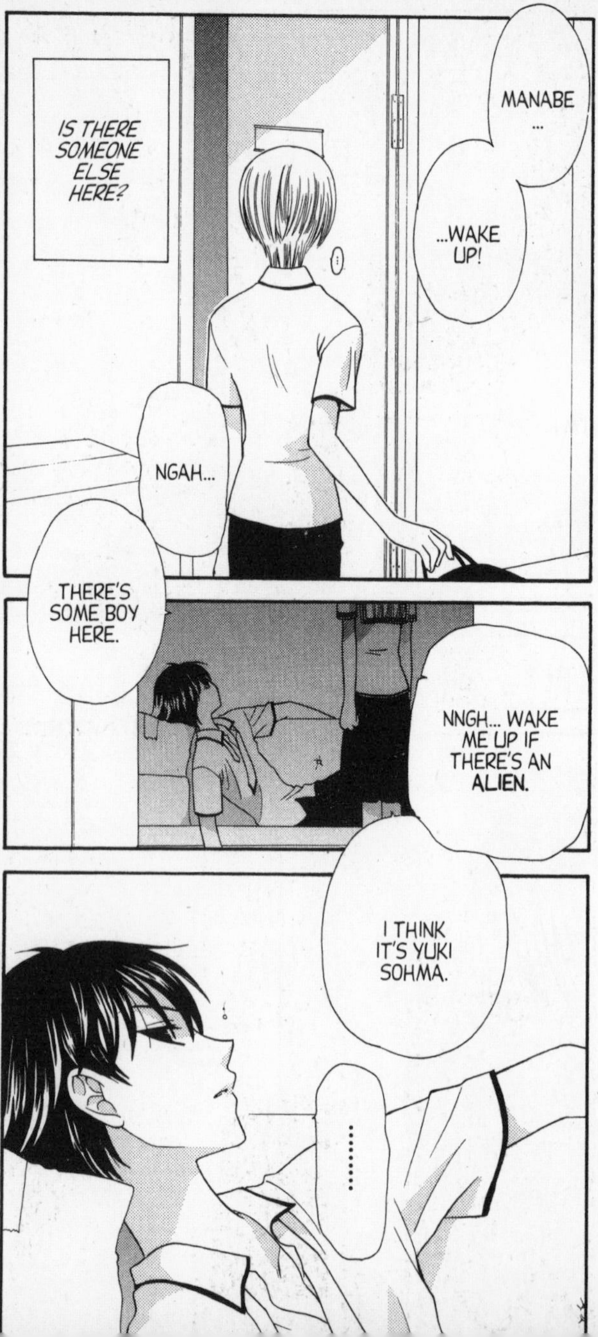
MANABE ...
...WAKE UP!
IS THERE SOMEONE ELSE HERE?
NGAH...
THERE'S SOME BOY HERE.
NNGH... WAKE ME UP IF THERE'S AN ALIEN.
I THINK IT'S YUKI SOHMA.
......

Fruits Basket 9
Part 1

Hajimemashite and konnichiwa! Takaya reporting for duty, here to present *Furuba* volume 9! This makes 21 volumes of manga that I've produced to date. (It doesn't feel so special anymore.) Volume 9 features "the King." Yup! It's Ayame. And now the Mabudachi Trio have all had their moment in the spotlight. Mabudachi fans, please line up volumes 4, 7, and 9. I guess no one really does that... Anyway, please enjoy volume 9.

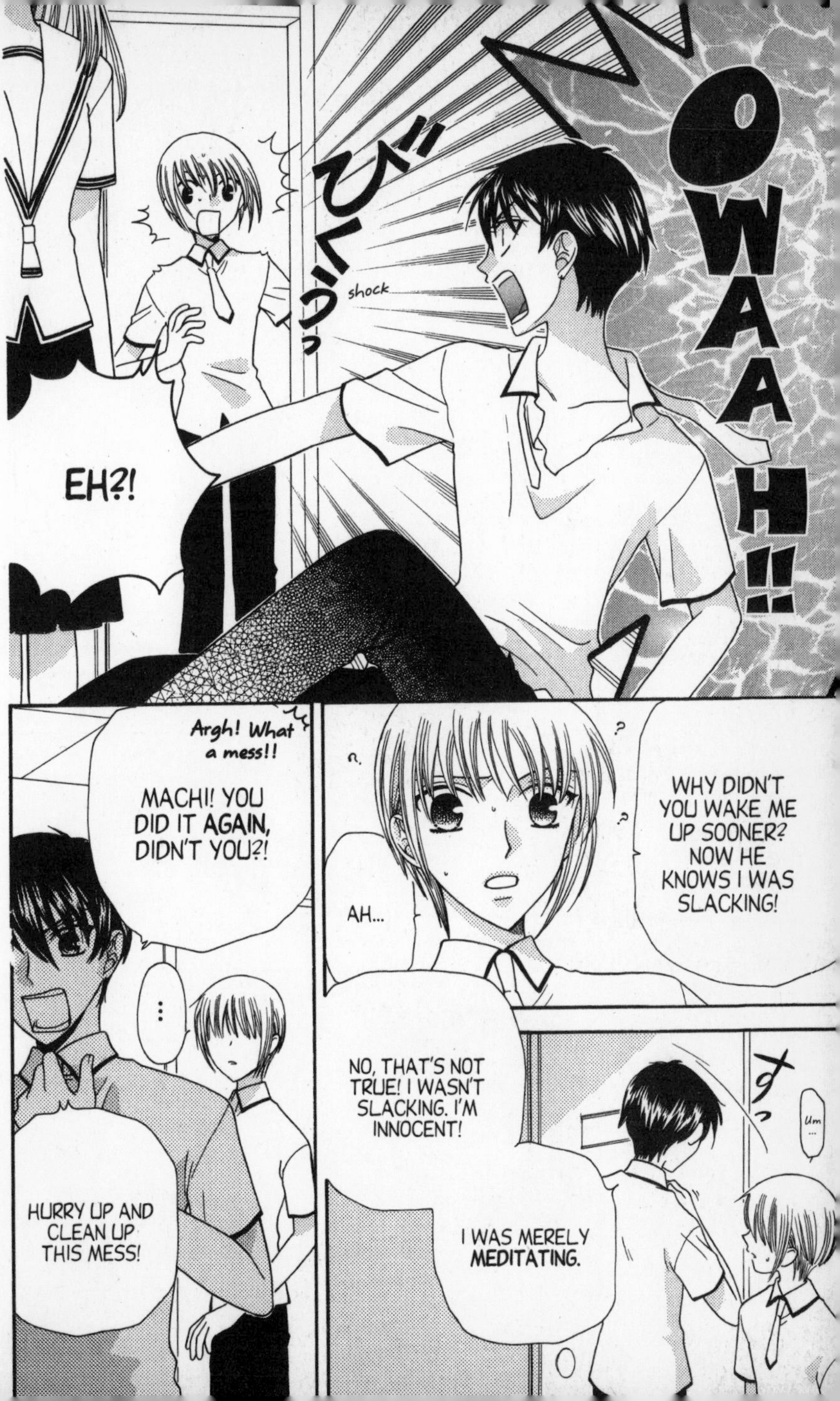
OWAAH!!
びくうっ
shock
EH?!
WHY DIDN'T YOU WAKE ME UP SOONER? NOW HE KNOWS I WAS SLACKING!
AH...
すっ
Um...
NO, THAT'S NOT TRUE! I WASN'T SLACKING. I'M INNOCENT!
I WAS MERELY MEDITATING.
Argh! What a mess!!
MACHI! YOU DID IT AGAIN, DIDN'T YOU?!
...
HURRY UP AND CLEAN UP THIS MESS!

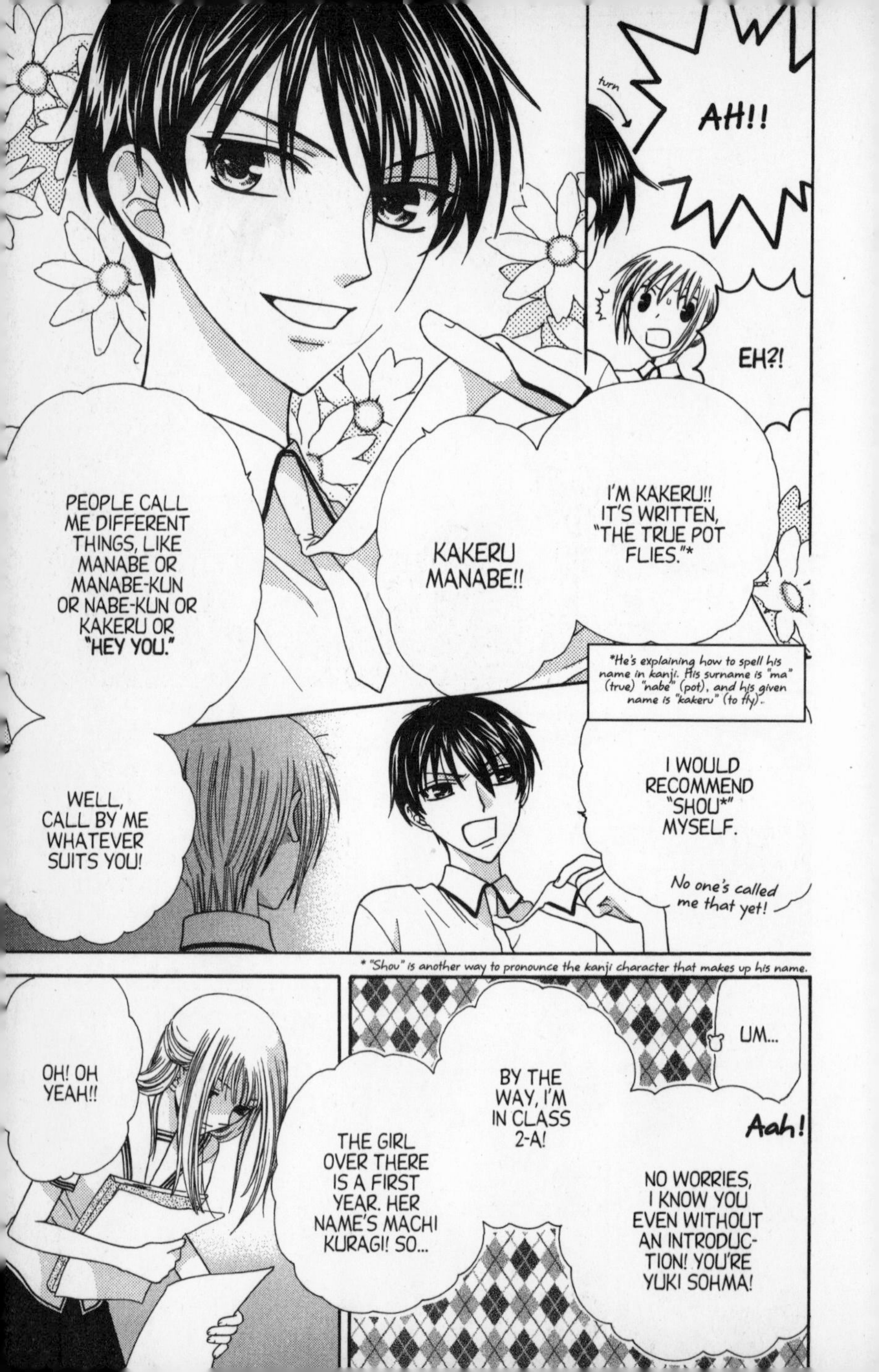
turn
AH!!
EH?!
I'M KAKERU!! IT'S WRITTEN, "THE TRUE POT FLIES."*
*He's explaining how to spell his name in kanji. His surname is "ma" (true) "nabe" (pot), and his given name is "kakeru" (to fly).
KAKERU MANABE!!
PEOPLE CALL ME DIFFERENT THINGS, LIKE MANABE OR MANABE-KUN OR NABE-KUN OR KAKERU OR "HEY YOU."
I WOULD RECOMMEND "SHOU*" MYSELF.
No one's called me that yet!
WELL, CALL BY ME WHATEVER SUITS YOU!
* "Shou" is another way to pronounce the kanji character that makes up his name.
UM...
Aah!
NO WORRIES, I KNOW YOU EVEN WITHOUT AN INTRODUC-TION! YOU'RE YUKI SOHMA!
BY THE WAY, I'M IN CLASS 2-A!
THE GIRL OVER THERE IS A FIRST YEAR. HER NAME'S MACHI KURAGI! SO...
OH! OH YEAH!!

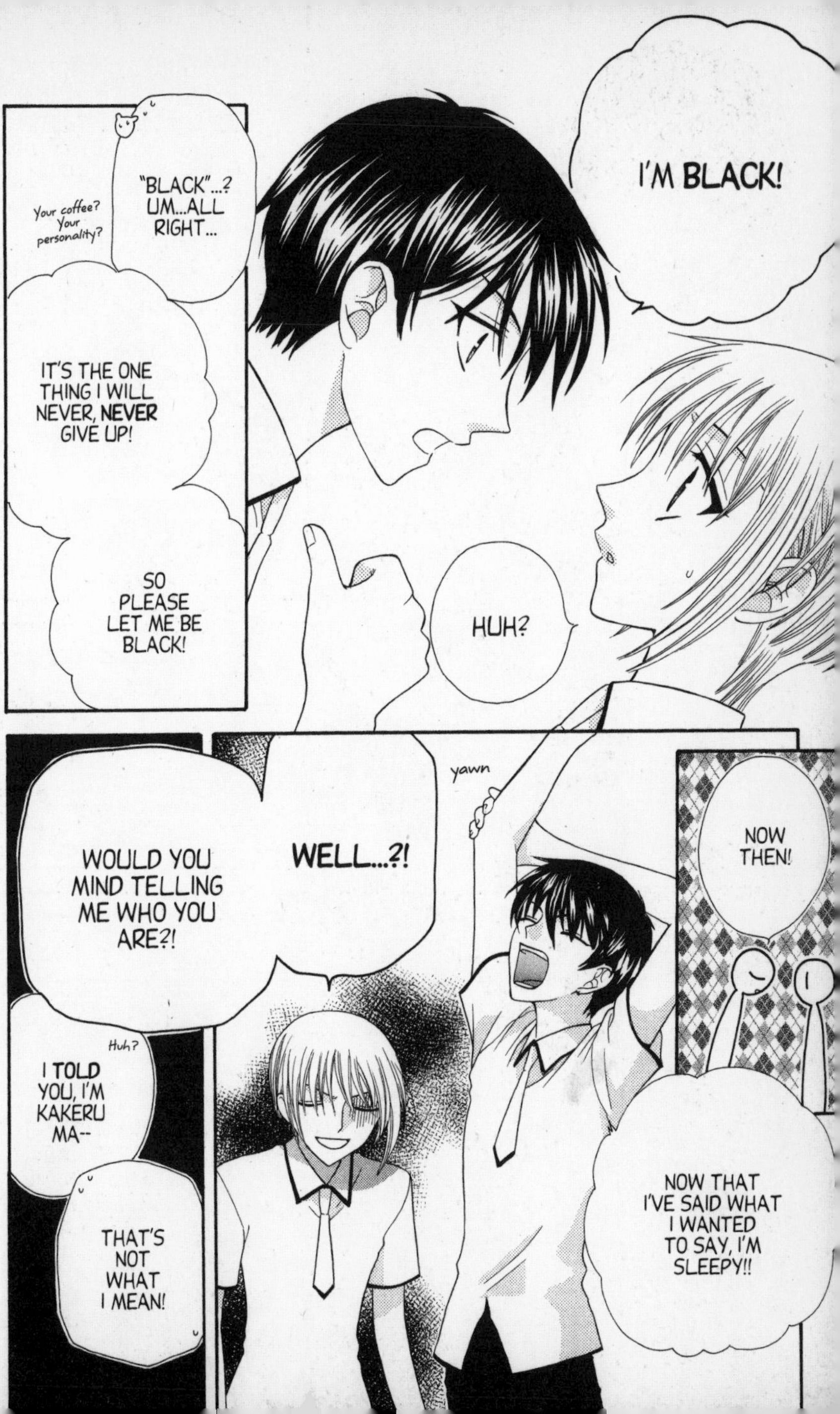
I'M BLACK!
HUH?
"BLACK"...? UM...ALL RIGHT...
Your coffee? Your personality?
IT'S THE ONE THING I WILL NEVER, NEVER GIVE UP!
SO PLEASE LET ME BE BLACK!
NOW THEN!
NOW THAT I'VE SAID WHAT I WANTED TO SAY, I'M SLEEPY!!
yawn
WELL...?!
WOULD YOU MIND TELLING ME WHO YOU ARE?!
Huh?
I TOLD YOU, I'M KAKERU MA--
THAT'S NOT WHAT I MEAN!

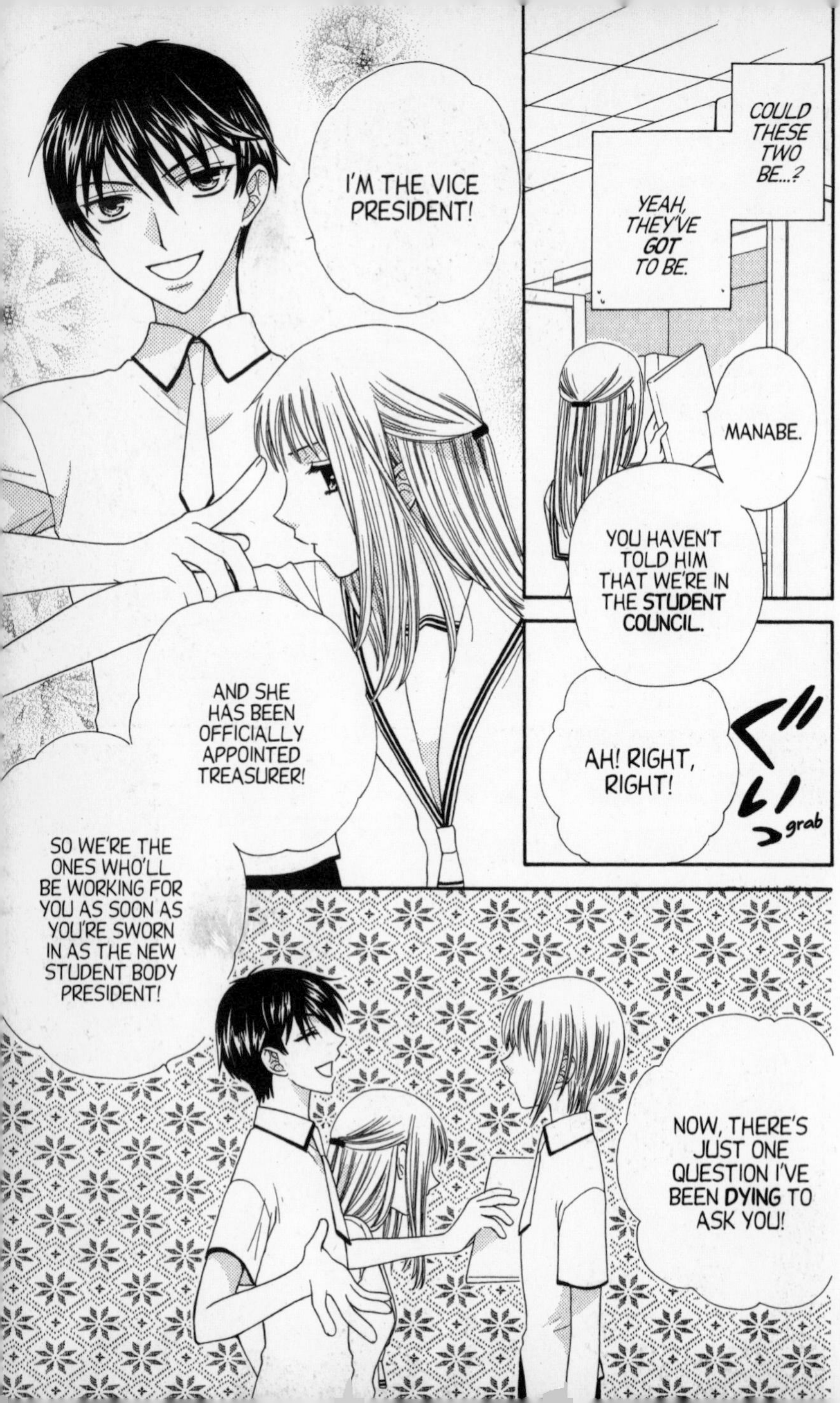
COULD THESE TWO BE...?
YEAH, THEY'VE GOT TO BE.
MANABE.
YOU HAVEN'T TOLD HIM THAT WE'RE IN THE STUDENT COUNCIL.
AH! RIGHT, RIGHT!
grab
I'M THE VICE PRESIDENT!
AND SHE HAS BEEN OFFICIALLY APPOINTED TREASURER!
SO WE'RE THE ONES WHO'LL BE WORKING FOR YOU AS SOON AS YOU'RE SWORN IN AS THE NEW STUDENT BODY PRESIDENT!
NOW, THERE'S JUST ONE QUESTION I'VE BEEN DYING TO ASK YOU!

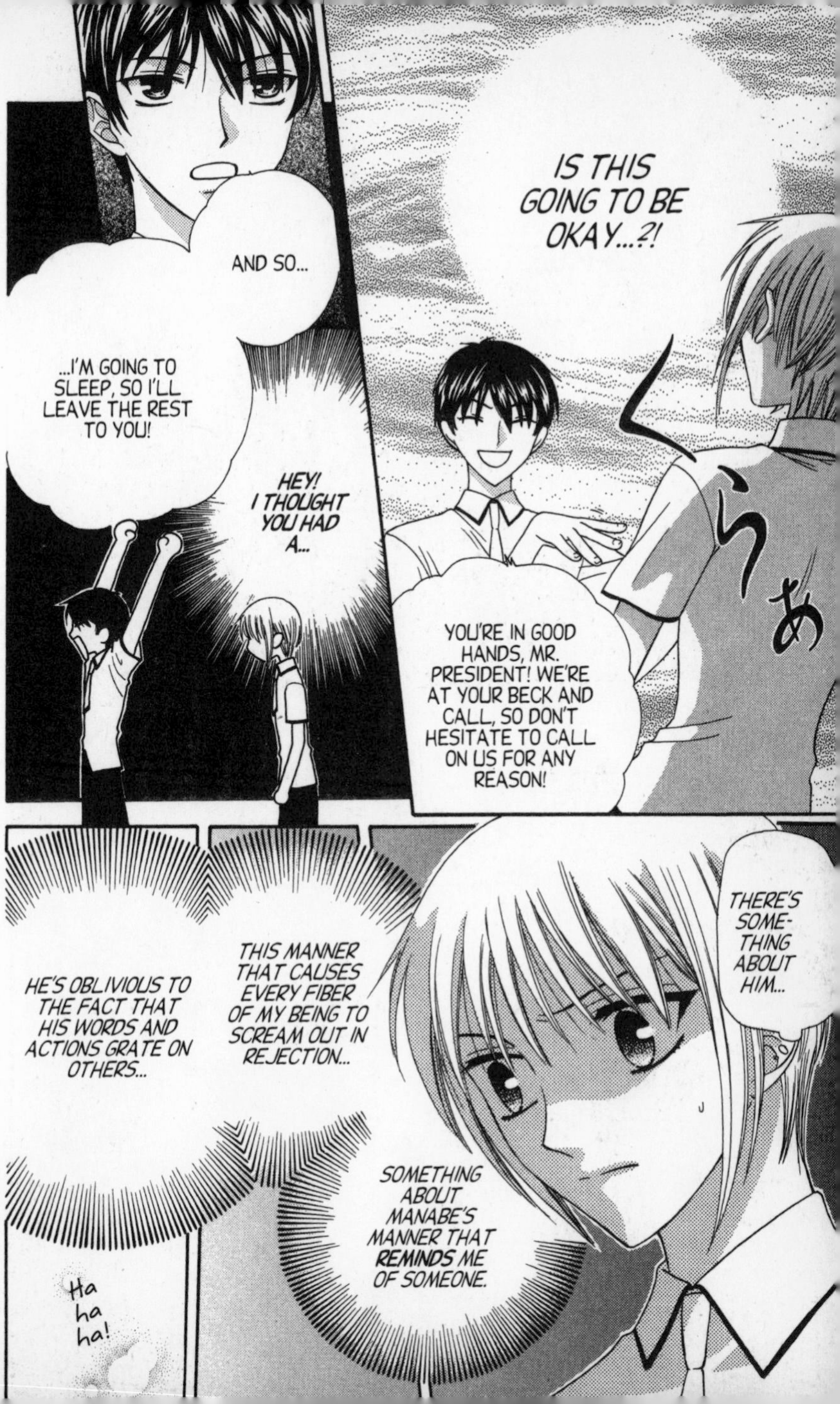
IS THIS GOING TO BE OKAY...?!
YOU'RE IN GOOD HANDS, MR. PRESIDENT! WE'RE AT YOUR BECK AND CALL, SO DON'T HESITATE TO CALL ON US FOR ANY REASON!
くらぁ
AND SO...
...I'M GOING TO SLEEP, SO I'LL LEAVE THE REST TO YOU!
HEY! I THOUGHT YOU HAD A...
THERE'S SOME-THING ABOUT HIM...
SOMETHING ABOUT MANABE'S MANNER THAT REMINDS ME OF SOMEONE.
THIS MANNER THAT CAUSES EVERY FIBER OF MY BEING TO SCREAM OUT IN REJECTION...
HE'S OBLIVIOUS TO THE FACT THAT HIS WORDS AND ACTIONS GRATE ON OTHERS...
Ha ha ha!

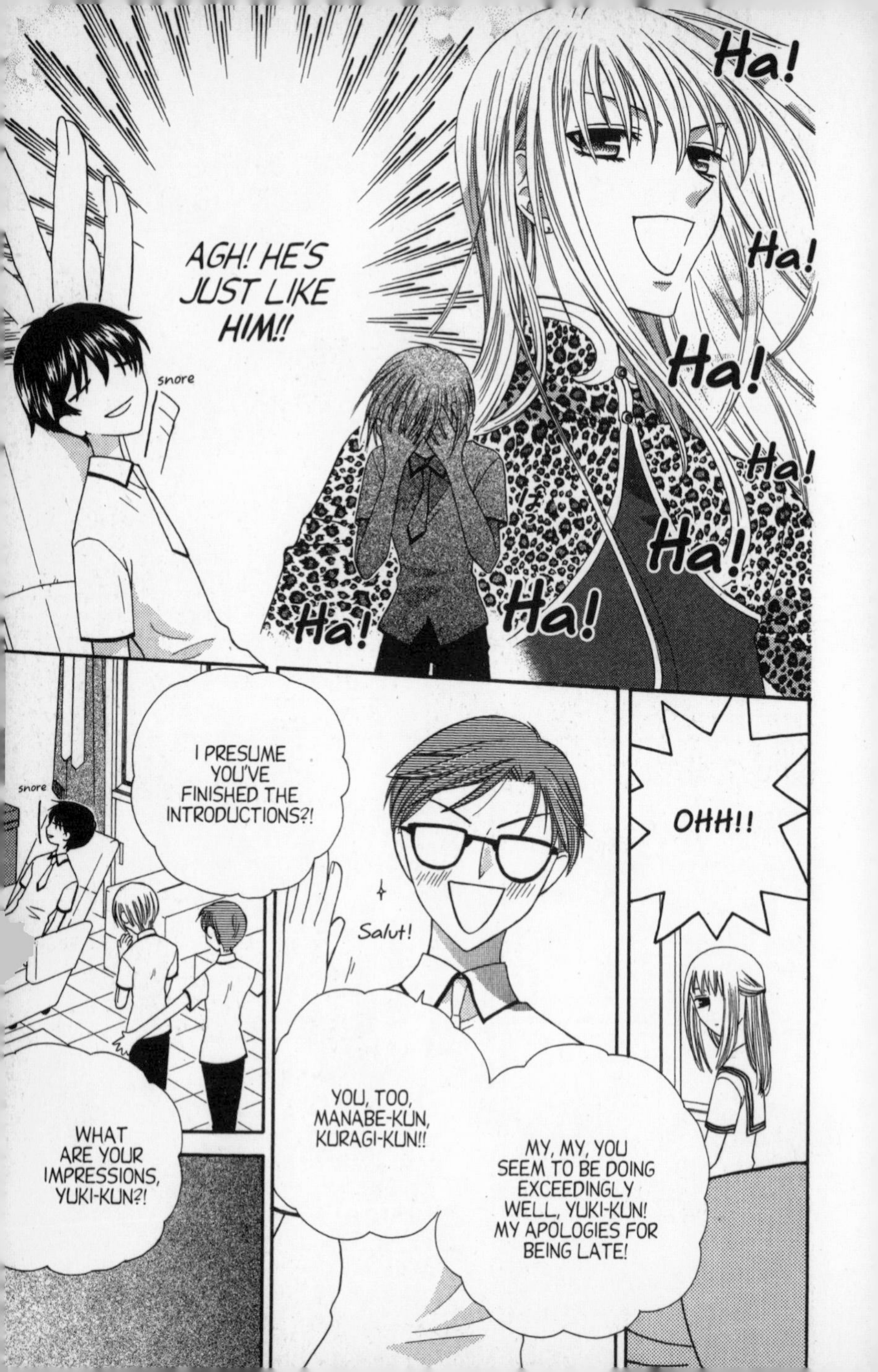
Ha!
Ha!
Ha!
Ha!
Ha!
Ha!
Ha!
AGH! HE'S JUST LIKE HIM!!
snore
OHH!!
Salut!
MY, MY, YOU SEEM TO BE DOING EXCEEDINGLY WELL, YUKI-KUN! MY APOLOGIES FOR BEING LATE!
YOU, TOO, MANABE-KUN, KURAGI-KUN!!
I PRESUME YOU'VE FINISHED THE INTRODUCTIONS?!
snore
WHAT ARE YOUR IMPRESSIONS, YUKI-KUN?!

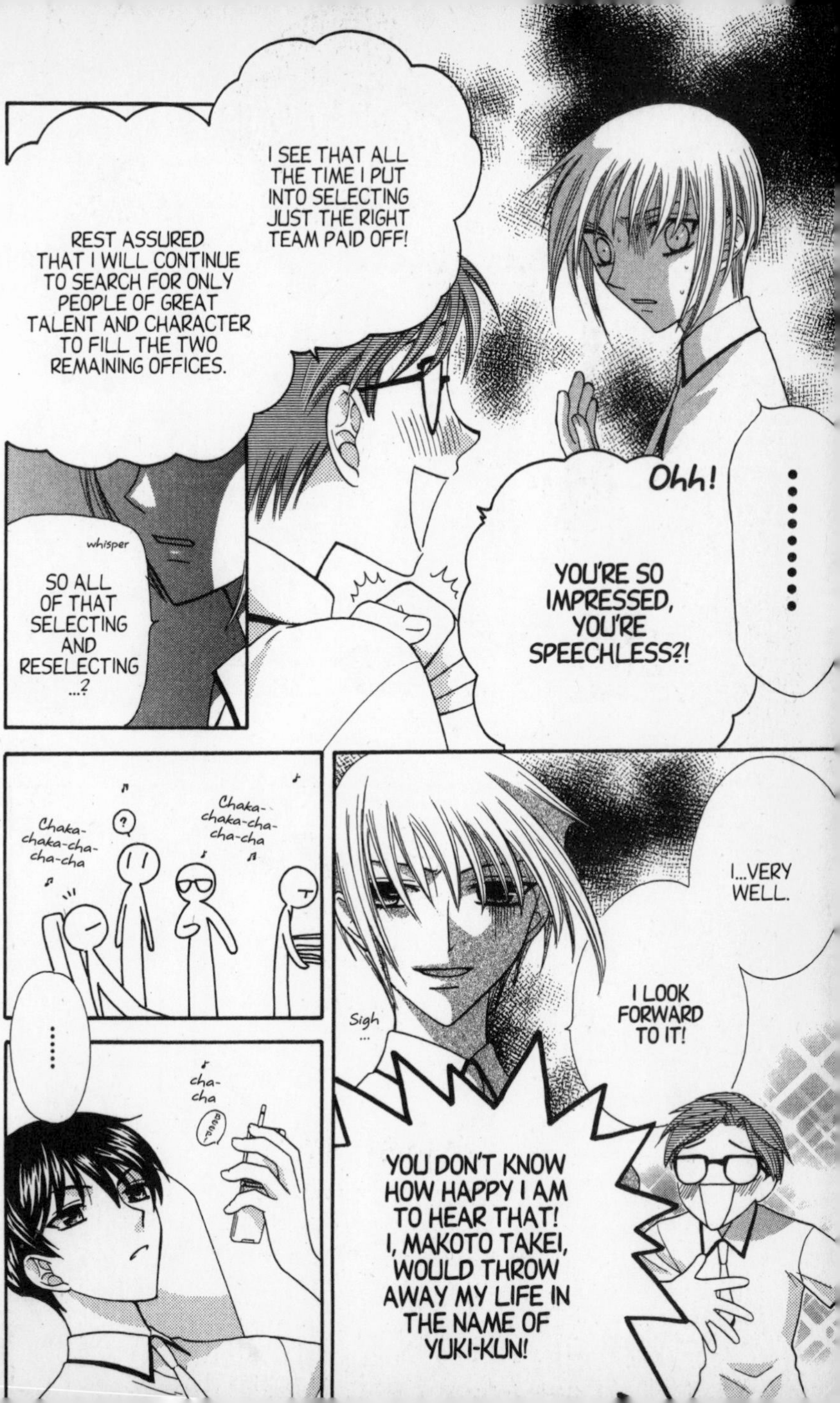
I SEE THAT ALL THE TIME I PUT INTO SELECTING JUST THE RIGHT TEAM PAID OFF!
REST ASSURED THAT I WILL CONTINUE TO SEARCH FOR ONLY PEOPLE OF GREAT TALENT AND CHARACTER TO FILL THE TWO REMAINING OFFICES.
....
Ohh!
YOU'RE SO IMPRESSED, YOU'RE SPEECHLESS?!
whisper
SO ALL OF THAT SELECTING AND RESELECTING ...?
I...VERY WELL.
I LOOK FORWARD TO IT!
Sigh ...
YOU DON'T KNOW HOW HAPPY I AM TO HEAR THAT! I, MAKOTO TAKEI, WOULD THROW AWAY MY LIFE IN THE NAME OF YUKI-KUN!
Chaka-chaka-cha-cha-cha
?
Chaka-chaka-cha-cha-cha
......
cha-cha

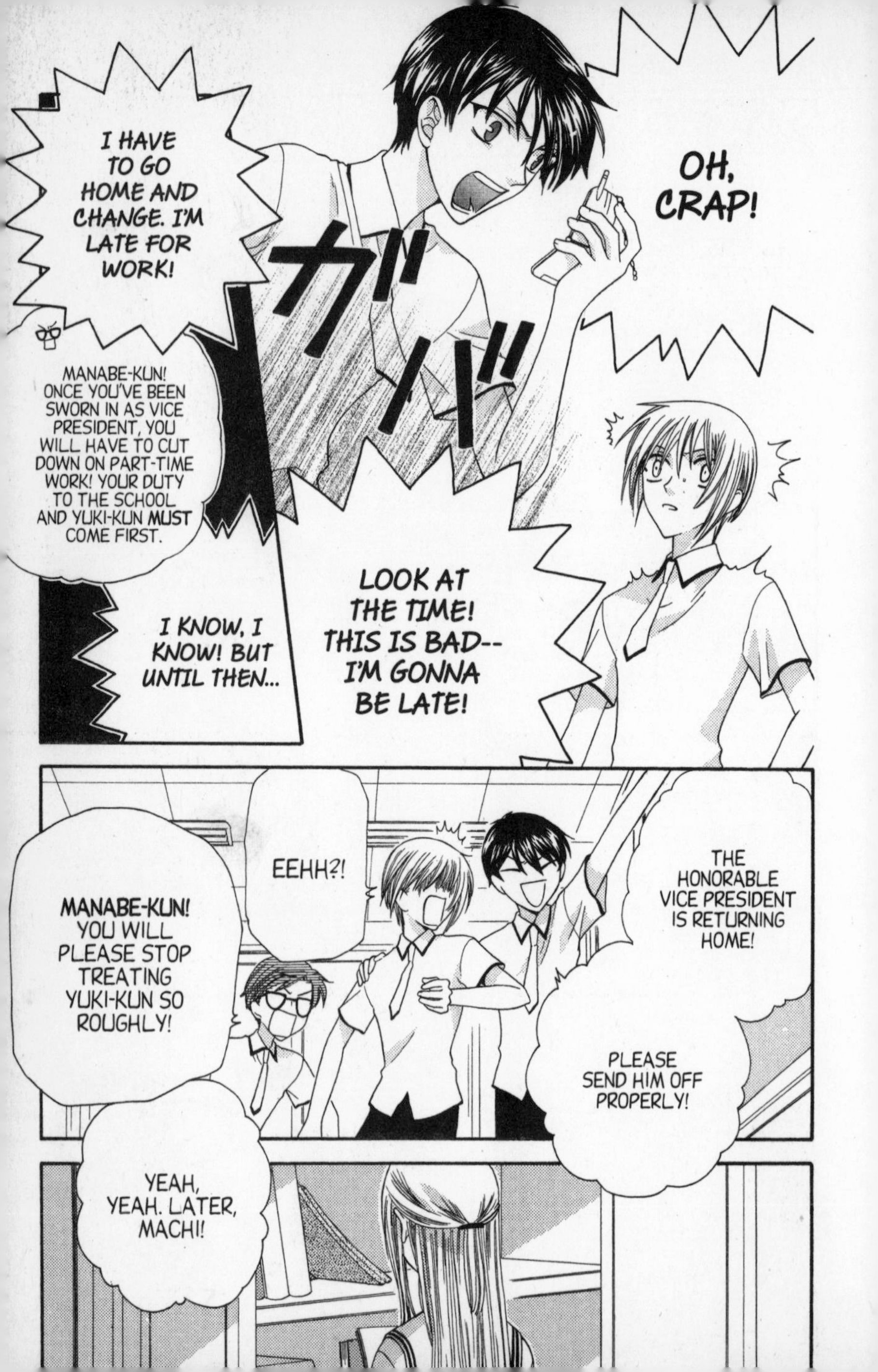
OH, CRAP!
I HAVE TO GO HOME AND CHANGE. I'M LATE FOR WORK!
MANABE-KUN! ONCE YOU'VE BEEN SWORN IN AS VICE PRESIDENT, YOU WILL HAVE TO CUT DOWN ON PART-TIME WORK! YOUR DUTY TO THE SCHOOL AND YUKI-KUN MUST COME FIRST.
LOOK AT THE TIME! THIS IS BAD-- I'M GONNA BE LATE!
I KNOW, I KNOW! BUT UNTIL THEN...
THE HONORABLE VICE PRESIDENT IS RETURNING HOME!
PLEASE SEND HIM OFF PROPERLY!
EEHH?!
MANABE-KUN! YOU WILL PLEASE STOP TREATING YUKI-KUN SO ROUGHLY!
YEAH, YEAH. LATER, MACHI!

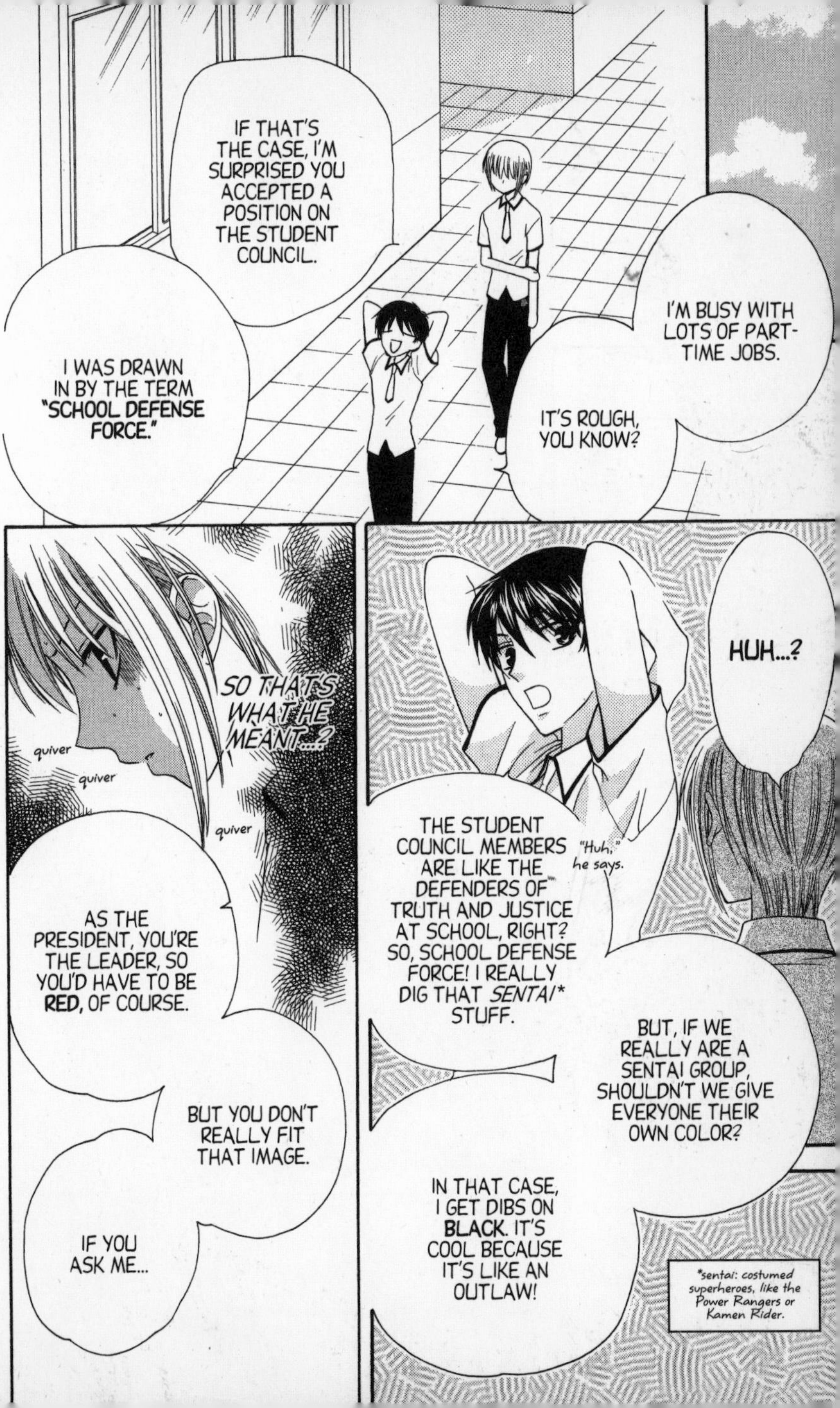
I'M BUSY WITH LOTS OF PART-TIME JOBS.
IT'S ROUGH, YOU KNOW?
IF THAT'S THE CASE, I'M SURPRISED YOU ACCEPTED A POSITION ON THE STUDENT COUNCIL.
I WAS DRAWN IN BY THE TERM "SCHOOL DEFENSE FORCE."
HUH...?
THE STUDENT COUNCIL MEMBERS ARE LIKE THE DEFENDERS OF TRUTH AND JUSTICE AT SCHOOL, RIGHT? SO, SCHOOL DEFENSE FORCE! I REALLY DIG THAT *SENTAI** STUFF.
"Huh," he says.
BUT, IF WE REALLY ARE A SENTAI GROUP, SHOULDN'T WE GIVE EVERYONE THEIR OWN COLOR?
IN THAT CASE, I GET DIBS ON **BLACK**. IT'S COOL BECAUSE IT'S LIKE AN OUTLAW!
*sentai: costumed superheroes, like the Power Rangers or Kamen Rider.
SO THAT'S WHAT HE MEANT...?
quiver
quiver
quiver
AS THE PRESIDENT, YOU'RE THE LEADER, SO YOU'D HAVE TO BE **RED**, OF COURSE.
BUT YOU DON'T REALLY FIT THAT IMAGE.
IF YOU ASK ME...

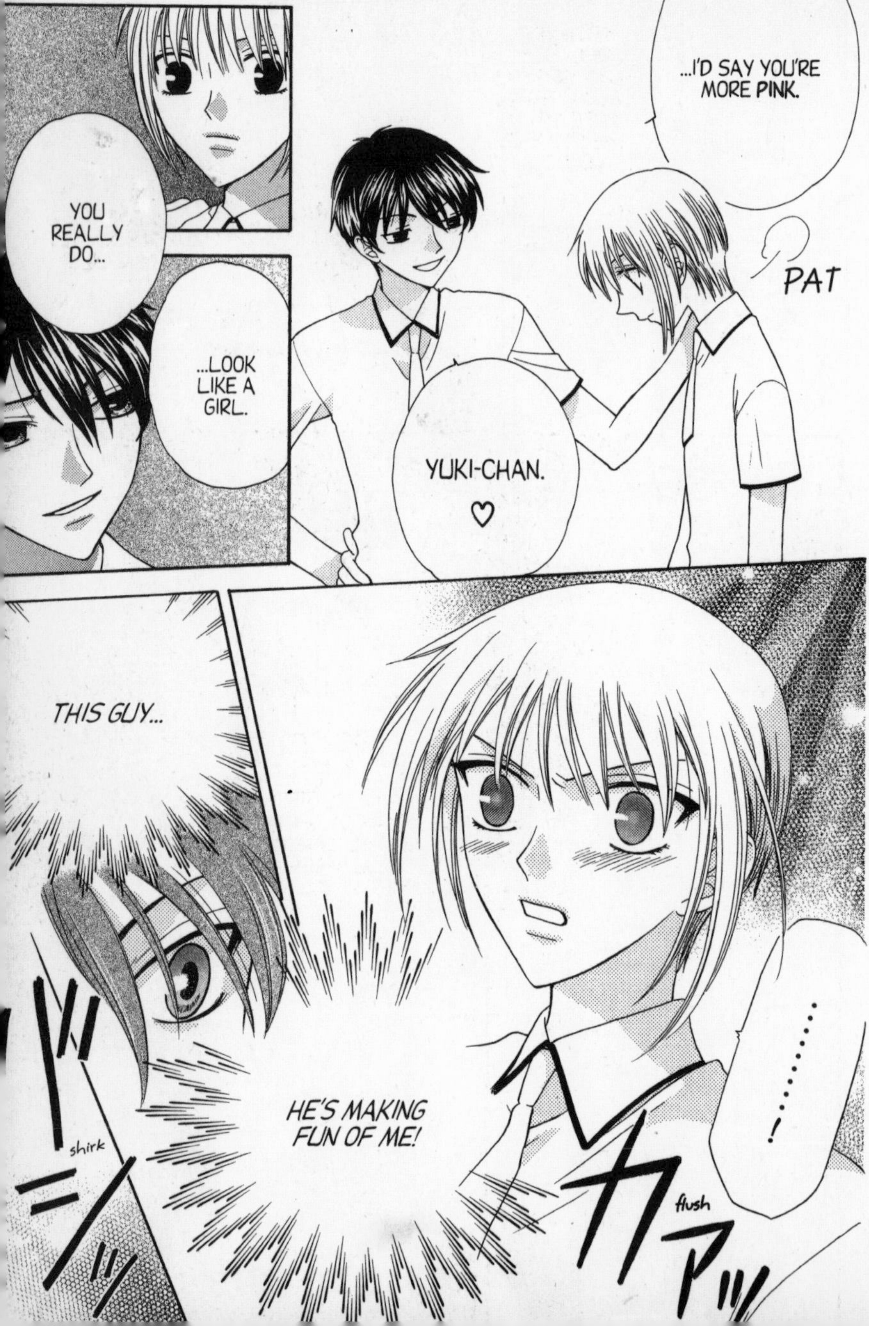
...I'D SAY YOU'RE MORE PINK.
PAT
YUKI-CHAN. ♡
YOU REALLY DO...
...LOOK LIKE A GIRL.
!......
flush
THIS GUY...
HE'S MAKING FUN OF ME!
shirk

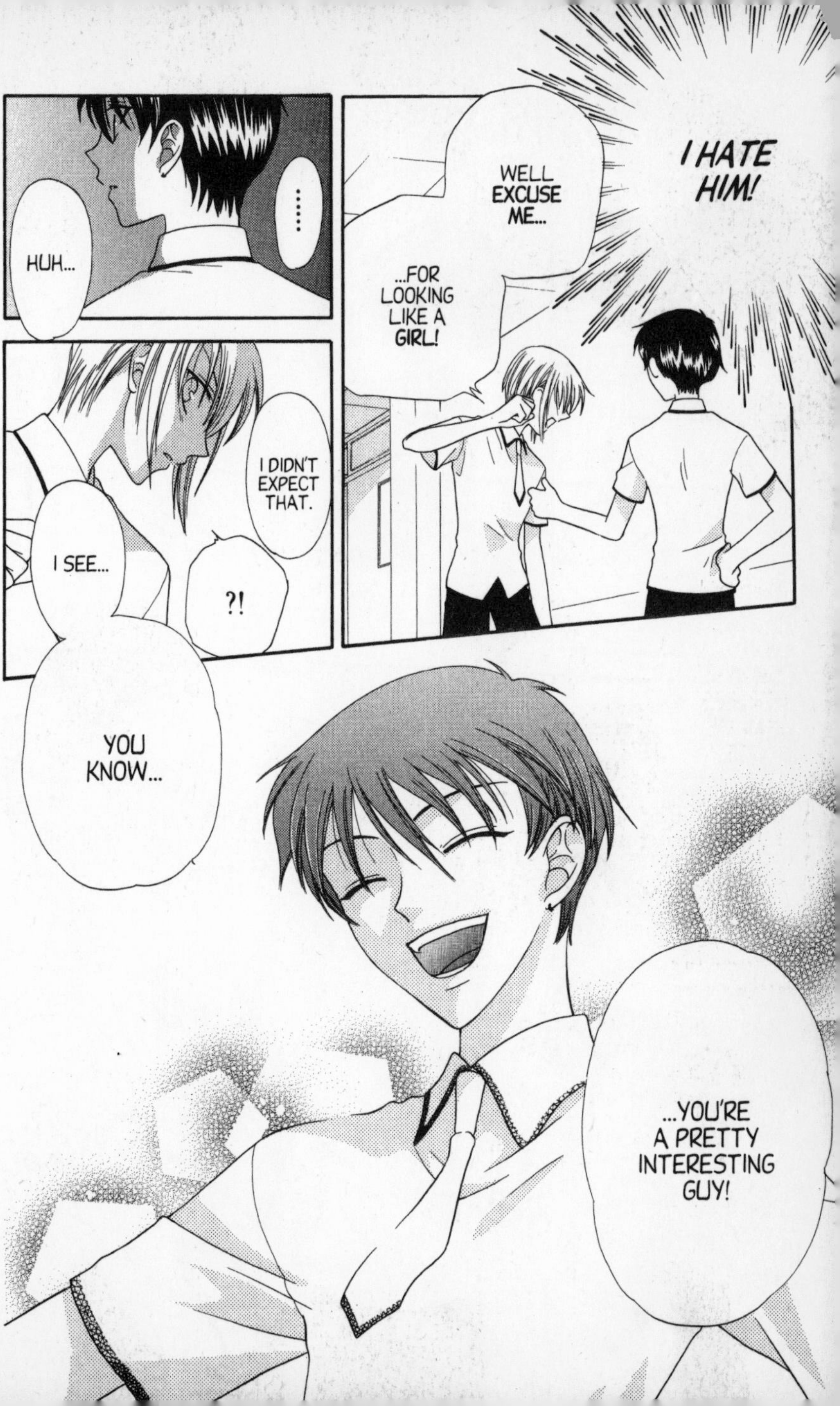
WELL EXCUSE ME...
...FOR LOOKING LIKE A GIRL!
I HATE HIM!
......
HUH...
I DIDN'T EXPECT THAT.
?!
I SEE...
YOU KNOW...
...YOU'RE A PRETTY INTERESTING GUY!

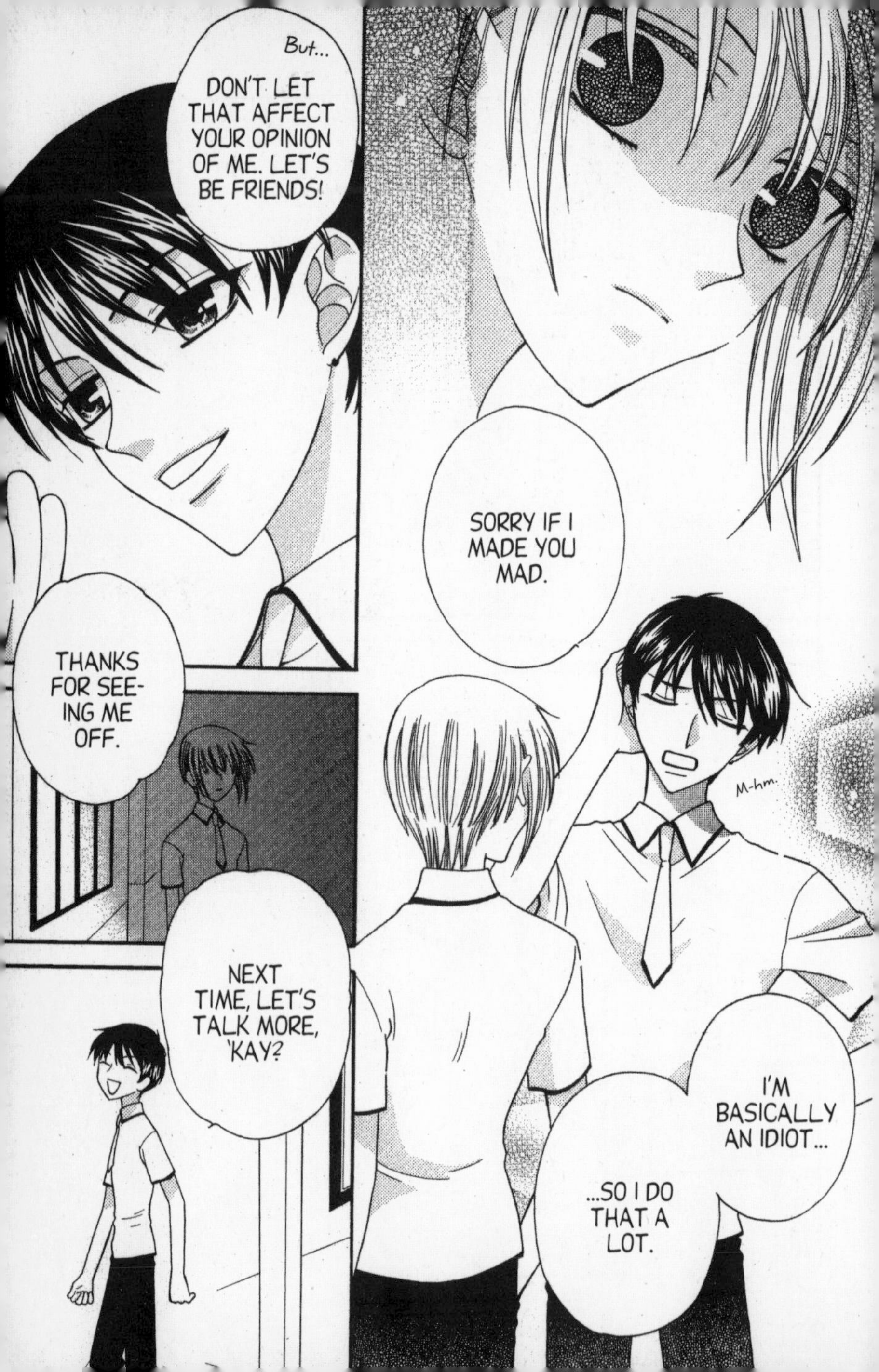
SORRY IF I MADE YOU MAD.
M-hm.
I'M BASICALLY AN IDIOT...
...SO I DO THAT A LOT.
But...
DON'T LET THAT AFFECT YOUR OPINION OF ME. LET'S BE FRIENDS!
THANKS FOR SEEING ME OFF.
NEXT TIME, LET'S TALK MORE, 'KAY?

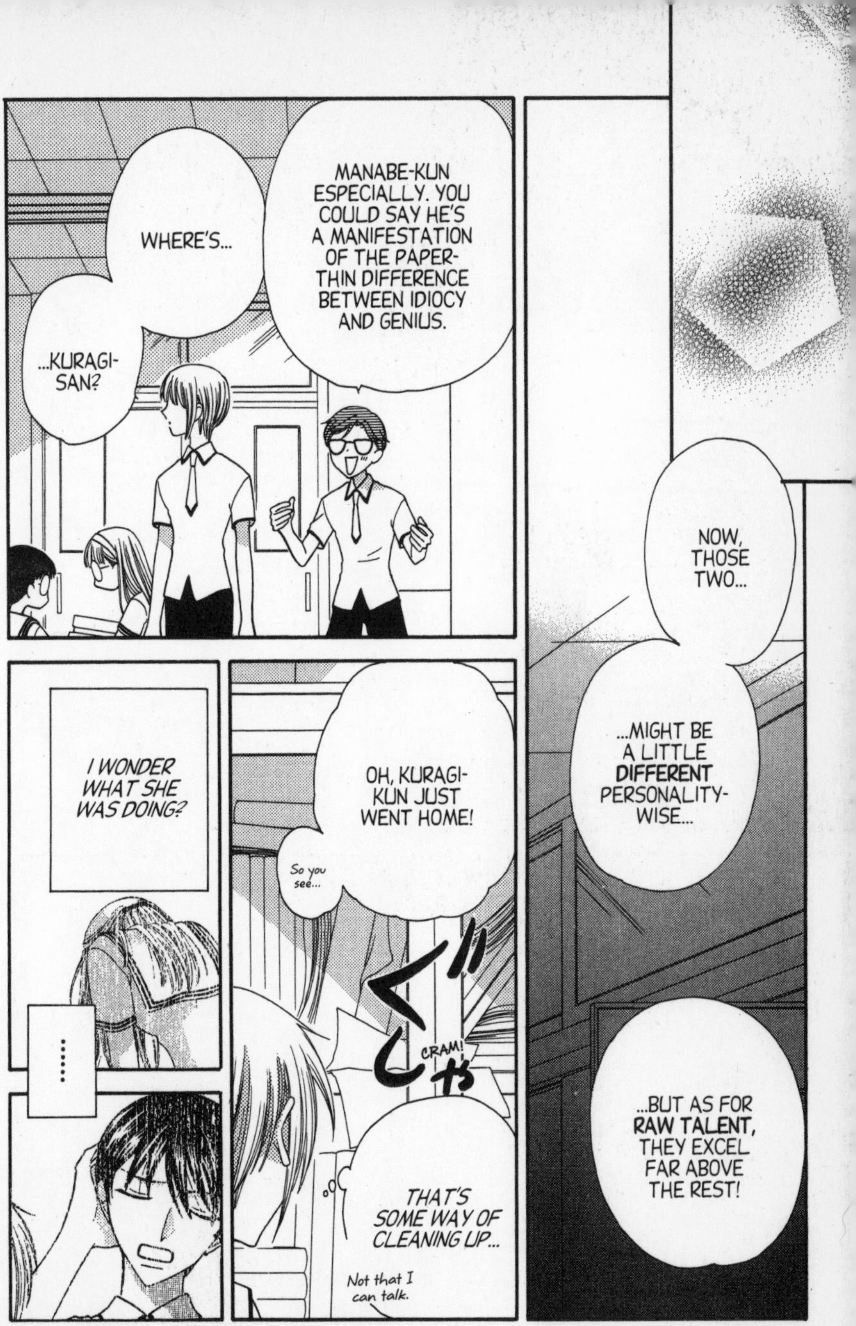
NOW, THOSE TWO...
...MIGHT BE A LITTLE DIFFERENT PERSONALITY-WISE...
...BUT AS FOR RAW TALENT, THEY EXCEL FAR ABOVE THE REST!
MANABE-KUN ESPECIALLY. YOU COULD SAY HE'S A MANIFESTATION OF THE PAPER-THIN DIFFERENCE BETWEEN IDIOCY AND GENIUS.
WHERE'S...
...KURAGI-SAN?
OH, KURAGI-KUN JUST WENT HOME!
So you see...
CRAM!
THAT'S SOME WAY OF CLEANING UP...
Not that I can talk.
I WONDER WHAT SHE WAS DOING?
......

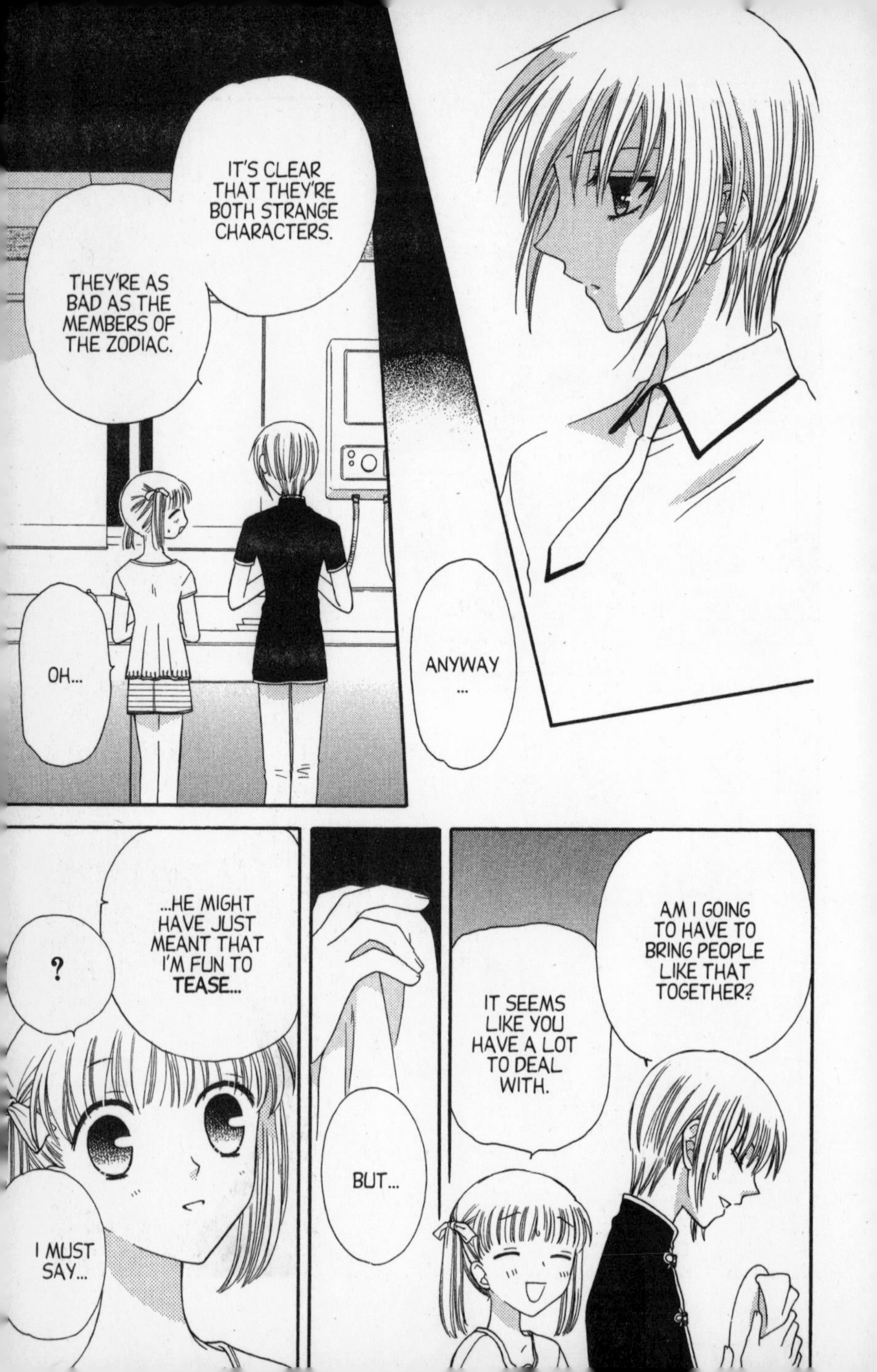
ANYWAY ...
IT'S CLEAR THAT THEY'RE BOTH STRANGE CHARACTERS.
THEY'RE AS BAD AS THE MEMBERS OF THE ZODIAC.
OH...
AM I GOING TO HAVE TO BRING PEOPLE LIKE THAT TOGETHER?
IT SEEMS LIKE YOU HAVE A LOT TO DEAL WITH.
BUT...
...HE MIGHT HAVE JUST MEANT THAT I'M FUN TO TEASE...
?
I MUST SAY...

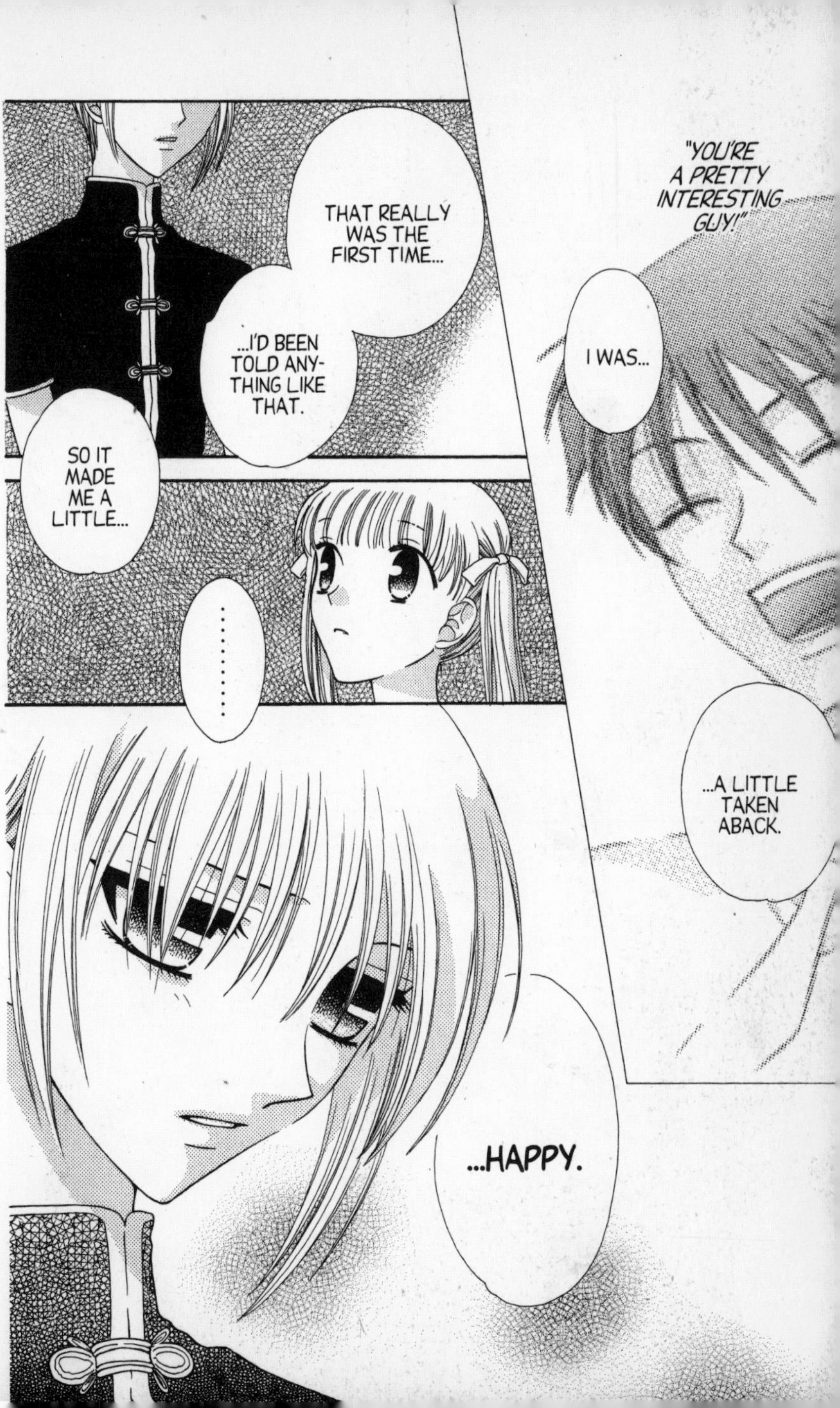
"YOU'RE A PRETTY INTERESTING GUY!"
I WAS...
...A LITTLE TAKEN ABACK.
THAT REALLY WAS THE FIRST TIME...
...I'D BEEN TOLD ANYTHING LIKE THAT.
SO IT MADE ME A LITTLE...
....
...HAPPY.

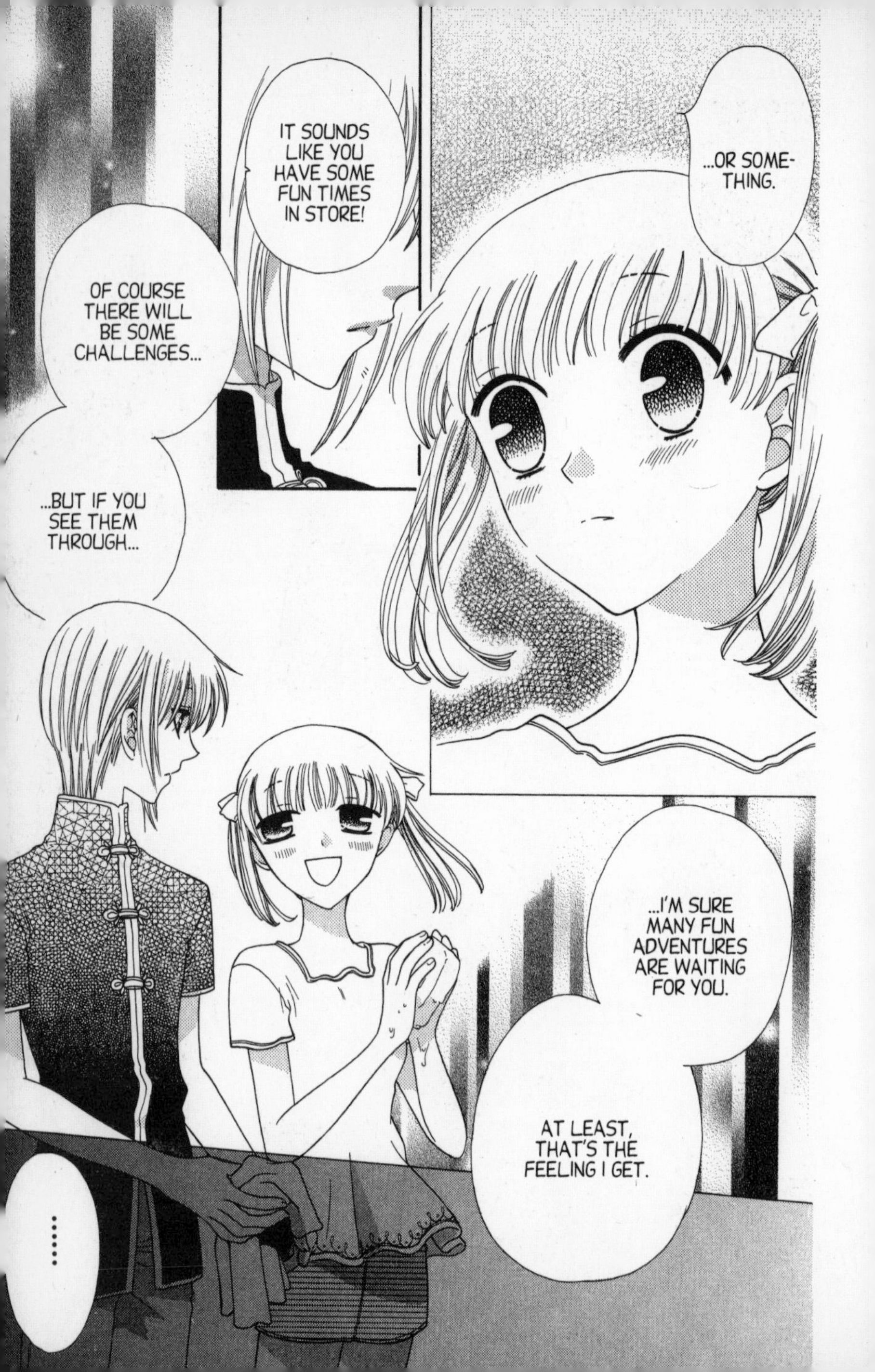
...OR SOME-THING.
IT SOUNDS LIKE YOU HAVE SOME FUN TIMES IN STORE!
OF COURSE THERE WILL BE SOME CHALLENGES...
...BUT IF YOU SEE THEM THROUGH...
...I'M SURE MANY FUN ADVENTURES ARE WAITING FOR YOU.
AT LEAST, THAT'S THE FEELING I GET.
......

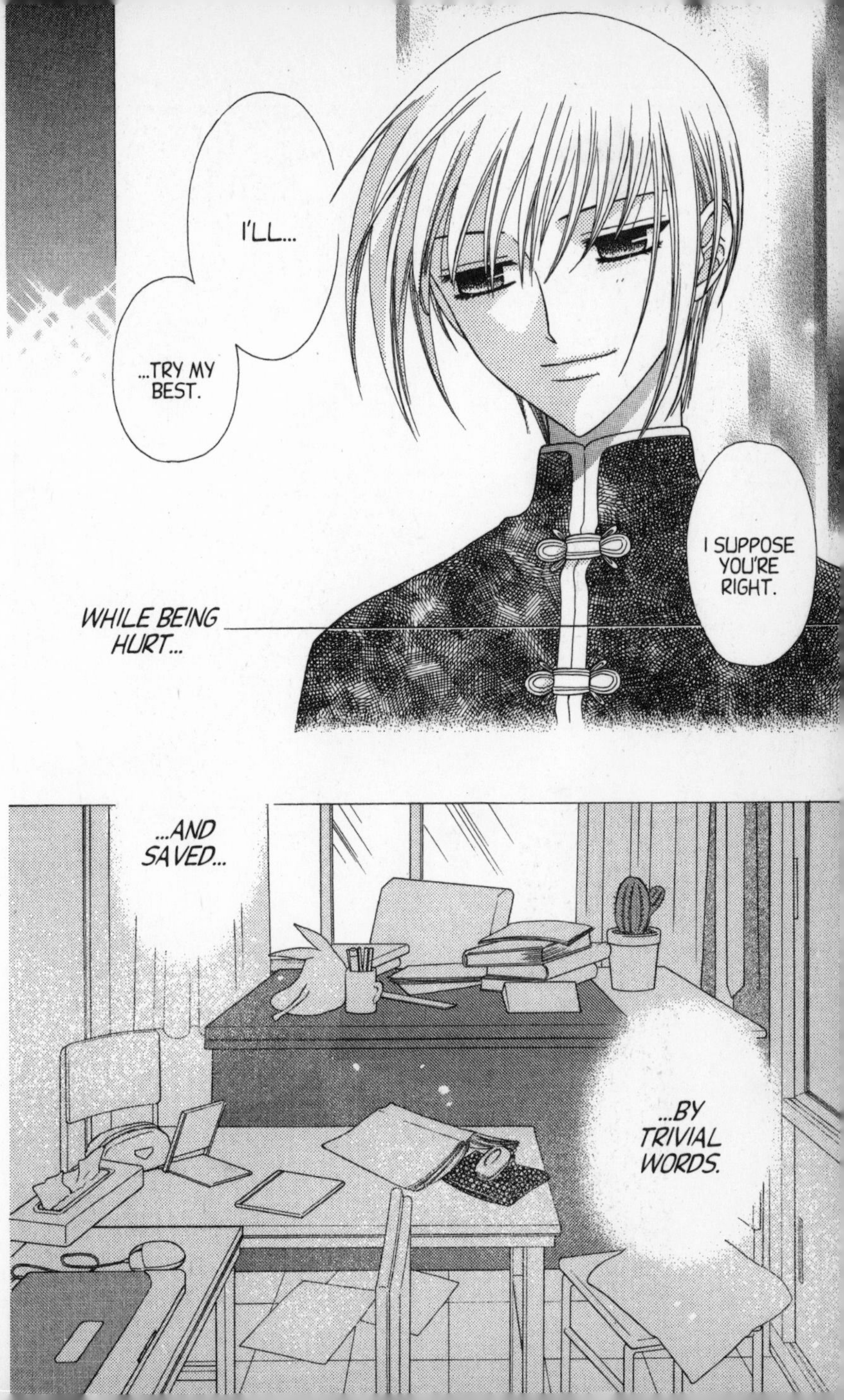
I SUPPOSE YOU'RE RIGHT.
I'LL...
...TRY MY BEST.
WHILE BEING HURT...
...AND SAVED...
...BY TRIVIAL WORDS.

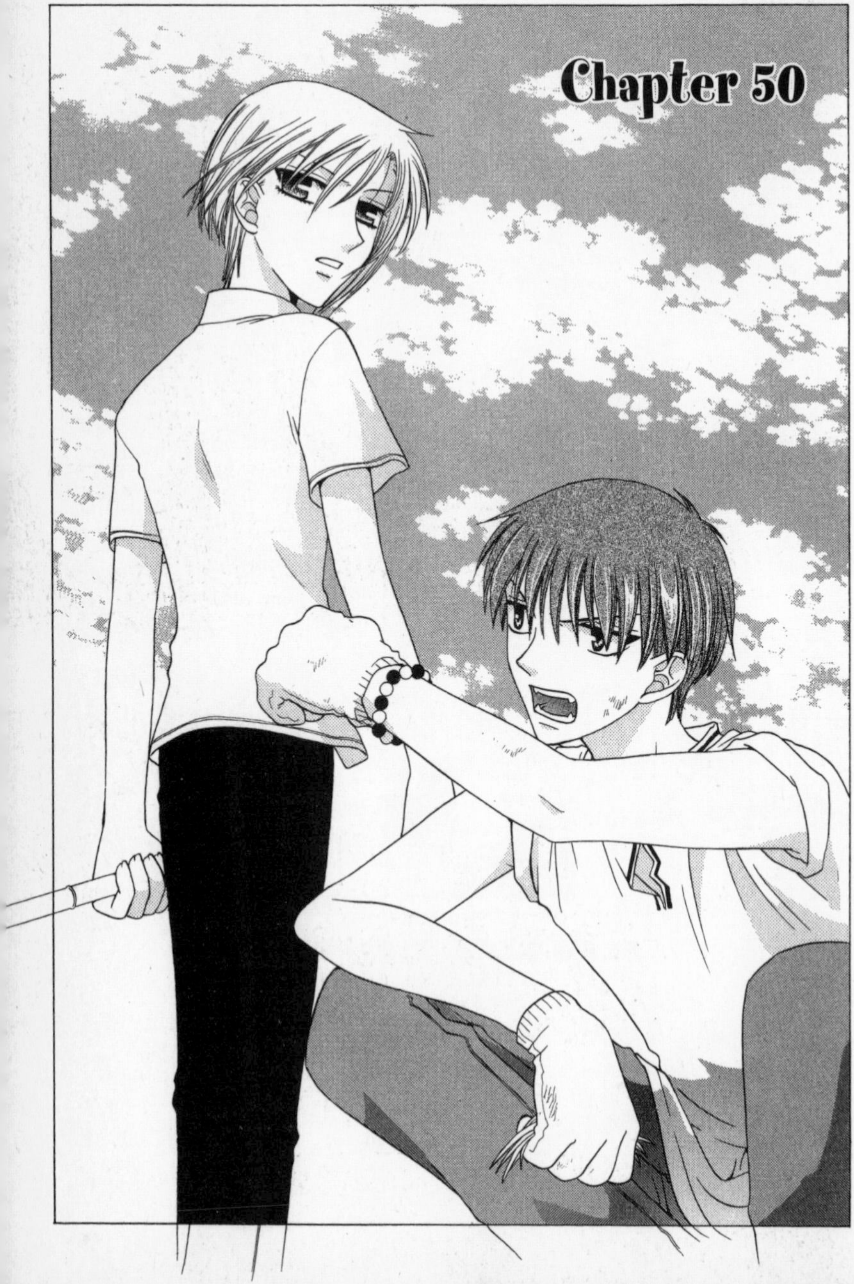
Chapter 50

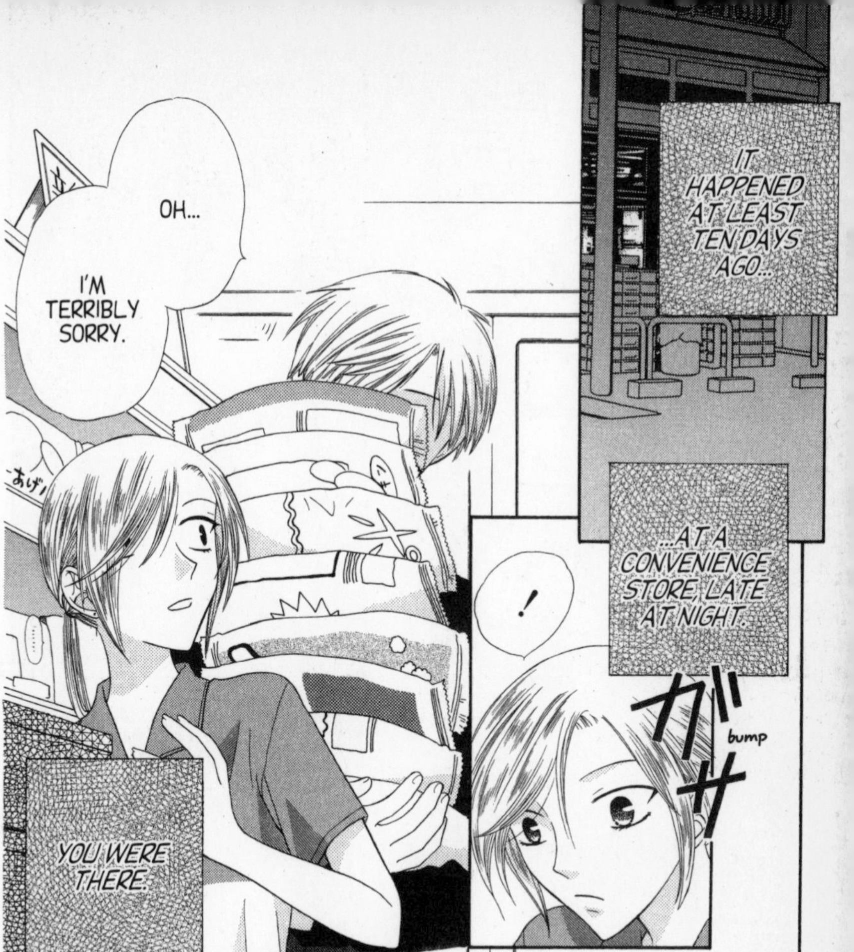
IT HAPPENED AT LEAST TEN DAYS AGO...
...AT A CONVENIENCE STORE, LATE AT NIGHT.
!
ガザ
bump
OH...
I'M TERRIBLY SORRY.
YOU WERE THERE.

BLAH, BLAH, BLAH 2

We've arrived at Chapter 50! My feelings upon arriving at this milestone are..."Wow, I've drawn a lot."

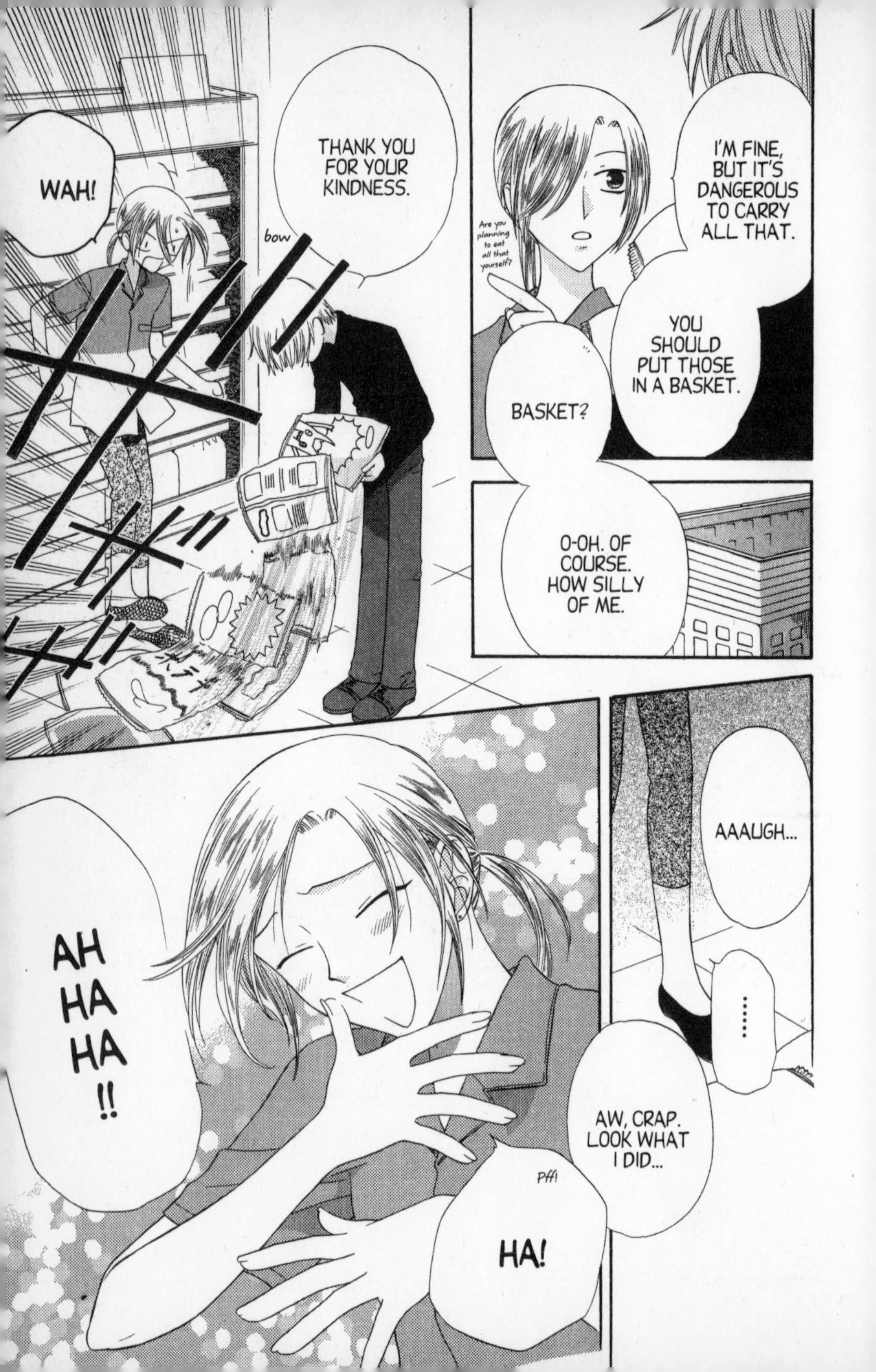
I'M FINE, BUT IT'S DANGEROUS TO CARRY ALL THAT.
YOU SHOULD PUT THOSE IN A BASKET.
Are you planning to eat all that yourself?
BASKET?
O-OH. OF COURSE. HOW SILLY OF ME.
THANK YOU FOR YOUR KINDNESS.
bow
WAH!
AAAUGH...
......
AW, CRAP. LOOK WHAT I DID...
Pff!
HA!
AH HA HA HA !!

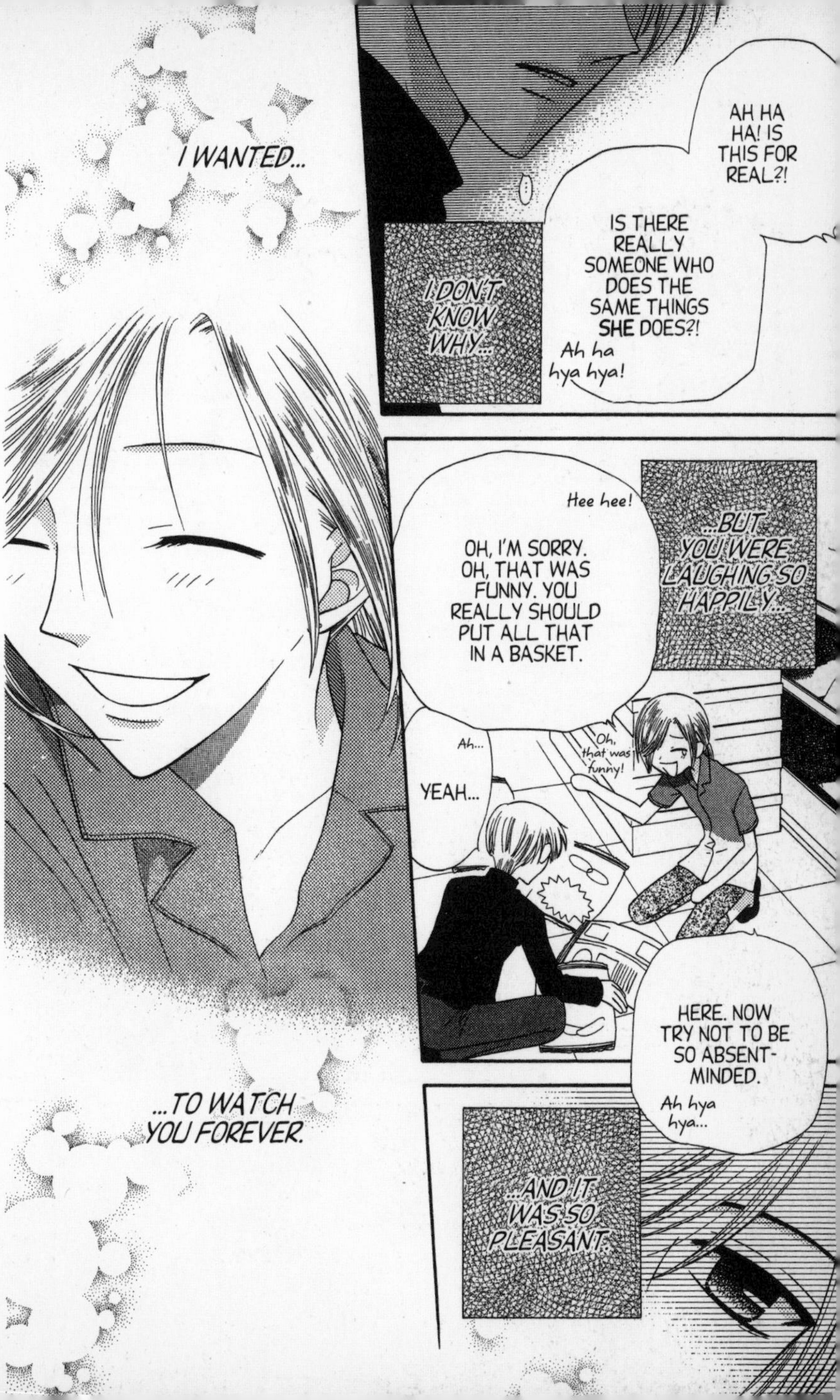
AH HA HA! IS THIS FOR REAL?!
IS THERE REALLY SOMEONE WHO DOES THE SAME THINGS SHE DOES?!
Ah ha hya hya!
I DON'T KNOW WHY...
...BUT YOU WERE LAUGHING SO HAPPILY...
Hee hee!
OH, I'M SORRY. OH, THAT WAS FUNNY. YOU REALLY SHOULD PUT ALL THAT IN A BASKET.
Oh, that was funny!
Ah...
YEAH...
HERE. NOW TRY NOT TO BE SO ABSENT-MINDED.
Ah hya hya...
...AND IT WAS SO PLEASANT.
I WANTED...
...TO WATCH YOU FOREVER.

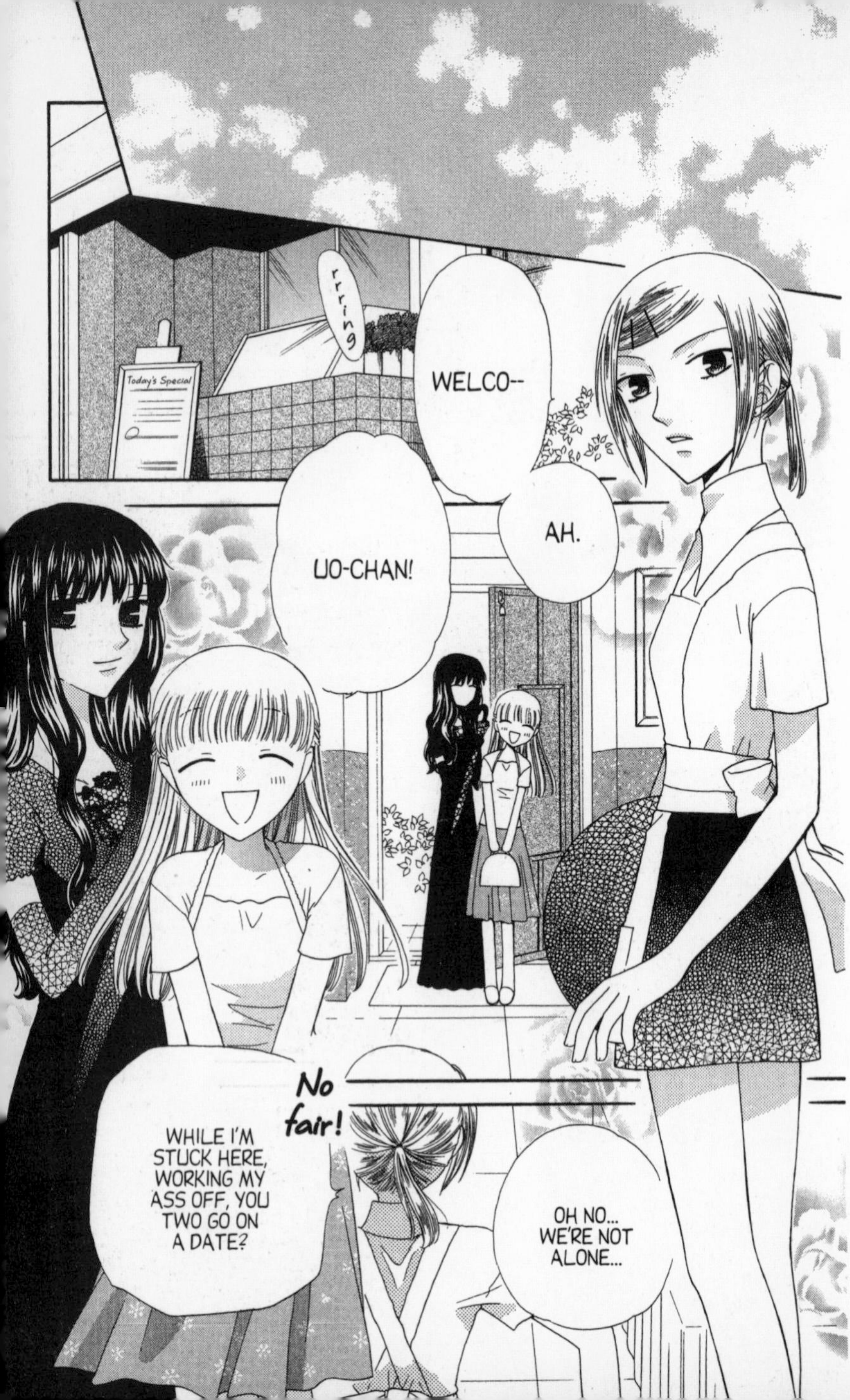
rrring
WELCO--
AH.
UO-CHAN!
OH NO... WE'RE NOT ALONE...
No fair!
WHILE I'M STUCK HERE, WORKING MY ASS OFF, YOU TWO GO ON A DATE?
Today's Special

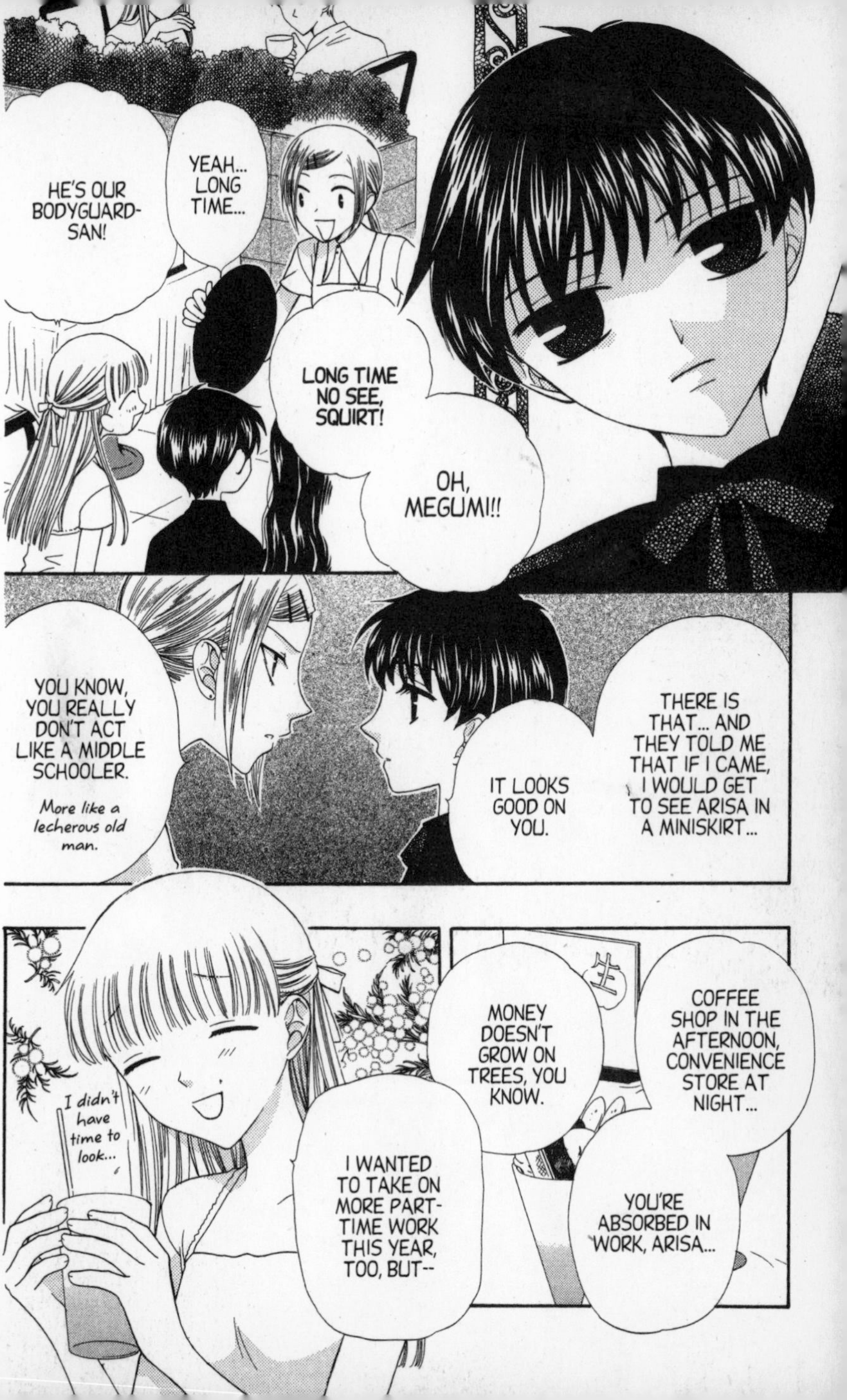
OH, MEGUMI!!
LONG TIME NO SEE, SQUIRT!
YEAH... LONG TIME...
HE'S OUR BODYGUARD-SAN!
THERE IS THAT... AND THEY TOLD ME THAT IF I CAME, I WOULD GET TO SEE ARISA IN A MINISKIRT...
IT LOOKS GOOD ON YOU.
YOU KNOW, YOU REALLY DON'T ACT LIKE A MIDDLE SCHOOLER.
More like a lecherous old man.
COFFEE SHOP IN THE AFTERNOON, CONVENIENCE STORE AT NIGHT...
MONEY DOESN'T GROW ON TREES, YOU KNOW.
YOU'RE ABSORBED IN WORK, ARISA...
I WANTED TO TAKE ON MORE PART-TIME WORK THIS YEAR, TOO, BUT--
I didn't have time to look...

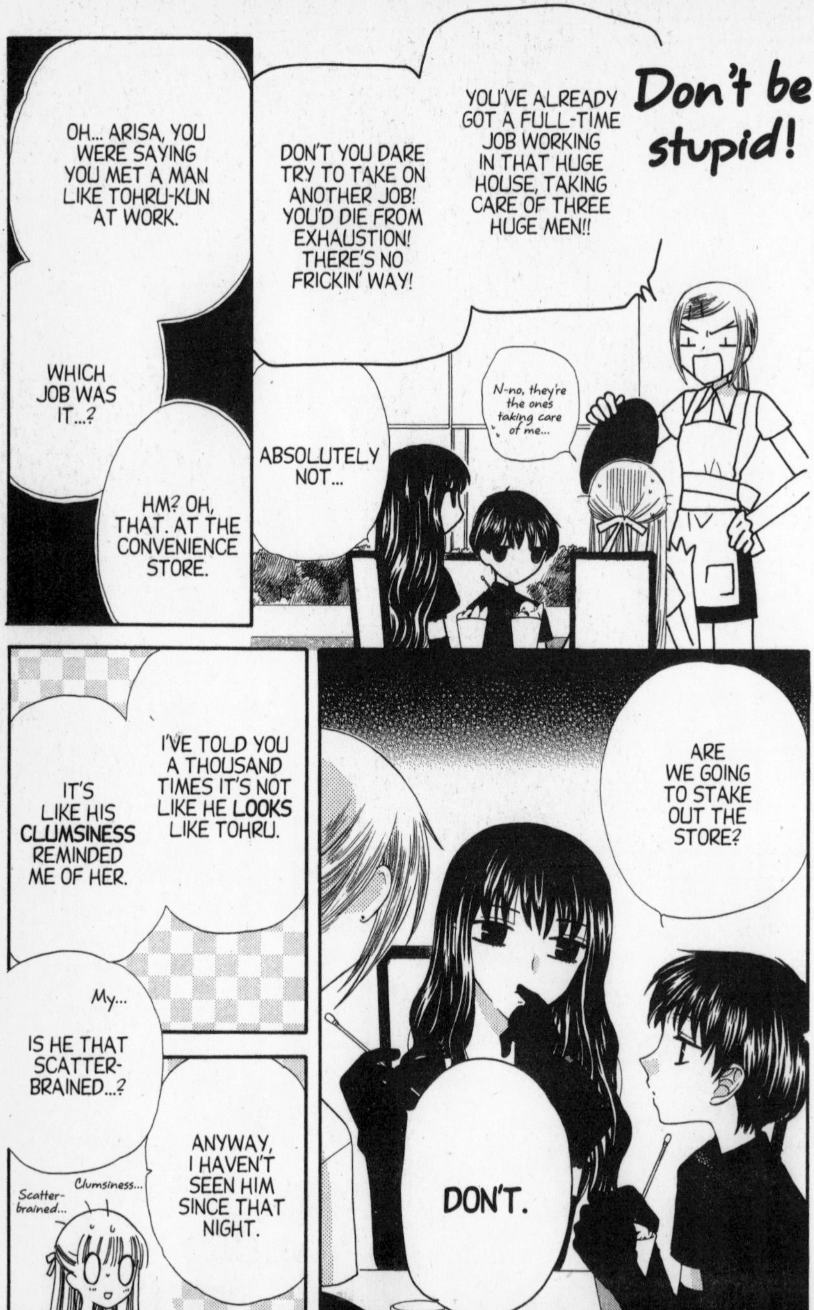
Don't be stupid!
YOU'VE ALREADY GOT A FULL-TIME JOB WORKING IN THAT HUGE HOUSE, TAKING CARE OF THREE HUGE MEN!!
DON'T YOU DARE TRY TO TAKE ON ANOTHER JOB! YOU'D DIE FROM EXHAUSTION! THERE'S NO FRICKIN' WAY!
N-no, they're the ones taking care of me...
ABSOLUTELY NOT...
OH... ARISA, YOU WERE SAYING YOU MET A MAN LIKE TOHRU-KUN AT WORK.
WHICH JOB WAS IT...?
HM? OH, THAT. AT THE CONVENIENCE STORE.
ARE WE GOING TO STAKE OUT THE STORE?
DON'T.
I'VE TOLD YOU A THOUSAND TIMES IT'S NOT LIKE HE LOOKS LIKE TOHRU.
IT'S LIKE HIS CLUMSINESS REMINDED ME OF HER.
My...
IS HE THAT SCATTER-BRAINED...?
ANYWAY, I HAVEN'T SEEN HIM SINCE THAT NIGHT.
Clumsiness...
Scatter-brained...

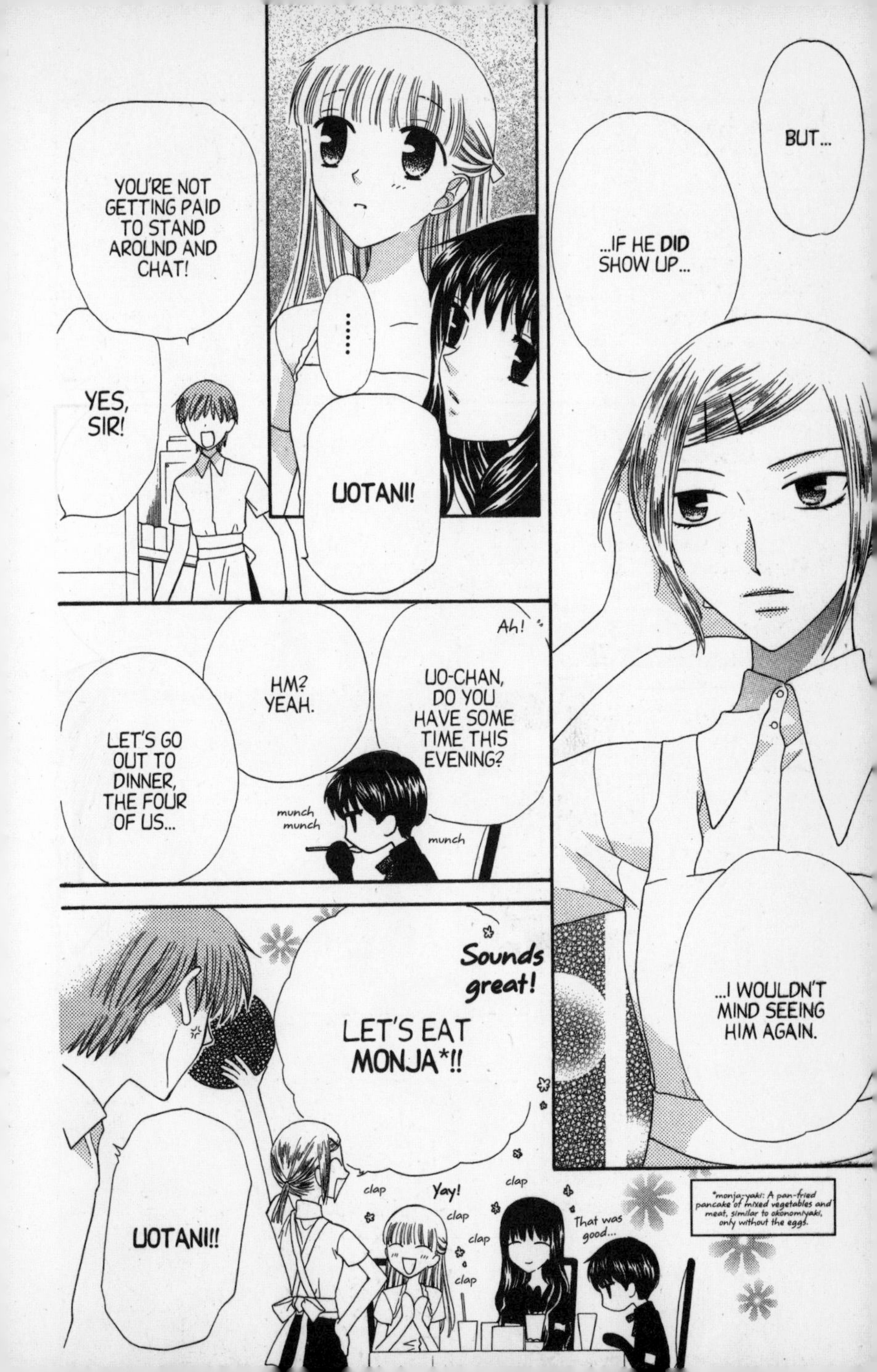
BUT...
...IF HE DID SHOW UP...
...I WOULDN'T MIND SEEING HIM AGAIN.
......
UOTANI!
YOU'RE NOT GETTING PAID TO STAND AROUND AND CHAT!
YES, SIR!
Ah!
UO-CHAN, DO YOU HAVE SOME TIME THIS EVENING?
HM? YEAH.
LET'S GO OUT TO DINNER, THE FOUR OF US...
munch munch
munch
Sounds great!
LET'S EAT MONJA*!!
UOTANI!!
clap
Yay!
clap
clap
clap
clap
That was good...
*monja-yaki: A pan-fried pancake of mixed vegetables and meat, similar to okonomiyaki, only without the eggs.

Fruits Basket 9 Part 2:

So I bought a new tracing table. People kept telling me, "Buy a new one!" "That one's too small," "No manga artist has such a cheap tracing table these days," etc. I finally gave in. My old one was pretty cheap... I chose it and bought it when I was drawing the first chapter of Gen'ei Musou, which I will never forget. I had no money, but I wanted to buy the best one I could.

To be continued...

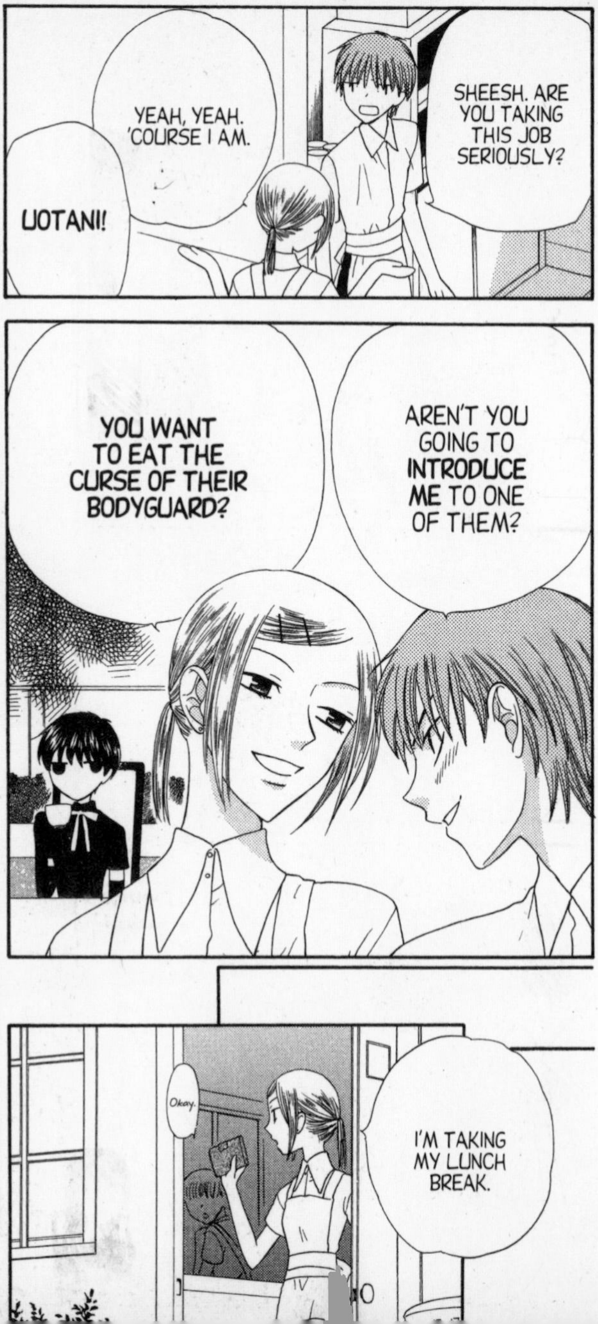
SHEESH. ARE YOU TAKING THIS JOB SERIOUSLY?
YEAH, YEAH. 'COURSE I AM.
UOTANI!
AREN'T YOU GOING TO INTRODUCE ME TO ONE OF THEM?
YOU WANT TO EAT THE CURSE OF THEIR BODYGUARD?
I'M TAKING MY LUNCH BREAK.
Okay.

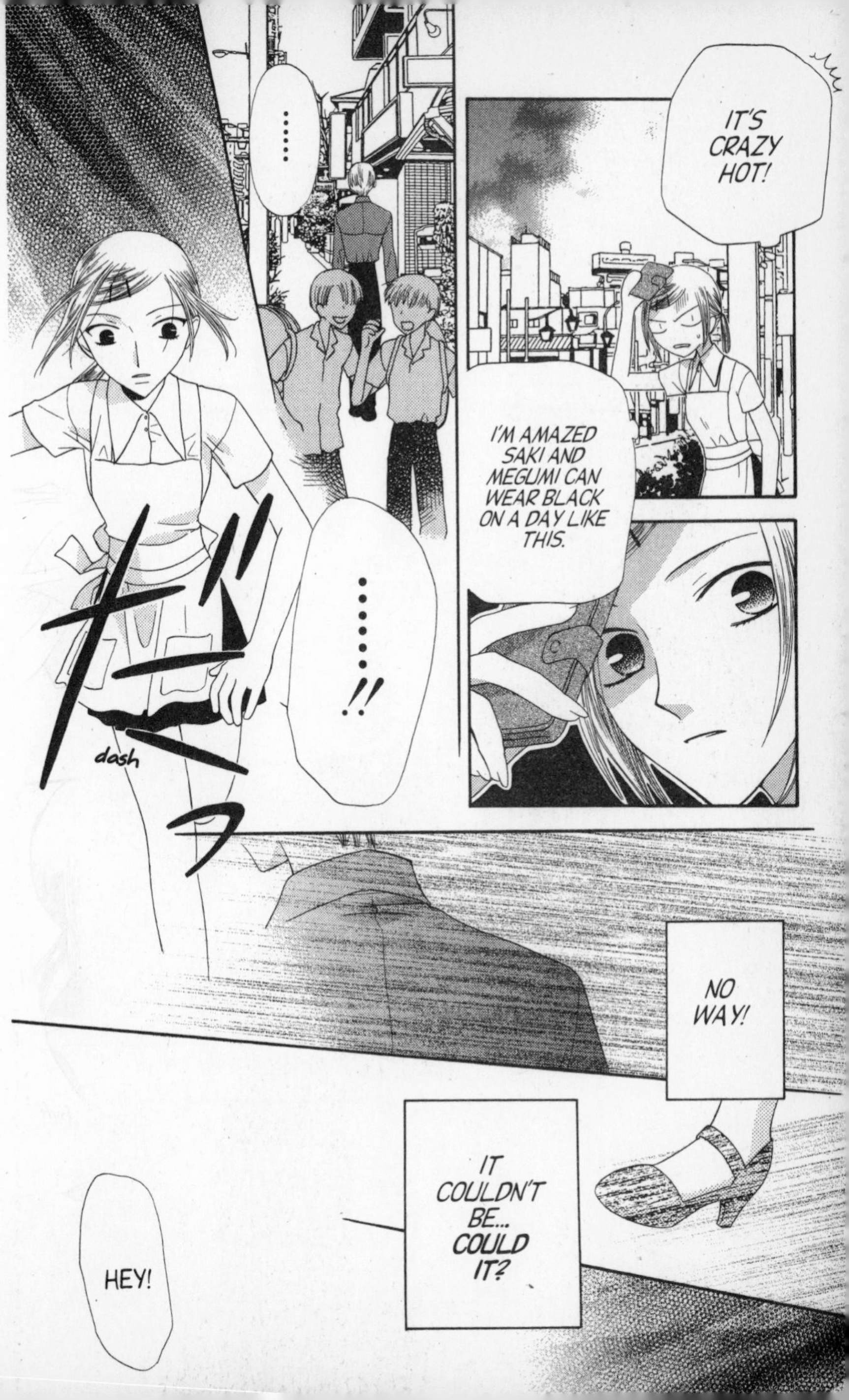
IT'S CRAZY HOT!
I'M AMAZED SAKI AND MEGUMI CAN WEAR BLACK ON A DAY LIKE THIS.
......
......!!
dash
NO WAY!
IT COULDN'T BE... COULD IT?
HEY!

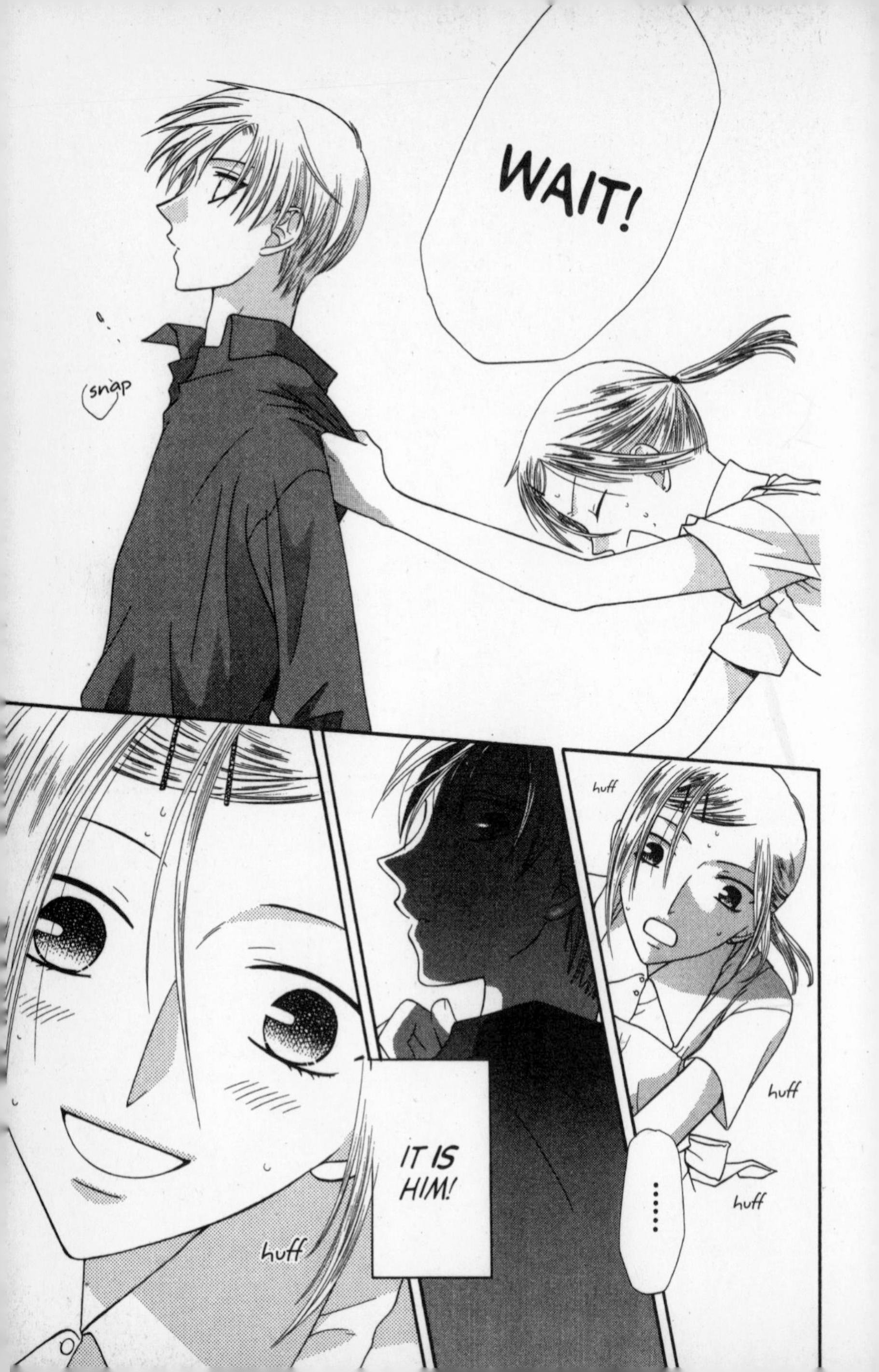
WAIT!
snap
huff
huff
huff
......
IT IS HIM!
huff

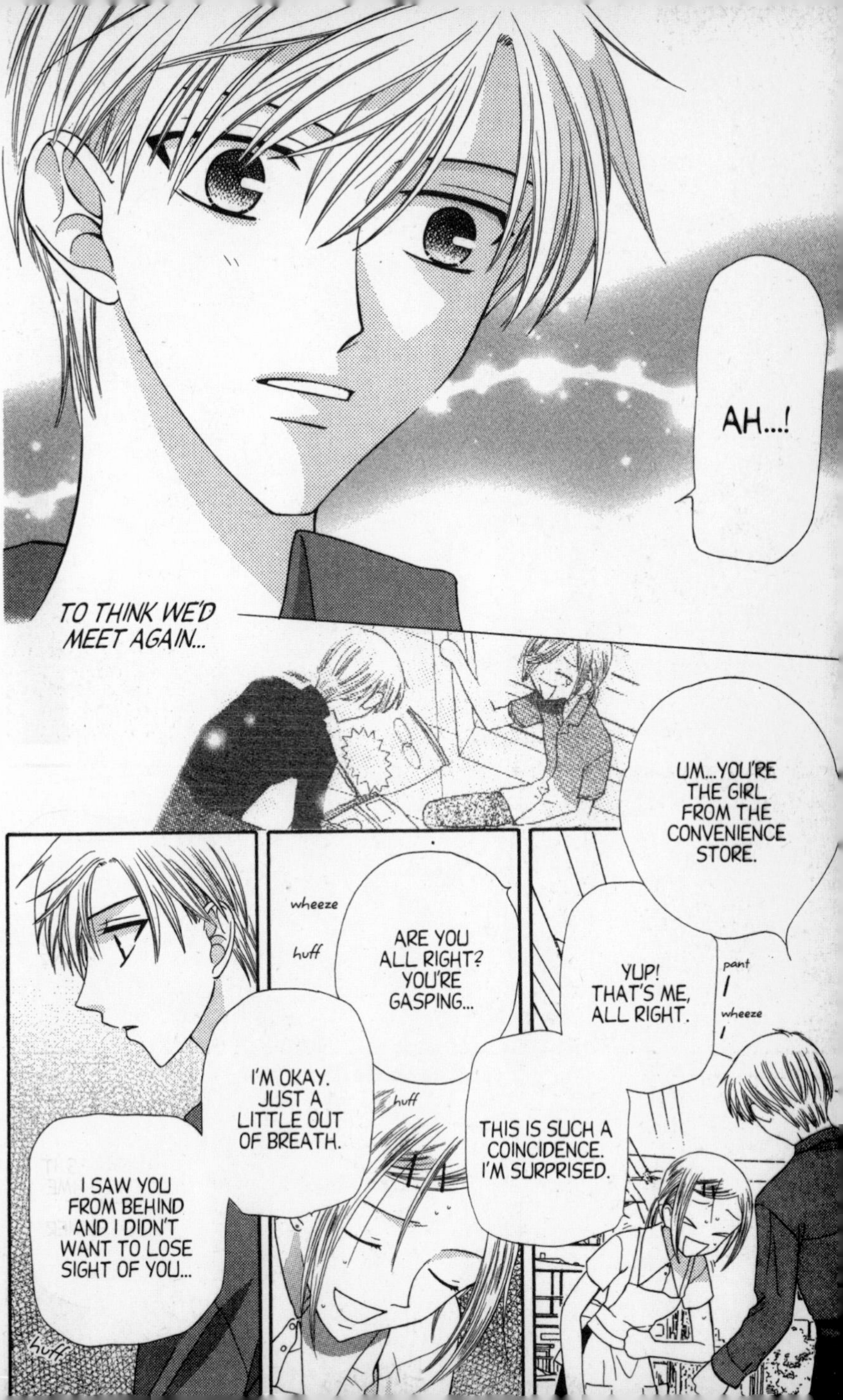
AH...!
TO THINK WE'D MEET AGAIN...
UM...YOU'RE THE GIRL FROM THE CONVENIENCE STORE.
pant
wheeze
YUP! THAT'S ME, ALL RIGHT.
THIS IS SUCH A COINCIDENCE. I'M SURPRISED.
wheeze
huff
ARE YOU ALL RIGHT? YOU'RE GASPING...
huff
I'M OKAY. JUST A LITTLE OUT OF BREATH.
I SAW YOU FROM BEHIND AND I DIDN'T WANT TO LOSE SIGHT OF YOU...
huff

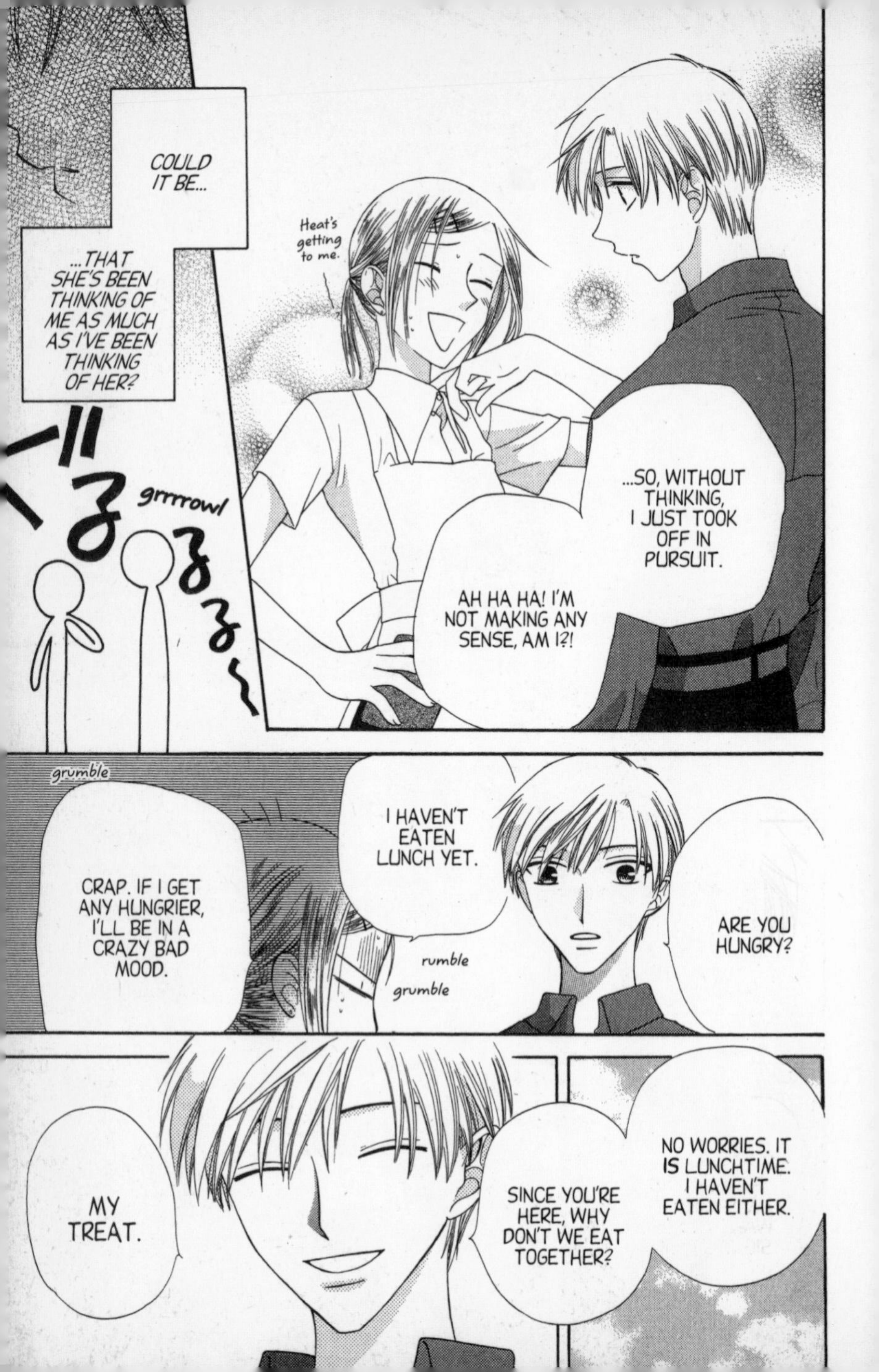
...SO, WITHOUT THINKING, I JUST TOOK OFF IN PURSUIT.
Heat's getting to me.
AH HA HA! I'M NOT MAKING ANY SENSE, AM I?!
COULD IT BE...
...THAT SHE'S BEEN THINKING OF ME AS MUCH AS I'VE BEEN THINKING OF HER?
grrrrowl
ARE YOU HUNGRY?
I HAVEN'T EATEN LUNCH YET.
rumble
grumble
grumble
CRAP. IF I GET ANY HUNGRIER, I'LL BE IN A CRAZY BAD MOOD.
NO WORRIES. IT **IS** LUNCHTIME. I HAVEN'T EATEN EITHER.
SINCE YOU'RE HERE, WHY DON'T WE EAT TOGETHER?
MY TREAT.

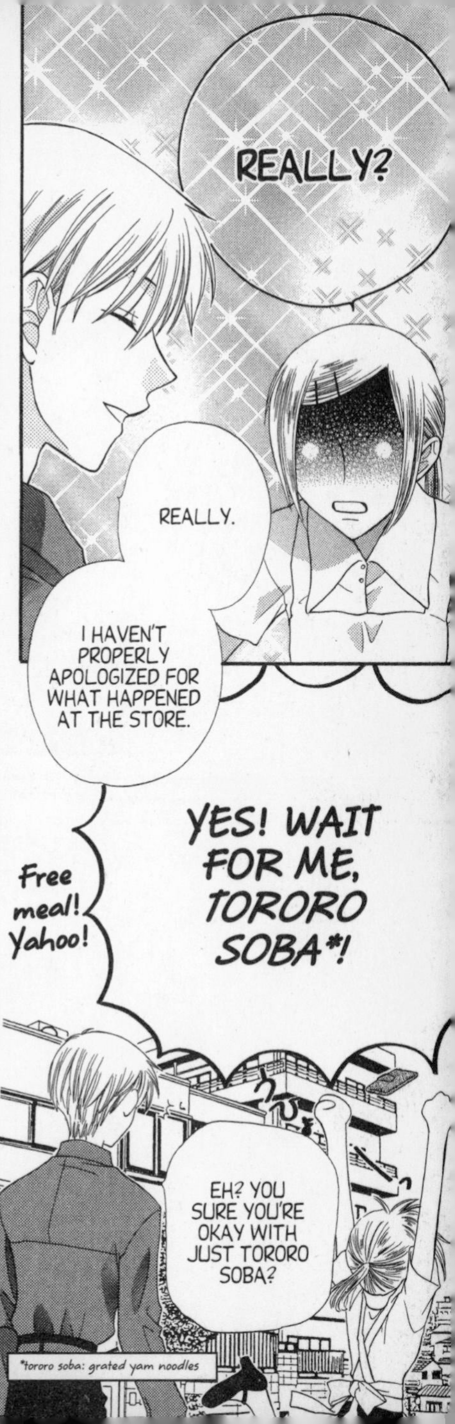
REALLY?
REALLY.
I HAVEN'T PROPERLY APOLOGIZED FOR WHAT HAPPENED AT THE STORE.
YES! WAIT FOR ME, TORORO SOBA*!
Free meal! Yahoo!
EH? YOU SURE YOU'RE OKAY WITH JUST TORORO SOBA?
*tororo soba: grated yam noodles

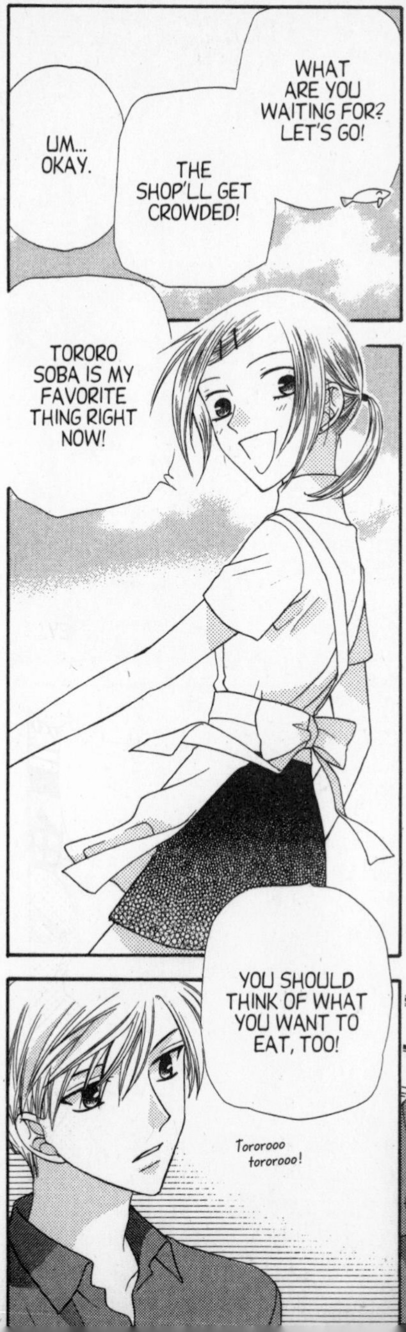
WHAT ARE YOU WAITING FOR? LET'S GO!
THE SHOP'LL GET CROWDED!
UM... OKAY.
TORORO SOBA IS MY FAVORITE THING RIGHT NOW!
YOU SHOULD THINK OF WHAT YOU WANT TO EAT, TOO!
Tororooo tororooo!

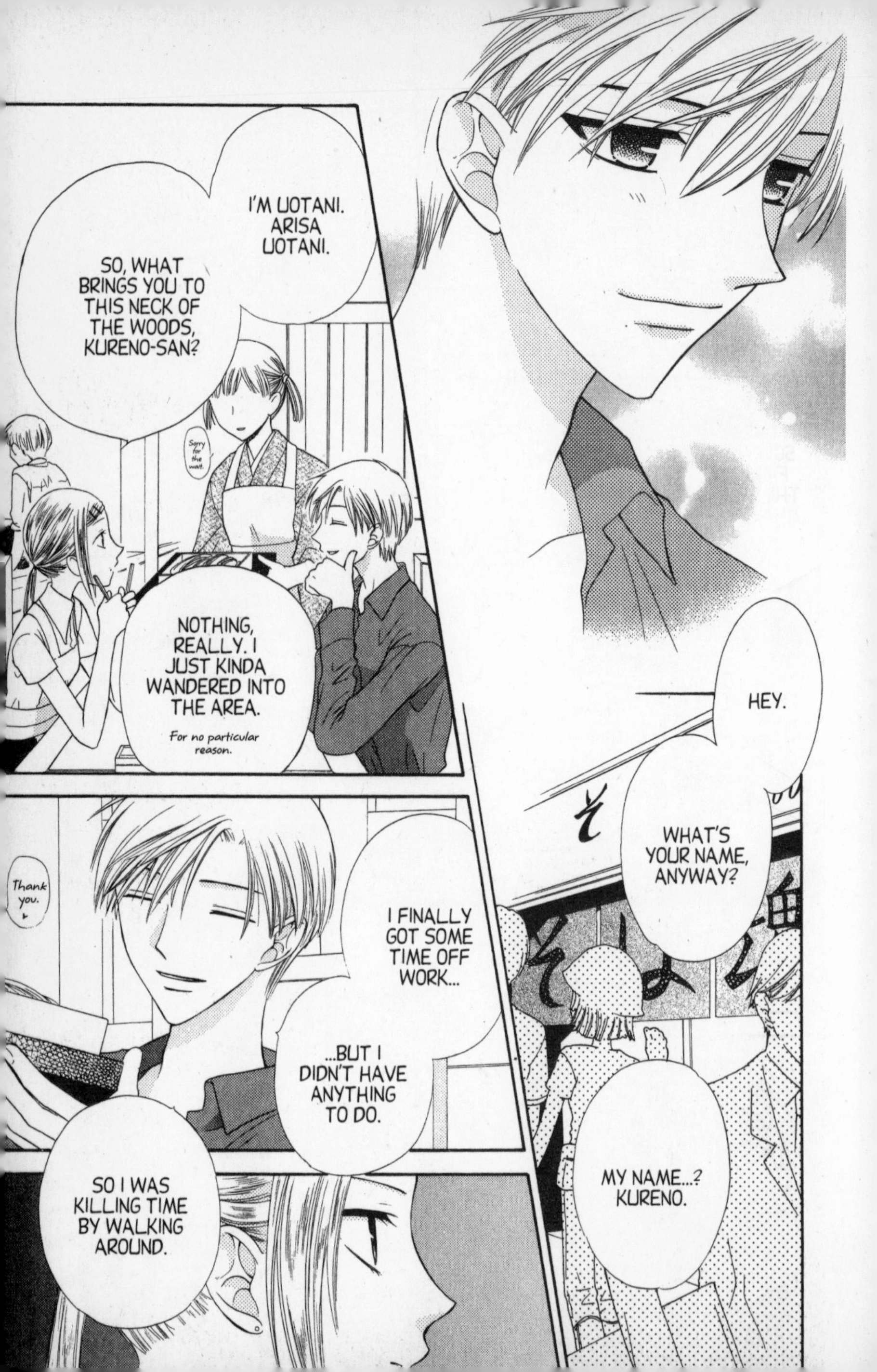
HEY.
WHAT'S YOUR NAME, ANYWAY?
MY NAME...? KURENO.
I'M UOTANI. ARISA UOTANI.
SO, WHAT BRINGS YOU TO THIS NECK OF THE WOODS, KURENO-SAN?
Sorry for the wait.
NOTHING, REALLY. I JUST KINDA WANDERED INTO THE AREA.
For no particular reason.
I FINALLY GOT SOME TIME OFF WORK...
...BUT I DIDN'T HAVE ANYTHING TO DO.
Thank you.
SO I WAS KILLING TIME BY WALKING AROUND.

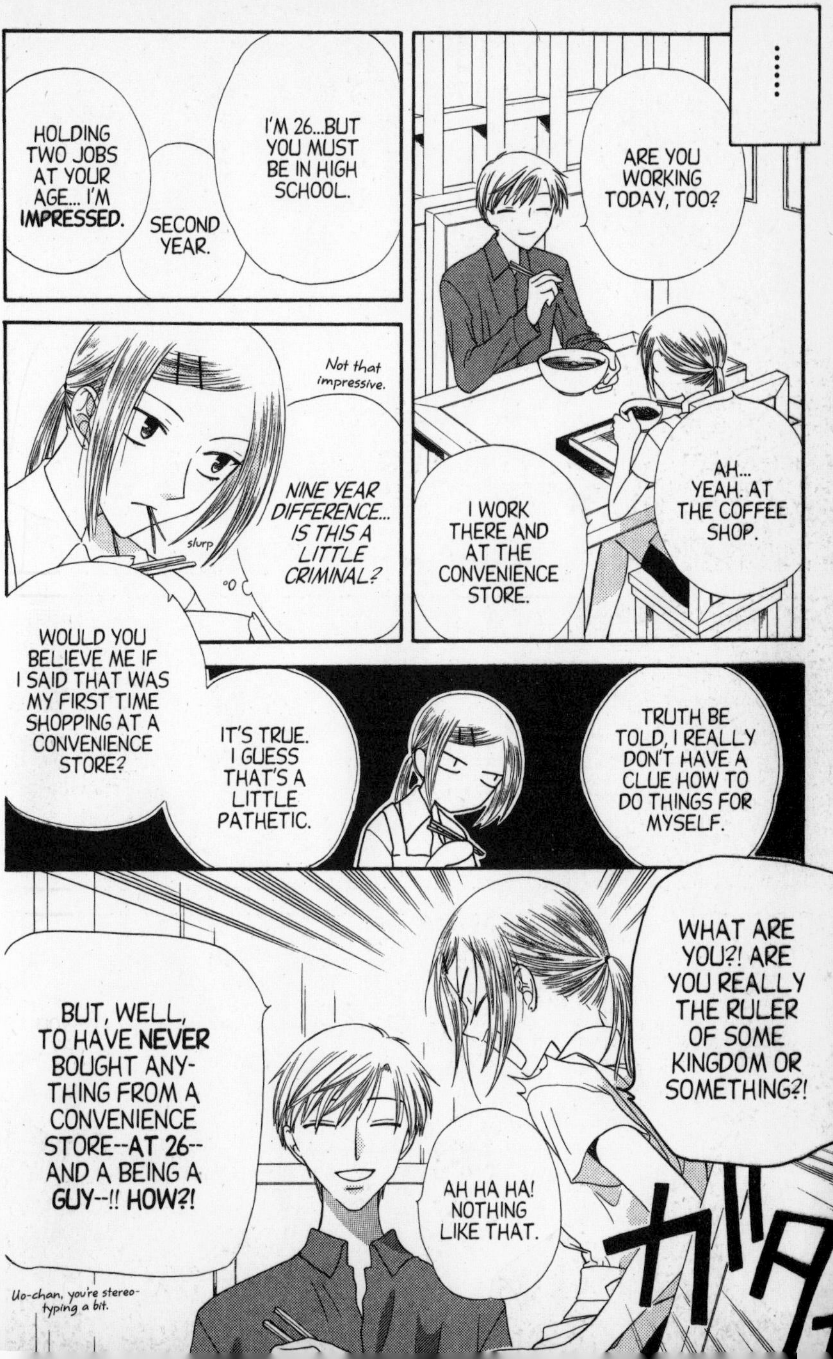
......
ARE YOU WORKING TODAY, TOO?
AH... YEAH. AT THE COFFEE SHOP.
I WORK THERE AND AT THE CONVENIENCE STORE.
I'M 26...BUT YOU MUST BE IN HIGH SCHOOL.
SECOND YEAR.
HOLDING TWO JOBS AT YOUR AGE... I'M **IMPRESSED.**
Not that impressive.
NINE YEAR DIFFERENCE... IS THIS A LITTLE CRIMINAL?
slurp
TRUTH BE TOLD, I REALLY DON'T HAVE A CLUE HOW TO DO THINGS FOR MYSELF.
IT'S TRUE. I GUESS THAT'S A LITTLE PATHETIC.
WOULD YOU BELIEVE ME IF I SAID THAT WAS MY FIRST TIME SHOPPING AT A CONVENIENCE STORE?
WHAT ARE YOU?! ARE YOU REALLY THE RULER OF SOME KINGDOM OR SOMETHING?!
BUT, WELL, TO HAVE **NEVER** BOUGHT ANY-THING FROM A CONVENIENCE STORE--**AT 26**--AND A BEING A **GUY**--!! **HOW?!**
AH HA HA! NOTHING LIKE THAT.
Uo-chan, you're stereo-typing a bit.

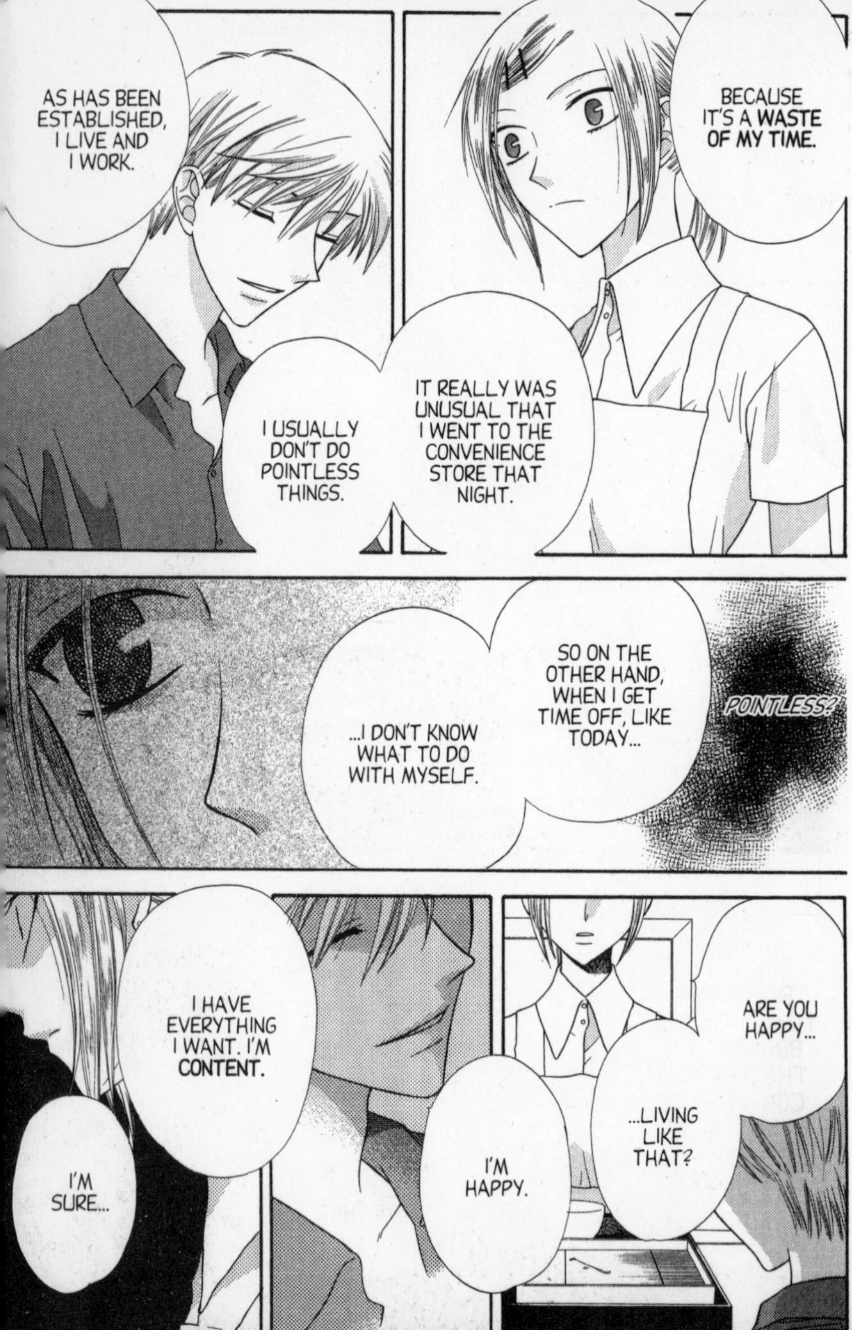
BECAUSE IT'S A **WASTE OF MY TIME.**
AS HAS BEEN ESTABLISHED, I LIVE AND I WORK.
IT REALLY WAS UNUSUAL THAT I WENT TO THE CONVENIENCE STORE THAT NIGHT.
I USUALLY DON'T DO POINTLESS THINGS.
POINTLESS?
SO ON THE OTHER HAND, WHEN I GET TIME OFF, LIKE TODAY...
...I DON'T KNOW WHAT TO DO WITH MYSELF.
ARE YOU HAPPY...
...LIVING LIKE THAT?
I'M HAPPY.
I HAVE EVERYTHING I WANT. I'M **CONTENT.**
I'M SURE...

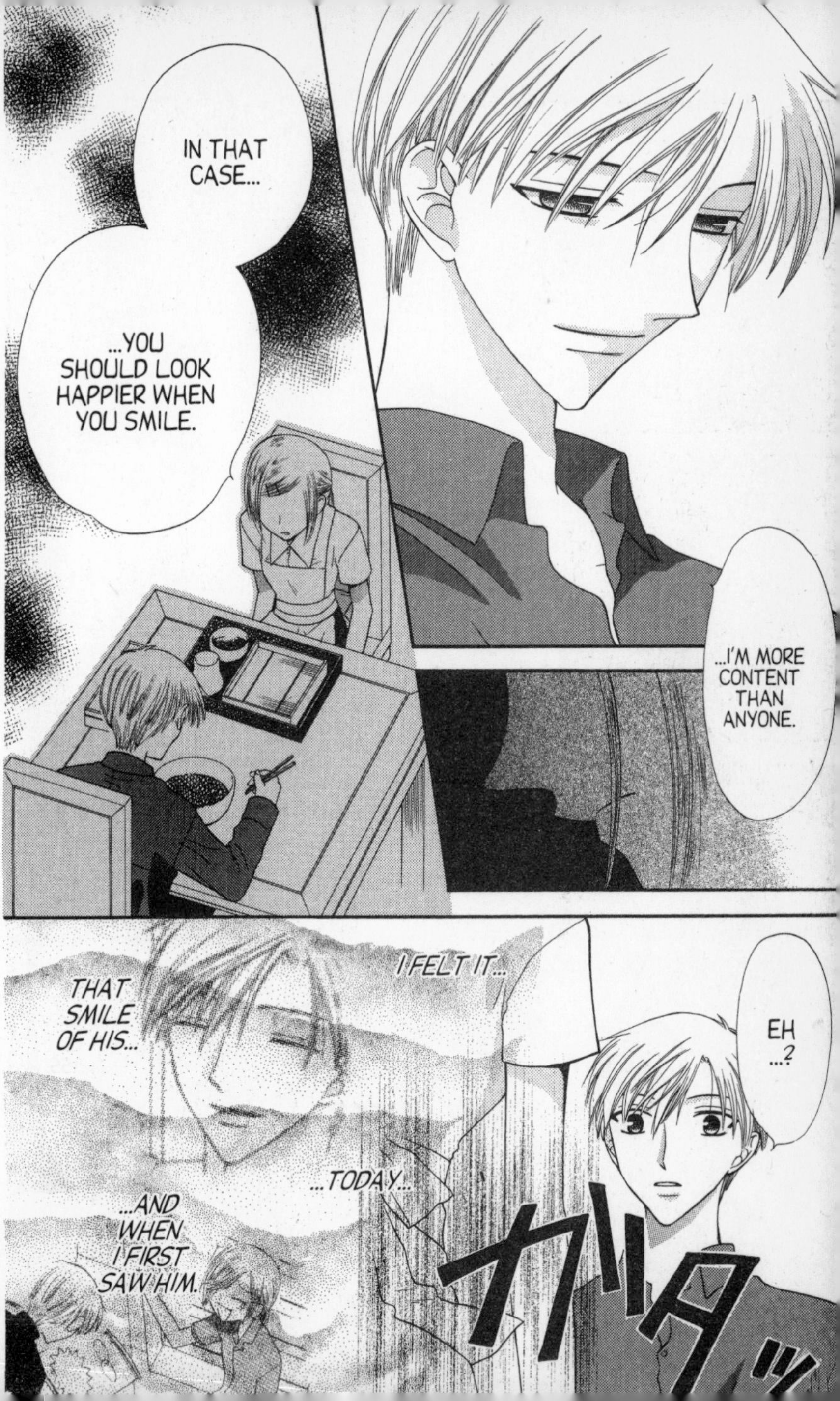
...I'M MORE CONTENT THAN ANYONE.
IN THAT CASE...
...YOU SHOULD LOOK HAPPIER WHEN YOU SMILE.
EH ...?
I FELT IT...
THAT SMILE OF HIS...
...TODAY...
...AND WHEN I FIRST SAW HIM.
ガタッ

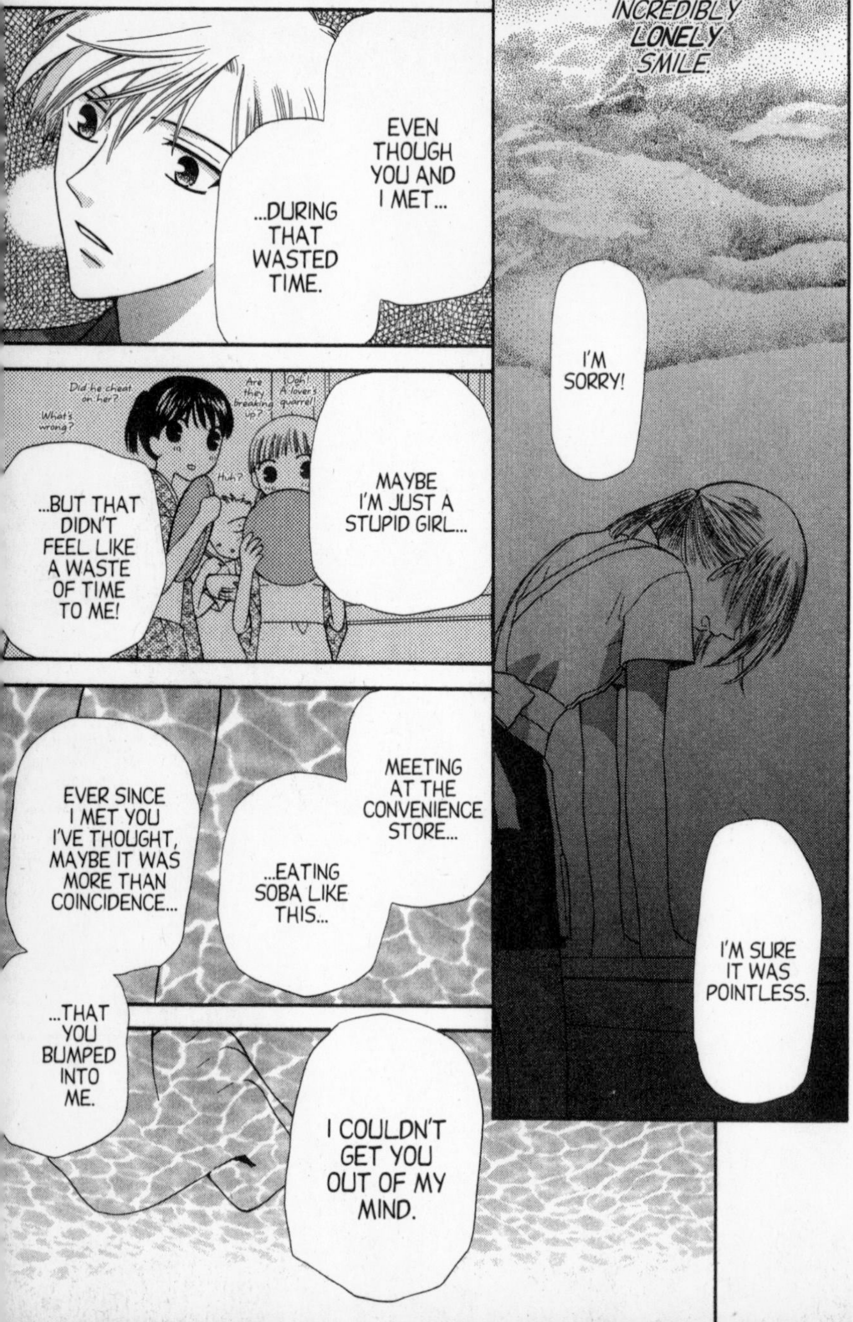
IT'S AN INCREDIBLY LONELY SMILE.
I'M SORRY!
I'M SURE IT WAS POINTLESS.
EVEN THOUGH YOU AND I MET...
...DURING THAT WASTED TIME.
MAYBE I'M JUST A STUPID GIRL...
Ooh! A lover's quarrel!
Are they breaking up?
Did he cheat on her?
What's wrong?
Huh?
...BUT THAT DIDN'T FEEL LIKE A WASTE OF TIME TO ME!
MEETING AT THE CONVENIENCE STORE...
...EATING SOBA LIKE THIS...
EVER SINCE I MET YOU I'VE THOUGHT, MAYBE IT WAS MORE THAN COINCIDENCE...
...THAT YOU BUMPED INTO ME.
I COULDN'T GET YOU OUT OF MY MIND.

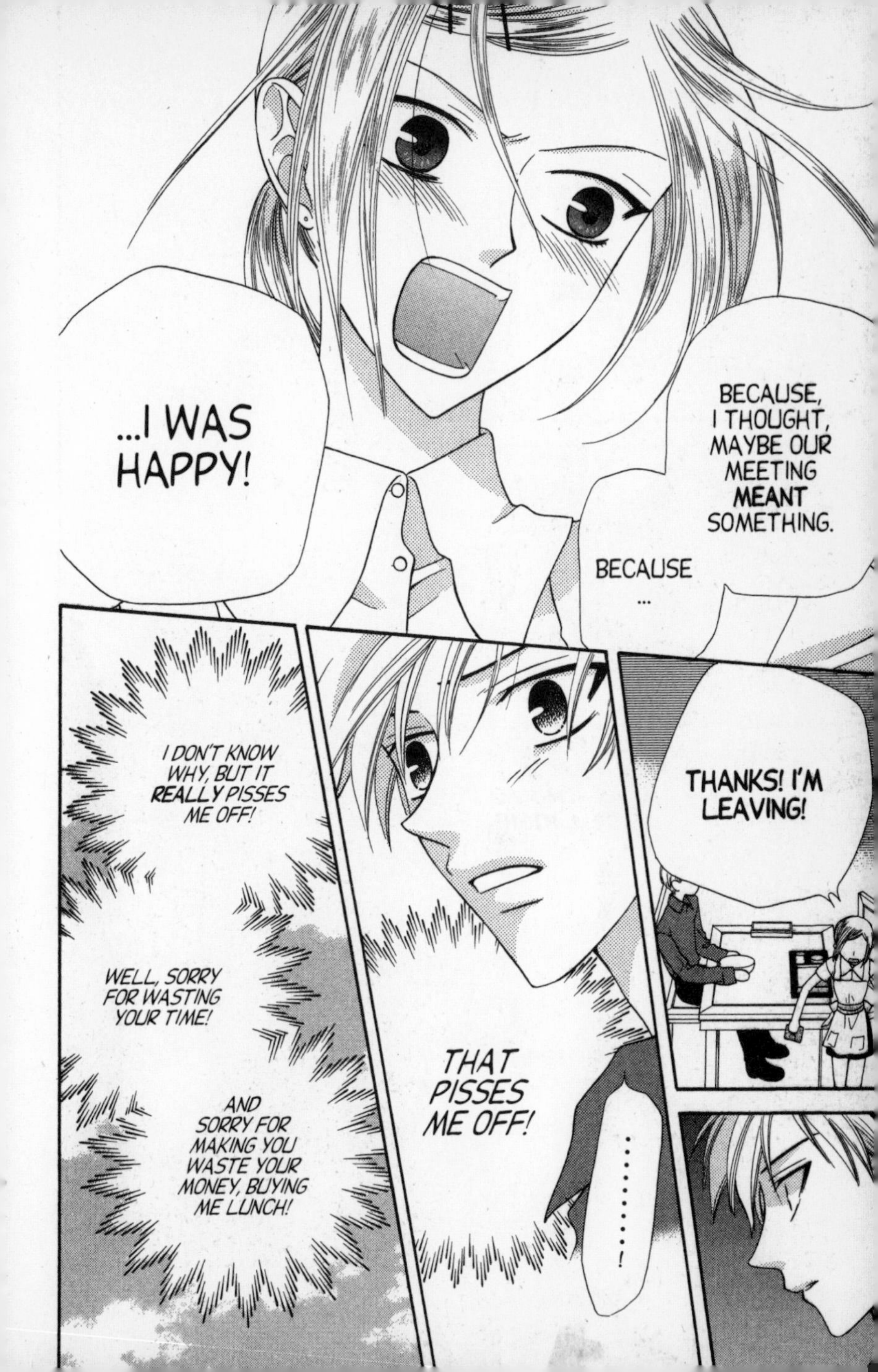
BECAUSE, I THOUGHT, MAYBE OUR MEETING MEANT SOMETHING.
BECAUSE ...
...I WAS HAPPY!
THANKS! I'M LEAVING!
THAT PISSES ME OFF!
..........!
I DON'T KNOW WHY, BUT IT REALLY PISSES ME OFF!
WELL, SORRY FOR WASTING YOUR TIME!
AND SORRY FOR MAKING YOU WASTE YOUR MONEY, BUYING ME LUNCH!

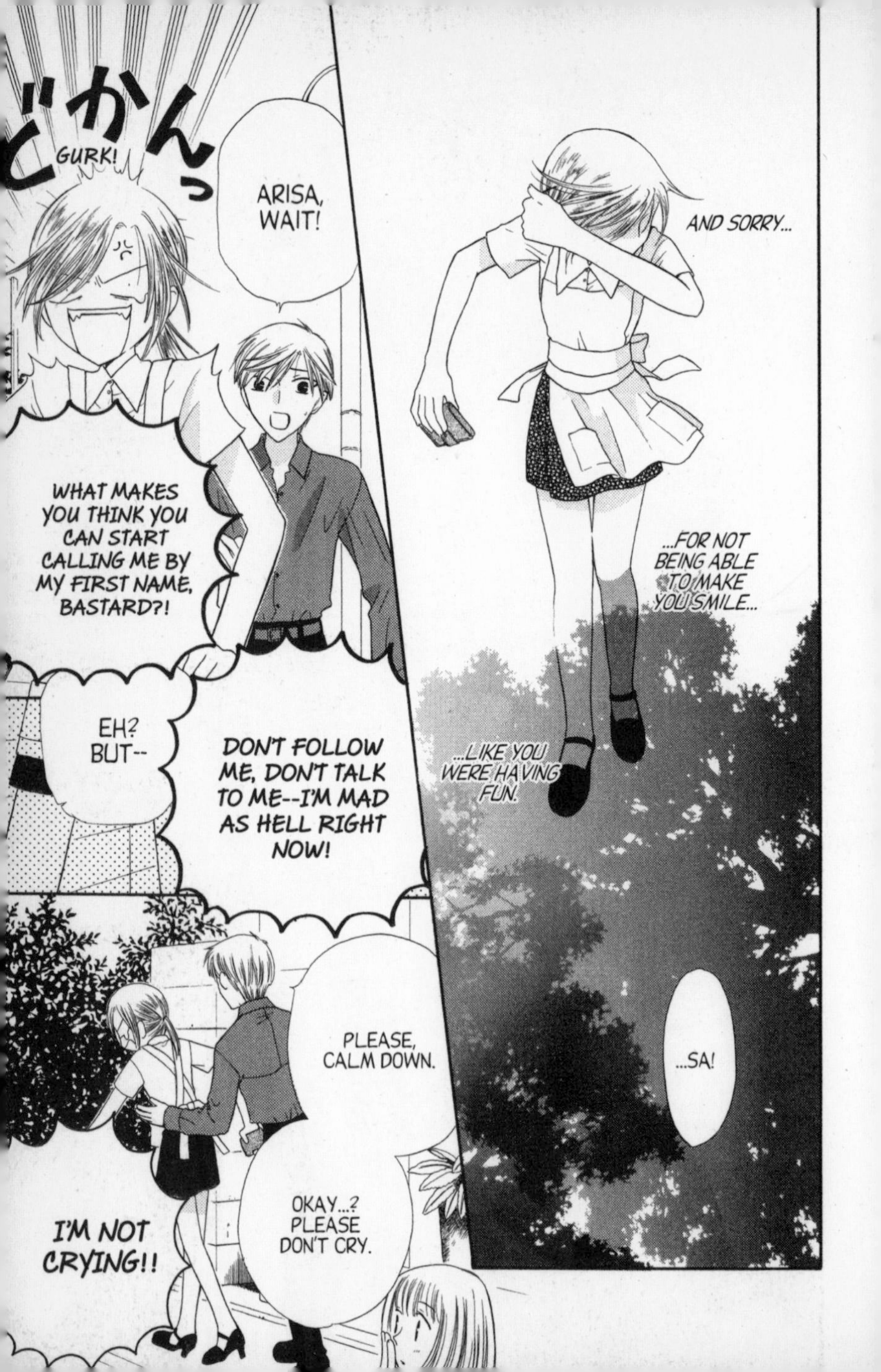
AND SORRY...
...FOR NOT BEING ABLE TO MAKE YOU SMILE...
...LIKE YOU WERE HAVING FUN.
...SA!
ARISA, WAIT!
どかんっ
GURK!
WHAT MAKES YOU THINK YOU CAN START CALLING ME BY MY FIRST NAME, BASTARD?!
EH? BUT--
DON'T FOLLOW ME, DON'T TALK TO ME--I'M MAD AS HELL RIGHT NOW!
PLEASE, CALM DOWN.
OKAY...? PLEASE DON'T CRY.
I'M NOT CRYING!!

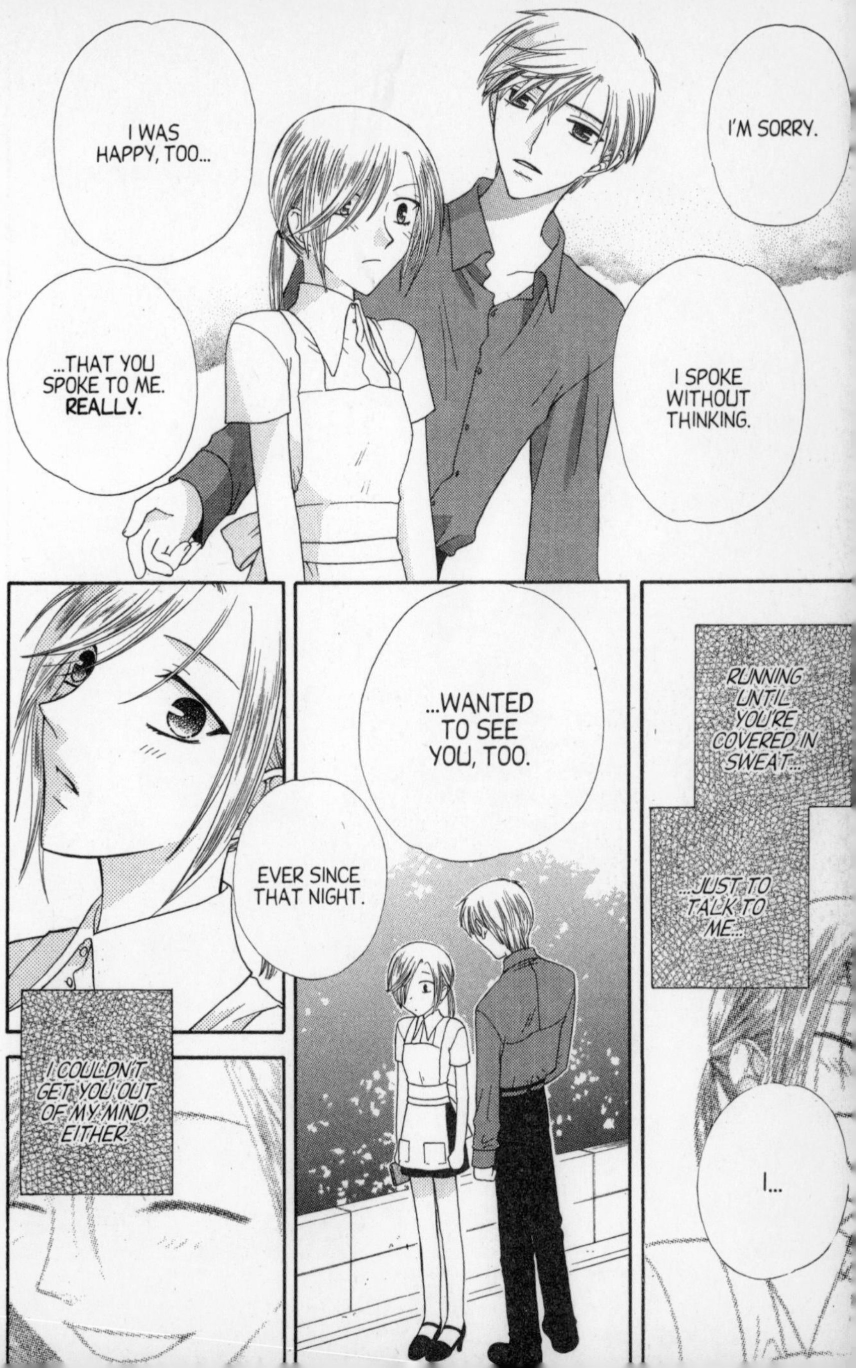
I'M SORRY.
I SPOKE WITHOUT THINKING.
I WAS HAPPY, TOO...
...THAT YOU SPOKE TO ME. REALLY.
RUNNING UNTIL YOU'RE COVERED IN SWEAT...
...JUST TO TALK TO ME...
I...
...WANTED TO SEE YOU, TOO.
EVER SINCE THAT NIGHT.
I COULDN'T GET YOU OUT OF MY MIND, EITHER.

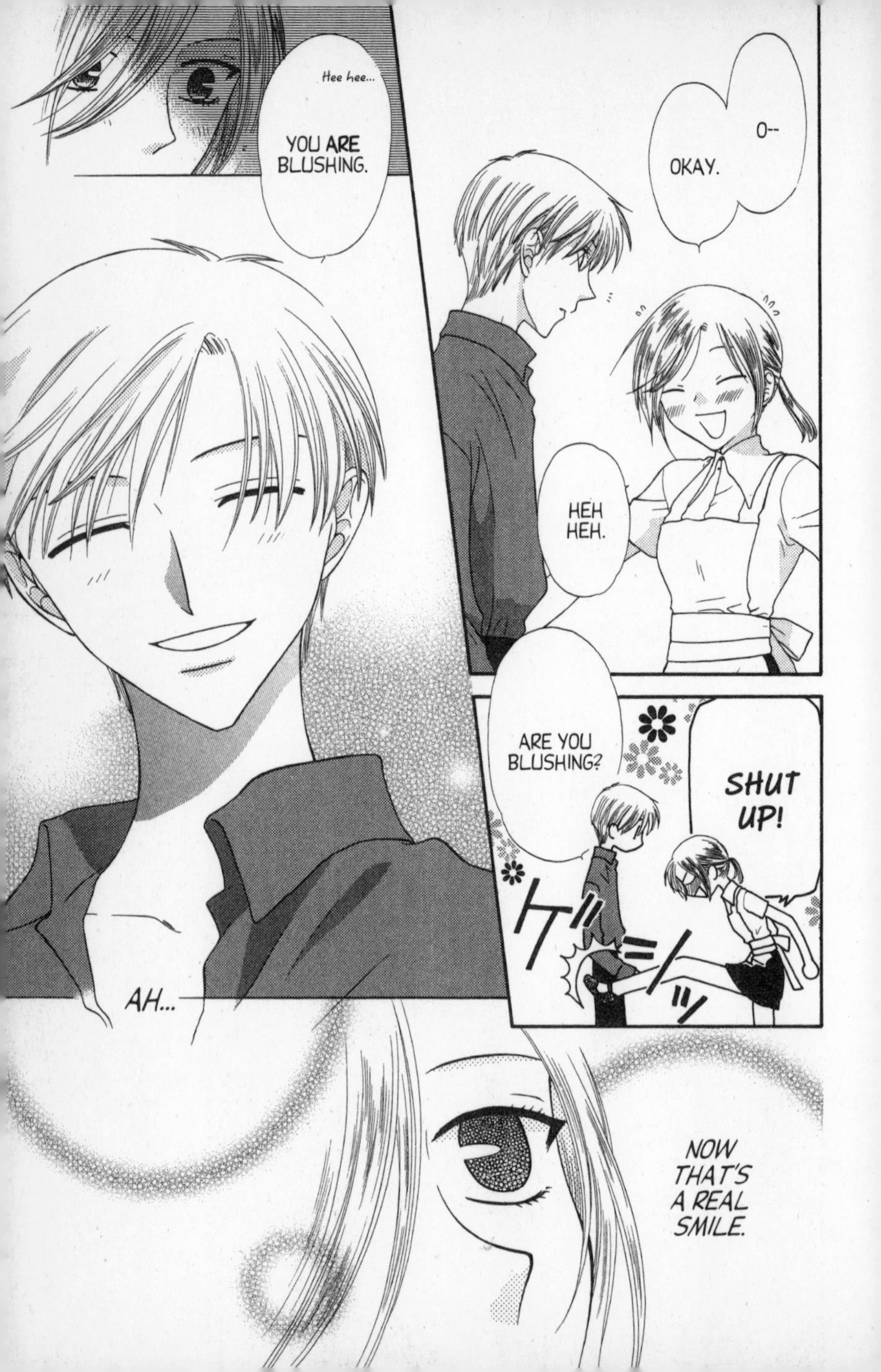
O--
OKAY.
HEH HEH.
ARE YOU BLUSHING?
SHUT UP!
Hee hee...
YOU ARE BLUSHING.
AH...
NOW THAT'S A REAL SMILE.

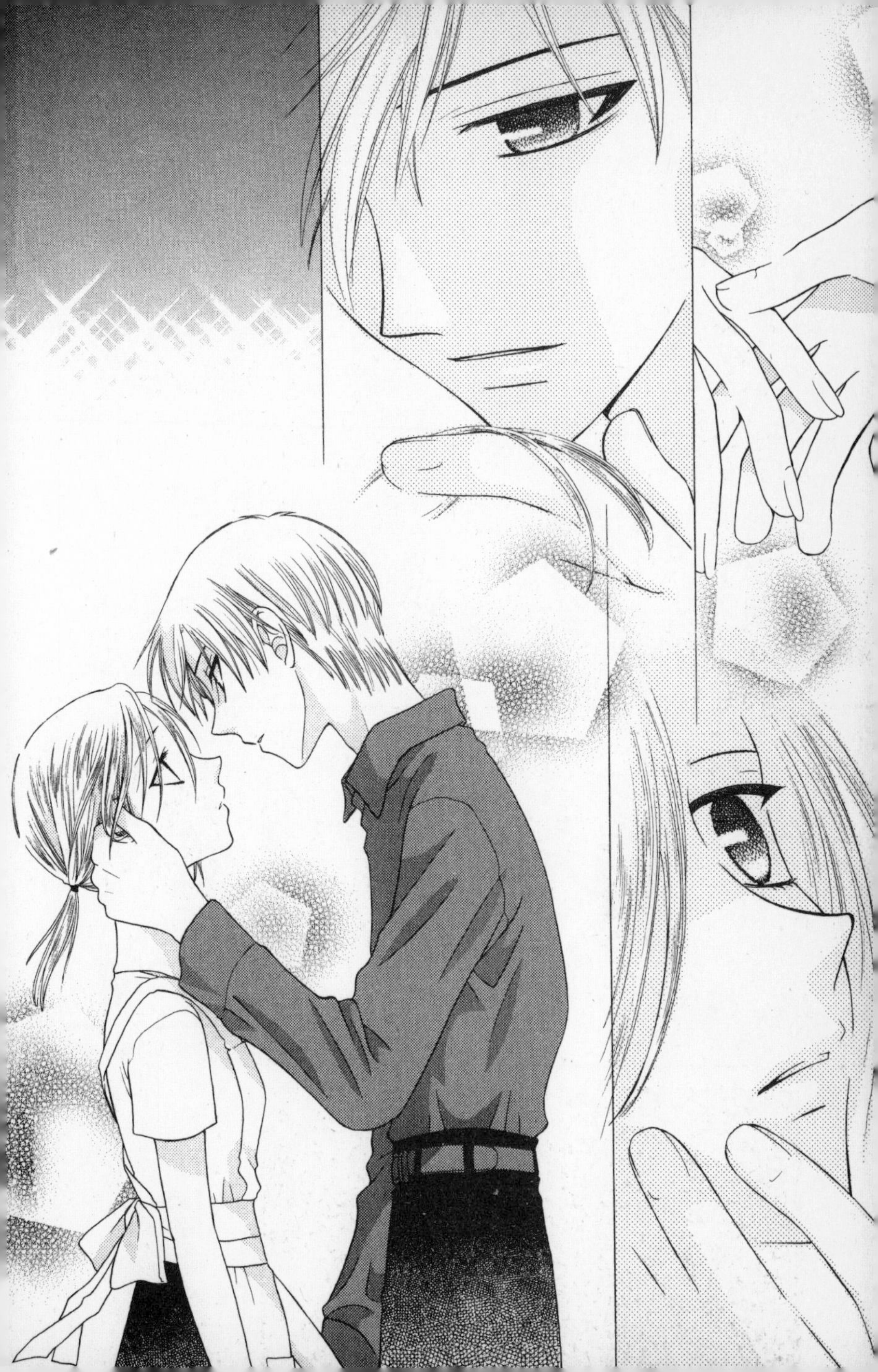

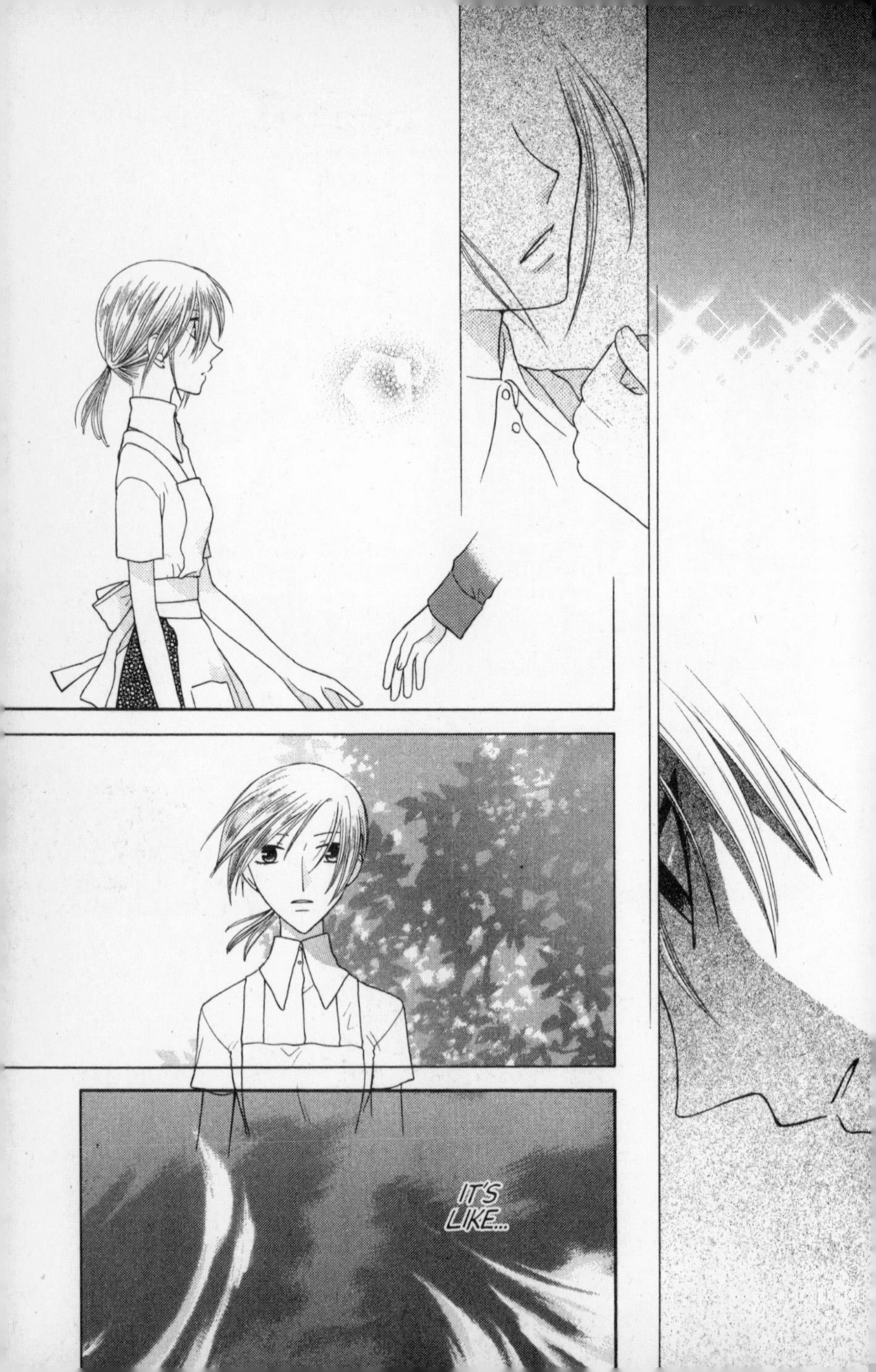
IT'S LIKE...

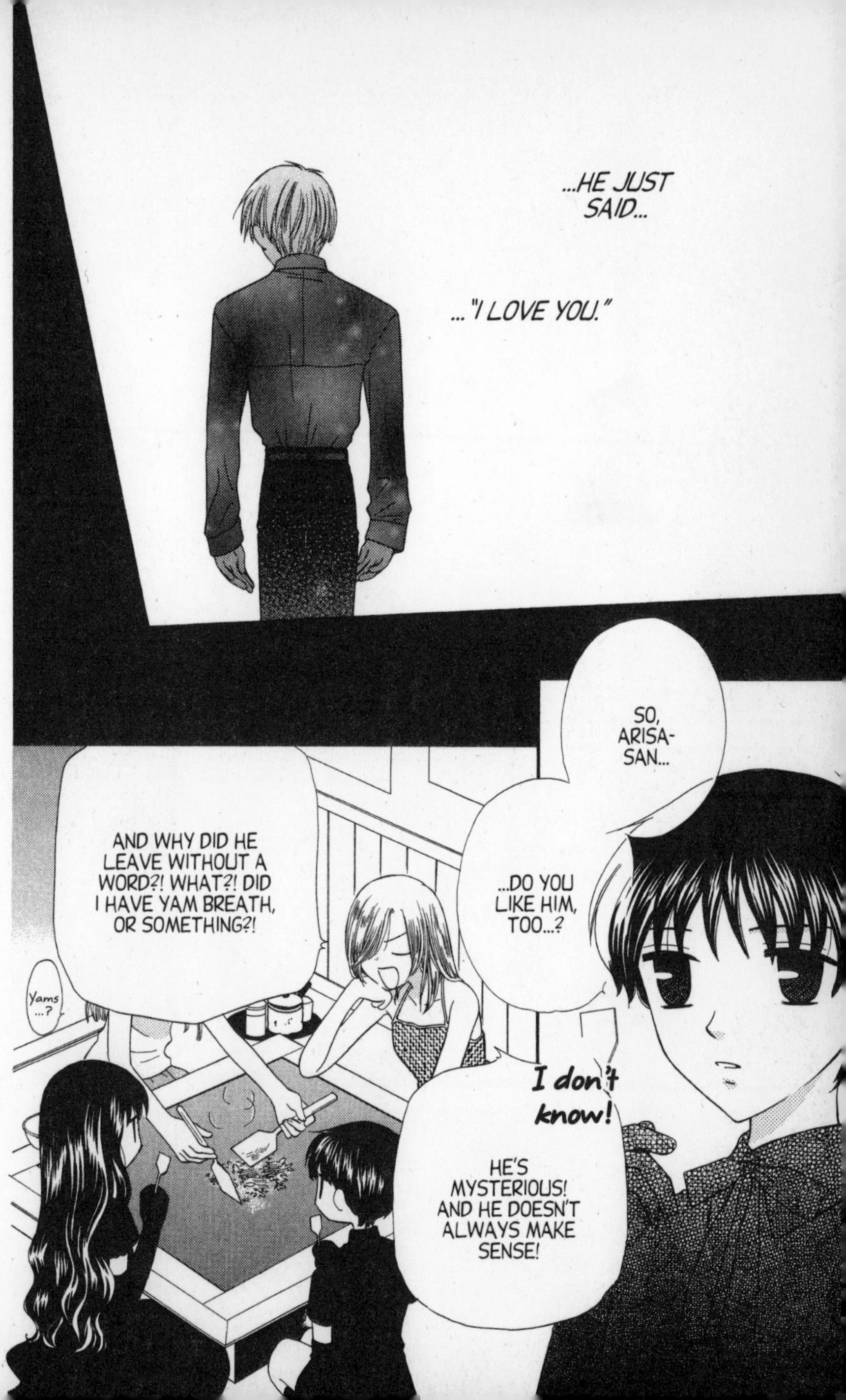
...HE JUST SAID...
..."I LOVE YOU."
SO, ARISA-SAN...
...DO YOU LIKE HIM, TOO...?
I don't know!
HE'S MYSTERIOUS! AND HE DOESN'T ALWAYS MAKE SENSE!
AND WHY DID HE LEAVE WITHOUT A WORD?! WHAT?! DID I HAVE YAM BREATH, OR SOMETHING?!
Yams ...?

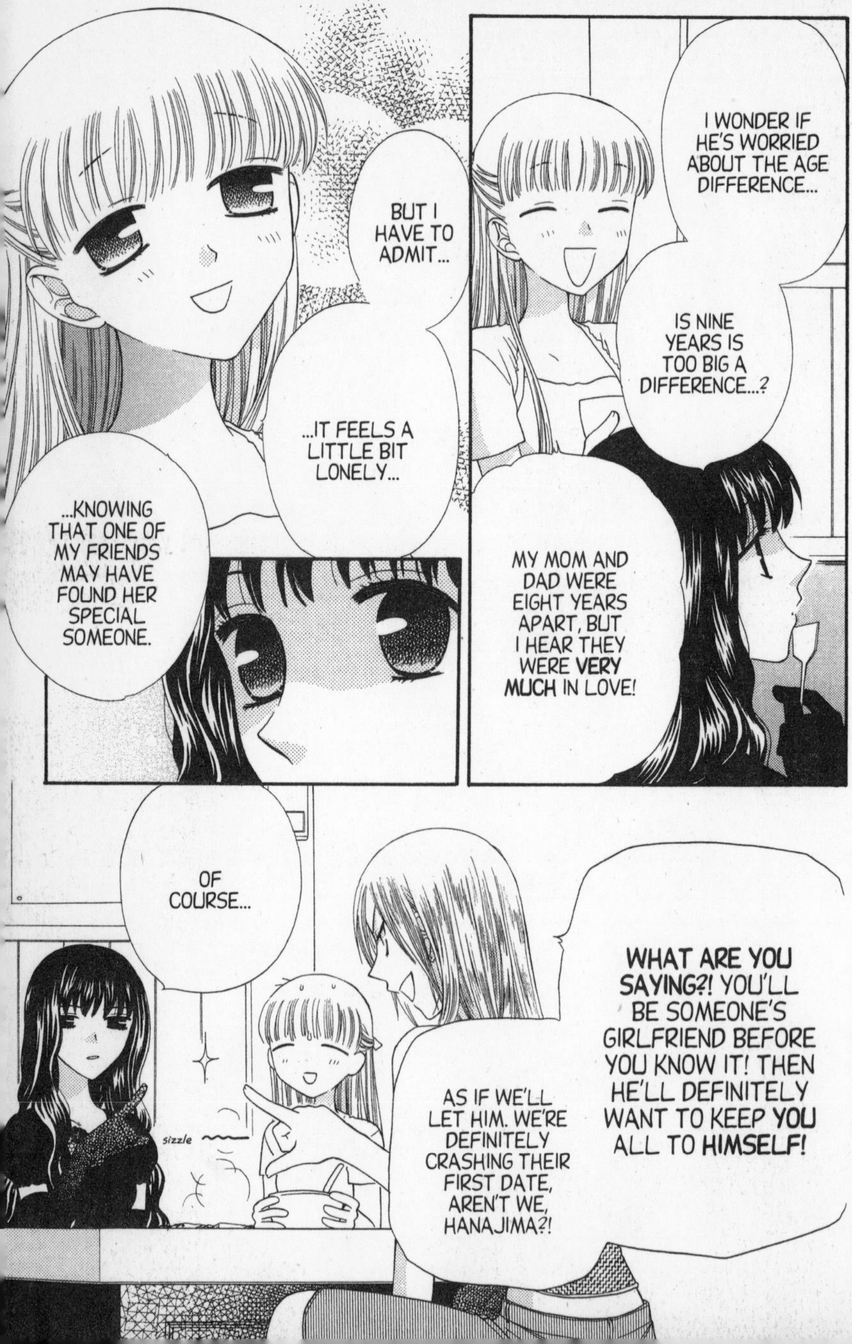
I WONDER IF HE'S WORRIED ABOUT THE AGE DIFFERENCE...
IS NINE YEARS IS TOO BIG A DIFFERENCE...?
MY MOM AND DAD WERE EIGHT YEARS APART, BUT I HEAR THEY WERE VERY MUCH IN LOVE!
BUT I HAVE TO ADMIT...
...IT FEELS A LITTLE BIT LONELY...
...KNOWING THAT ONE OF MY FRIENDS MAY HAVE FOUND HER SPECIAL SOMEONE.
WHAT ARE YOU SAYING?! YOU'LL BE SOMEONE'S GIRLFRIEND BEFORE YOU KNOW IT! THEN HE'LL DEFINITELY WANT TO KEEP YOU ALL TO HIMSELF!
AS IF WE'LL LET HIM. WE'RE DEFINITELY CRASHING THEIR FIRST DATE, AREN'T WE, HANAJIMA?!
OF COURSE...
sizzle

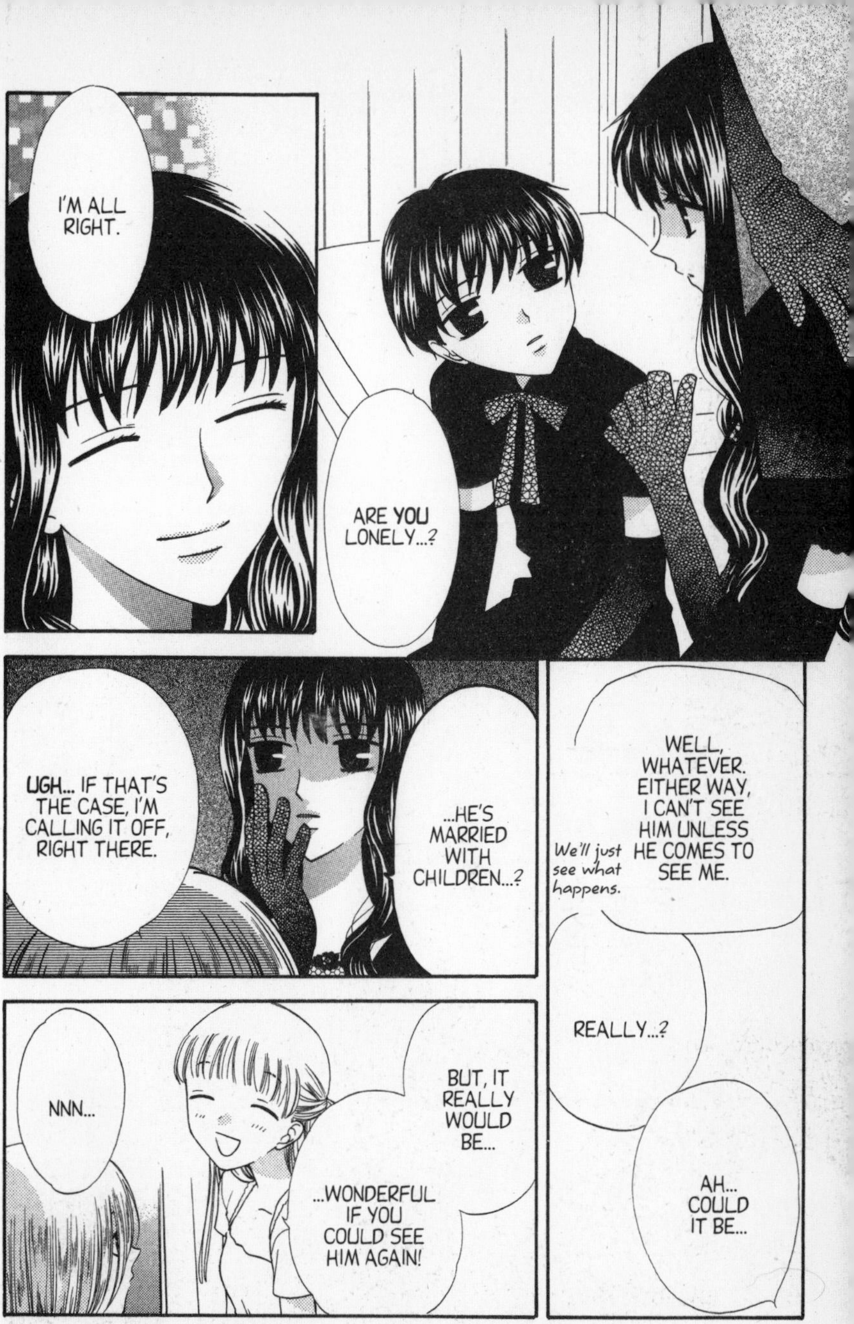
ARE YOU LONELY...?
I'M ALL RIGHT.
WELL, WHATEVER. EITHER WAY, I CAN'T SEE HIM UNLESS HE COMES TO SEE ME.
We'll just see what happens.
REALLY...?
AH... COULD IT BE...
...HE'S MARRIED WITH CHILDREN...?
UGH... IF THAT'S THE CASE, I'M CALLING IT OFF, RIGHT THERE.
BUT, IT REALLY WOULD BE...
...WONDERFUL IF YOU COULD SEE HIM AGAIN!
NNN...

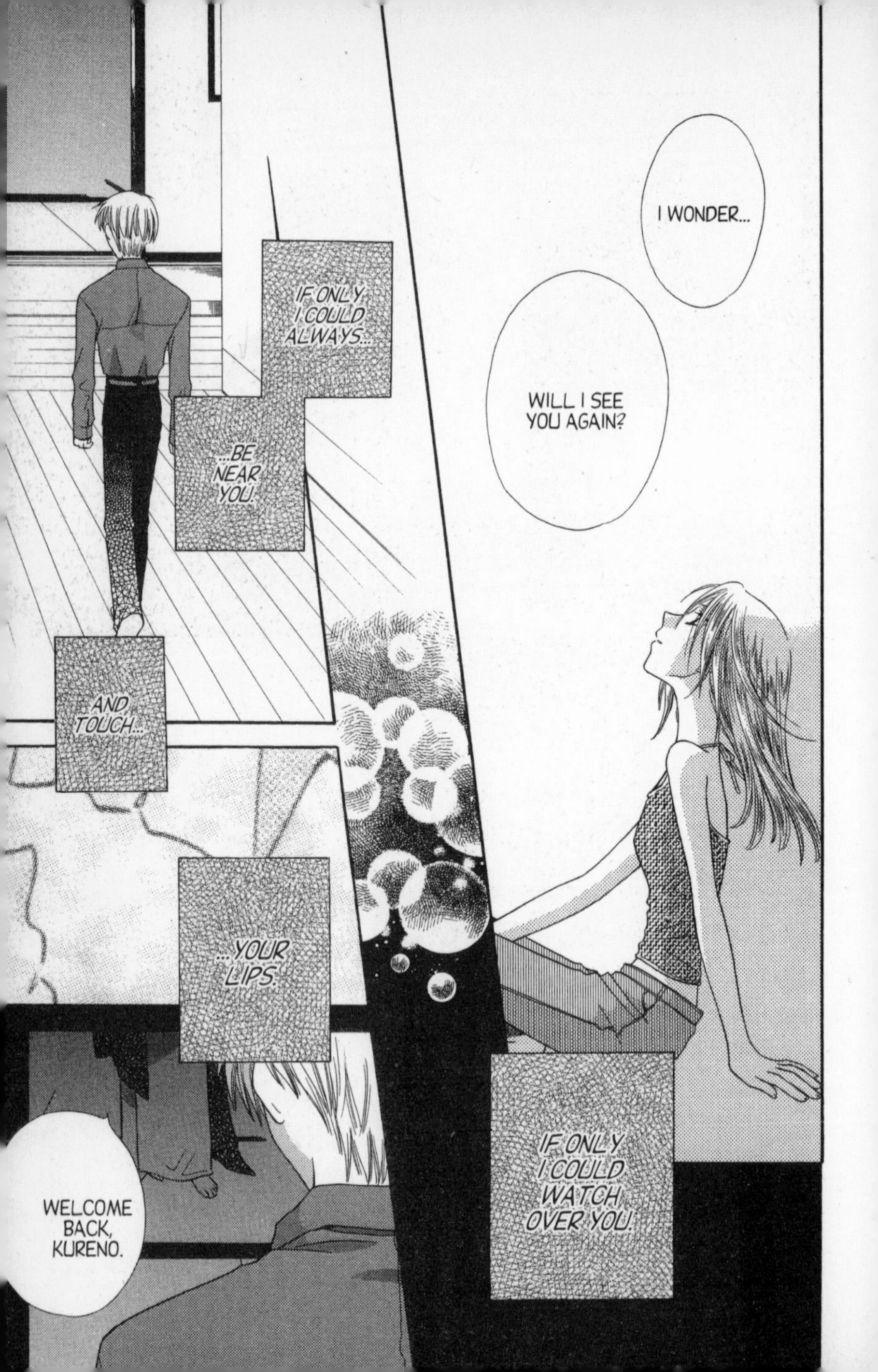

I WONDER...
WILL I SEE YOU AGAIN?
IF ONLY I COULD WATCH OVER YOU.
IF ONLY I COULD ALWAYS...
...BE NEAR YOU.
AND TOUCH...
...YOUR LIPS.
WELCOME BACK, KURENO.

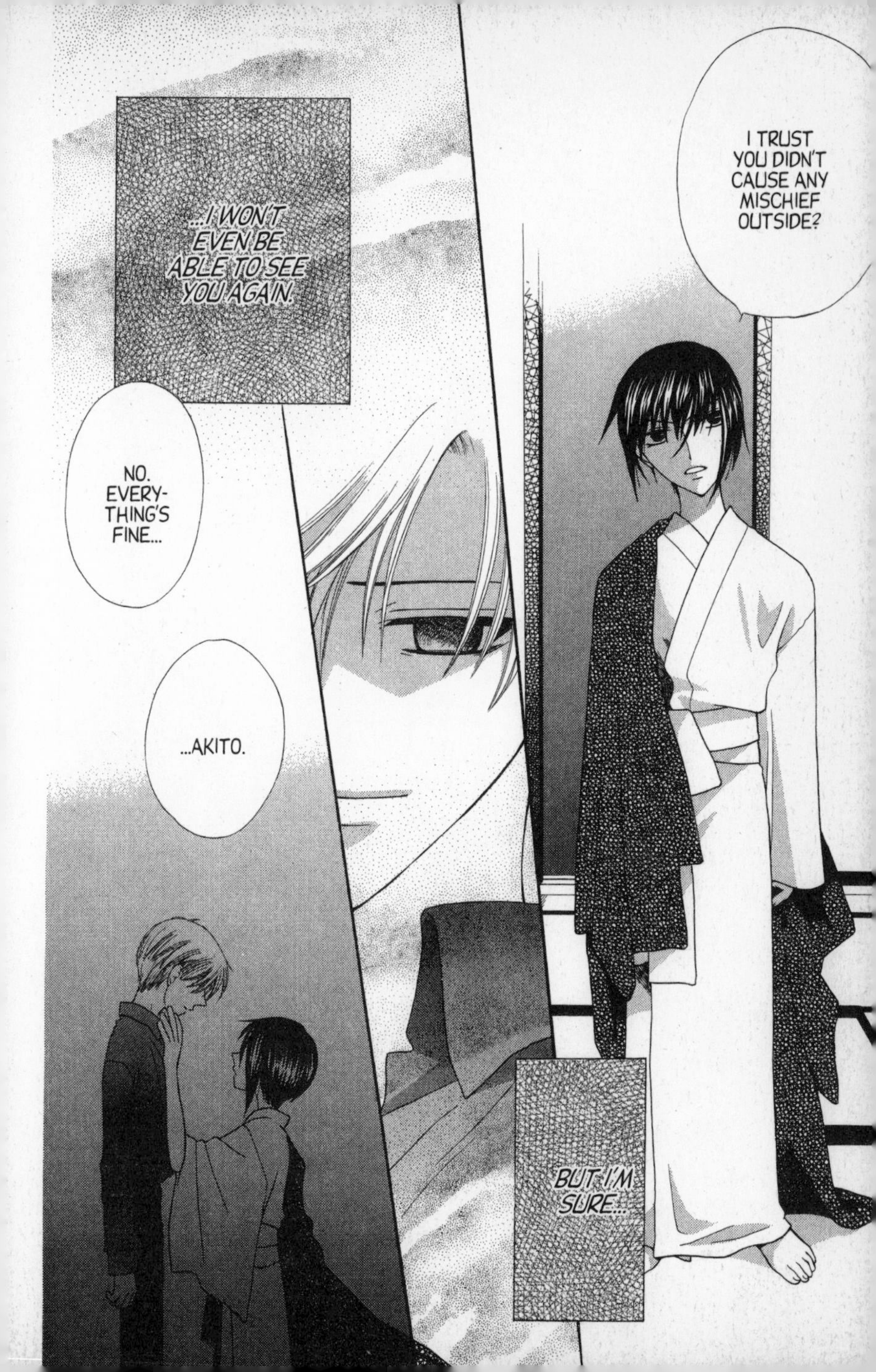
I TRUST YOU DIDN'T CAUSE ANY MISCHIEF OUTSIDE?
BUT I'M SURE...
...I WON'T EVEN BE ABLE TO SEE YOU AGAIN.
NO. EVERYTHING'S FINE...
...AKITO.

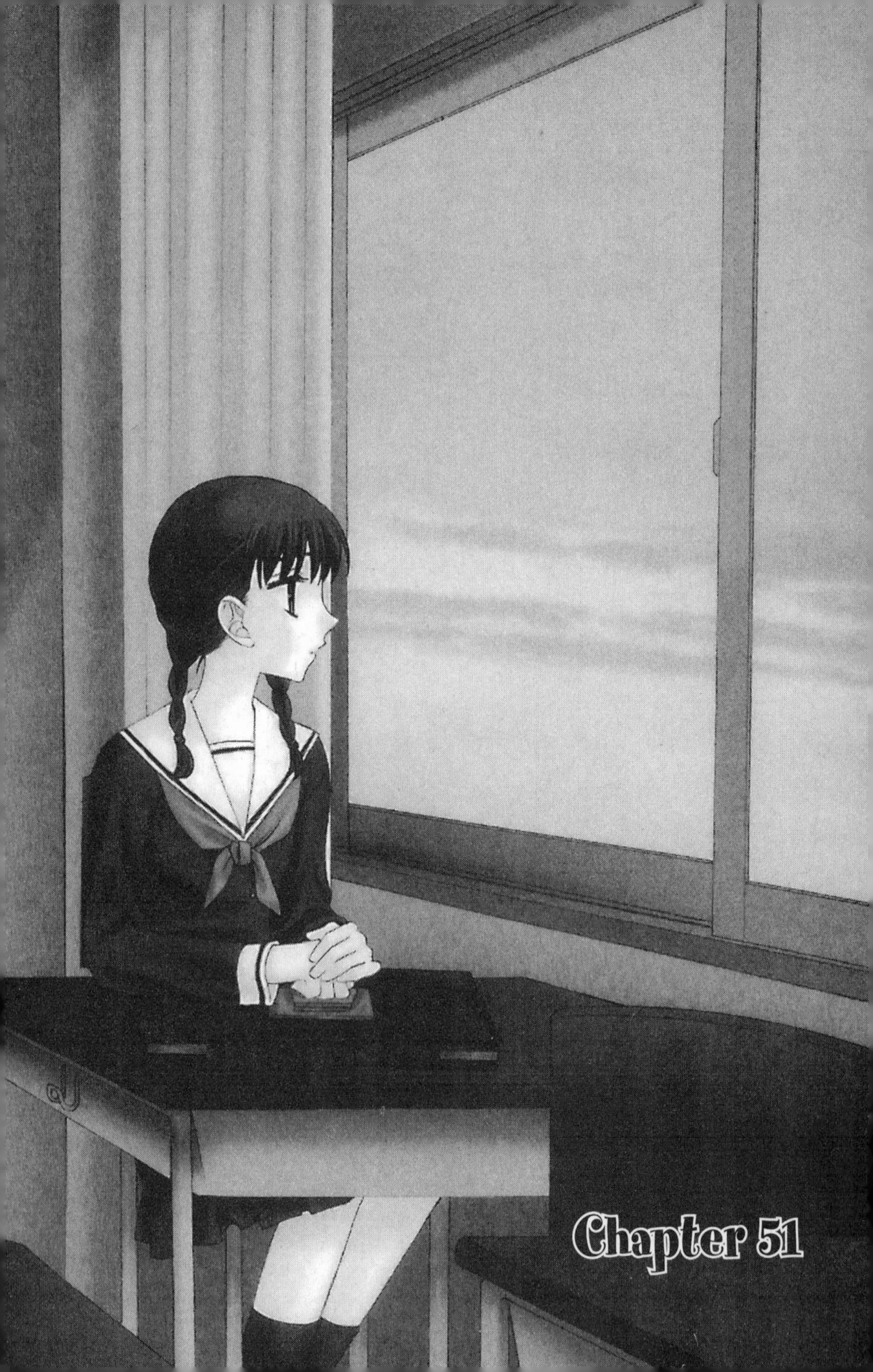
Chapter 51

I feel so grateful!

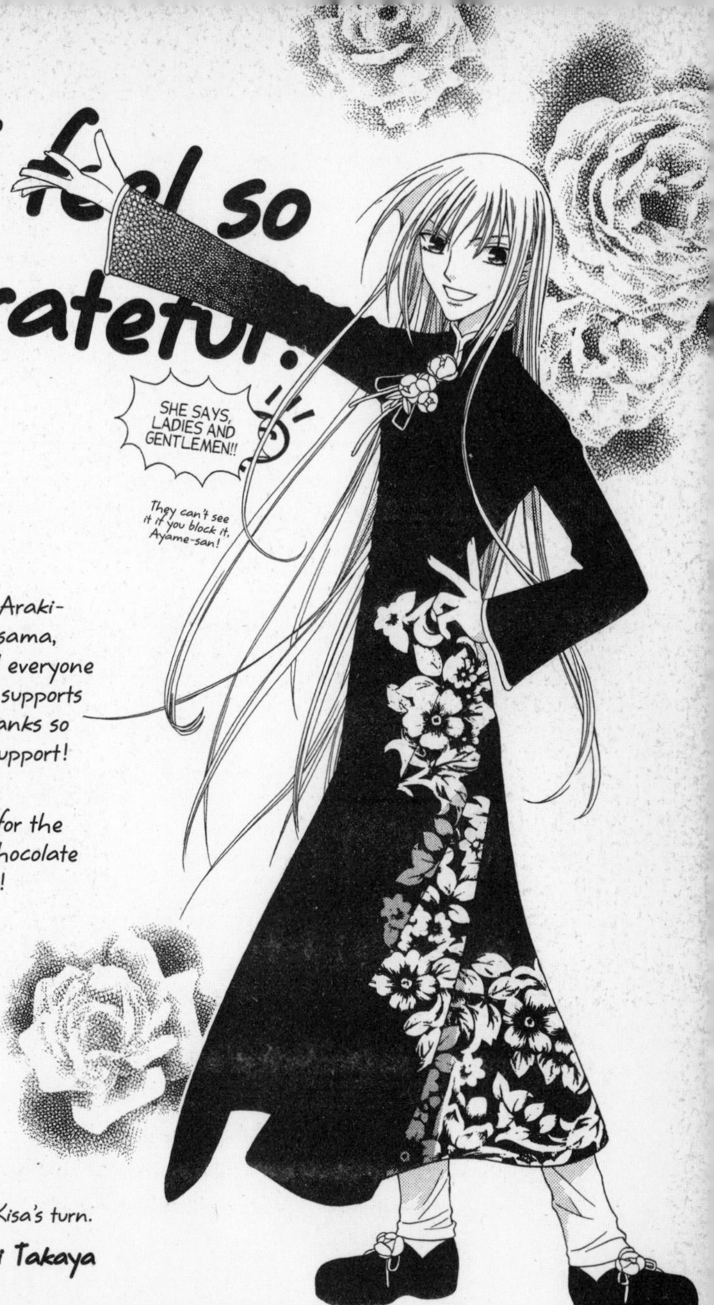
SHE SAYS, LADIES AND GENTLEMEN!!
They can't see it if you block it, Ayame-san!

Harada-sama, Araki-sama, Kawaai-sama, Mom, Dad and everyone who reads and supports this manga, thanks so much for your support!

And thanks for the Valentine's chocolate and presents!

And next it's Kisa's turn.

—Natsuki Takaya

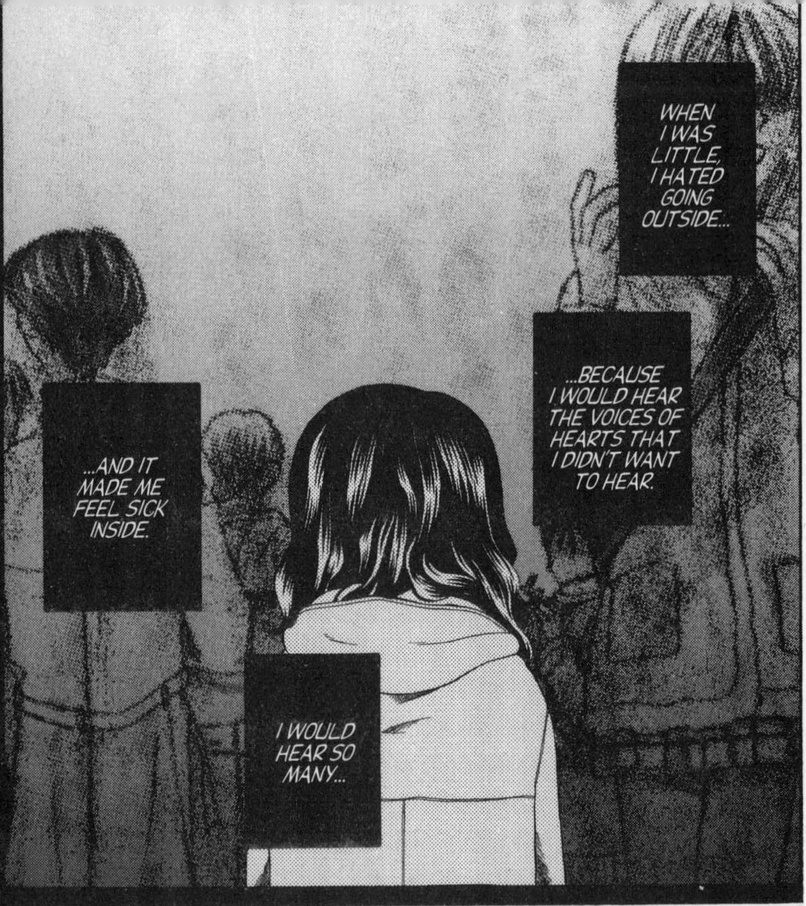
WHEN I WAS LITTLE, I HATED GOING OUTSIDE...
...BECAUSE I WOULD HEAR THE VOICES OF HEARTS THAT I DIDN'T WANT TO HEAR.
I WOULD HEAR SO MANY...
...AND IT MADE ME FEEL SICK INSIDE.

BLAH, BLAH, BLAH 3

The reason middle-school Arisa doesn't have blonde hair in this chapter is that she went back to her original color. She's rehabilitating...

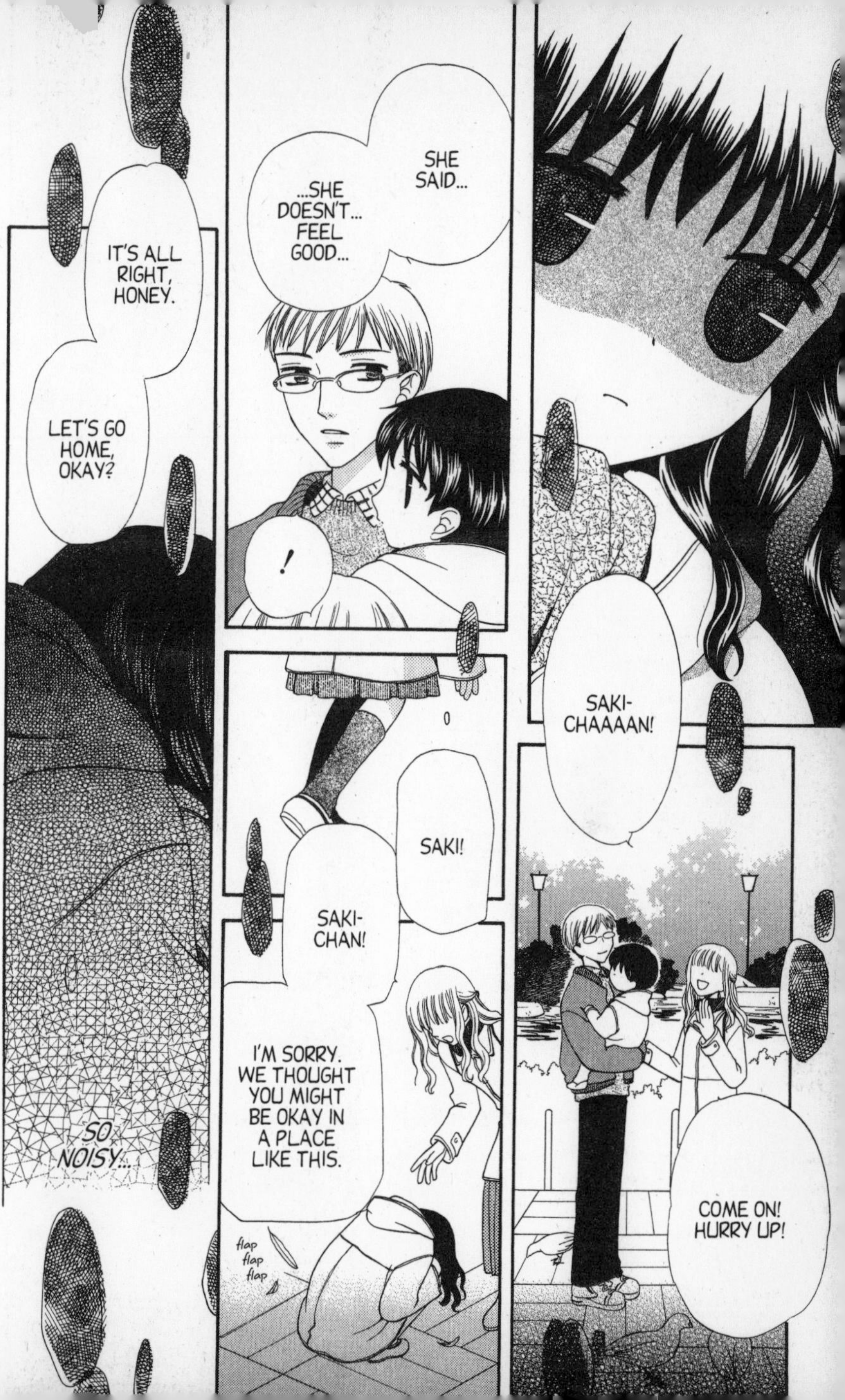
SAKI-CHAAAAN!
COME ON! HURRY UP!
SHE SAID...
...SHE DOESN'T... FEEL GOOD...
!
SAKI!
SAKI-CHAN!
I'M SORRY. WE THOUGHT YOU MIGHT BE OKAY IN A PLACE LIKE THIS.
flap flap flap
IT'S ALL RIGHT, HONEY.
LET'S GO HOME, OKAY?
SO NOISY...

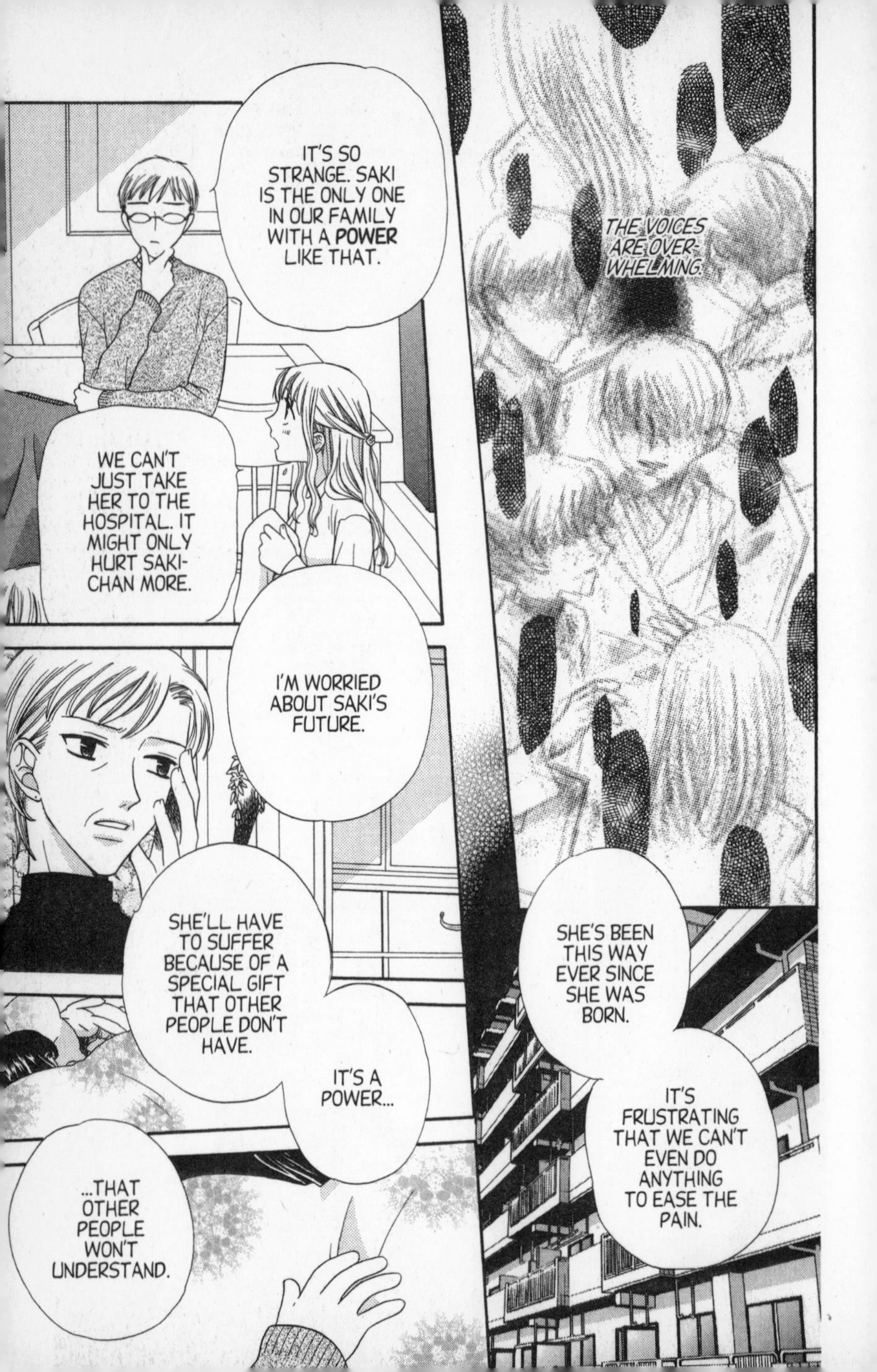
THE VOICES ARE OVER-WHELMING.
SHE'S BEEN THIS WAY EVER SINCE SHE WAS BORN.
IT'S FRUSTRATING THAT WE CAN'T EVEN DO ANYTHING TO EASE THE PAIN.
IT'S SO STRANGE. SAKI IS THE ONLY ONE IN OUR FAMILY WITH A **POWER** LIKE THAT.
WE CAN'T JUST TAKE HER TO THE HOSPITAL. IT MIGHT ONLY HURT SAKI-CHAN MORE.
I'M WORRIED ABOUT SAKI'S FUTURE.
SHE'LL HAVE TO SUFFER BECAUSE OF A SPECIAL GIFT THAT OTHER PEOPLE DON'T HAVE.
IT'S A POWER...
...THAT OTHER PEOPLE WON'T UNDERSTAND.

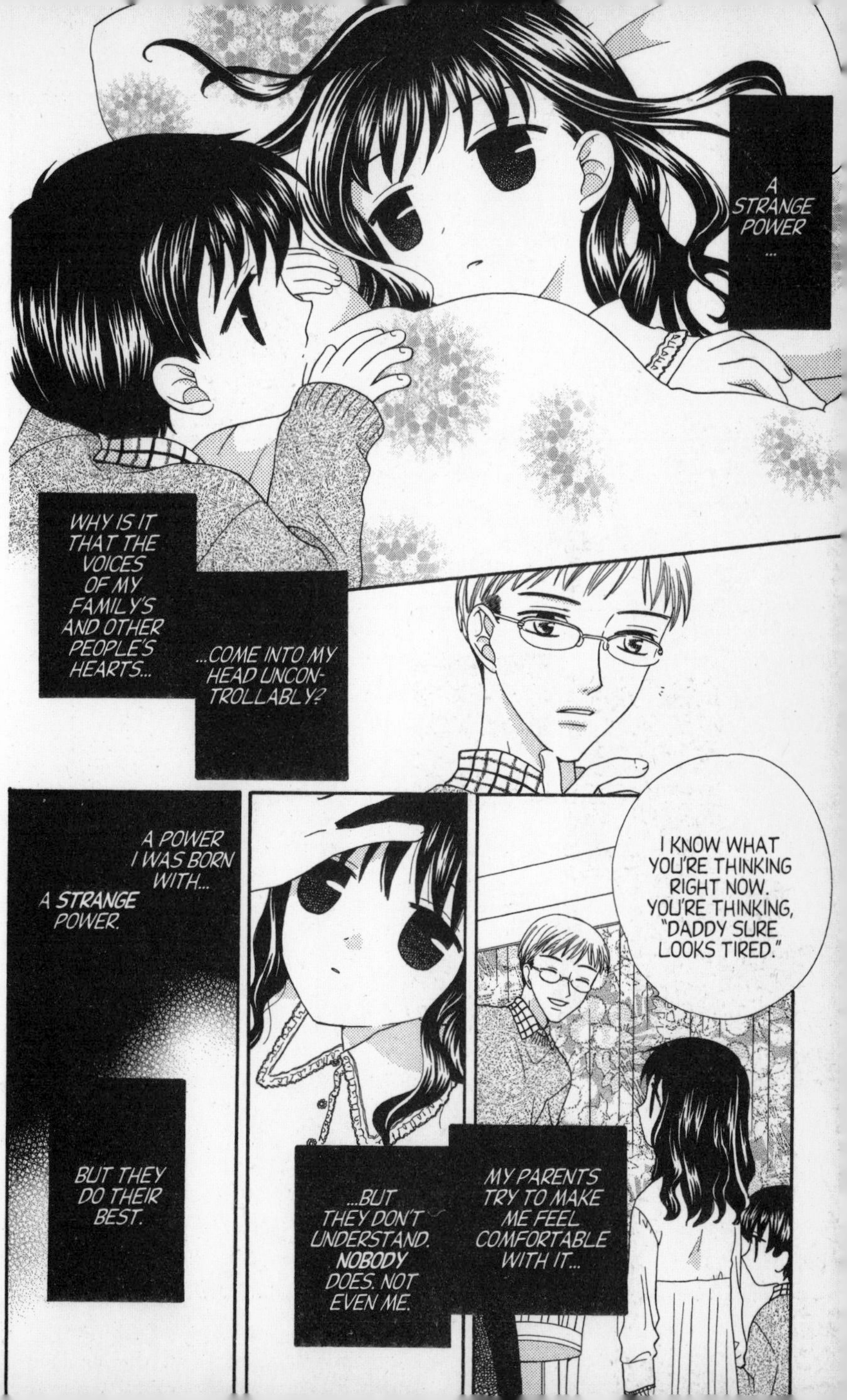
A STRANGE POWER ...
WHY IS IT THAT THE VOICES OF MY FAMILY'S AND OTHER PEOPLE'S HEARTS...
...COME INTO MY HEAD UNCONTROLLABLY?
I KNOW WHAT YOU'RE THINKING RIGHT NOW. YOU'RE THINKING, "DADDY SURE LOOKS TIRED."
MY PARENTS TRY TO MAKE ME FEEL COMFORTABLE WITH IT...
...BUT THEY DON'T UNDERSTAND. NOBODY DOES. NOT EVEN ME.
A POWER I WAS BORN WITH...
A STRANGE POWER.
BUT THEY DO THEIR BEST.

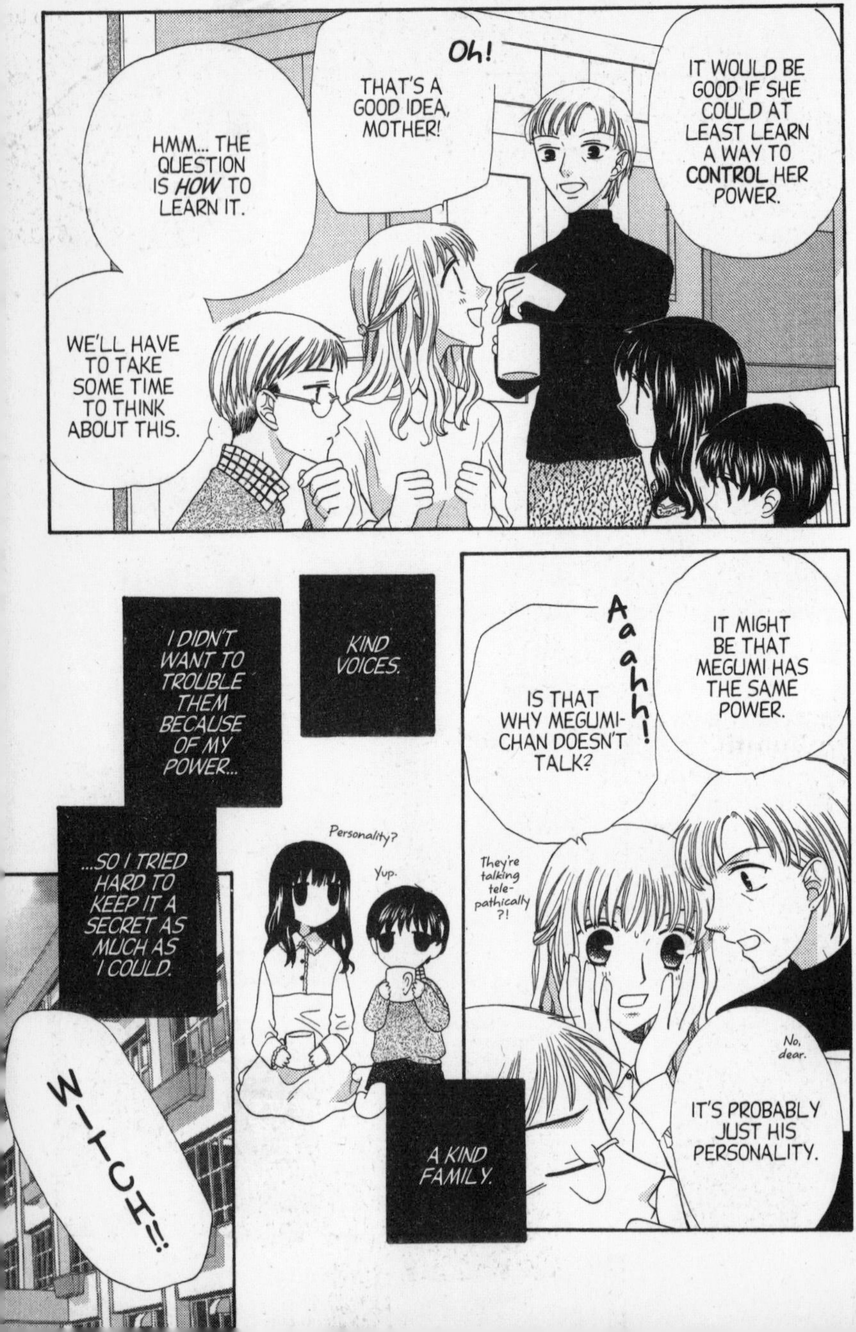
IT WOULD BE GOOD IF SHE COULD AT LEAST LEARN A WAY TO CONTROL HER POWER.
Oh!
THAT'S A GOOD IDEA, MOTHER!
HMM... THE QUESTION IS HOW TO LEARN IT.
WE'LL HAVE TO TAKE SOME TIME TO THINK ABOUT THIS.
IT MIGHT BE THAT MEGUMI HAS THE SAME POWER.
Aaahh!
IS THAT WHY MEGUMI-CHAN DOESN'T TALK?
They're talking telepathically?!
No, dear.
IT'S PROBABLY JUST HIS PERSONALITY.
KIND VOICES.
Personality?
Yup.
A KIND FAMILY.
I DIDN'T WANT TO TROUBLE THEM BECAUSE OF MY POWER...
...SO I TRIED HARD TO KEEP IT A SECRET AS MUCH AS I COULD.
WITCH!!

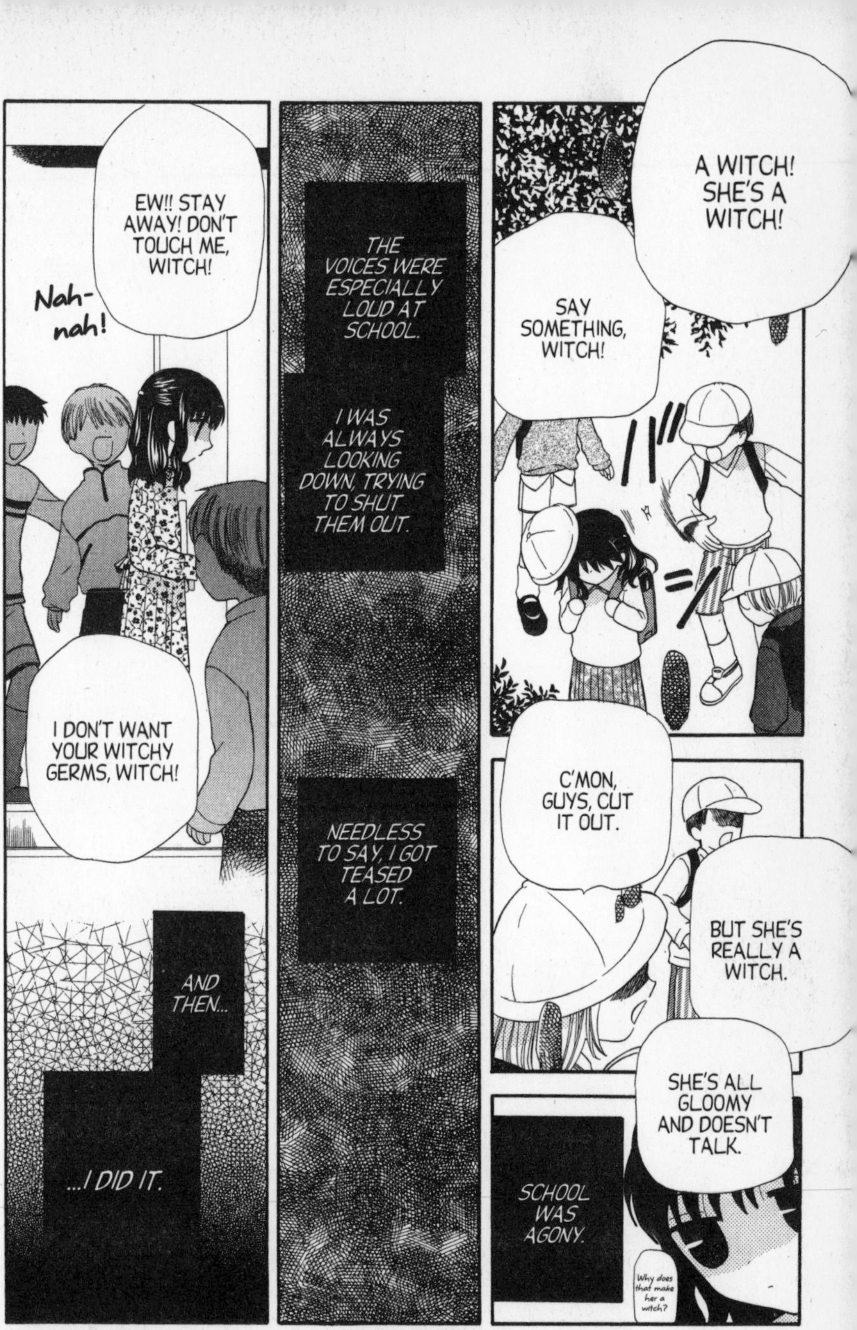
A WITCH! SHE'S A WITCH!
SAY SOMETHING, WITCH!
C'MON, GUYS, CUT IT OUT.
BUT SHE'S REALLY A WITCH.
SHE'S ALL GLOOMY AND DOESN'T TALK.
SCHOOL WAS AGONY.
Why does that make her a witch?
THE VOICES WERE ESPECIALLY LOUD AT SCHOOL.
I WAS ALWAYS LOOKING DOWN, TRYING TO SHUT THEM OUT.
NEEDLESS TO SAY, I GOT TEASED A LOT.
EW!! STAY AWAY! DON'T TOUCH ME, WITCH!
Nah-nah!
I DON'T WANT YOUR WITCHY GERMS, WITCH!
AND THEN...
...I DID IT.

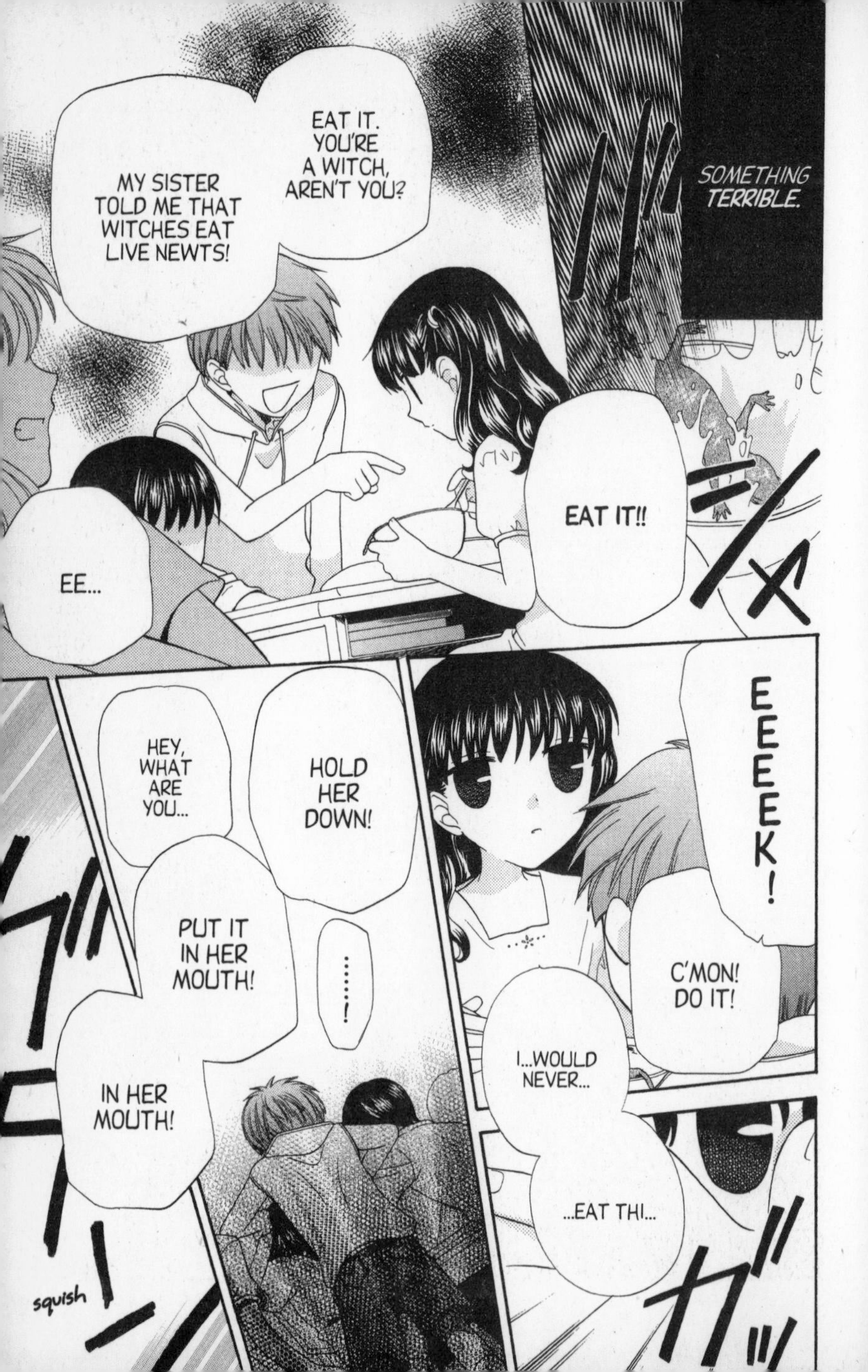
SOMETHING TERRIBLE.
EAT IT. YOU'RE A WITCH, AREN'T YOU?
MY SISTER TOLD ME THAT WITCHES EAT LIVE NEWTS!
EAT IT!!
EE...
EEEEK!
C'MON! DO IT!
I...WOULD NEVER...
...EAT THI...
HOLD HER DOWN!
HEY, WHAT ARE YOU...
......!
PUT IT IN HER MOUTH!
IN HER MOUTH!
squish

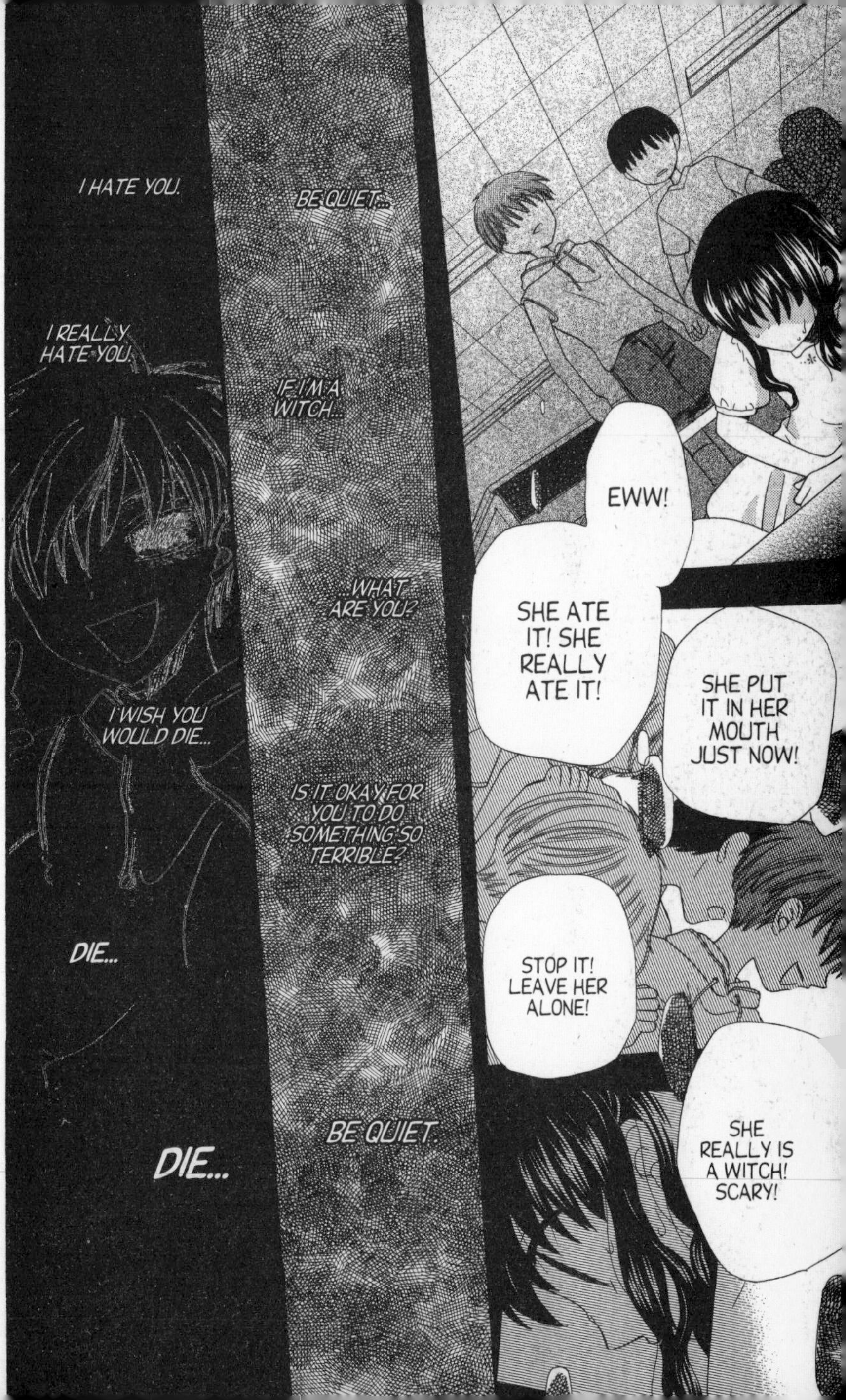
EWW!
SHE ATE IT! SHE REALLY ATE IT!
SHE PUT IT IN HER MOUTH JUST NOW!
STOP IT! LEAVE HER ALONE!
SHE REALLY IS A WITCH! SCARY!
BE QUIET...
IF I'M A WITCH...
...WHAT ARE YOU?
IS IT OKAY FOR YOU TO DO SOMETHING SO TERRIBLE?
BE QUIET.
I HATE YOU.
I REALLY HATE YOU.
I WISH YOU WOULD DIE...
DIE...
DIE...

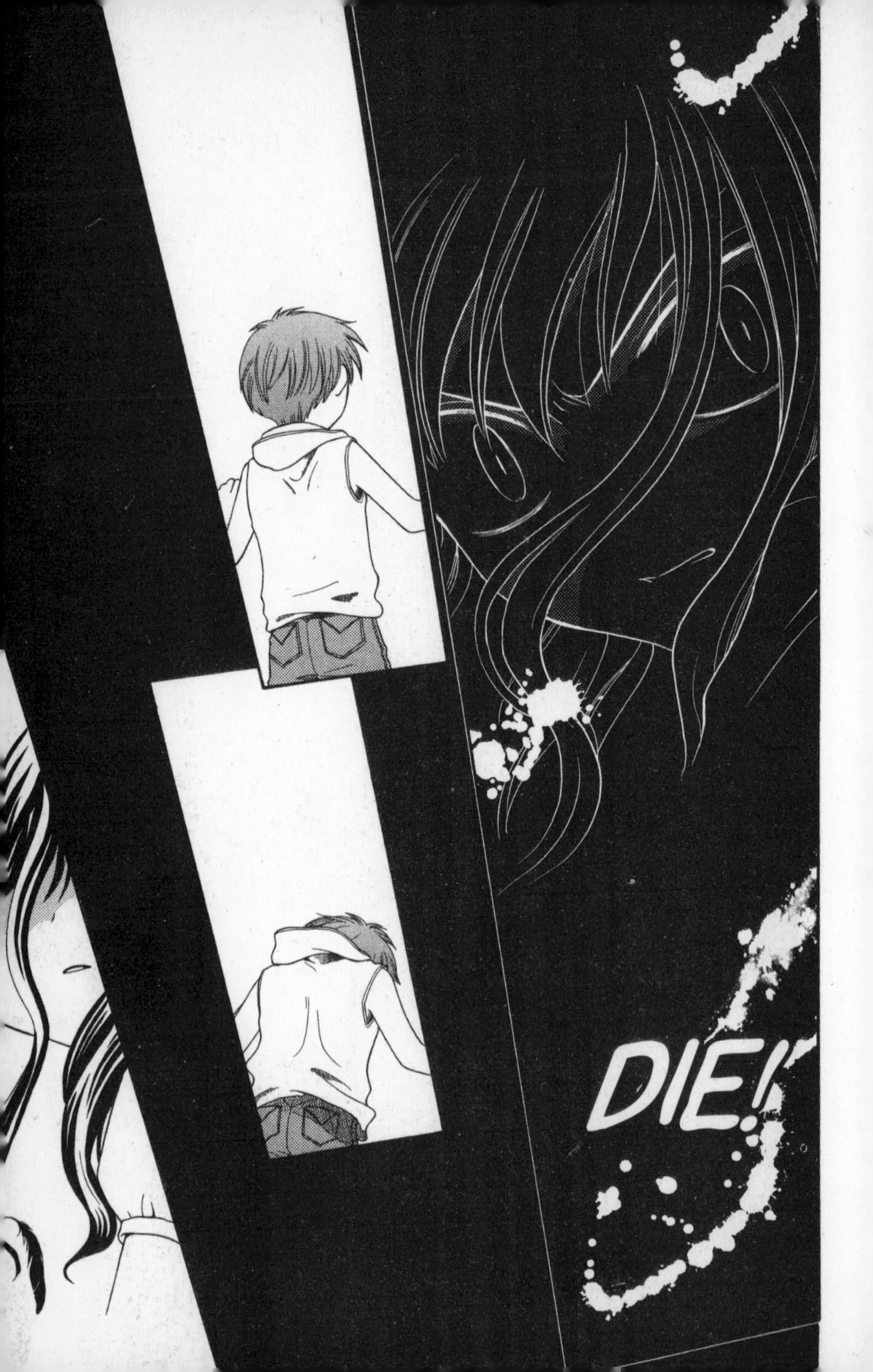
DIE!!

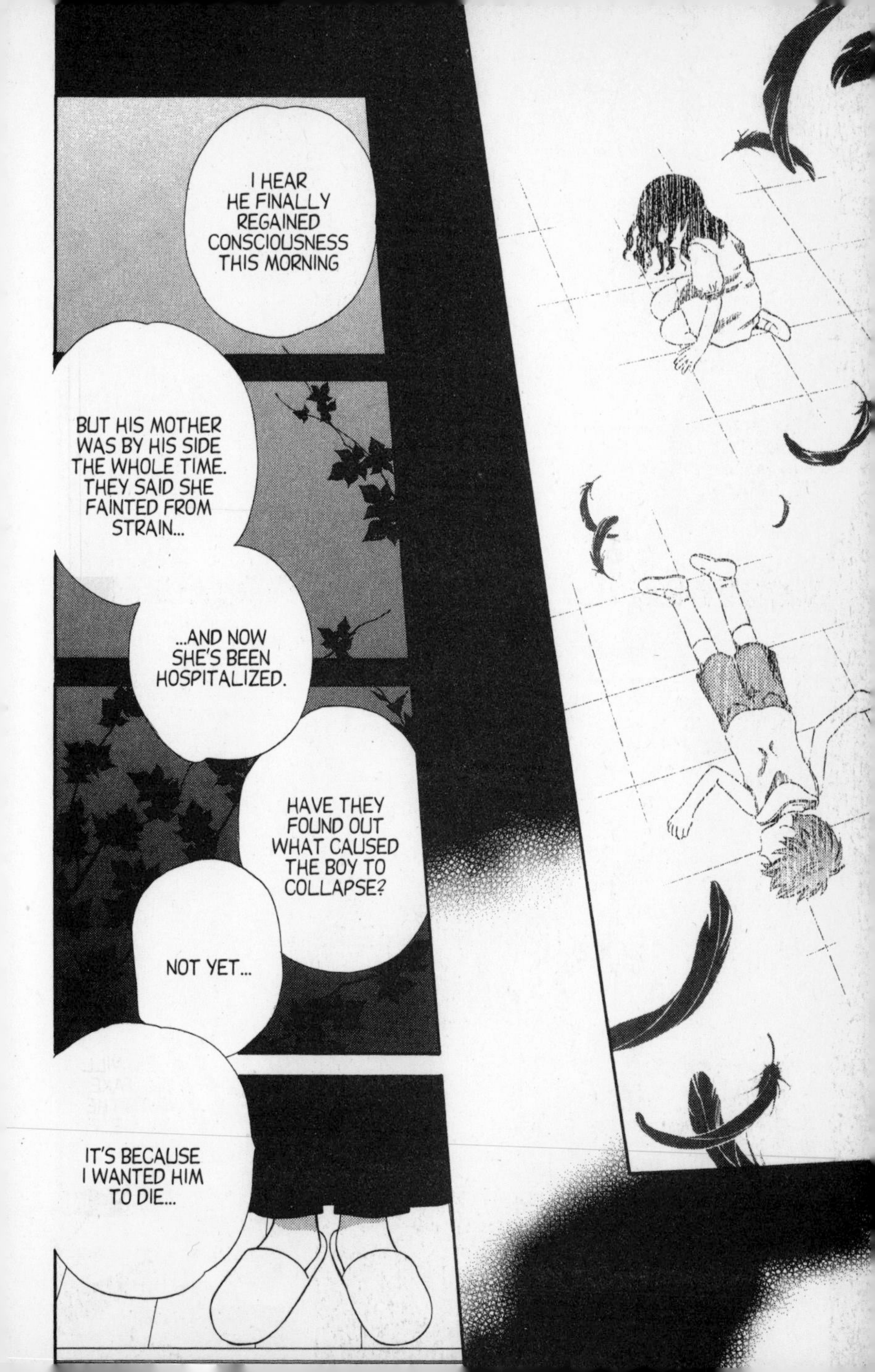
I HEAR HE FINALLY REGAINED CONSCIOUSNESS THIS MORNING
BUT HIS MOTHER WAS BY HIS SIDE THE WHOLE TIME. THEY SAID SHE FAINTED FROM STRAIN...
...AND NOW SHE'S BEEN HOSPITALIZED.
HAVE THEY FOUND OUT WHAT CAUSED THE BOY TO COLLAPSE?
NOT YET...
IT'S BECAUSE I WANTED HIM TO DIE...

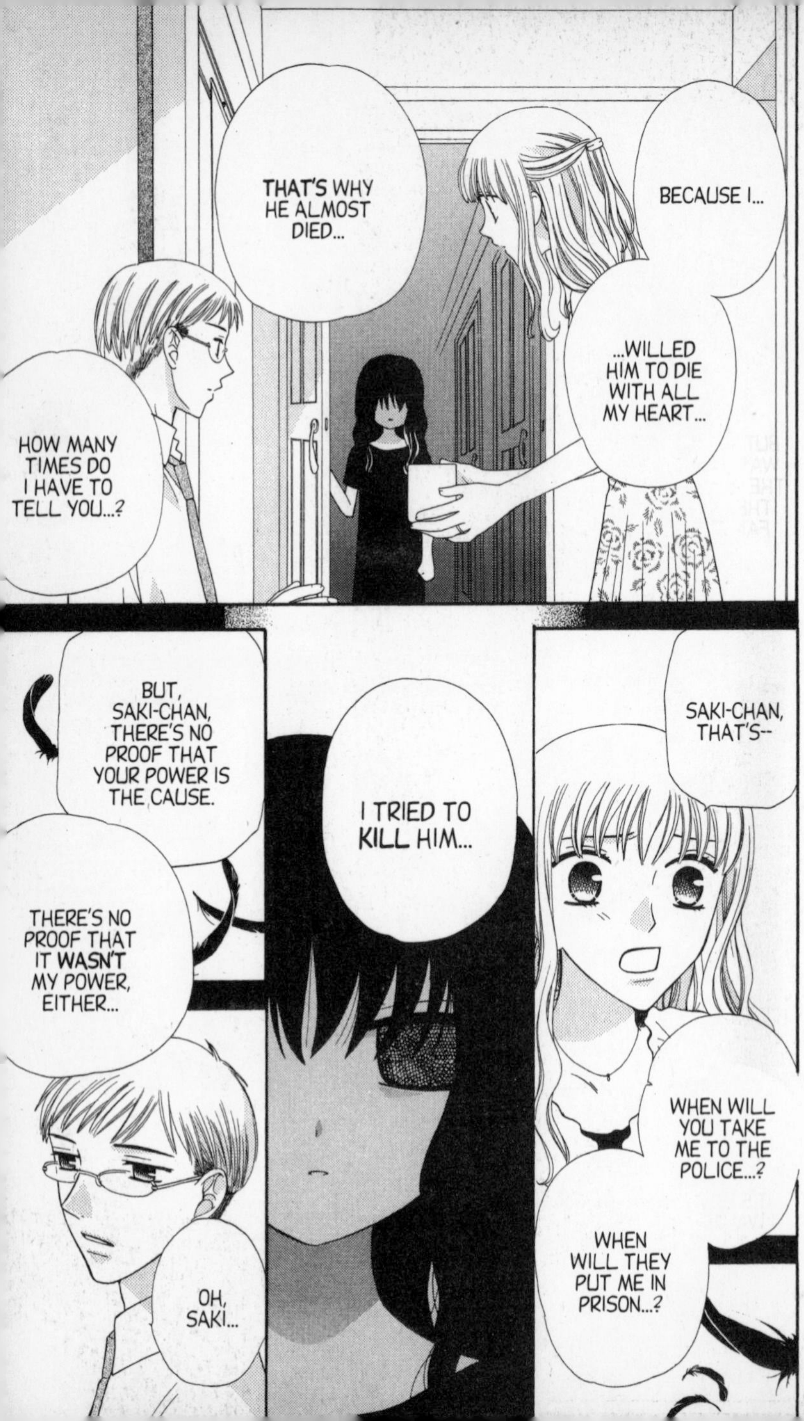
BECAUSE I...
...WILLED HIM TO DIE WITH ALL MY HEART...
THAT'S WHY HE ALMOST DIED...
HOW MANY TIMES DO I HAVE TO TELL YOU...?
SAKI-CHAN, THAT'S--
WHEN WILL YOU TAKE ME TO THE POLICE...?
WHEN WILL THEY PUT ME IN PRISON...?
I TRIED TO KILL HIM...
BUT, SAKI-CHAN, THERE'S NO PROOF THAT YOUR POWER IS THE CAUSE.
THERE'S NO PROOF THAT IT WASN'T MY POWER, EITHER...
OH, SAKI...

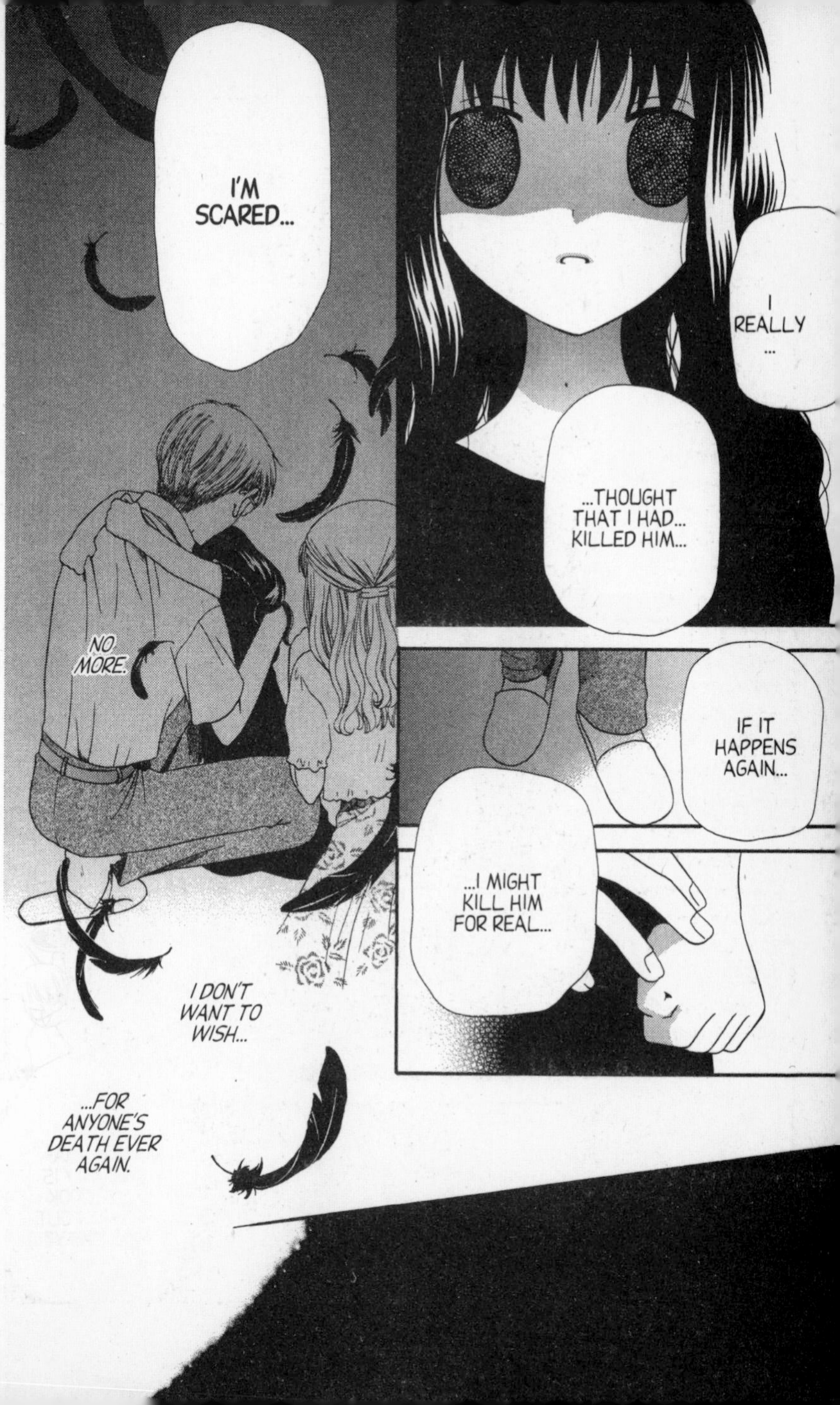
I REALLY ...
...THOUGHT THAT I HAD... KILLED HIM...
IF IT HAPPENS AGAIN...
...I MIGHT KILL HIM FOR REAL...
I'M SCARED...
NO MORE.
I DON'T WANT TO WISH...
...FOR ANYONE'S DEATH EVER AGAIN.

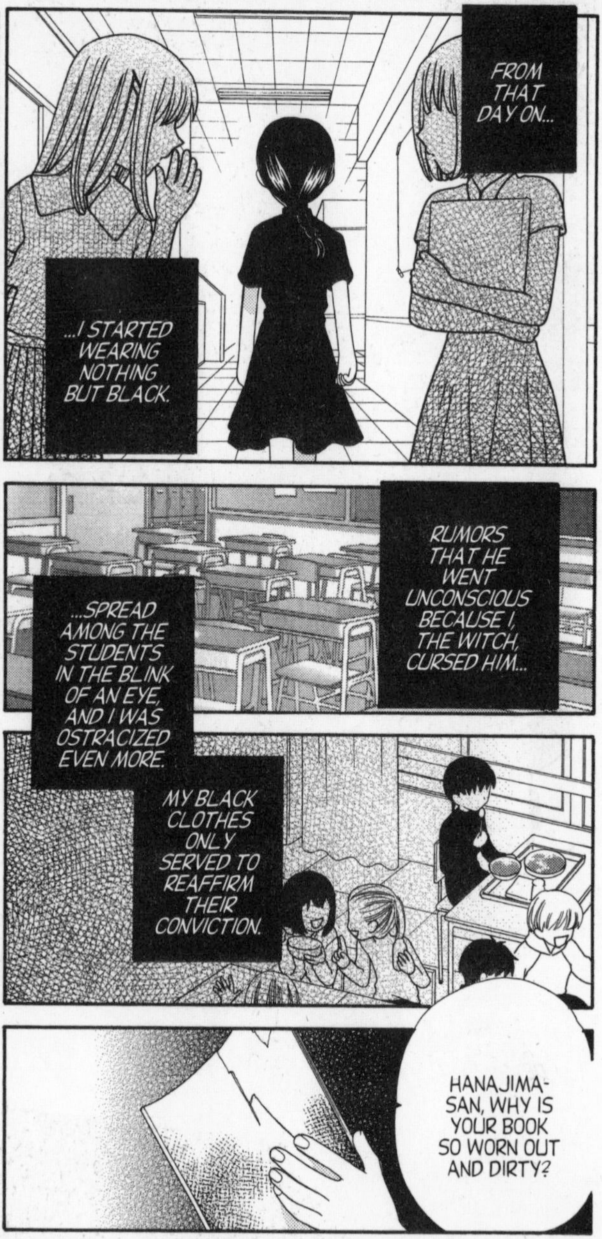
FROM THAT DAY ON...
...I STARTED WEARING NOTHING BUT BLACK.
RUMORS THAT HE WENT UNCONSCIOUS BECAUSE I, THE WITCH, CURSED HIM...
...SPREAD AMONG THE STUDENTS IN THE BLINK OF AN EYE, AND I WAS OSTRACIZED EVEN MORE.
MY BLACK CLOTHES ONLY SERVED TO REAFFIRM THEIR CONVICTION.
HANAJIMA-SAN, WHY IS YOUR BOOK SO WORN OUT AND DIRTY?

Fruits Basket 9
Part 3:

Continued...

Yup. Over the years that table had absorbed my blood, sweat, and tears...I don't really like that phrase. Anyway, it was my beloved table that had worked hard with me for nearly eight years. You understand why it was so hard to let go? The new tracing table is enshrined on my desk, but I couldn't throw the old one away, so it's at my feet. Sometimes I kick it, though.

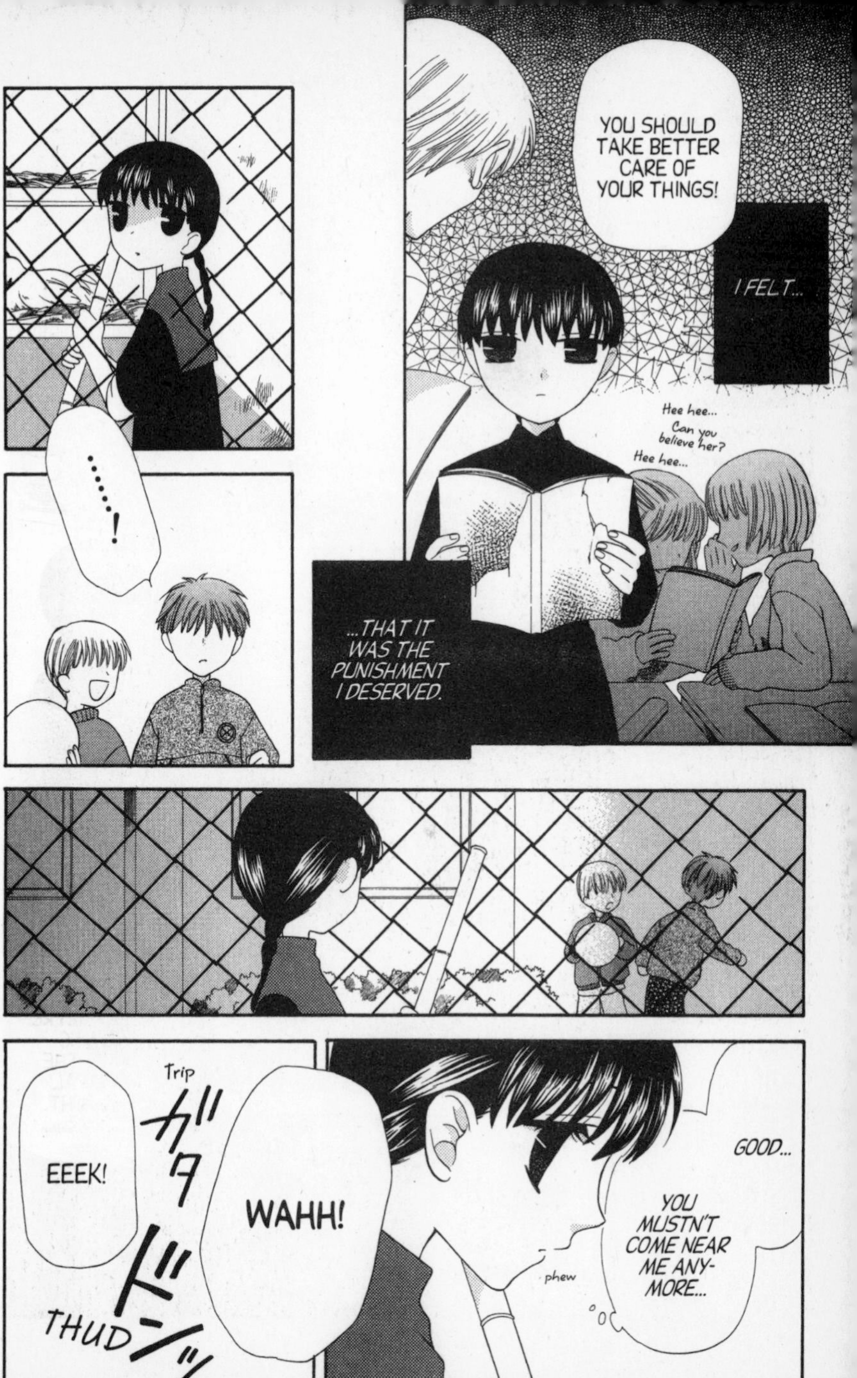
YOU SHOULD TAKE BETTER CARE OF YOUR THINGS!
I FELT...
Hee hee... Can you believe her? Hee hee...
...THAT IT WAS THE PUNISHMENT I DESERVED.
......!
GOOD...
YOU MUSTN'T COME NEAR ME ANY-MORE...
phew
WAHH!
Trip
EEEK!
THUD

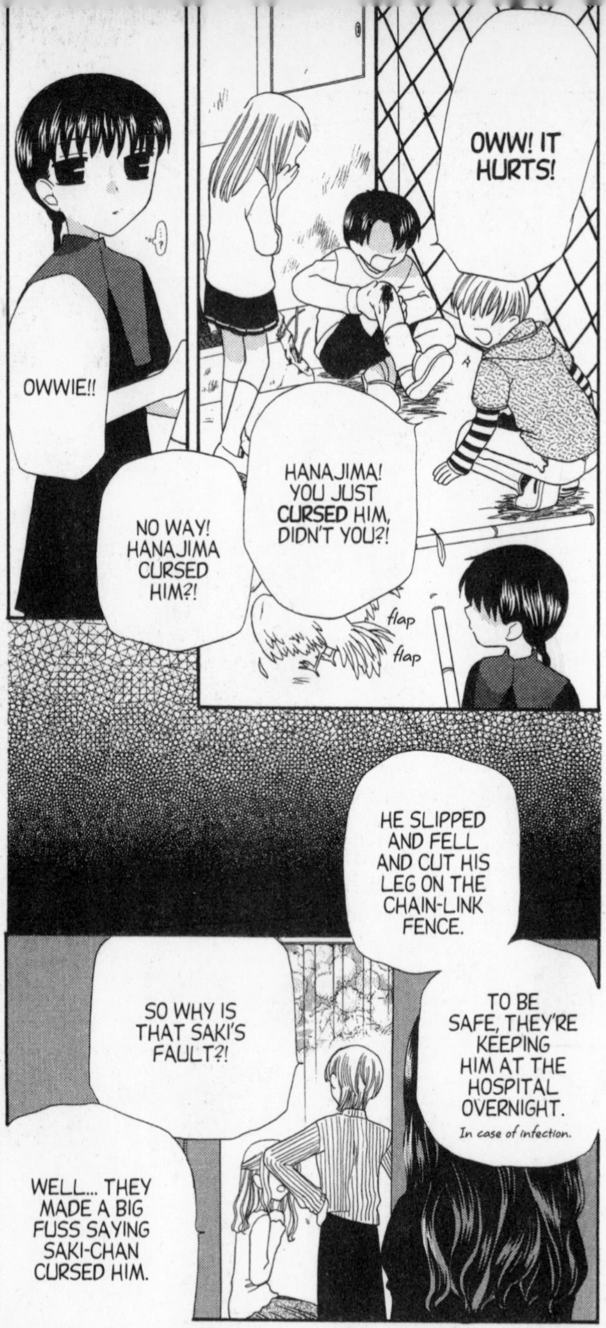
OWW! IT HURTS!
HANAJIMA! YOU JUST CURSED HIM, DIDN'T YOU?!
flap
flap
OWWIE!!
NO WAY! HANAJIMA CURSED HIM?!
HE SLIPPED AND FELL AND CUT HIS LEG ON THE CHAIN-LINK FENCE.
TO BE SAFE, THEY'RE KEEPING HIM AT THE HOSPITAL OVERNIGHT.
In case of infection.
SO WHY IS THAT SAKI'S FAULT?!
WELL... THEY MADE A BIG FUSS SAYING SAKI-CHAN CURSED HIM.

Fruits Basket 9 Part 4:

This is about dreams. Until now, none of the characters from my stories have appeared in my dreams, but I guess because I've been working on *Furuba* for so long, for the first time Yuki and Kyo appeared. There they were, just walking by minding their own business. I thought, "Why isn't Tohru in my dream?" I was impressed to see them in three dimensions. No, it was a dream though. And never again! (laugh)

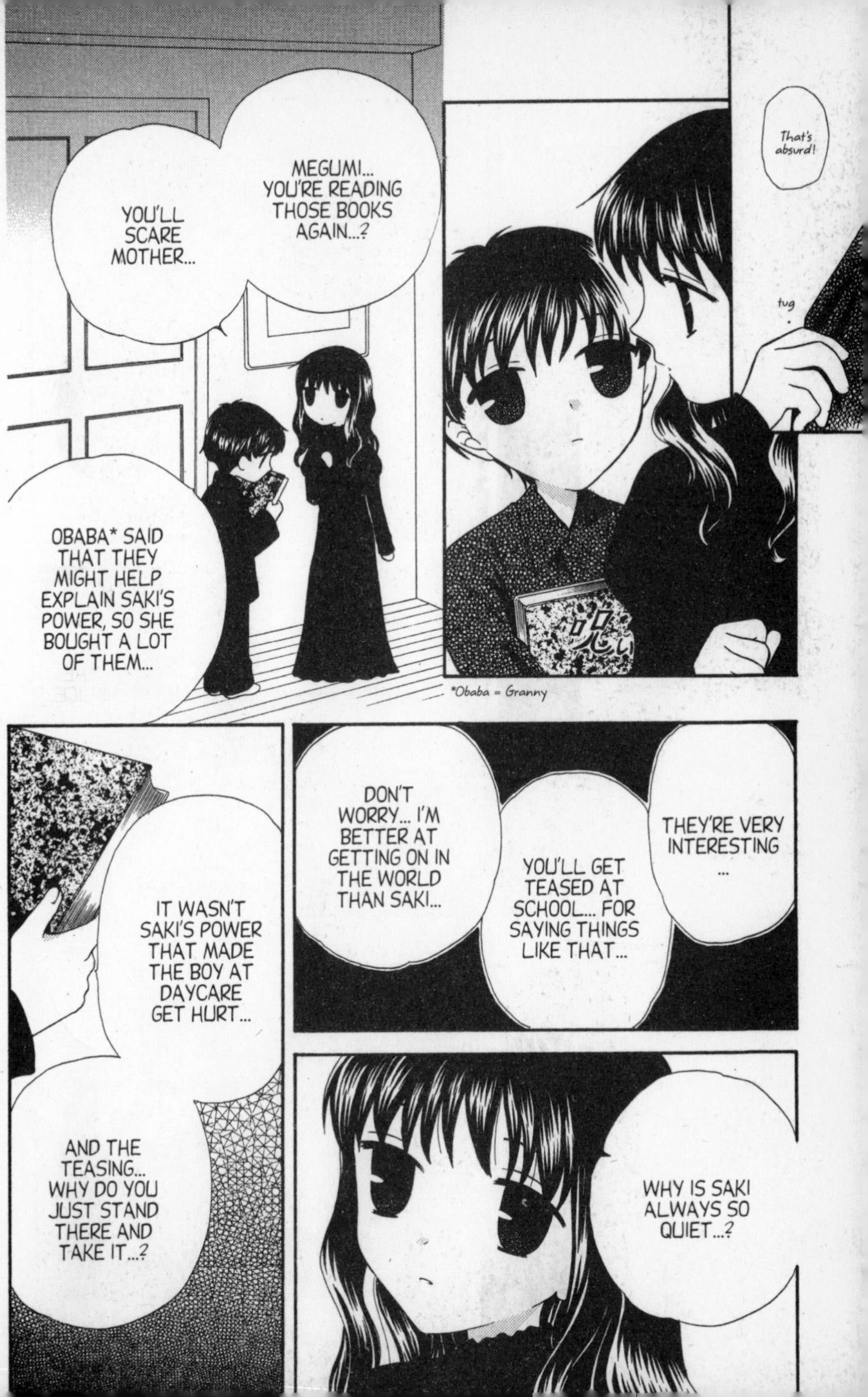
That's absurd!
tug
MEGUMI... YOU'RE READING THOSE BOOKS AGAIN...?
YOU'LL SCARE MOTHER...
OBABA* SAID THAT THEY MIGHT HELP EXPLAIN SAKI'S POWER, SO SHE BOUGHT A LOT OF THEM...
*Obaba = Granny
THEY'RE VERY INTERESTING ...
YOU'LL GET TEASED AT SCHOOL... FOR SAYING THINGS LIKE THAT...
DON'T WORRY... I'M BETTER AT GETTING ON IN THE WORLD THAN SAKI...
WHY IS SAKI ALWAYS SO QUIET...?
IT WASN'T SAKI'S POWER THAT MADE THE BOY AT DAYCARE GET HURT...
AND THE TEASING... WHY DO YOU JUST STAND THERE AND TAKE IT...?

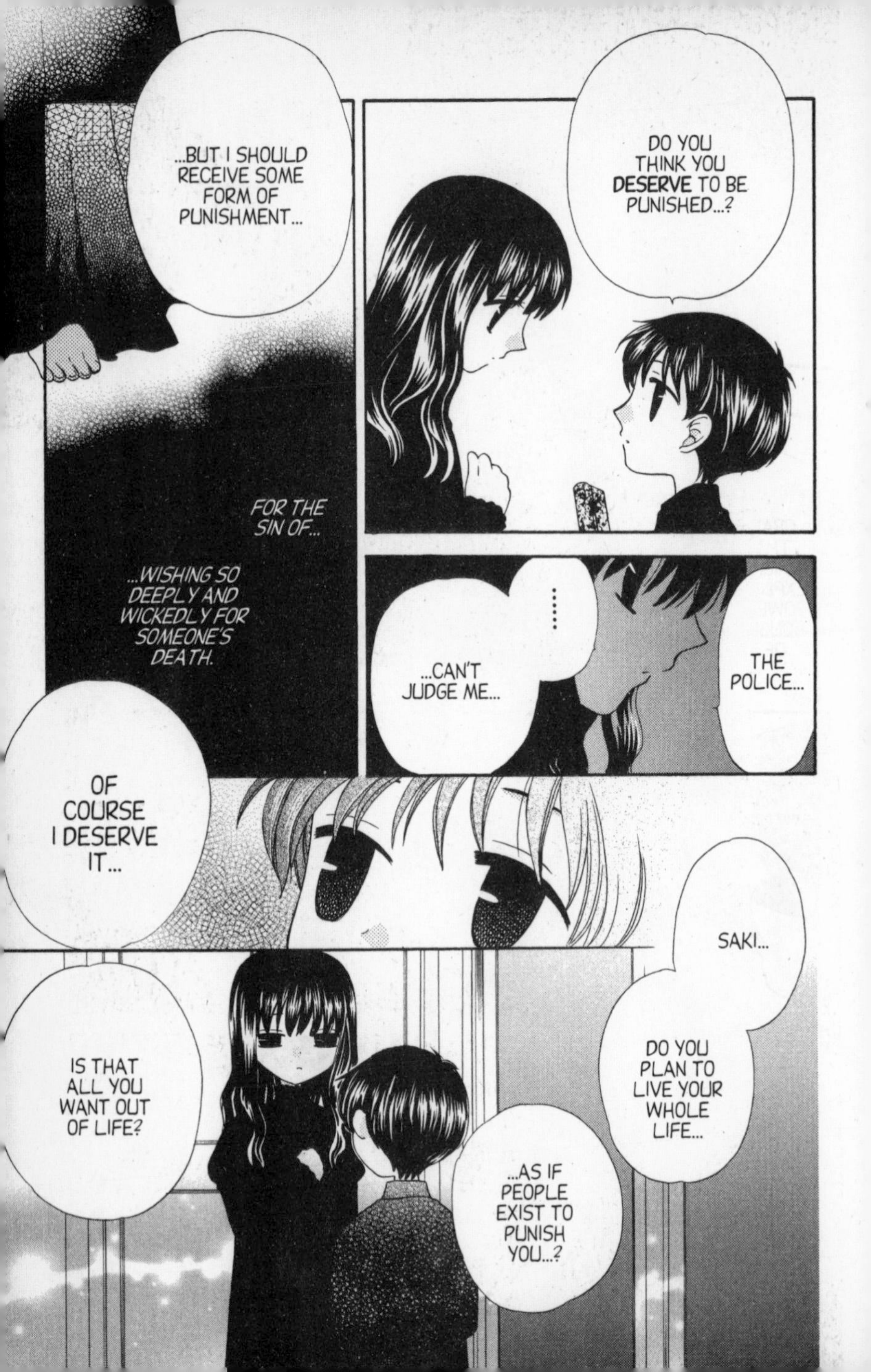
DO YOU THINK YOU DESERVE TO BE PUNISHED...?
THE POLICE...
...CAN'T JUDGE ME...
......
...BUT I SHOULD RECEIVE SOME FORM OF PUNISHMENT...
FOR THE SIN OF...
...WISHING SO DEEPLY AND WICKEDLY FOR SOMEONE'S DEATH.
OF COURSE I DESERVE IT...
SAKI...
DO YOU PLAN TO LIVE YOUR WHOLE LIFE...
...AS IF PEOPLE EXIST TO PUNISH YOU...?
IS THAT ALL YOU WANT OUT OF LIFE?

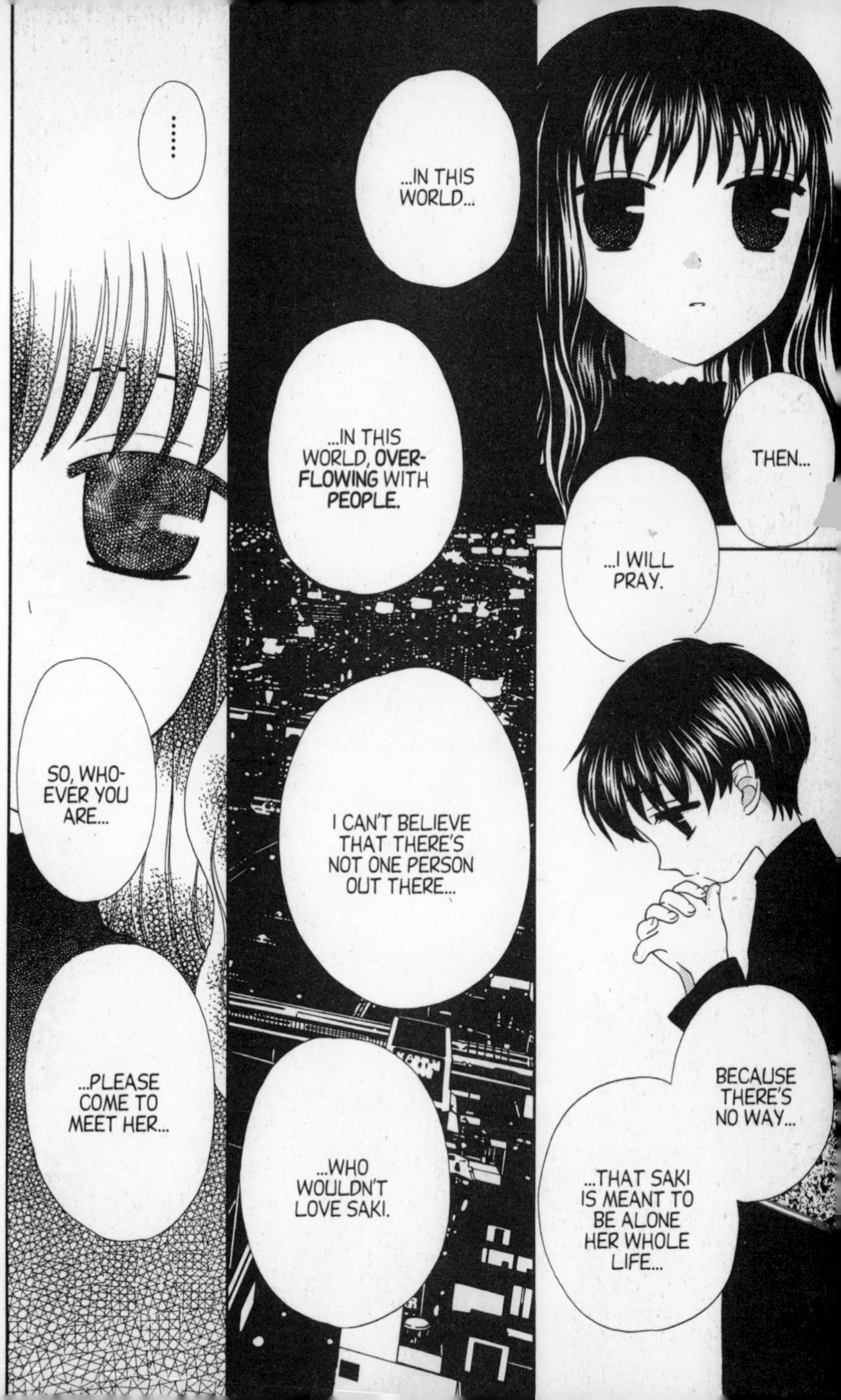
THEN...
...I WILL PRAY.
BECAUSE THERE'S NO WAY...
...THAT SAKI IS MEANT TO BE ALONE HER WHOLE LIFE...
...IN THIS WORLD...
...IN THIS WORLD, OVER-FLOWING WITH PEOPLE.
I CAN'T BELIEVE THAT THERE'S NOT ONE PERSON OUT THERE...
...WHO WOULDN'T LOVE SAKI.
......
SO, WHO-EVER YOU ARE...
...PLEASE COME TO MEET HER...

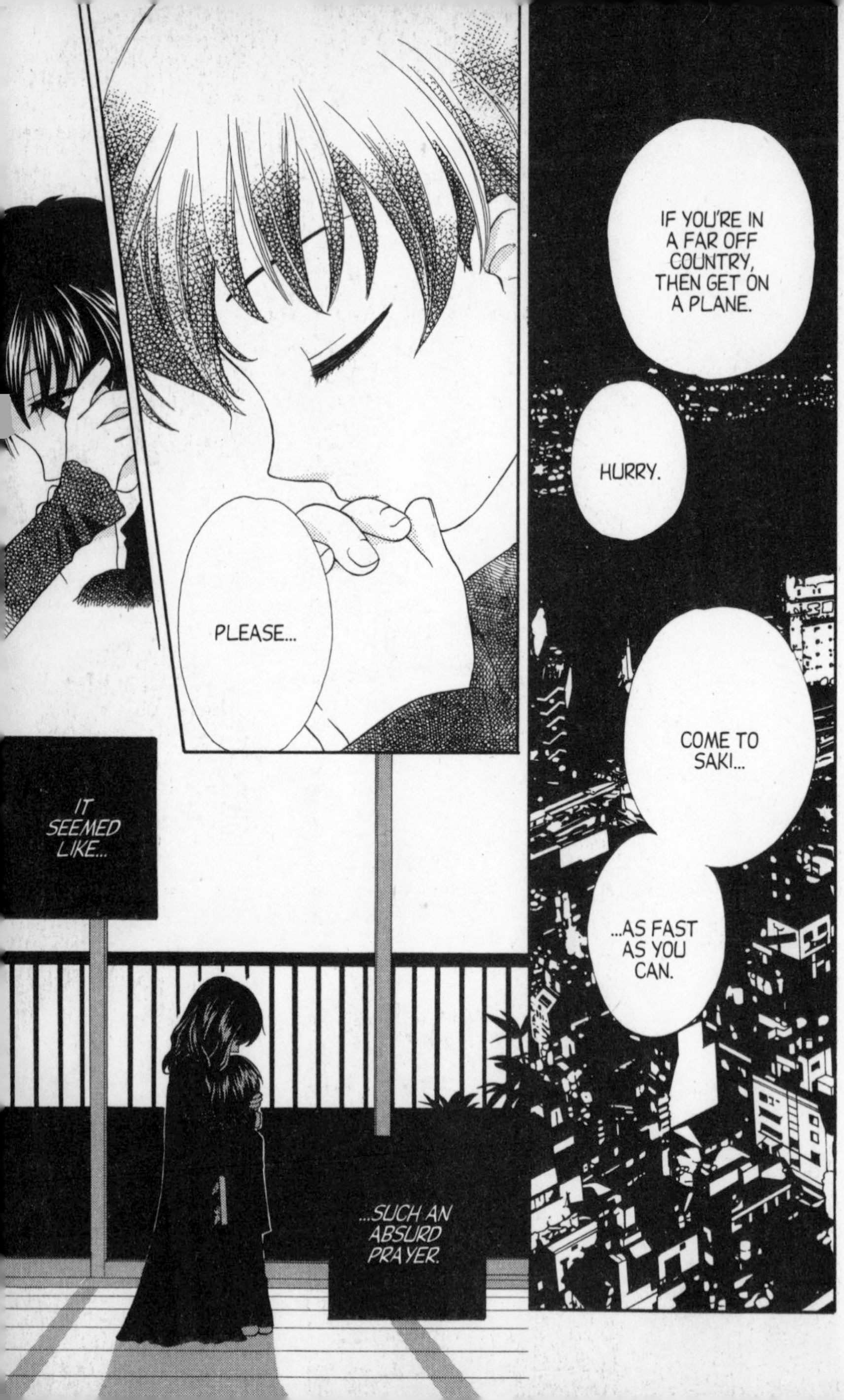
IF YOU'RE IN A FAR OFF COUNTRY, THEN GET ON A PLANE.
HURRY.
COME TO SAKI...
...AS FAST AS YOU CAN.
PLEASE...
IT SEEMED LIKE...
...SUCH AN ABSURD PRAYER.

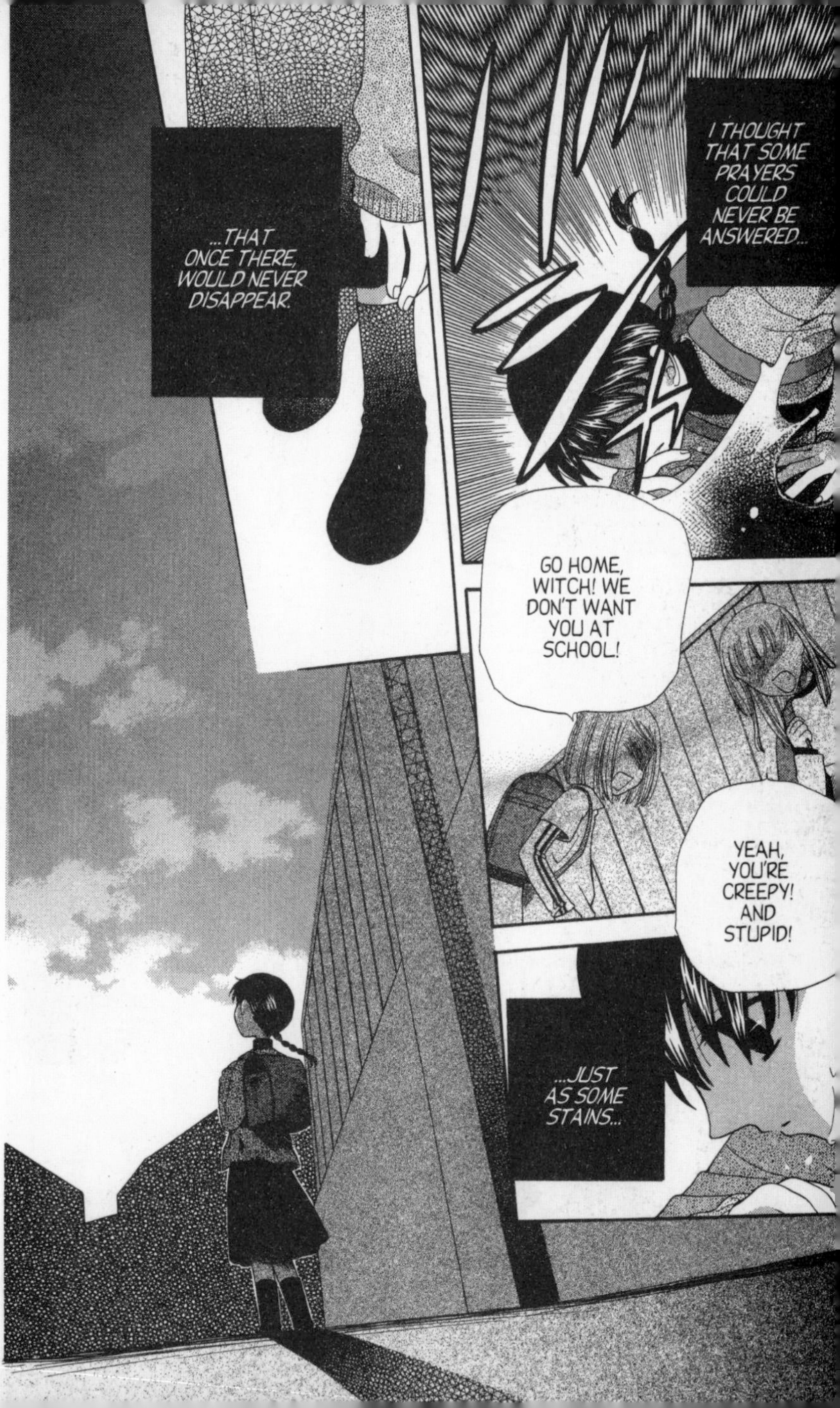
I THOUGHT THAT SOME PRAYERS COULD NEVER BE ANSWERED...
GO HOME, WITCH! WE DON'T WANT YOU AT SCHOOL!
YEAH, YOU'RE CREEPY! AND STUPID!
...JUST AS SOME STAINS...
...THAT ONCE THERE, WOULD NEVER DISAPPEAR.

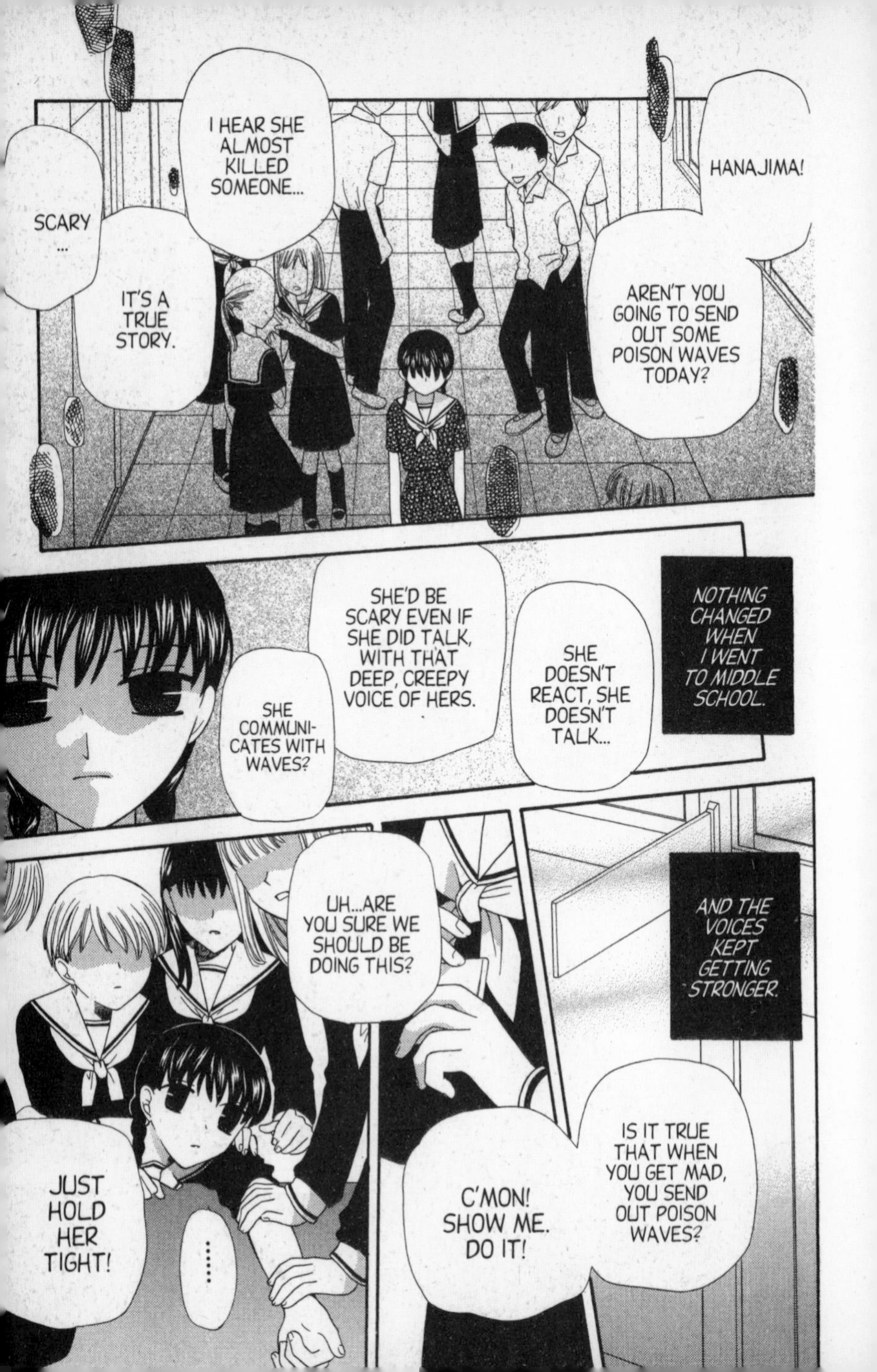
HANAJIMA!
AREN'T YOU GOING TO SEND OUT SOME POISON WAVES TODAY?
I HEAR SHE ALMOST KILLED SOMEONE...
SCARY...
IT'S A TRUE STORY.
NOTHING CHANGED WHEN I WENT TO MIDDLE SCHOOL.
SHE DOESN'T REACT, SHE DOESN'T TALK...
SHE'D BE SCARY EVEN IF SHE DID TALK, WITH THAT DEEP, CREEPY VOICE OF HERS.
SHE COMMUNI-CATES WITH WAVES?
AND THE VOICES KEPT GETTING STRONGER.
IS IT TRUE THAT WHEN YOU GET MAD, YOU SEND OUT POISON WAVES?
C'MON! SHOW ME. DO IT!
UH...ARE YOU SURE WE SHOULD BE DOING THIS?
JUST HOLD HER TIGHT!
......

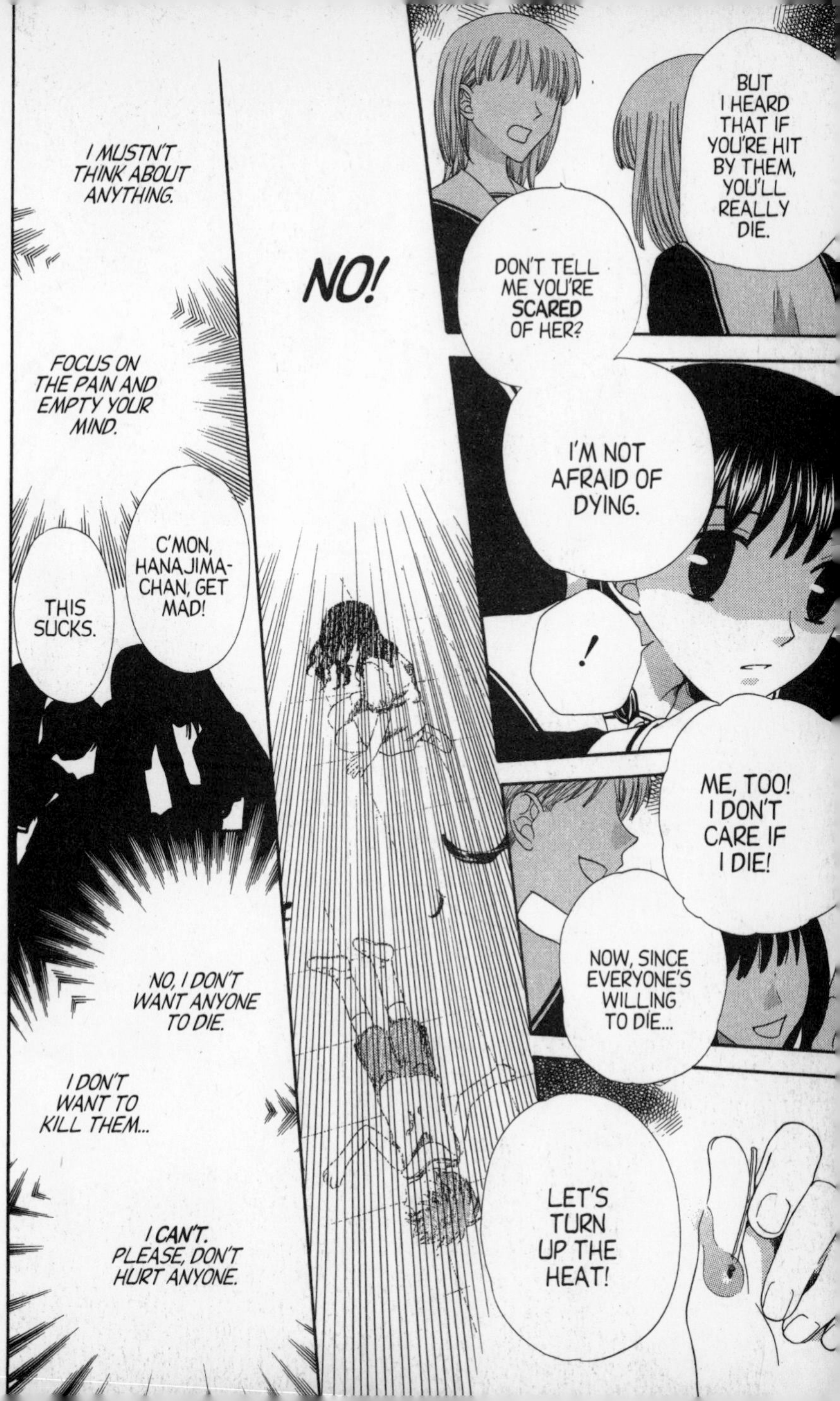
BUT I HEARD THAT IF YOU'RE HIT BY THEM, YOU'LL REALLY DIE.
DON'T TELL ME YOU'RE SCARED OF HER?
I'M NOT AFRAID OF DYING.
!
ME, TOO! I DON'T CARE IF I DIE!
NOW, SINCE EVERYONE'S WILLING TO DIE...
LET'S TURN UP THE HEAT!
NO!
I MUSTN'T THINK ABOUT ANYTHING.
FOCUS ON THE PAIN AND EMPTY YOUR MIND.
C'MON, HANAJIMA-CHAN, GET MAD!
THIS SUCKS.
NO, I DON'T WANT ANYONE TO DIE.
I DON'T WANT TO KILL THEM...
I CAN'T. PLEASE, DON'T HURT ANYONE.

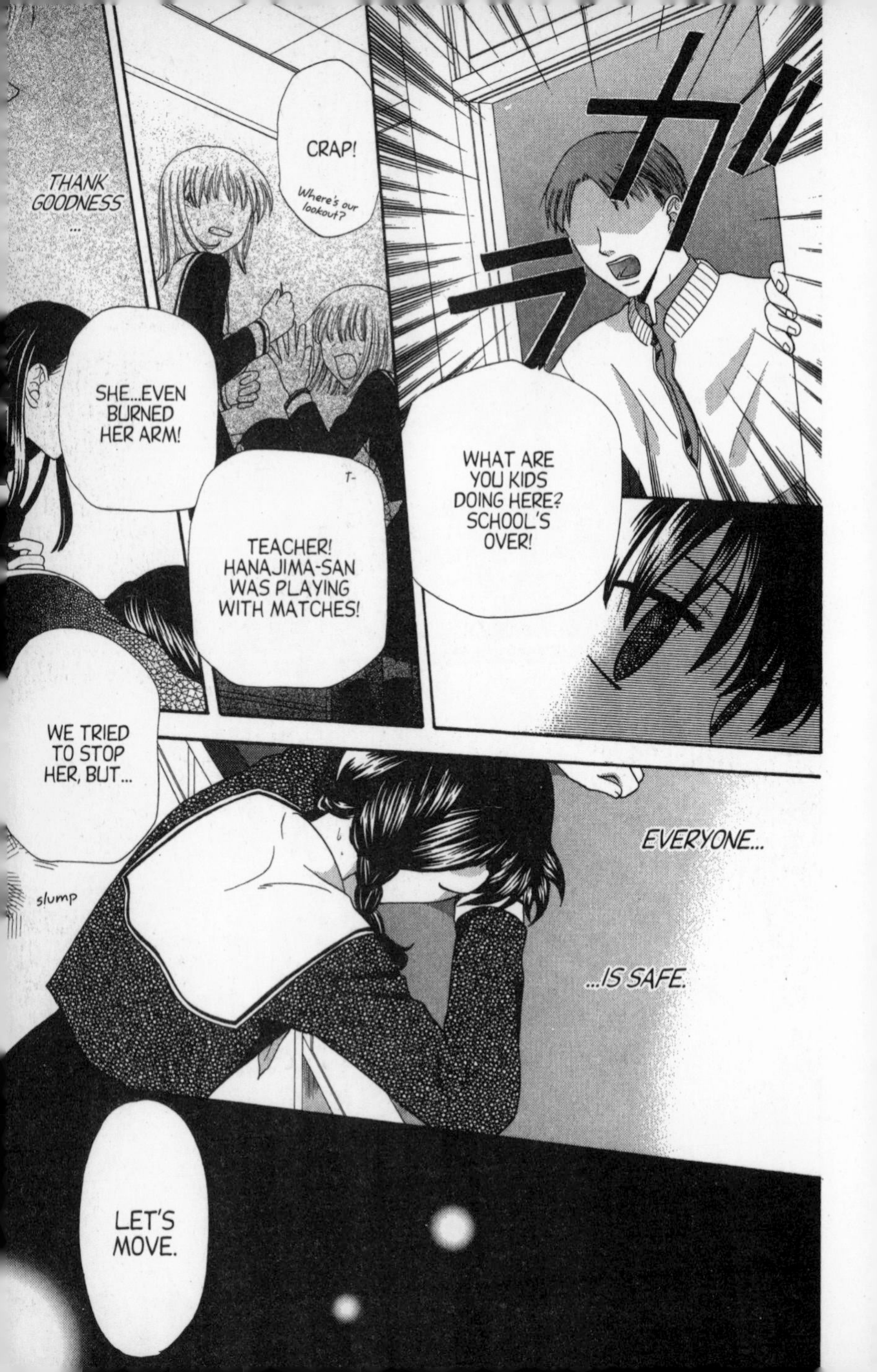
ガラ
WHAT ARE YOU KIDS DOING HERE? SCHOOL'S OVER!
CRAP!
Where's our lookout?
THANK GOODNESS ...
T-
TEACHER! HANAJIMA-SAN WAS PLAYING WITH MATCHES!
SHE...EVEN BURNED HER ARM!
WE TRIED TO STOP HER, BUT...
slump
EVERYONE...
...IS SAFE.
LET'S MOVE.

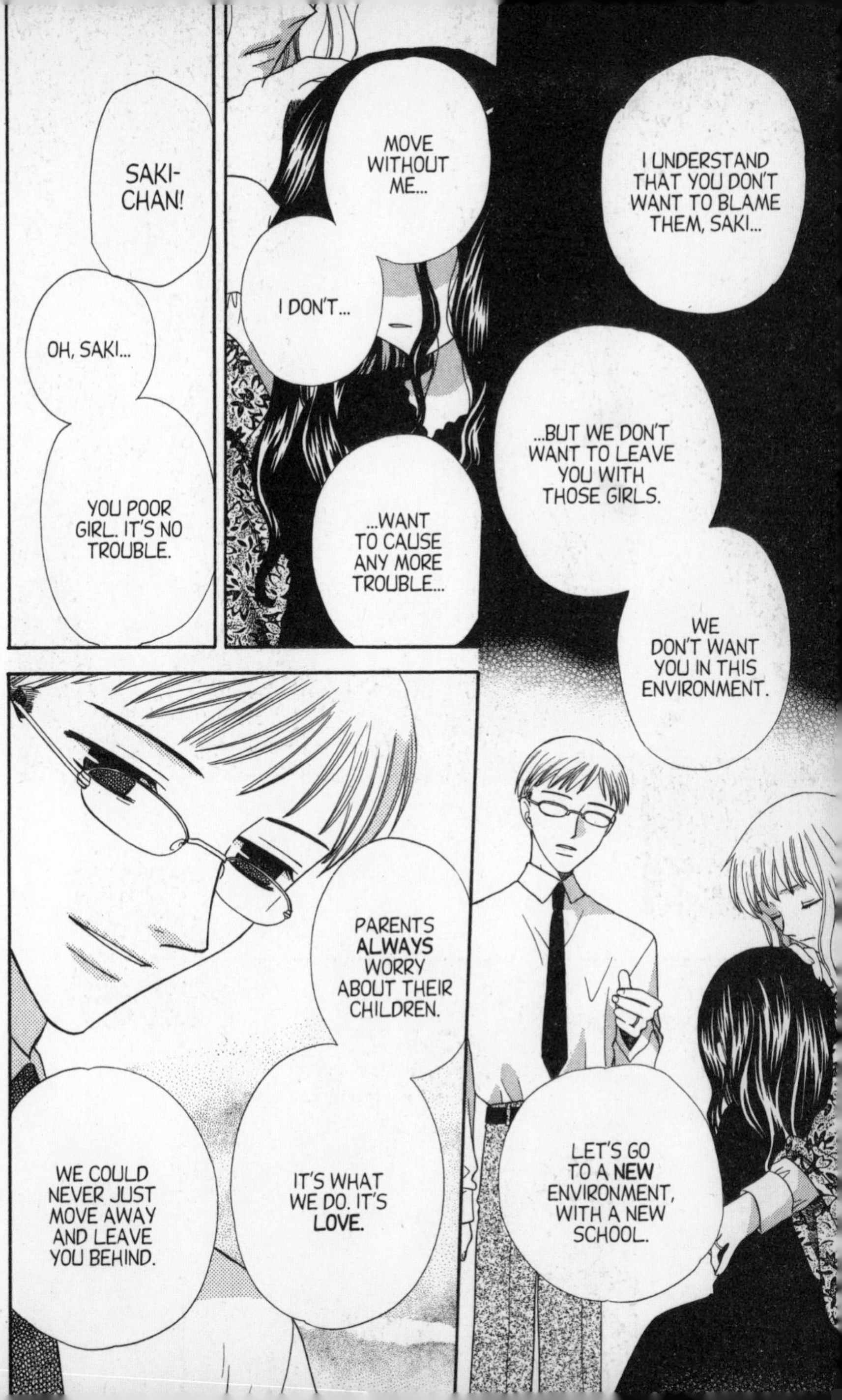
I UNDERSTAND THAT YOU DON'T WANT TO BLAME THEM, SAKI...
...BUT WE DON'T WANT TO LEAVE YOU WITH THOSE GIRLS.
WE DON'T WANT YOU IN THIS ENVIRONMENT.
MOVE WITHOUT ME...
I DON'T...
...WANT TO CAUSE ANY MORE TROUBLE...
SAKI-CHAN!
OH, SAKI...
YOU POOR GIRL. IT'S NO TROUBLE.
LET'S GO TO A **NEW** ENVIRONMENT, WITH A NEW SCHOOL.
PARENTS **ALWAYS** WORRY ABOUT THEIR CHILDREN.
IT'S WHAT WE DO. IT'S **LOVE.**
WE COULD NEVER JUST MOVE AWAY AND LEAVE YOU BEHIND.

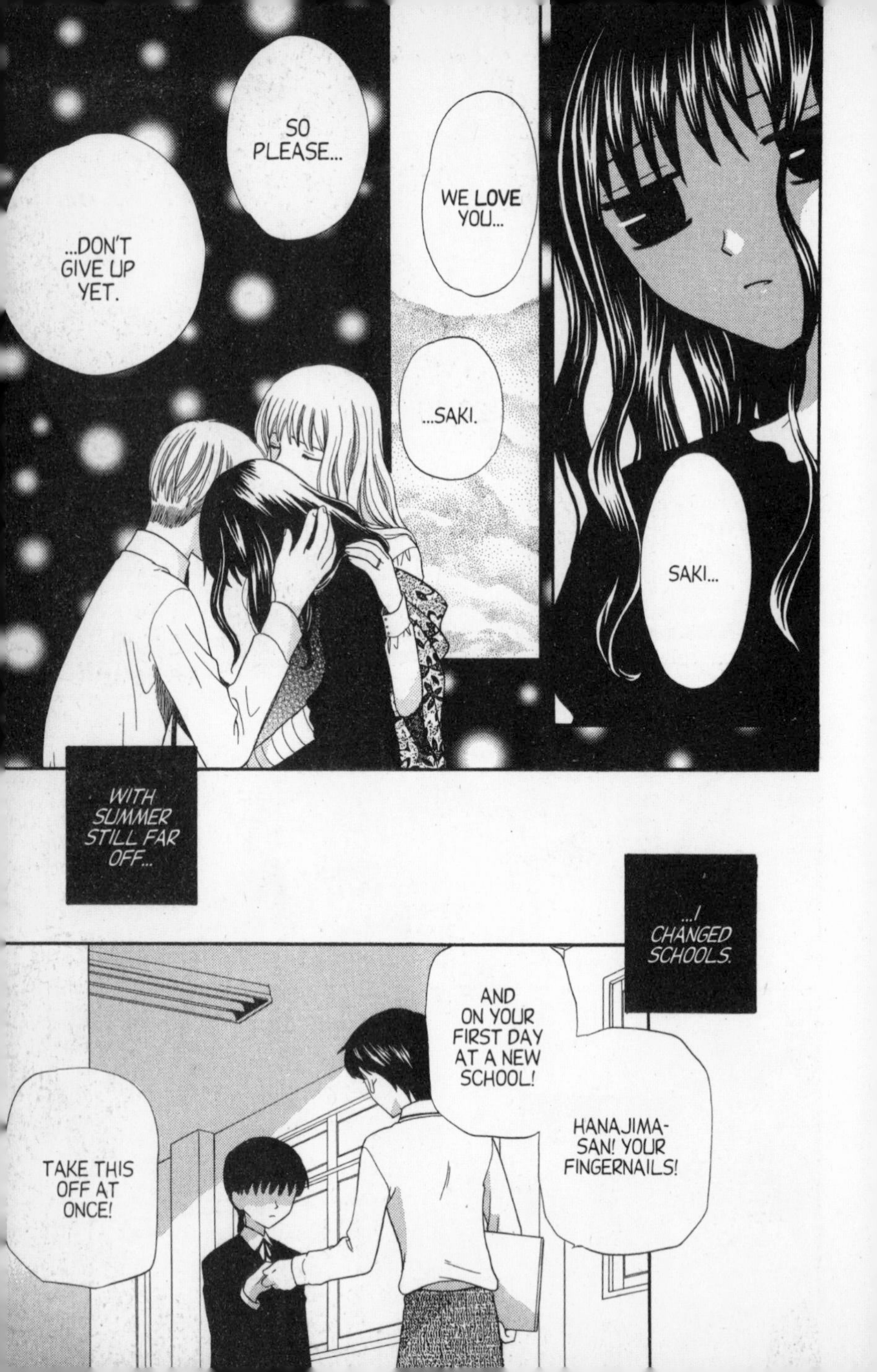
SAKI...
WE LOVE YOU...
...SAKI.
SO PLEASE...
...DON'T GIVE UP YET.
WITH SUMMER STILL FAR OFF...
...I CHANGED SCHOOLS.
HANAJIMA-SAN! YOUR FINGERNAILS!
AND ON YOUR FIRST DAY AT A NEW SCHOOL!
TAKE THIS OFF AT ONCE!

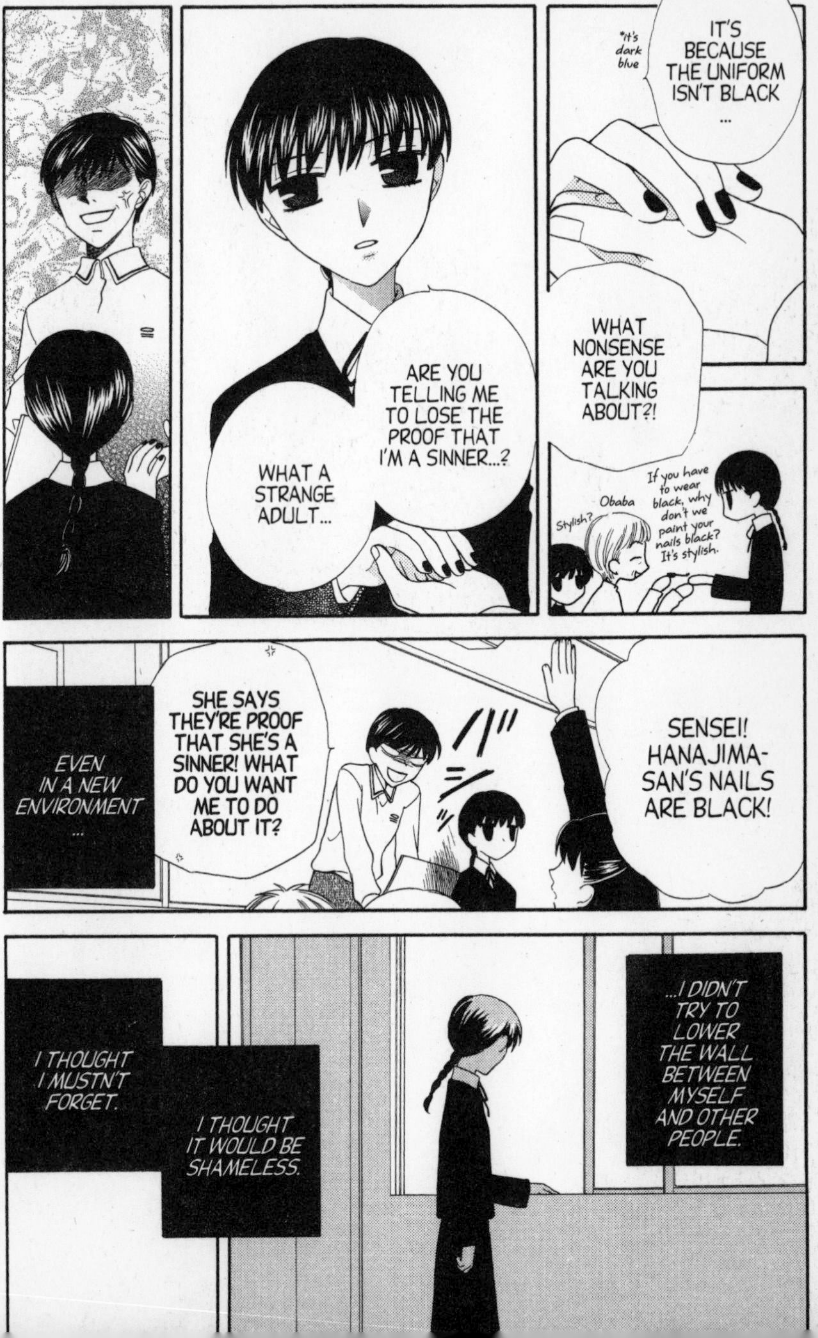
*it's dark blue
IT'S BECAUSE THE UNIFORM ISN'T BLACK ...
WHAT NONSENSE ARE YOU TALKING ABOUT?!
If you have to wear black, why don't we paint your nails black? It's stylish.
Obaba
Stylish?
ARE YOU TELLING ME TO LOSE THE PROOF THAT I'M A SINNER...?
WHAT A STRANGE ADULT...
SENSEI! HANAJIMA-SAN'S NAILS ARE BLACK!
SHE SAYS THEY'RE PROOF THAT SHE'S A SINNER! WHAT DO YOU WANT ME TO DO ABOUT IT?
EVEN IN A NEW ENVIRONMENT ...
...I DIDN'T TRY TO LOWER THE WALL BETWEEN MYSELF AND OTHER PEOPLE.
I THOUGHT IT WOULD BE SHAMELESS.
I THOUGHT I MUSTN'T FORGET.

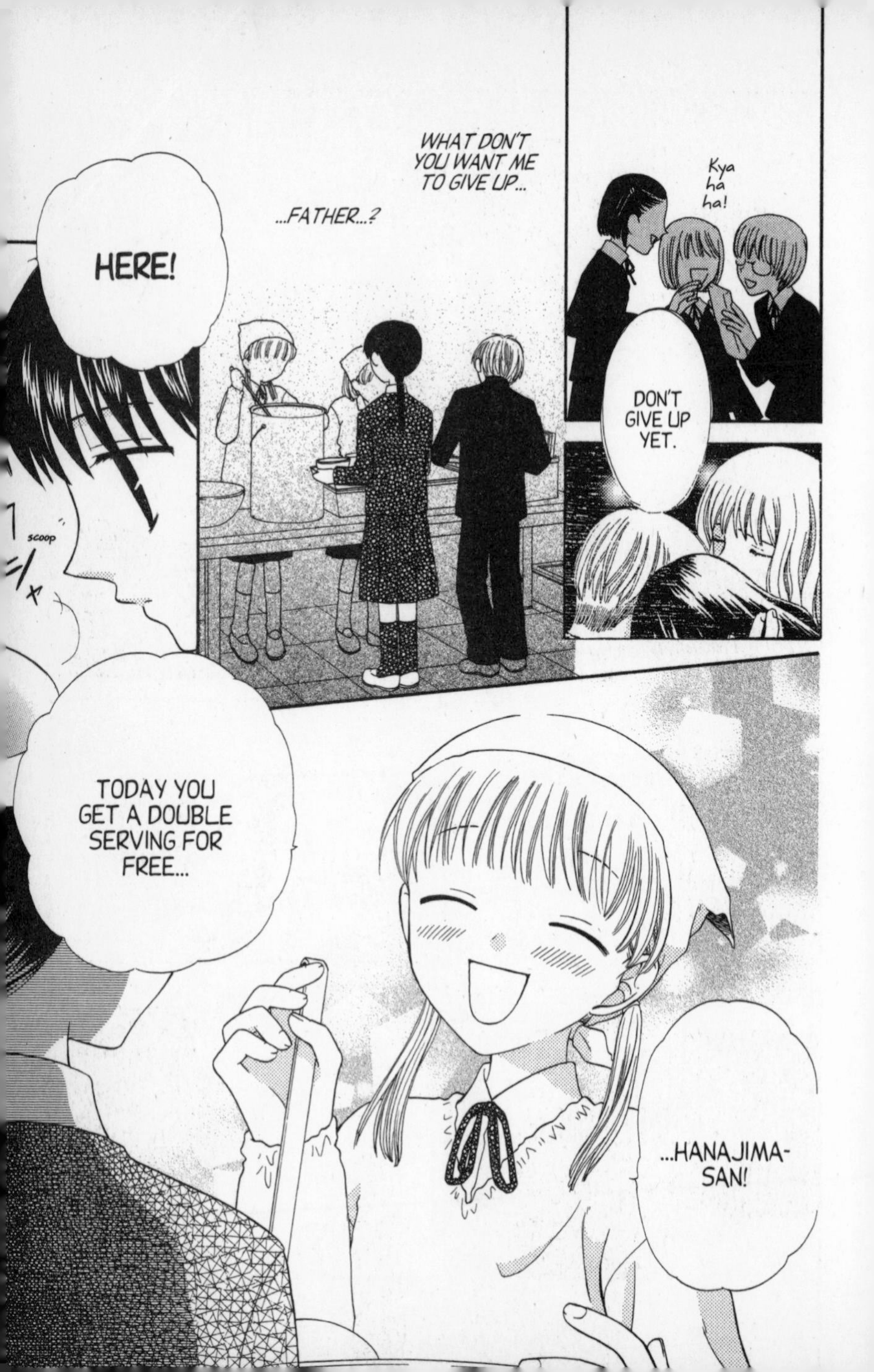
Kya ha ha!
DON'T GIVE UP YET.
WHAT DON'T YOU WANT ME TO GIVE UP...
...FATHER...?
HERE!
scoop
TODAY YOU GET A DOUBLE SERVING FOR FREE...
...HANAJIMA-SAN!

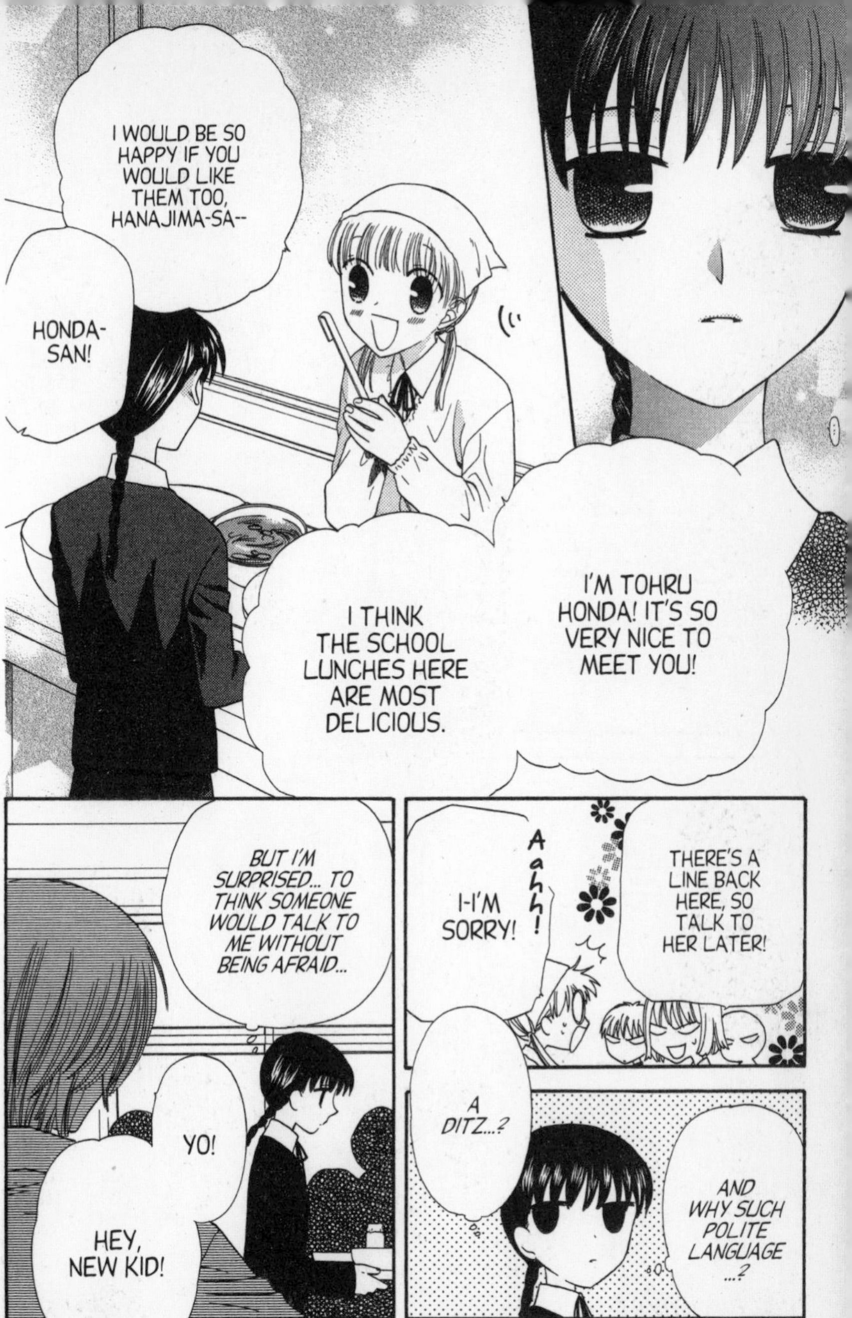
I'M TOHRU HONDA! IT'S SO VERY NICE TO MEET YOU!
I THINK THE SCHOOL LUNCHES HERE ARE MOST DELICIOUS.
I WOULD BE SO HAPPY IF YOU WOULD LIKE THEM TOO, HANAJIMA-SA--
HONDA-SAN!
THERE'S A LINE BACK HERE, SO TALK TO HER LATER!
Aahh!
I-I'M SORRY!
AND WHY SUCH POLITE LANGUAGE ...?
A DITZ...?
BUT I'M SURPRISED... TO THINK SOMEONE WOULD TALK TO ME WITHOUT BEING AFRAID...
YO!
HEY, NEW KID!

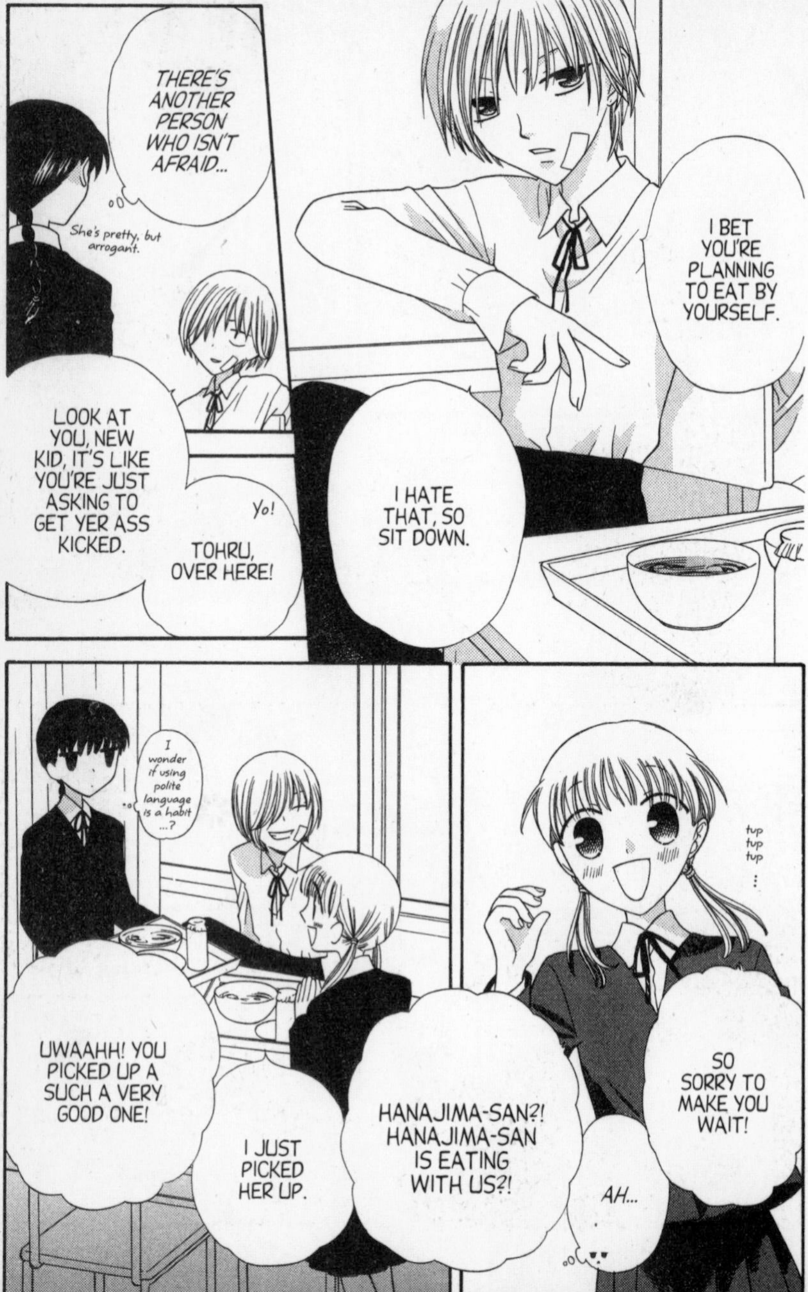
I BET YOU'RE PLANNING TO EAT BY YOURSELF.
I HATE THAT, SO SIT DOWN.
THERE'S ANOTHER PERSON WHO ISN'T AFRAID...
She's pretty, but arrogant.
LOOK AT YOU, NEW KID, IT'S LIKE YOU'RE JUST ASKING TO GET YER ASS KICKED.
Yo!
TOHRU, OVER HERE!
tup tup tup ...
SO SORRY TO MAKE YOU WAIT!
AH...
HANAJIMA-SAN?! HANAJIMA-SAN IS EATING WITH US?!
I JUST PICKED HER UP.
UWAAHH! YOU PICKED UP A SUCH A VERY GOOD ONE!
I wonder if using polite language is a habit ...?

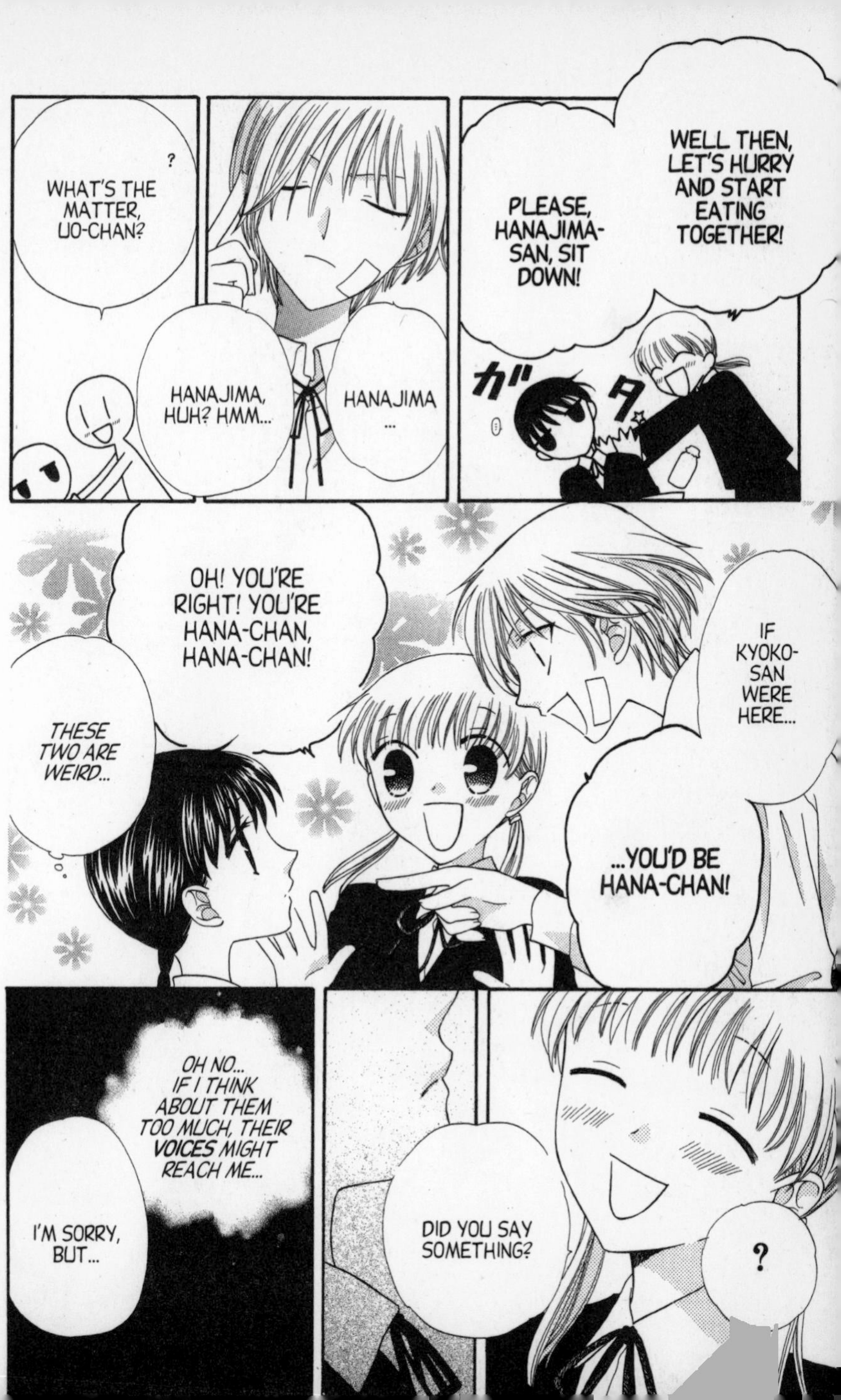
WELL THEN, LET'S HURRY AND START EATING TOGETHER!
PLEASE, HANAJIMA-SAN, SIT DOWN!
ガ
タ
HANAJIMA ...
HANAJIMA, HUH? HMM...
?
WHAT'S THE MATTER, UO-CHAN?
IF KYOKO-SAN WERE HERE...
...YOU'D BE HANA-CHAN!
OH! YOU'RE RIGHT! YOU'RE HANA-CHAN, HANA-CHAN!
THESE TWO ARE WEIRD...
?
DID YOU SAY SOMETHING?
OH NO... IF I THINK ABOUT THEM TOO MUCH, THEIR VOICES MIGHT REACH ME...
I'M SORRY, BUT...

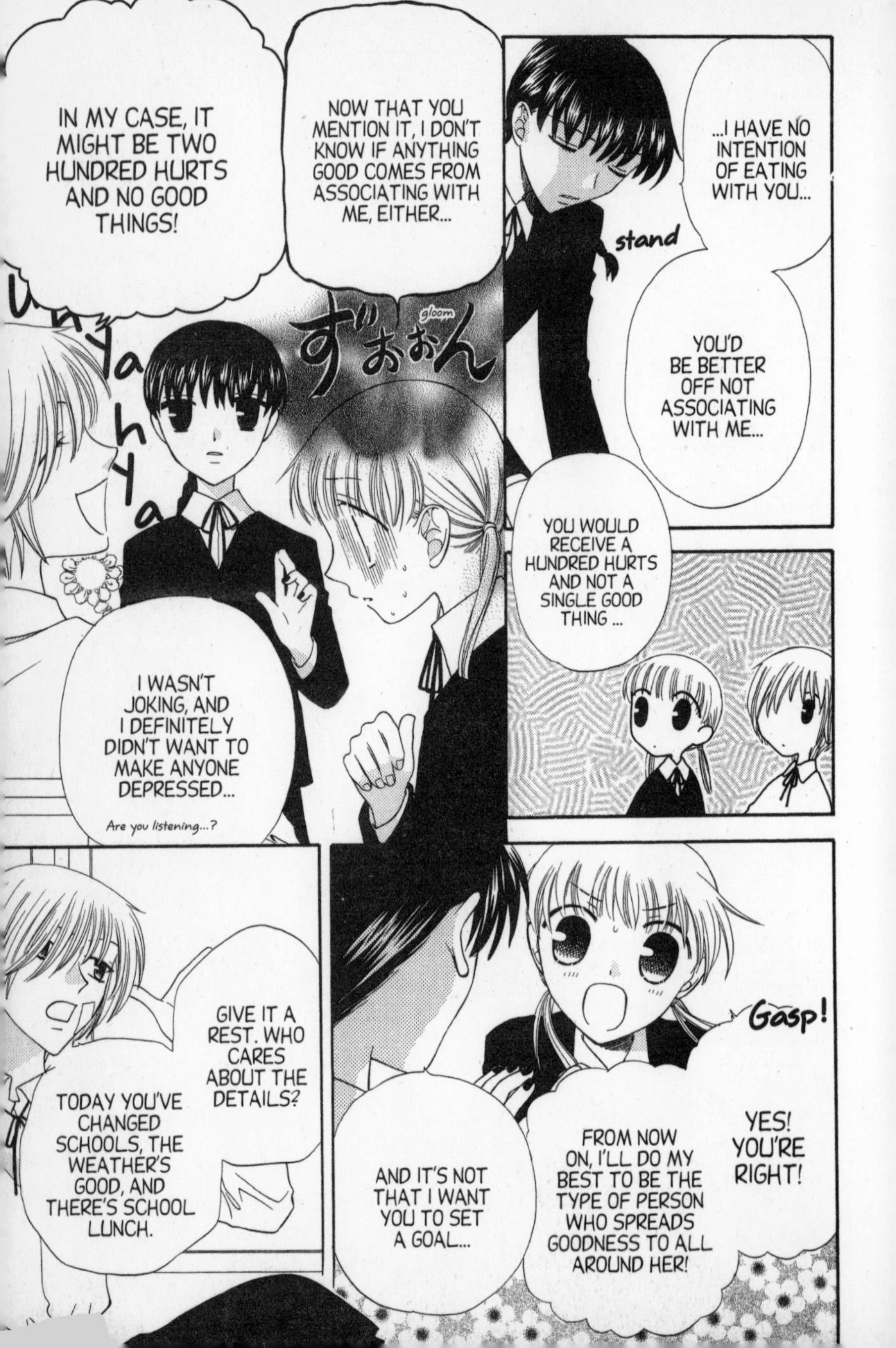

...I HAVE NO INTENTION OF EATING WITH YOU...
stand
YOU'D BE BETTER OFF NOT ASSOCIATING WITH ME...
YOU WOULD RECEIVE A HUNDRED HURTS AND NOT A SINGLE GOOD THING ...
NOW THAT YOU MENTION IT, I DON'T KNOW IF ANYTHING GOOD COMES FROM ASSOCIATING WITH ME, EITHER...
ずおぉん
gloom
IN MY CASE, IT MIGHT BE TWO HUNDRED HURTS AND NO GOOD THINGS!
I WASN'T JOKING, AND I DEFINITELY DIDN'T WANT TO MAKE ANYONE DEPRESSED...
Are you listening...?
Gasp!
YES! YOU'RE RIGHT!
FROM NOW ON, I'LL DO MY BEST TO BE THE TYPE OF PERSON WHO SPREADS GOODNESS TO ALL AROUND HER!
AND IT'S NOT THAT I WANT YOU TO SET A GOAL...
GIVE IT A REST. WHO CARES ABOUT THE DETAILS?
TODAY YOU'VE CHANGED SCHOOLS, THE WEATHER'S GOOD, AND THERE'S SCHOOL LUNCH.

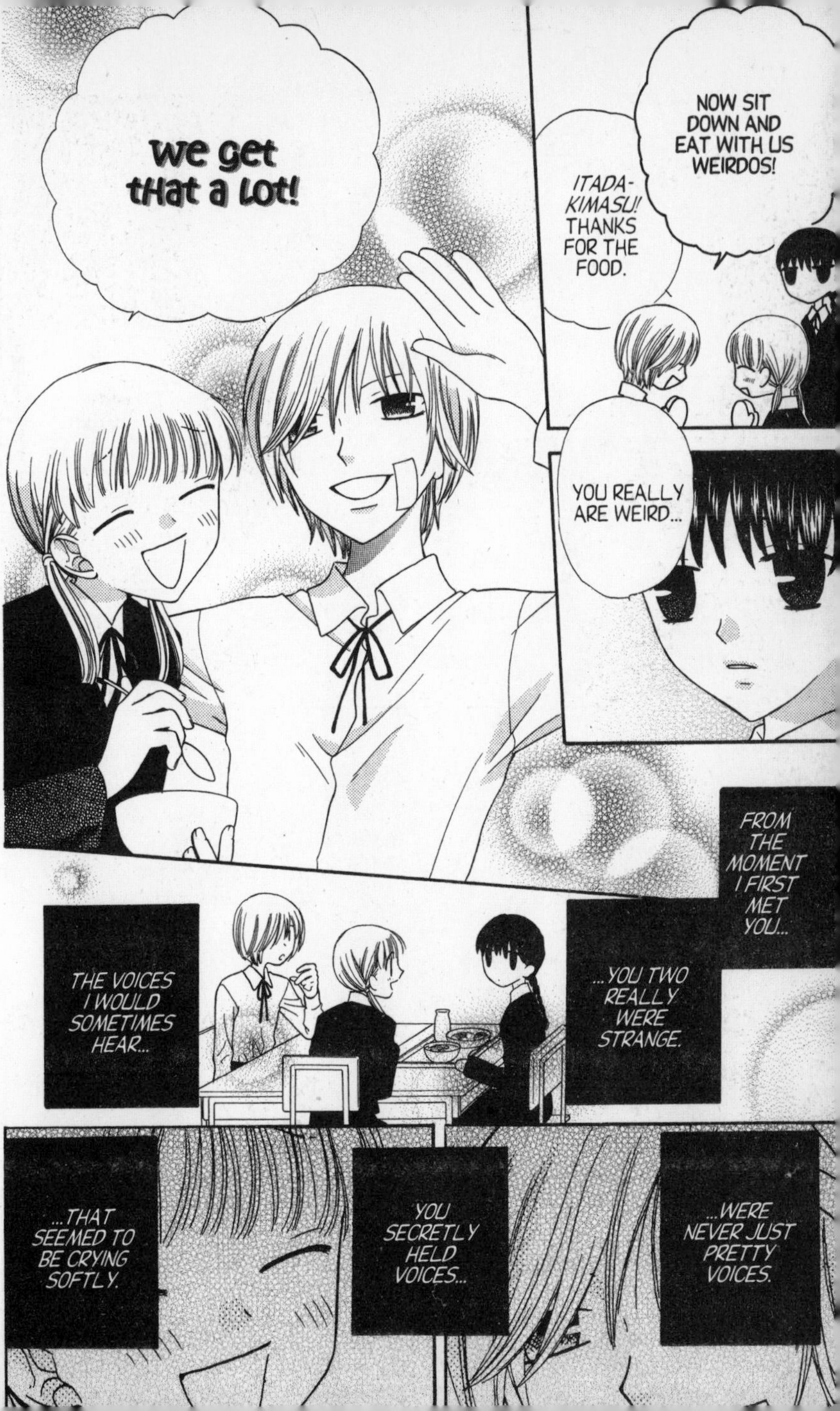
NOW SIT DOWN AND EAT WITH US WEIRDOS!
ITADA-KIMASU! THANKS FOR THE FOOD.
YOU REALLY ARE WEIRD...
we get tHat a Lot!
FROM THE MOMENT I FIRST MET YOU...
...YOU TWO REALLY WERE STRANGE.
THE VOICES I WOULD SOMETIMES HEAR...
...WERE NEVER JUST PRETTY VOICES.
YOU SECRETLY HELD VOICES...
...THAT SEEMED TO BE CRYING SOFTLY.

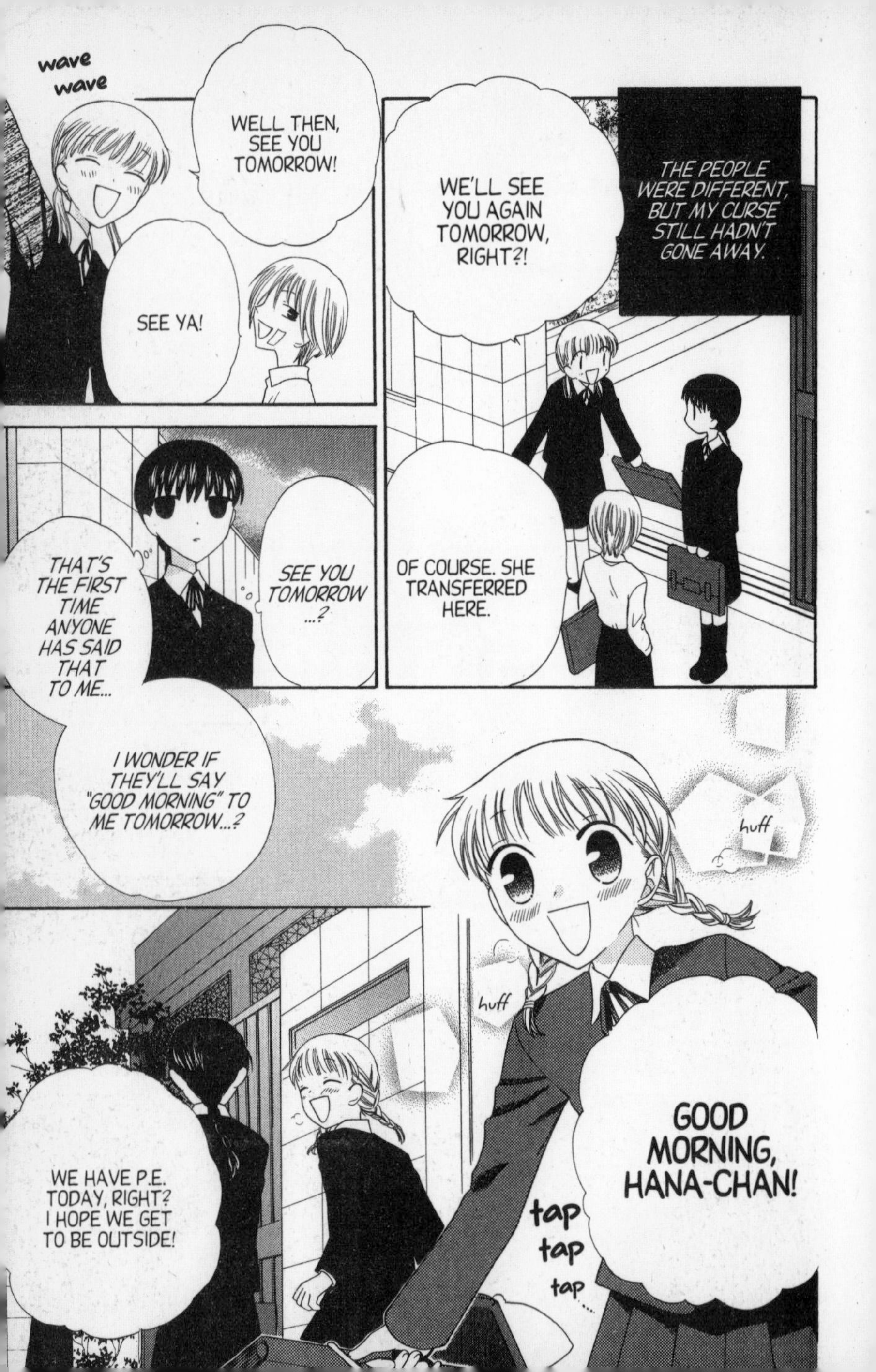
THE PEOPLE WERE DIFFERENT, BUT MY CURSE STILL HADN'T GONE AWAY.
WE'LL SEE YOU AGAIN TOMORROW, RIGHT?!
OF COURSE. SHE TRANSFERRED HERE.
wave wave
WELL THEN, SEE YOU TOMORROW!
SEE YA!
SEE YOU TOMORROW ...?
THAT'S THE FIRST TIME ANYONE HAS SAID THAT TO ME...
I WONDER IF THEY'LL SAY "GOOD MORNING" TO ME TOMORROW...?
huff
huff
GOOD MORNING, HANA-CHAN!
tap tap tap....
WE HAVE P.E. TODAY, RIGHT? I HOPE WE GET TO BE OUTSIDE!

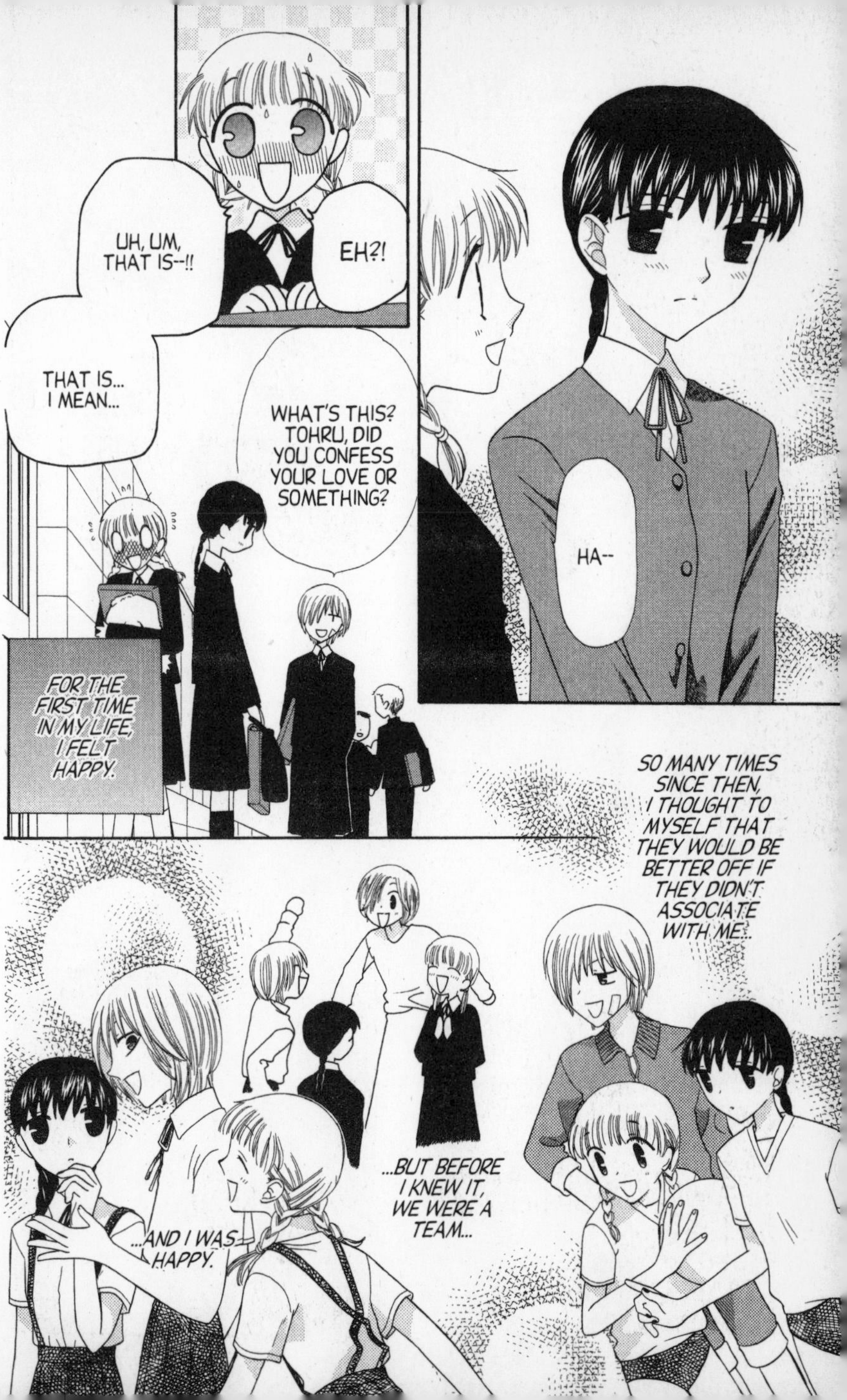
HA--
EH?!
UH, UM, THAT IS--!!
THAT IS... I MEAN...
WHAT'S THIS? TOHRU, DID YOU CONFESS YOUR LOVE OR SOMETHING?
FOR THE FIRST TIME IN MY LIFE, I FELT HAPPY.
SO MANY TIMES SINCE THEN, I THOUGHT TO MYSELF THAT THEY WOULD BE BETTER OFF IF THEY DIDN'T ASSOCIATE WITH ME...
...BUT BEFORE I KNEW IT, WE WERE A TEAM...
...AND I WAS HAPPY.

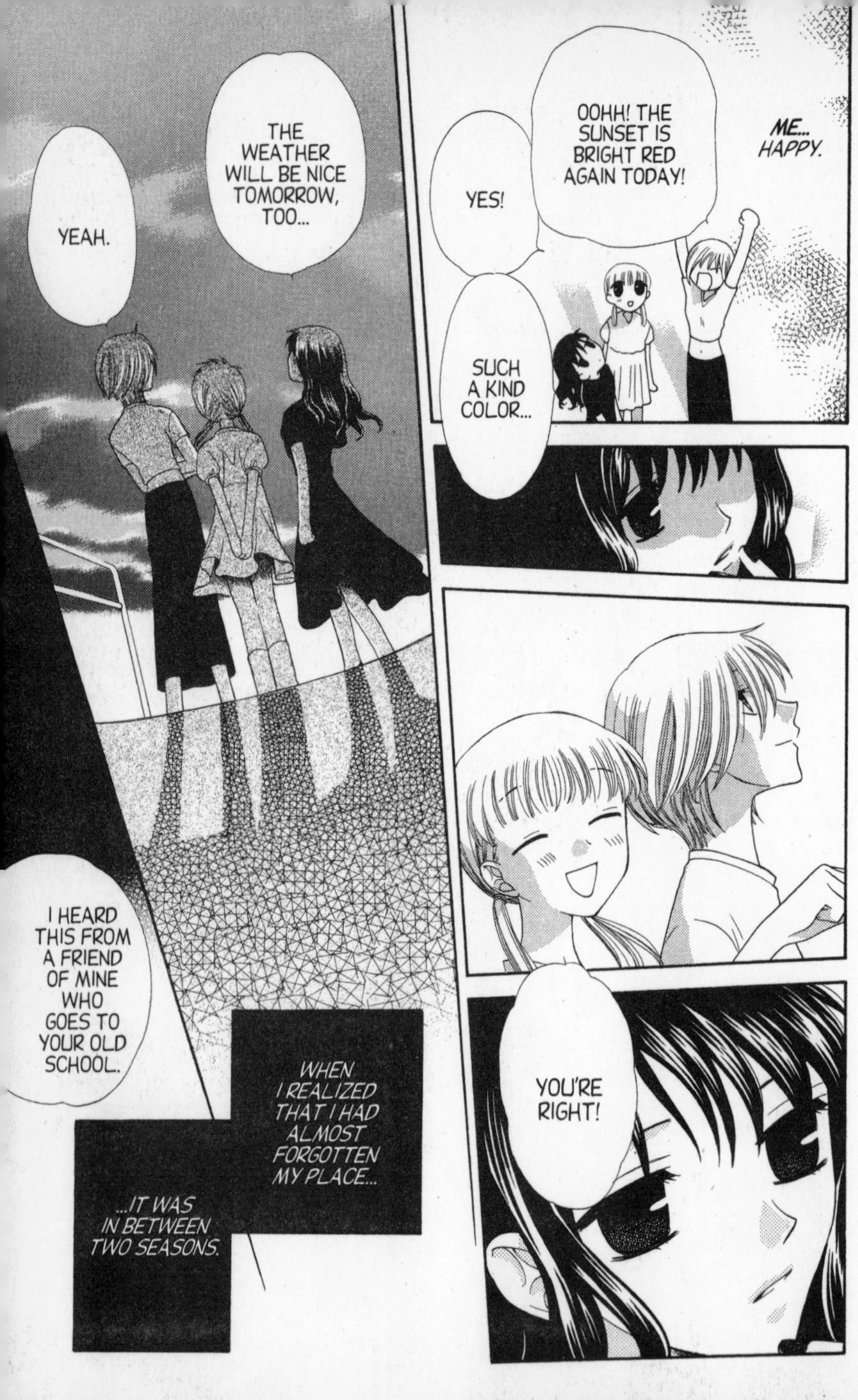

ME... HAPPY.
OOHH! THE SUNSET IS BRIGHT RED AGAIN TODAY!
YES!
SUCH A KIND COLOR...
YOU'RE RIGHT!
THE WEATHER WILL BE NICE TOMORROW, TOO...
YEAH.
I HEARD THIS FROM A FRIEND OF MINE WHO GOES TO YOUR OLD SCHOOL.
WHEN I REALIZED THAT I HAD ALMOST FORGOTTEN MY PLACE...
...IT WAS IN BETWEEN TWO SEASONS.

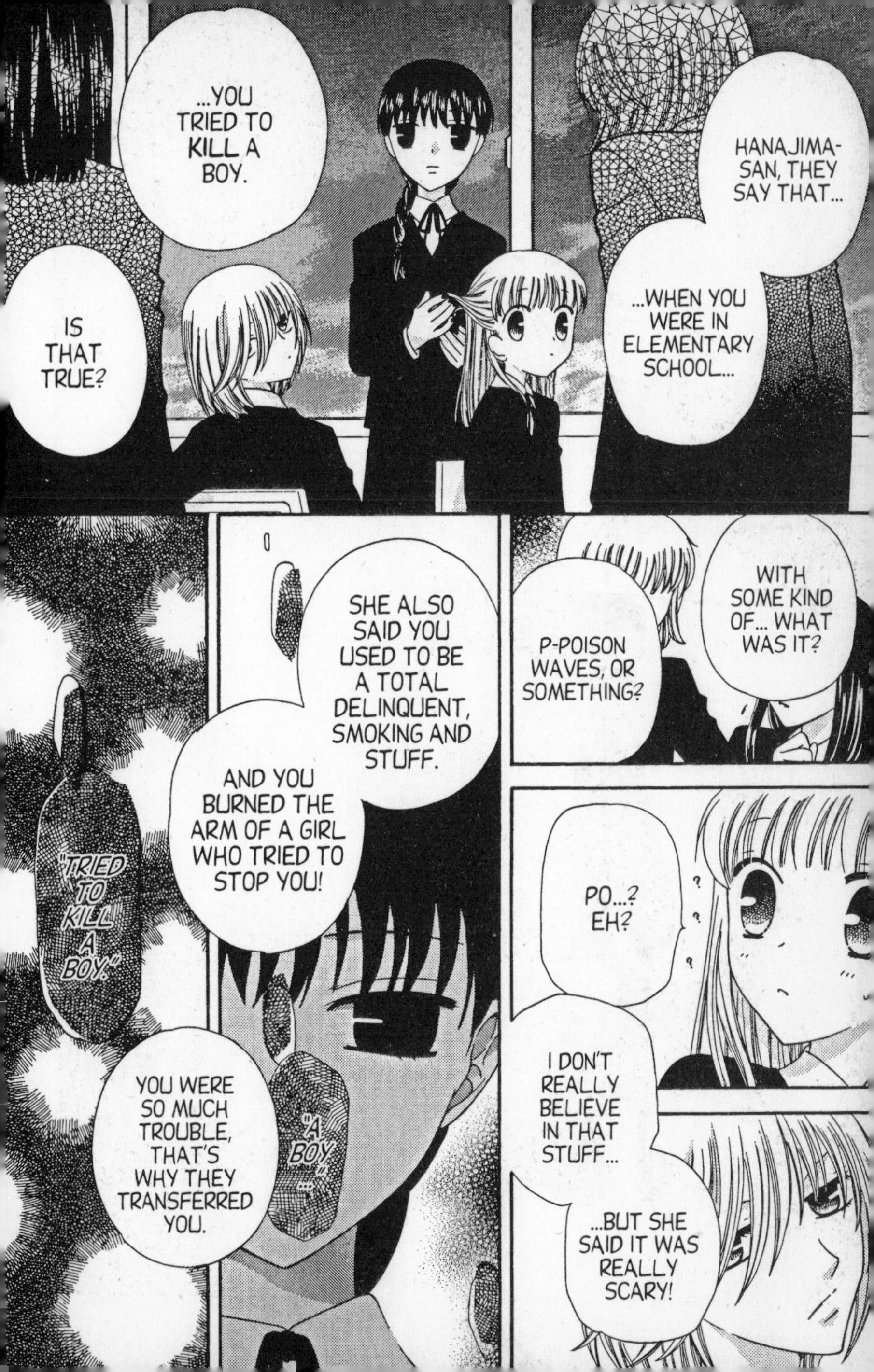

HANAJIMA-SAN, THEY SAY THAT...
...WHEN YOU WERE IN ELEMENTARY SCHOOL...
...YOU TRIED TO KILL A BOY.
IS THAT TRUE?
WITH SOME KIND OF... WHAT WAS IT?
P-POISON WAVES, OR SOMETHING?
PO...? EH?
I DON'T REALLY BELIEVE IN THAT STUFF...
...BUT SHE SAID IT WAS REALLY SCARY!
SHE ALSO SAID YOU USED TO BE A TOTAL DELINQUENT, SMOKING AND STUFF.
AND YOU BURNED THE ARM OF A GIRL WHO TRIED TO STOP YOU!
"TRIED TO KILL A BOY."
"A BOY"...
YOU WERE SO MUCH TROUBLE, THAT'S WHY THEY TRANSFERRED YOU.

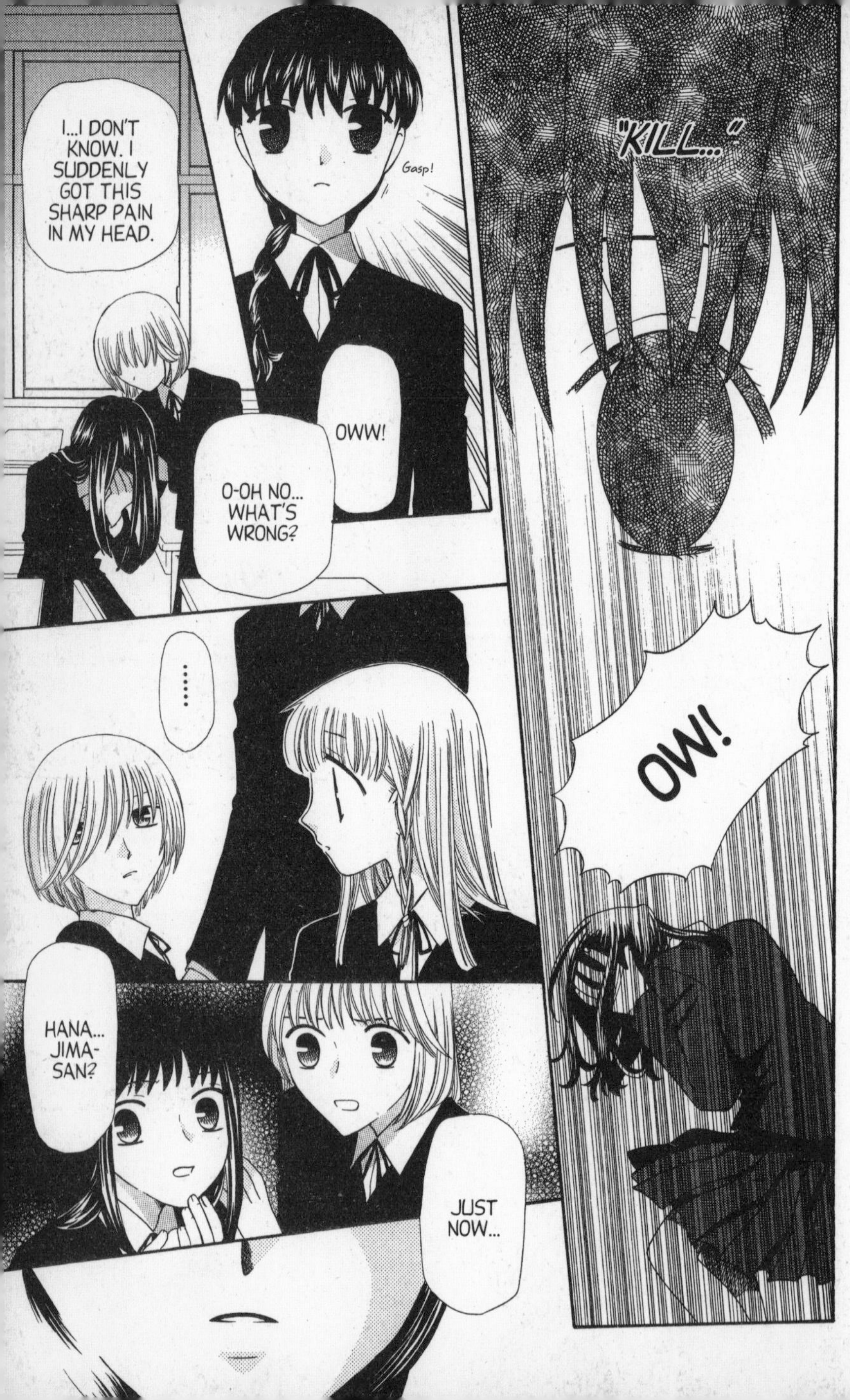
"KILL..."
OW!
Gasp!
OWW!
O-OH NO... WHAT'S WRONG?
I...I DON'T KNOW. I SUDDENLY GOT THIS SHARP PAIN IN MY HEAD.
......
HANA... JIMA-SAN?
JUST NOW...

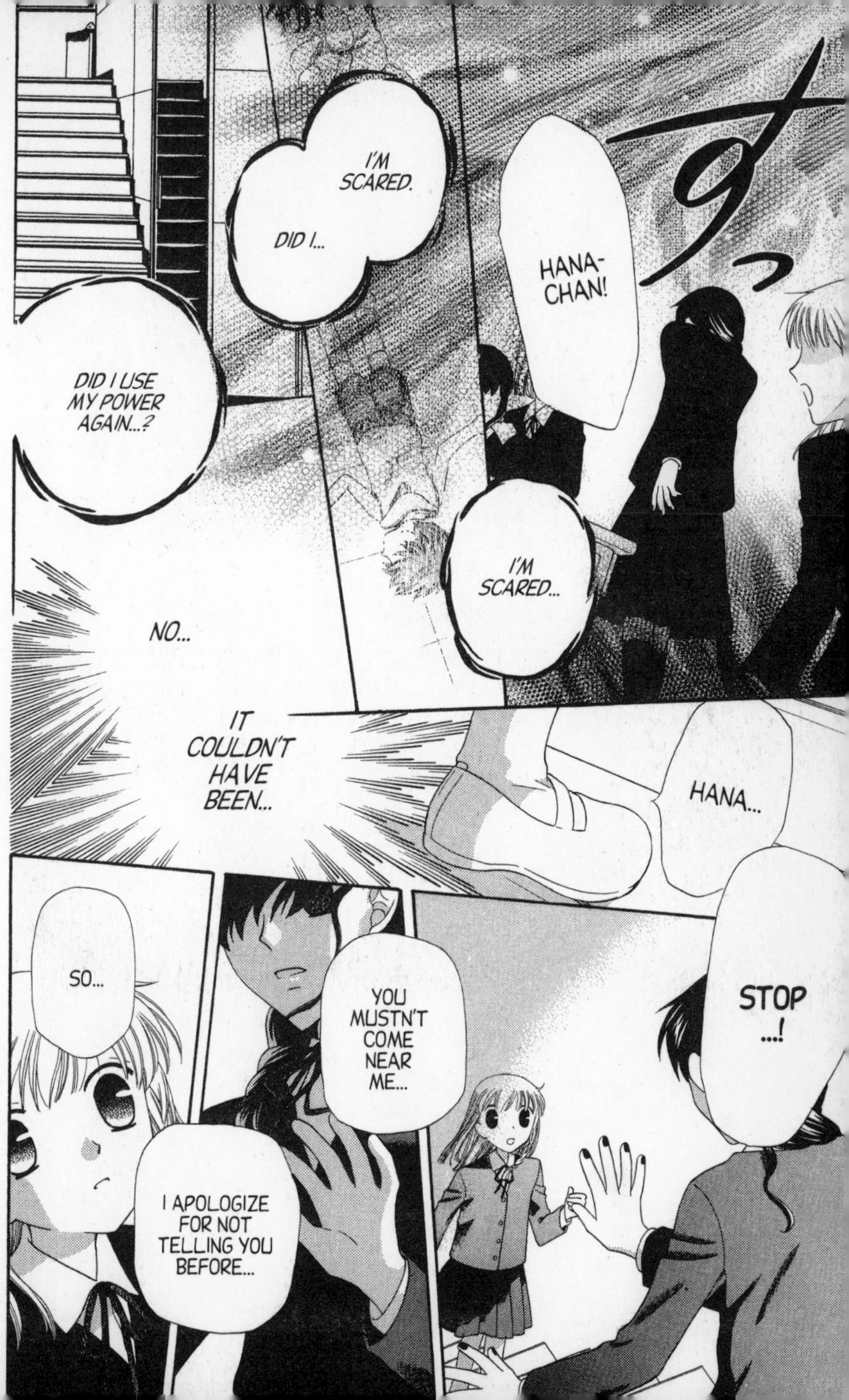
すっ
HANA-CHAN!
I'M SCARED...
I'M SCARED.
DID I...
DID I USE MY POWER AGAIN...?
HANA...
NO...
IT COULDN'T HAVE BEEN...
STOP ...!
YOU MUSTN'T COME NEAR ME...
I APOLOGIZE FOR NOT TELLING YOU BEFORE...
SO...

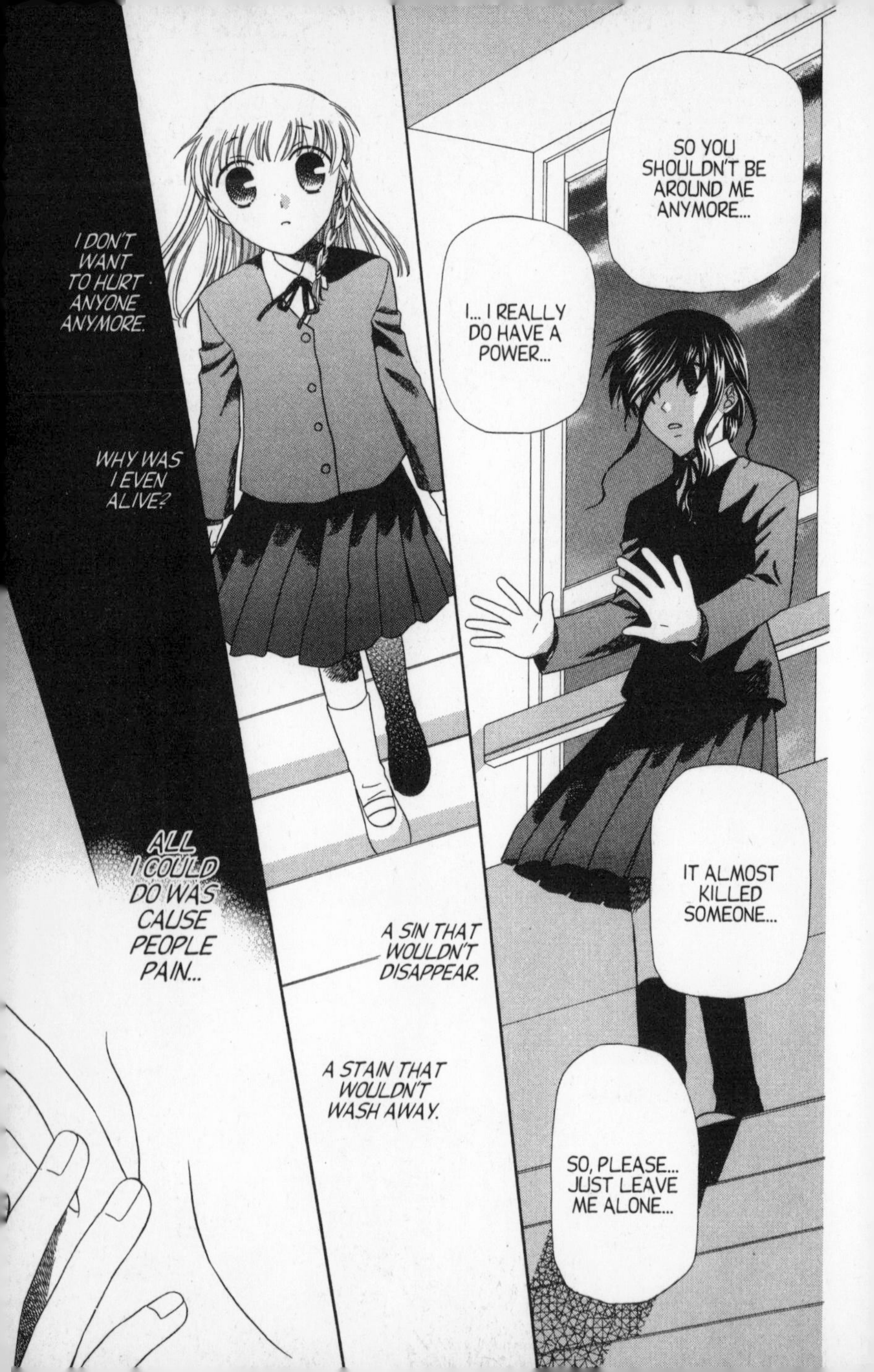
SO YOU SHOULDN'T BE AROUND ME ANYMORE...
I... I REALLY DO HAVE A POWER...
IT ALMOST KILLED SOMEONE...
SO, PLEASE... JUST LEAVE ME ALONE...
A SIN THAT WOULDN'T DISAPPEAR.
A STAIN THAT WOULDN'T WASH AWAY.
I DON'T WANT TO HURT ANYONE ANYMORE.
WHY WAS I EVEN ALIVE?
ALL I COULD DO WAS CAUSE PEOPLE PAIN...

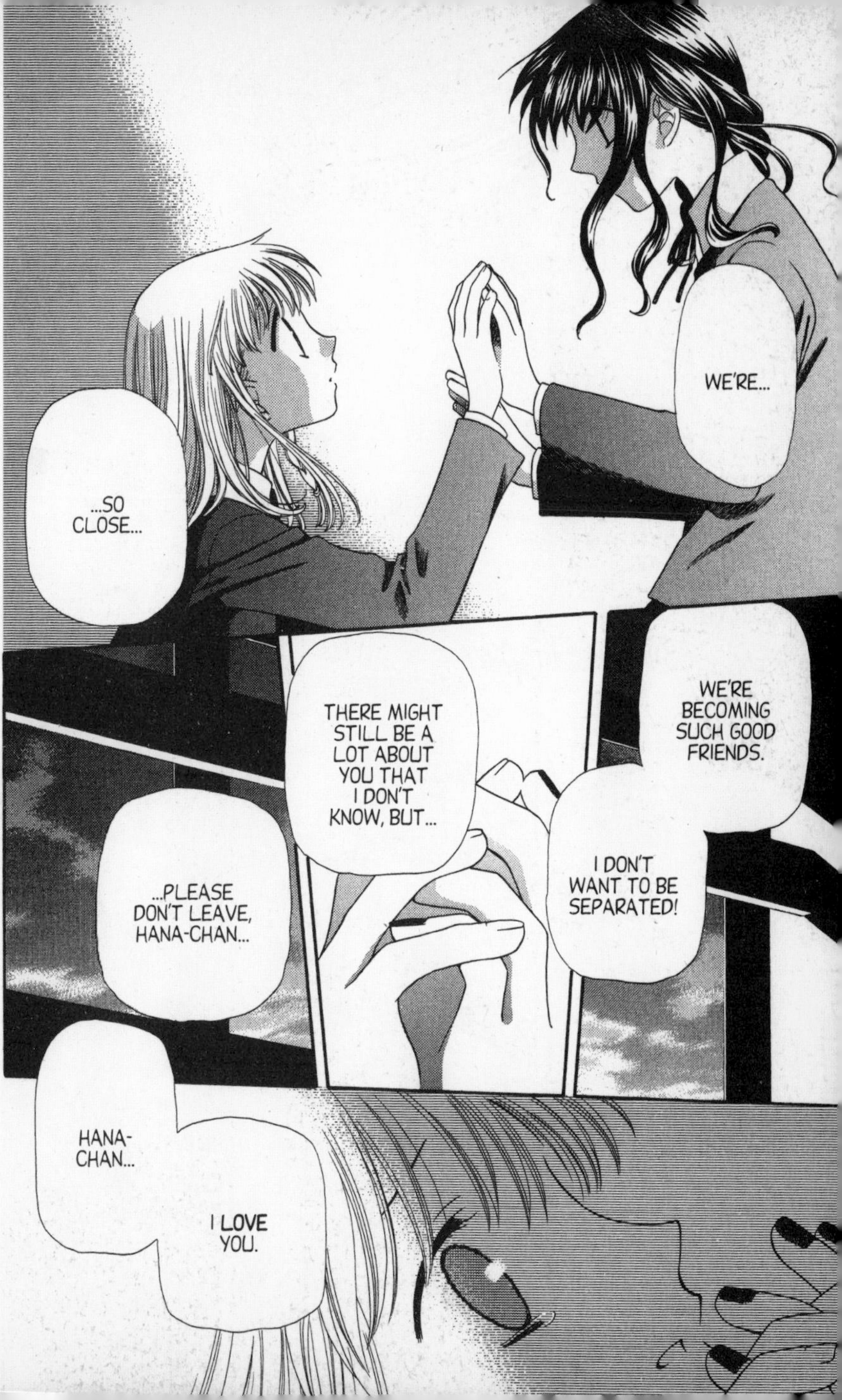
WE'RE...
...SO CLOSE...
WE'RE BECOMING SUCH GOOD FRIENDS.
I DON'T WANT TO BE SEPARATED!
THERE MIGHT STILL BE A LOT ABOUT YOU THAT I DON'T KNOW, BUT...
...PLEASE DON'T LEAVE, HANA-CHAN...
HANA-CHAN...
I LOVE YOU.

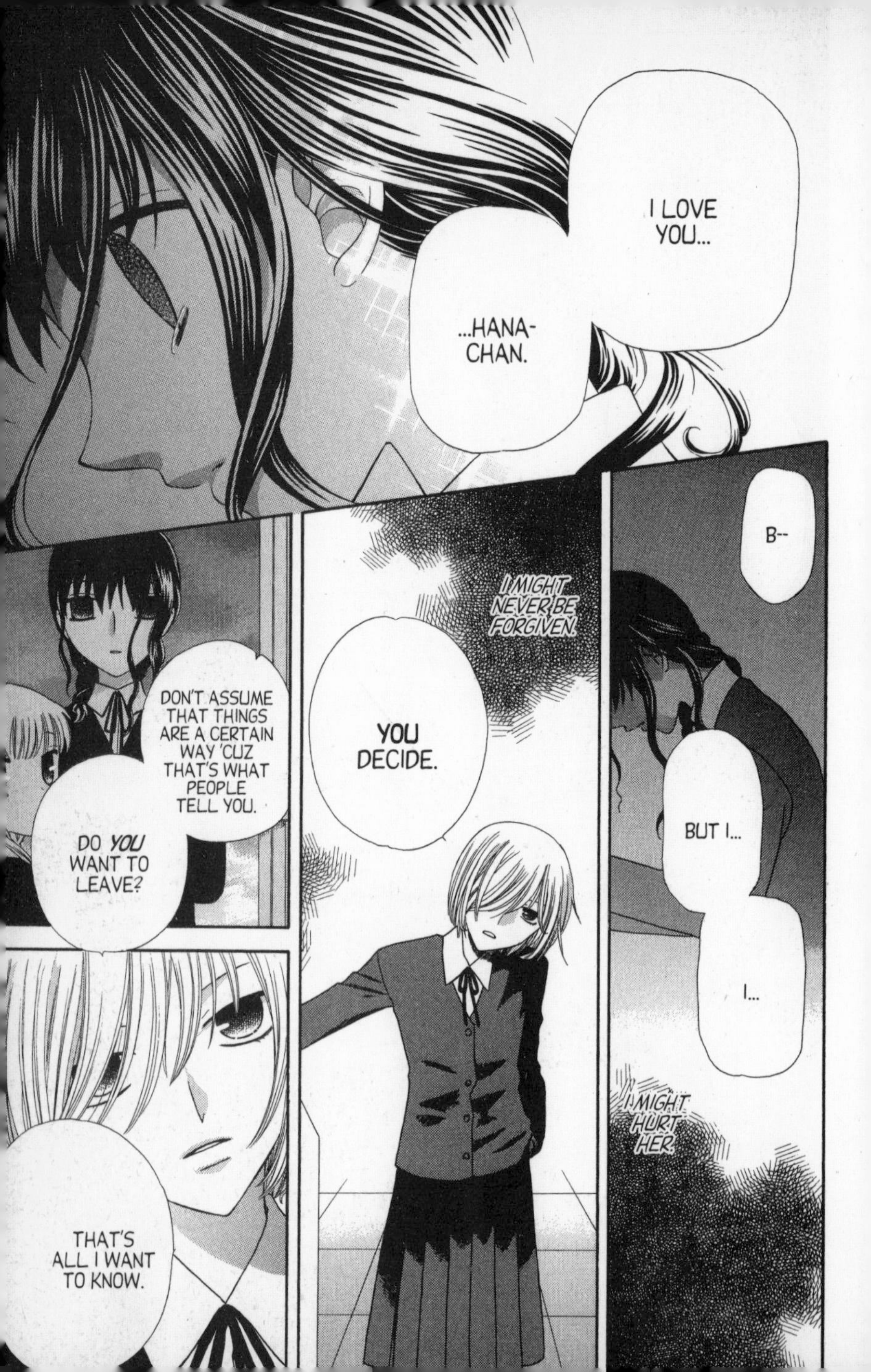
I LOVE YOU...
...HANA-CHAN.
B--
BUT I...
I...
I MIGHT HURT HER.
I MIGHT NEVER BE FORGIVEN.
YOU DECIDE.
DON'T ASSUME THAT THINGS ARE A CERTAIN WAY 'CUZ THAT'S WHAT PEOPLE TELL YOU.
DO *YOU* WANT TO LEAVE?
THAT'S ALL I WANT TO KNOW.

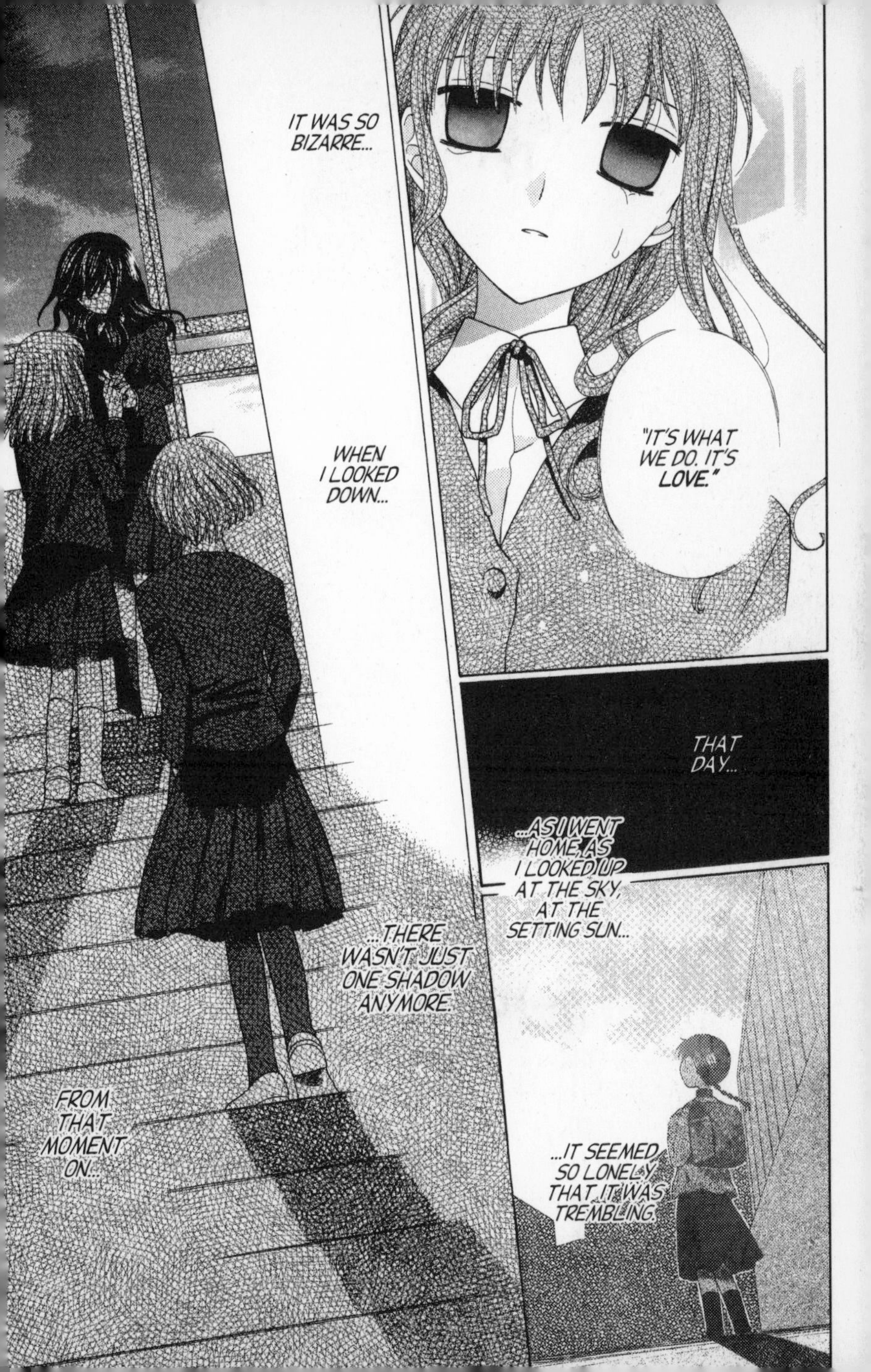
"IT'S WHAT WE DO. IT'S LOVE."
THAT DAY...
...AS I WENT HOME, AS I LOOKED UP AT THE SKY, AT THE SETTING SUN...
...IT SEEMED SO LONELY THAT IT WAS TREMBLING.
IT WAS SO BIZARRE...
WHEN I LOOKED DOWN...
...THERE WASN'T JUST ONE SHADOW ANYMORE.
FROM THAT MOMENT ON...

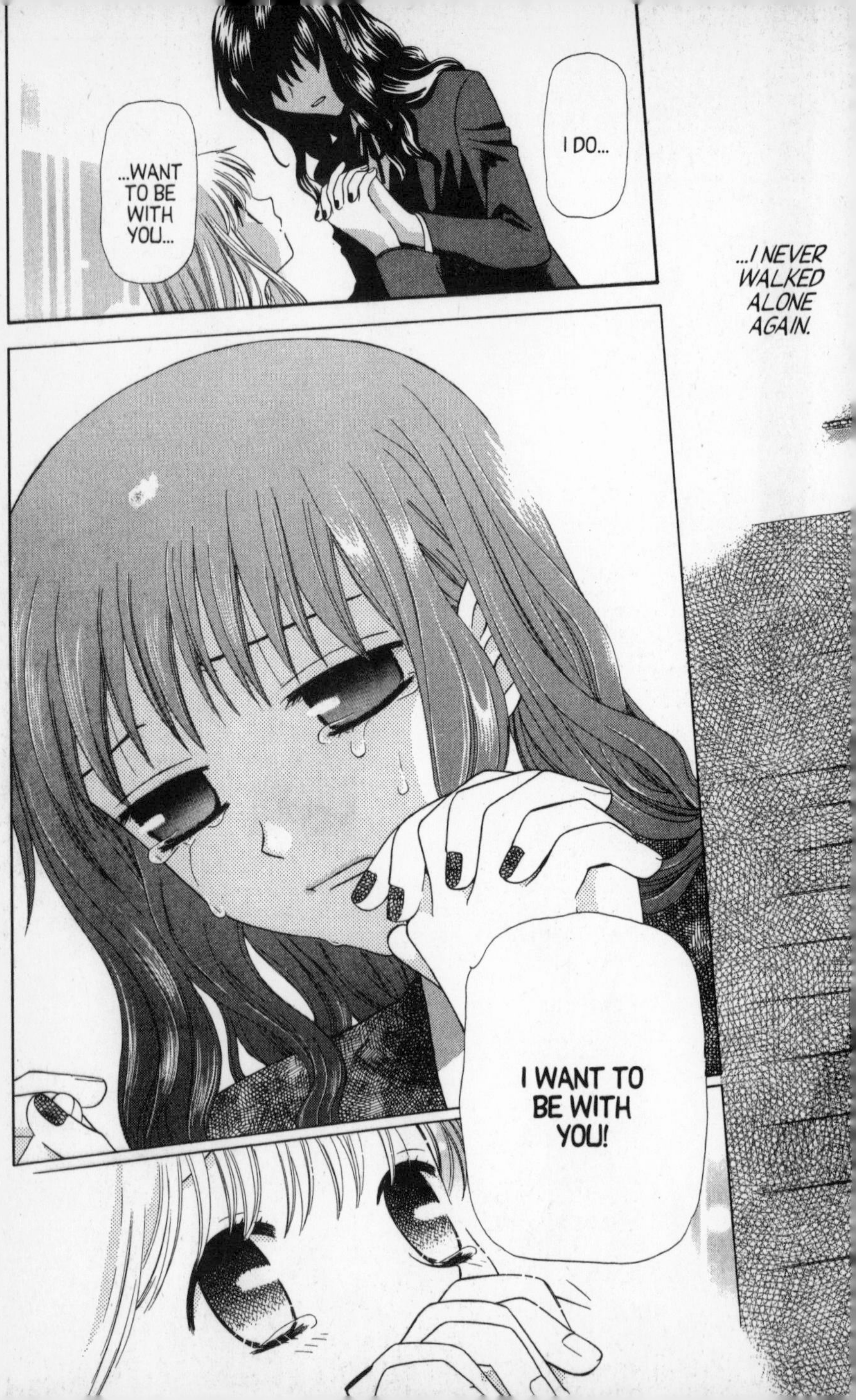
...I NEVER WALKED ALONE AGAIN.
I DO...
...WANT TO BE WITH YOU...
I WANT TO BE WITH YOU!

"I WILL PRAY."
"I CAN'T BELIEVE...
...THAT THERE'S NOT ONE PERSON OUT THERE...
...WHO WOULDN'T LOVE SAKI."
"I WILL PRAY...
...SO...

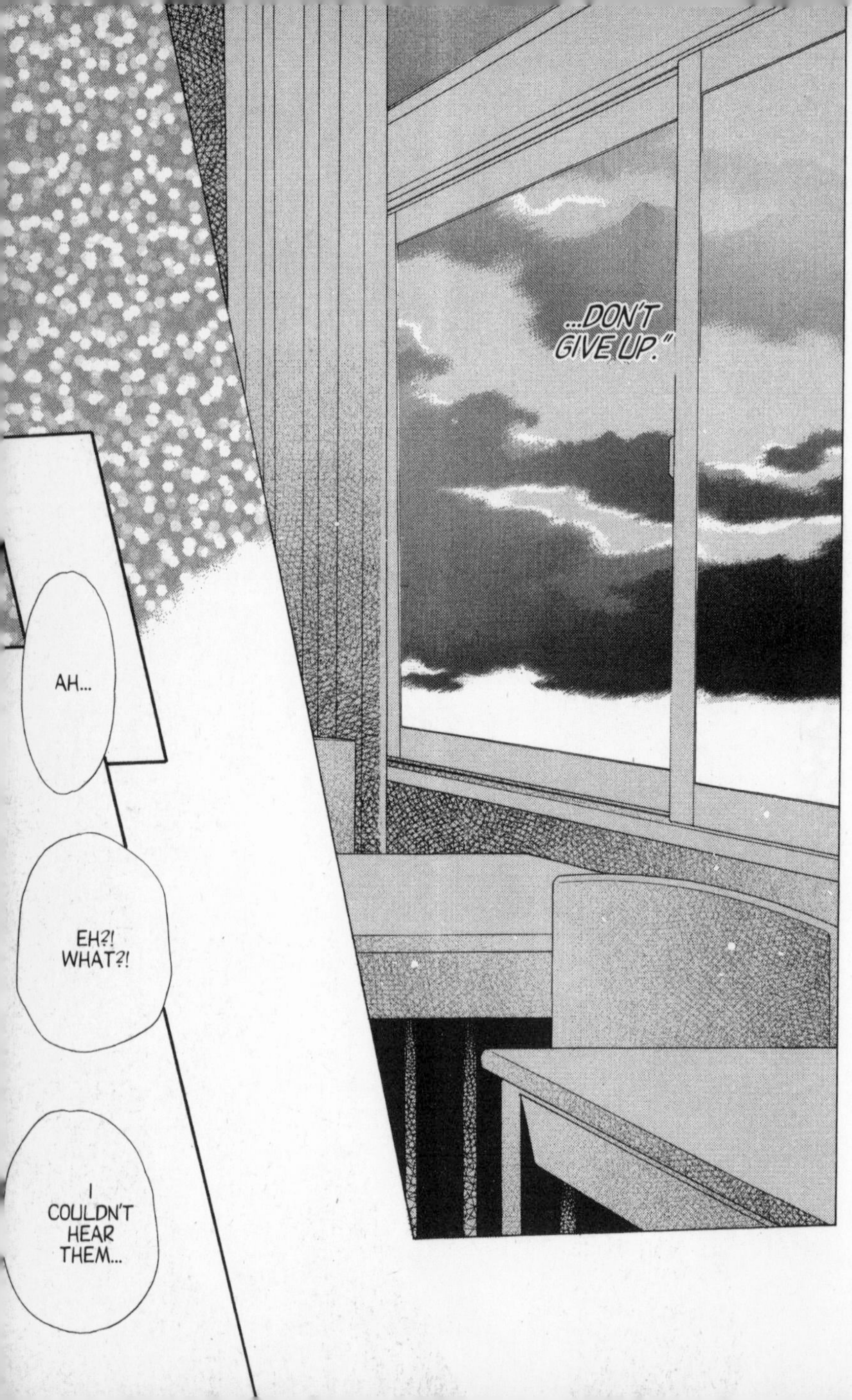
...DON'T GIVE UP."
AH...
EH?! WHAT?!
I COULDN'T HEAR THEM...

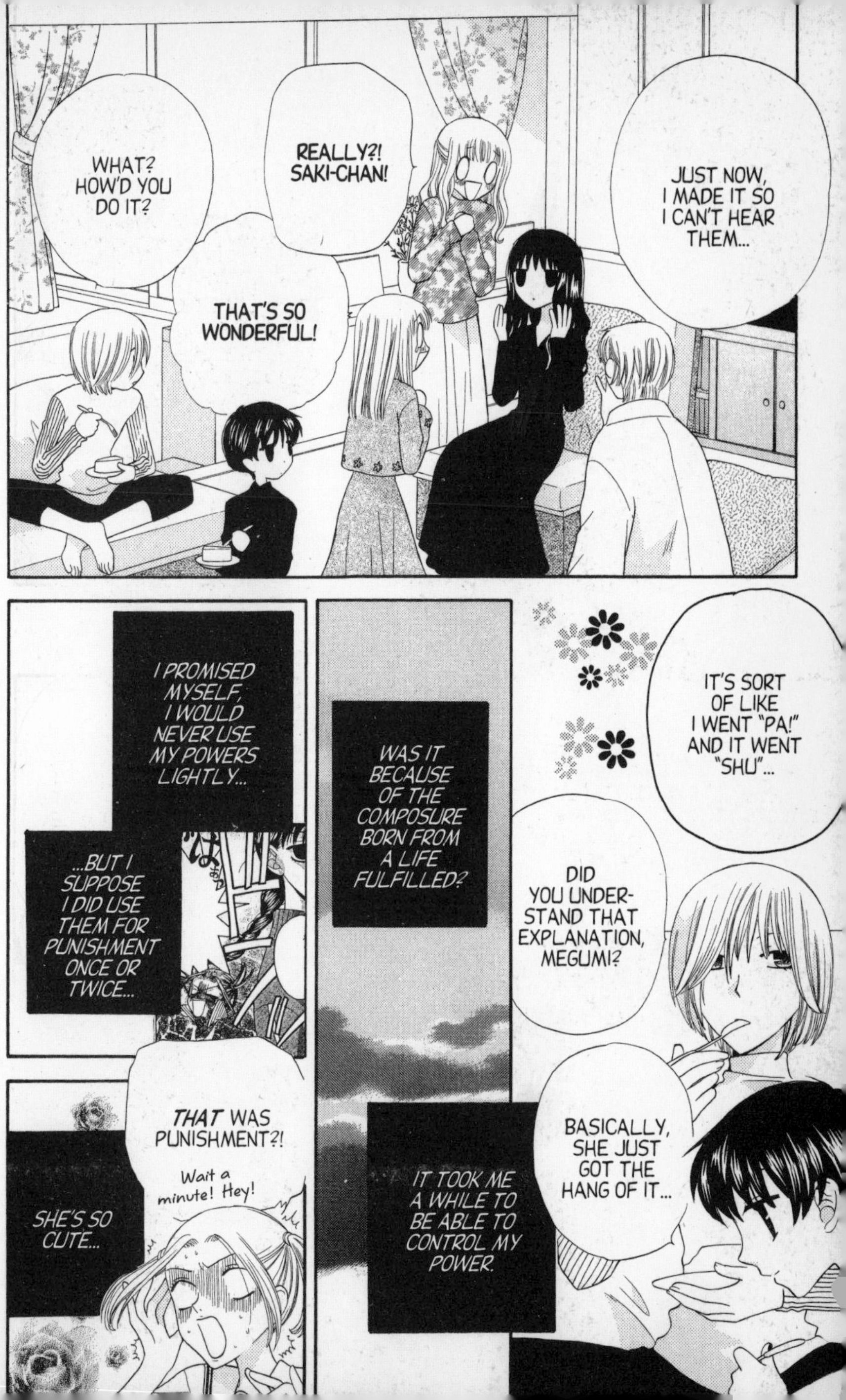
JUST NOW, I MADE IT SO I CAN'T HEAR THEM...
REALLY?! SAKI-CHAN!
WHAT? HOW'D YOU DO IT?
THAT'S SO WONDERFUL!
IT'S SORT OF LIKE I WENT "PA!" AND IT WENT "SHU"...
DID YOU UNDER-STAND THAT EXPLANATION, MEGUMI?
BASICALLY, SHE JUST GOT THE HANG OF IT...
WAS IT BECAUSE OF THE COMPOSURE BORN FROM A LIFE FULFILLED?
IT TOOK ME A WHILE TO BE ABLE TO CONTROL MY POWER.
I PROMISED MYSELF, I WOULD NEVER USE MY POWERS LIGHTLY...
...BUT I SUPPOSE I DID USE THEM FOR PUNISHMENT ONCE OR TWICE...
THAT WAS PUNISHMENT?!
Wait a minute! Hey!
SHE'S SO CUTE...

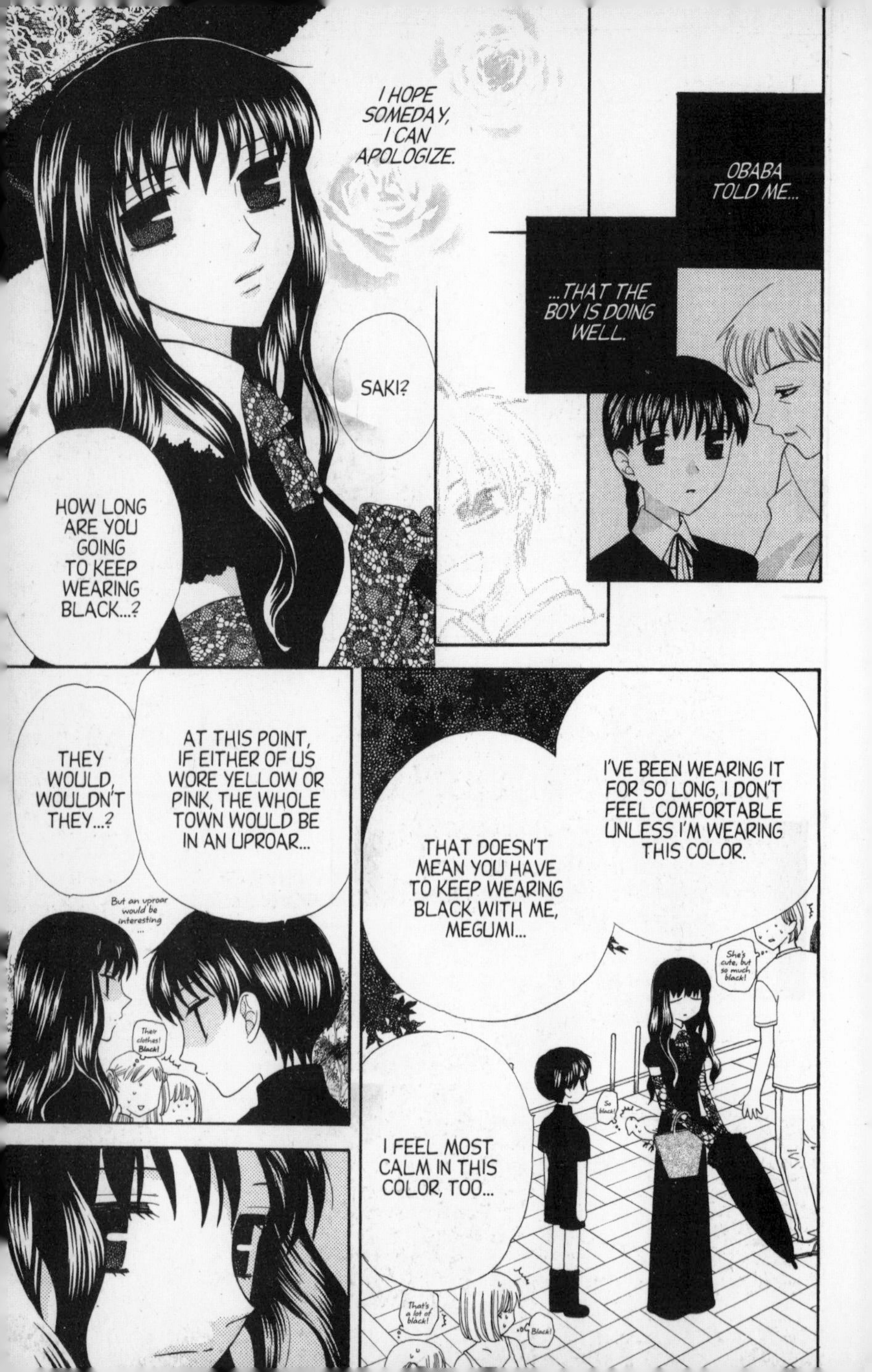
OBABA TOLD ME...
...THAT THE BOY IS DOING WELL.
I HOPE SOMEDAY, I CAN APOLOGIZE.
SAKI?
HOW LONG ARE YOU GOING TO KEEP WEARING BLACK...?
I'VE BEEN WEARING IT FOR SO LONG, I DON'T FEEL COMFORTABLE UNLESS I'M WEARING THIS COLOR.
THAT DOESN'T MEAN YOU HAVE TO KEEP WEARING BLACK WITH ME, MEGUMI...
She's cute, but so much black!
So black!
I FEEL MOST CALM IN THIS COLOR, TOO...
That's a lot of black!
Black!
AT THIS POINT, IF EITHER OF US WORE YELLOW OR PINK, THE WHOLE TOWN WOULD BE IN AN UPROAR...
THEY WOULD, WOULDN'T THEY...?
But an uproar would be interesting ...
Their clothes! Black!

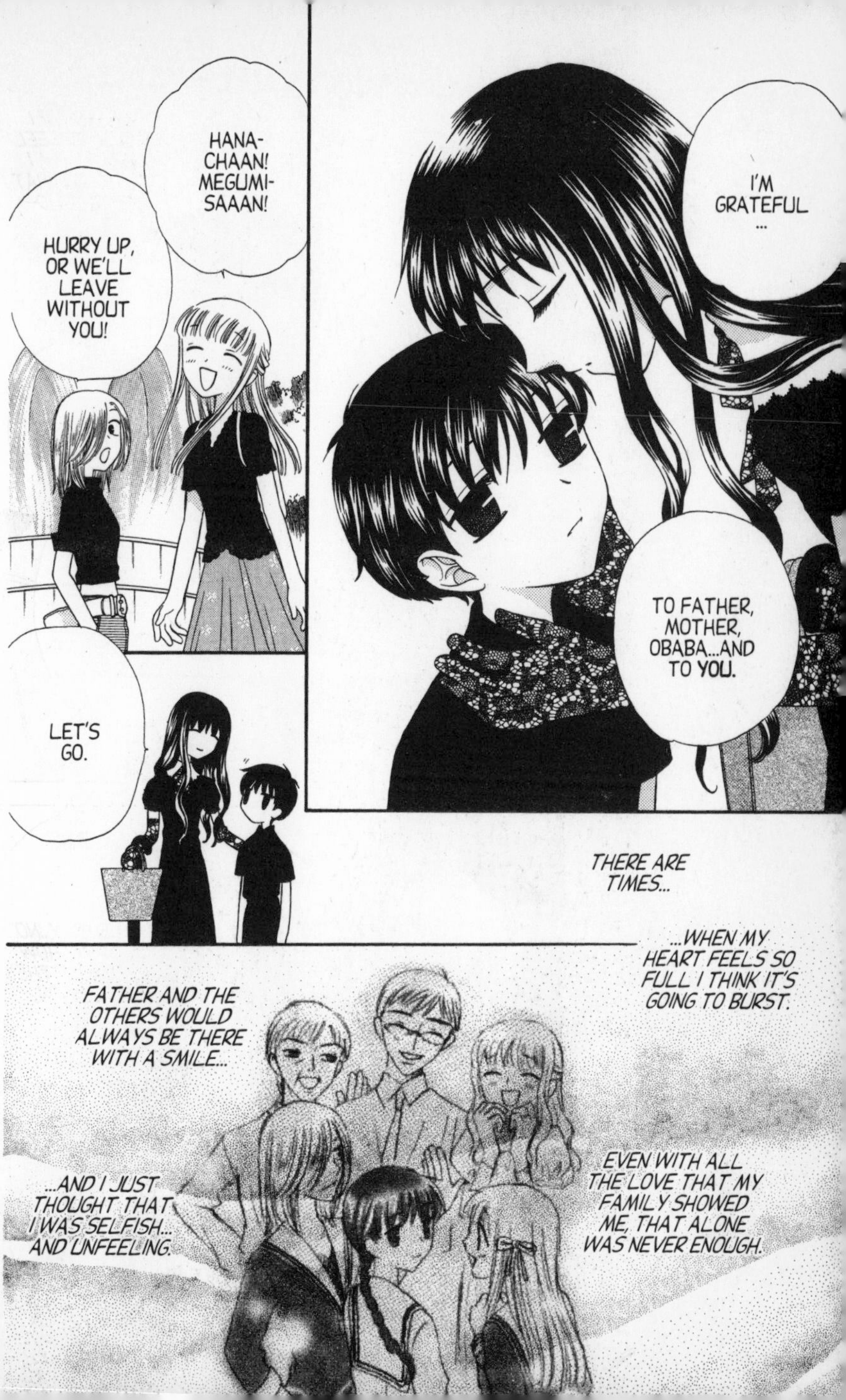
I'M GRATEFUL ...
TO FATHER, MOTHER, OBABA...AND TO YOU.
HANA-CHAAN! MEGUMI-SAAAN!
HURRY UP, OR WE'LL LEAVE WITHOUT YOU!
LET'S GO.
THERE ARE TIMES...
...WHEN MY HEART FEELS SO FULL I THINK IT'S GOING TO BURST.
EVEN WITH ALL THE LOVE THAT MY FAMILY SHOWED ME, THAT ALONE WAS NEVER ENOUGH.
FATHER AND THE OTHERS WOULD ALWAYS BE THERE WITH A SMILE...
...AND I JUST THOUGHT THAT I WAS SELFISH... AND UNFEELING.

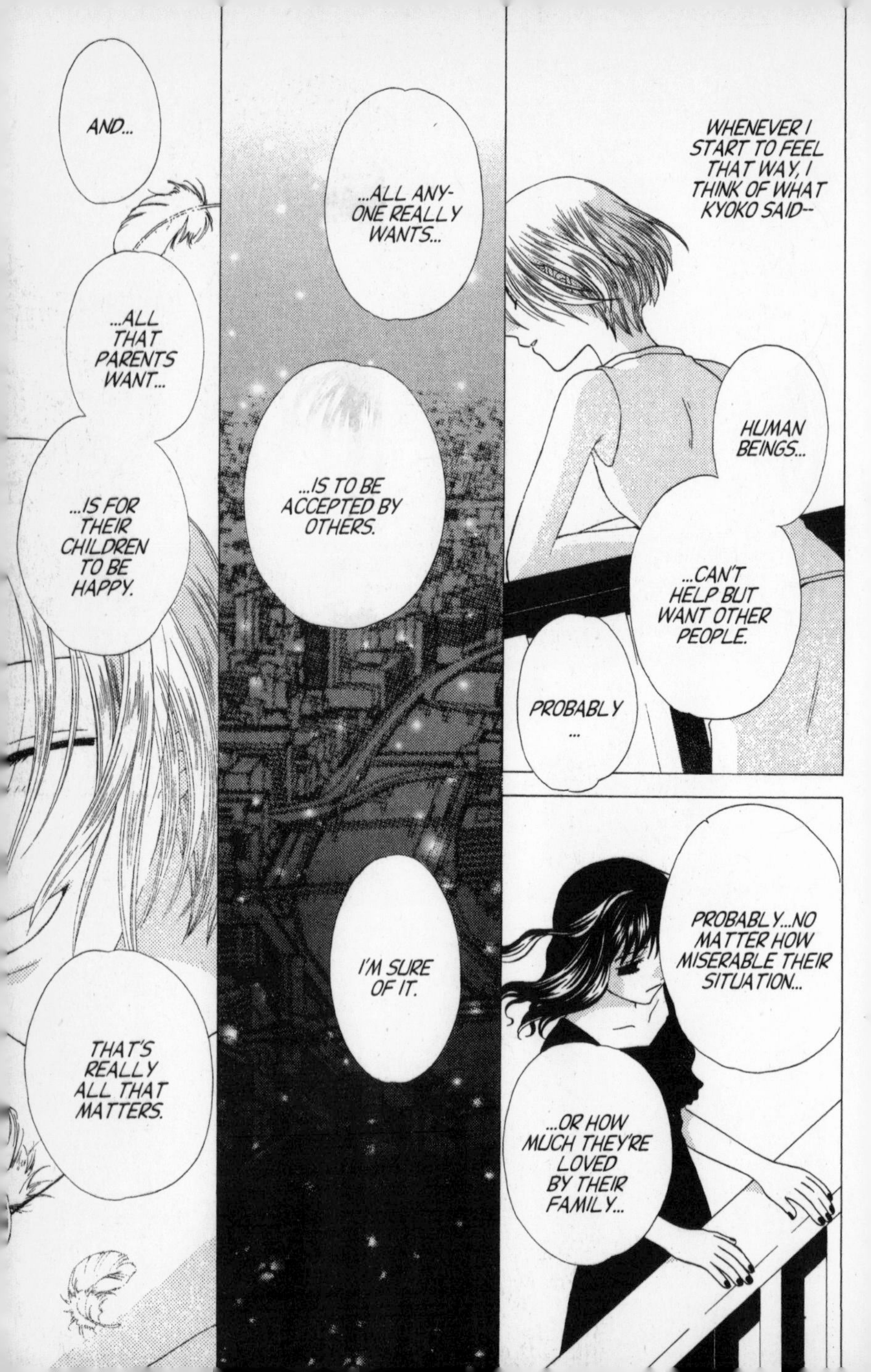
WHENEVER I START TO FEEL THAT WAY, I THINK OF WHAT KYOKO SAID--
HUMAN BEINGS...
...CAN'T HELP BUT WANT OTHER PEOPLE.
PROBABLY ...
PROBABLY...NO MATTER HOW MISERABLE THEIR SITUATION...
...OR HOW MUCH THEY'RE LOVED BY THEIR FAMILY...
...ALL ANY-ONE REALLY WANTS...
...IS TO BE ACCEPTED BY OTHERS.
I'M SURE OF IT.
AND...
...ALL THAT PARENTS WANT...
...IS FOR THEIR CHILDREN TO BE HAPPY.
THAT'S REALLY ALL THAT MATTERS.

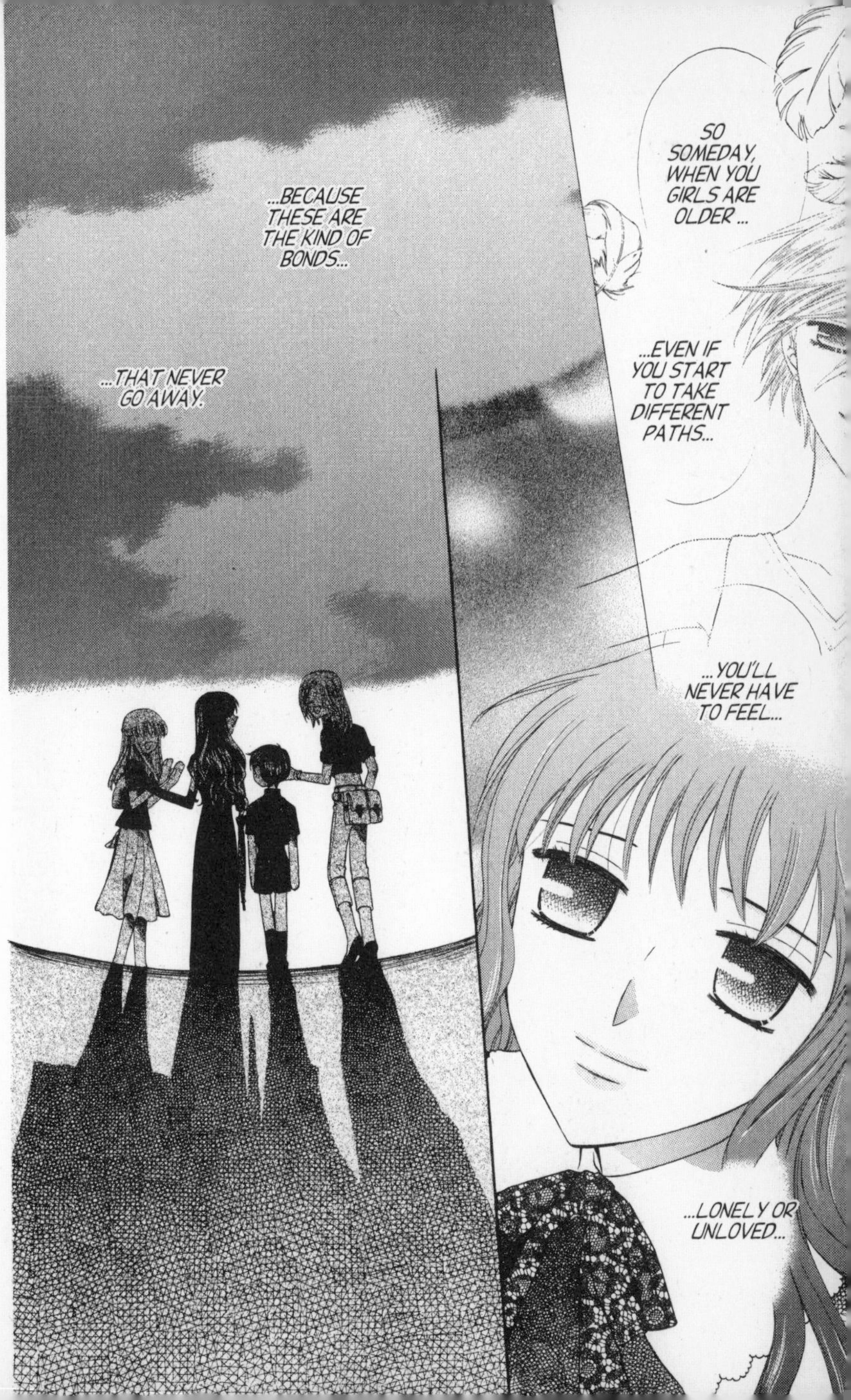
SO SOMEDAY, WHEN YOU GIRLS ARE OLDER ...
...EVEN IF YOU START TO TAKE DIFFERENT PATHS...
...YOU'LL NEVER HAVE TO FEEL...
...LONELY OR UNLOVED...
...BECAUSE THESE ARE THE KIND OF BONDS...
...THAT NEVER GO AWAY.

Chapter 52

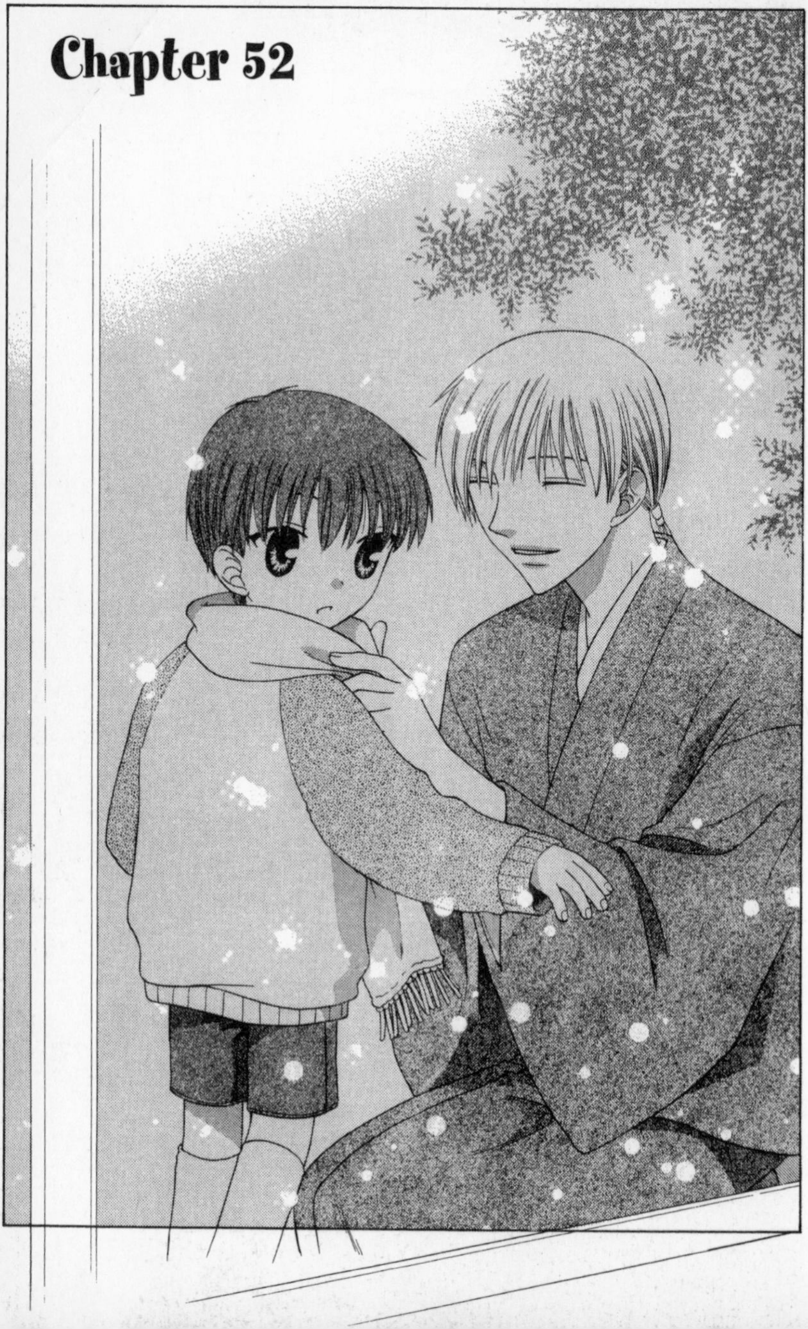

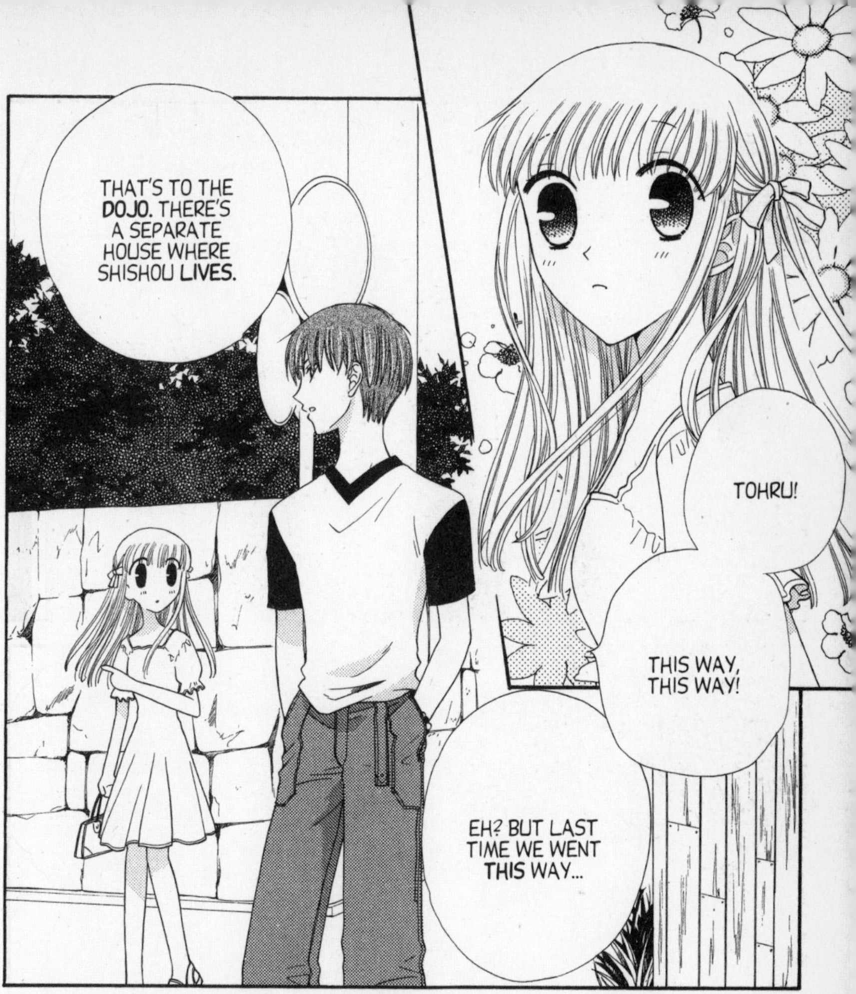
TOHRU!
THIS WAY, THIS WAY!
EH? BUT LAST TIME WE WENT THIS WAY...
THAT'S TO THE DOJO. THERE'S A SEPARATE HOUSE WHERE SHISHOU LIVES.

BLAH, BLAH, BLAH 4

Have you noticed how Kyo is steadily growing taller? Yuki, too. A lot of readers have noticed this, right?

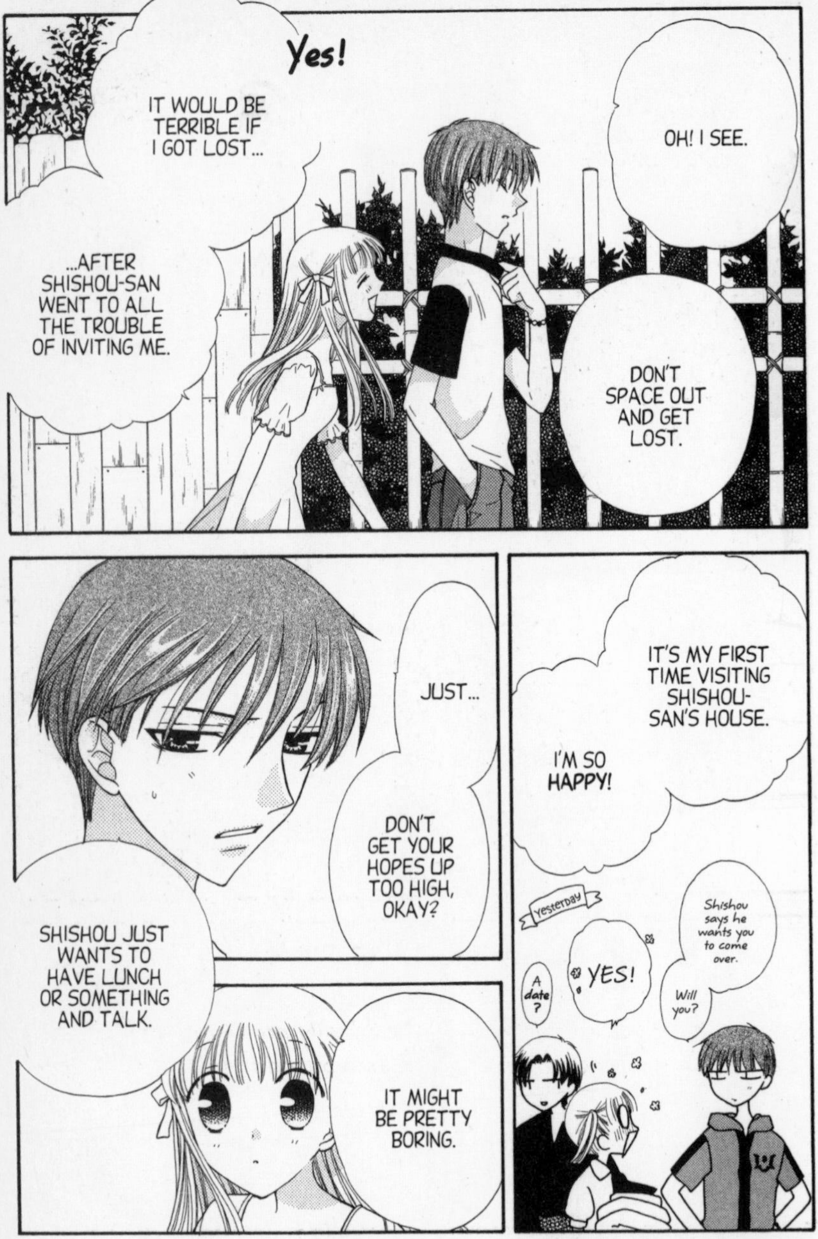
OH! I SEE.
Yes!
IT WOULD BE TERRIBLE IF I GOT LOST...
DON'T SPACE OUT AND GET LOST.
...AFTER SHISHOU-SAN WENT TO ALL THE TROUBLE OF INVITING ME.
IT'S MY FIRST TIME VISITING SHISHOU-SAN'S HOUSE.
I'M SO HAPPY!
Yesterday
Shishou says he wants you to come over.
Will you?
YES!
A date?
JUST...
DON'T GET YOUR HOPES UP TOO HIGH, OKAY?
SHISHOU JUST WANTS TO HAVE LUNCH OR SOMETHING AND TALK.
IT MIGHT BE PRETTY BORING.

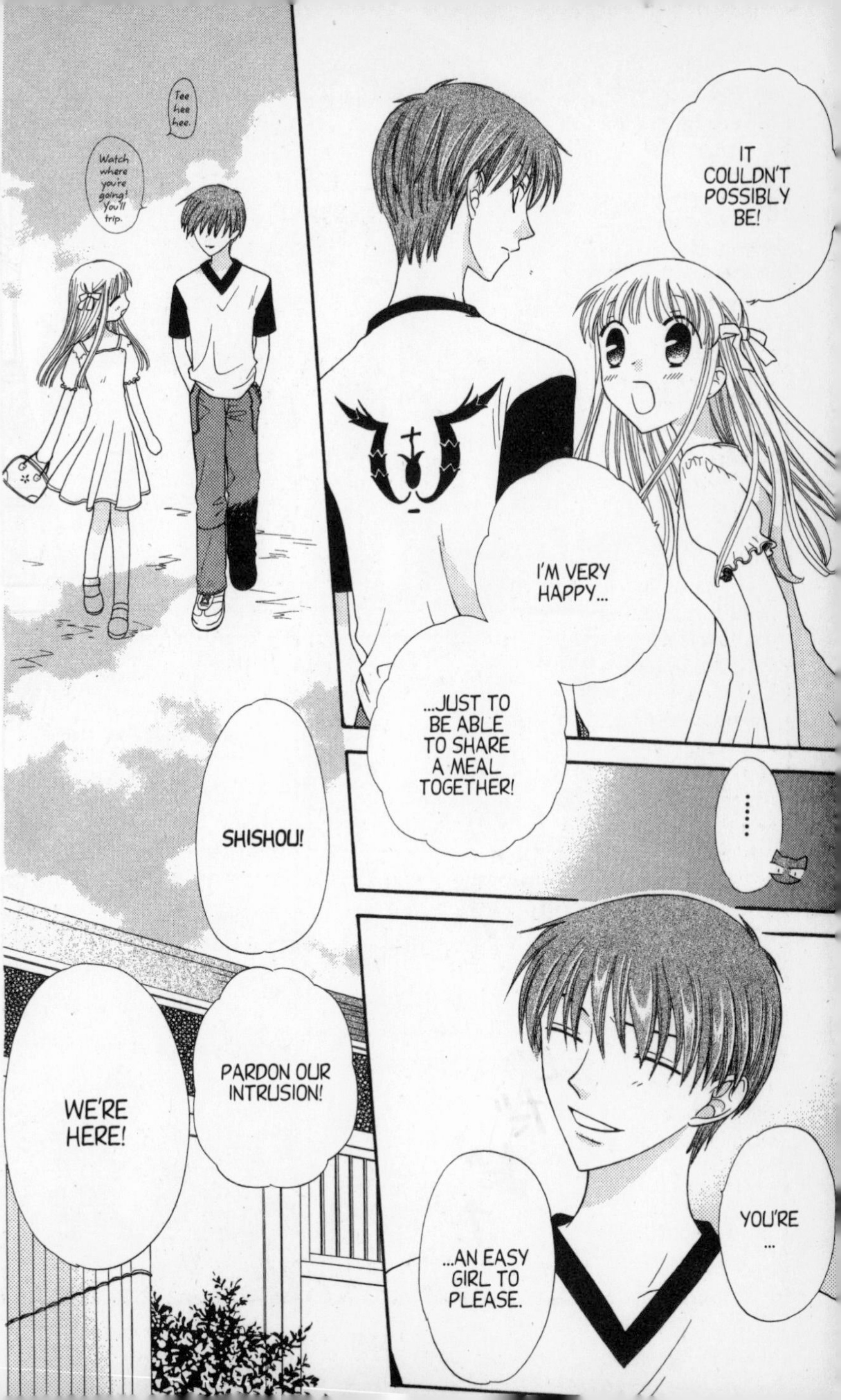
IT COULDN'T POSSIBLY BE!
I'M VERY HAPPY...
...JUST TO BE ABLE TO SHARE A MEAL TOGETHER!
......
YOU'RE ...
...AN EASY GIRL TO PLEASE.
Tee hee hee.
Watch where you're going! You'll trip.
SHISHOU!
PARDON OUR INTRUSION!
WE'RE HERE!

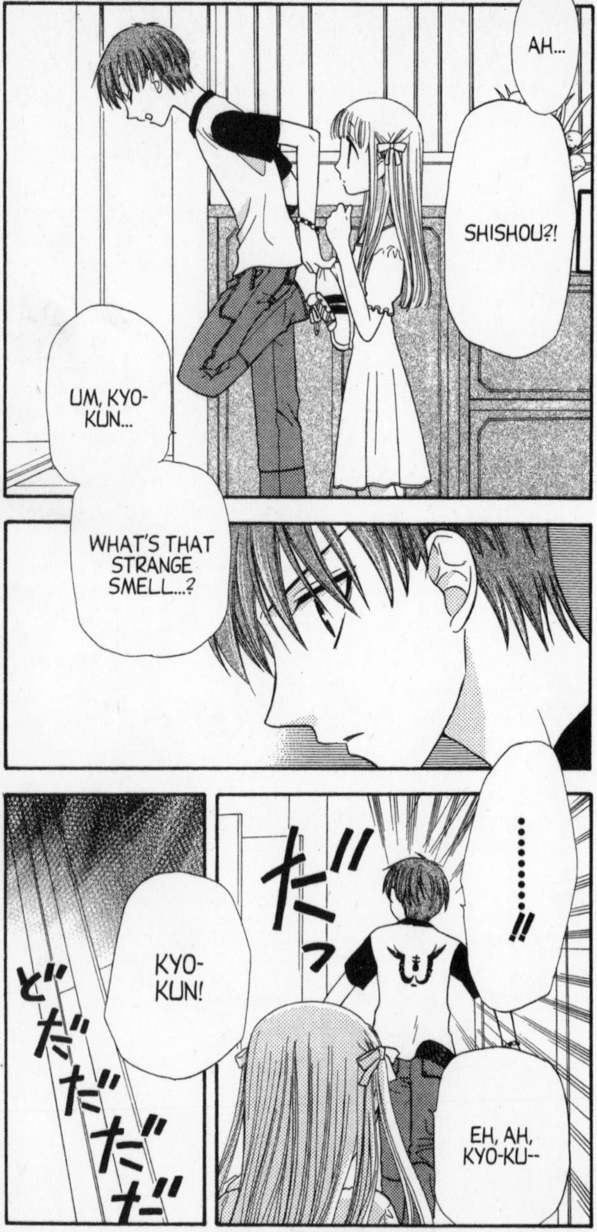
AH...
SHISHOU?!
UM, KYO-KUN...
WHAT'S THAT STRANGE SMELL...?
......!!
だっ
KYO-KUN!
どだだだだ
EH, AH, KYO-KU--

Fruits Basket 9 Part 5:

This time I'm back to video games. I've finished the PC version of **Harukanaru Toki no Nakade 2,** but I also bought the PS2 version and am playing through that. I really do seem to like this game (laugh). I'm also enjoying playing RPGs as usual, but I'm very hooked on the adventure game **ICO.** Silent kindness, silent loneliness, being so close and yet so far...um, I can't really explain it (laugh). It's a great game. I highly recommend it. As long as I'm recommending things, the **Resident Evil** remake for the GameCube brought back a lot of memories!

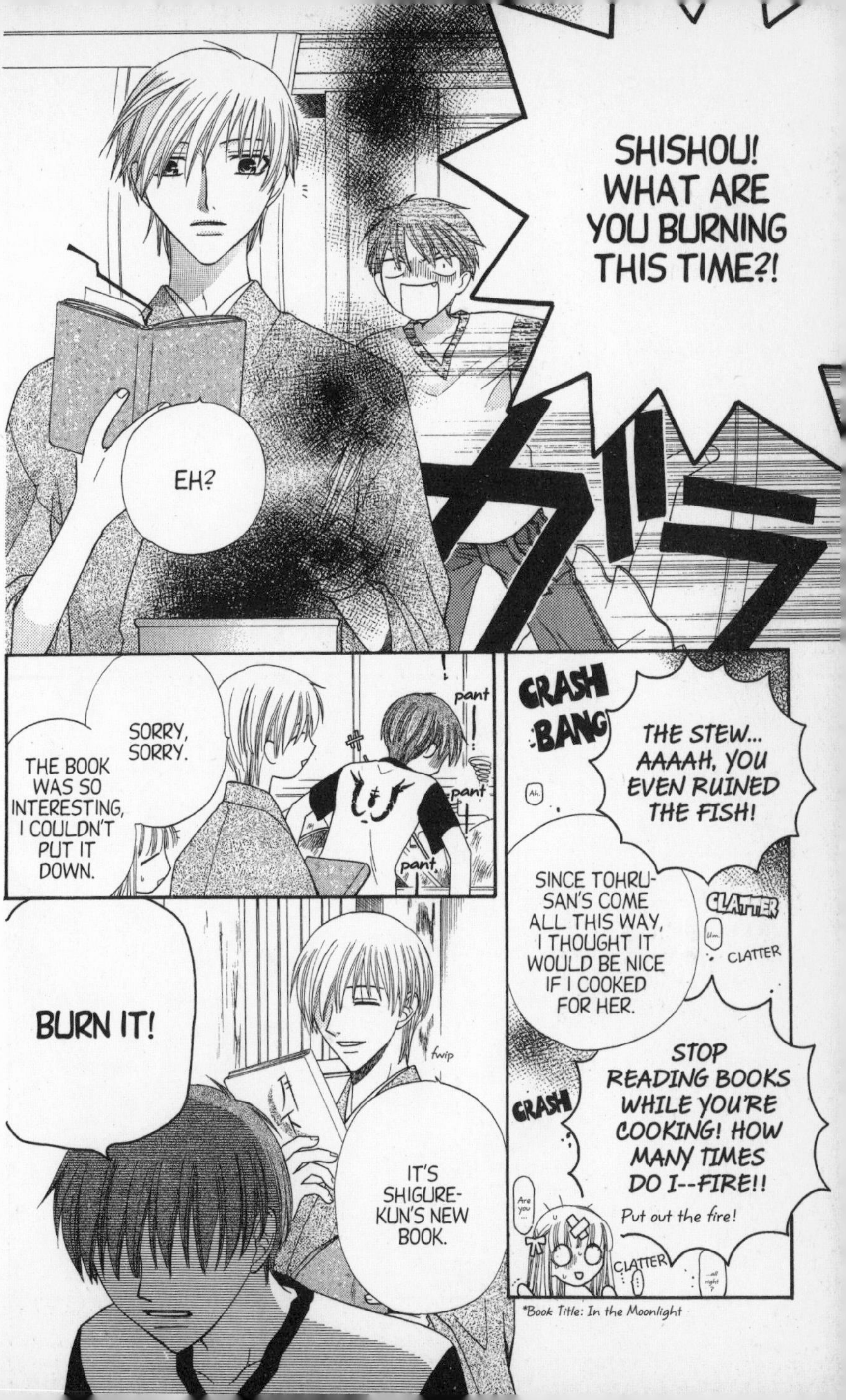
SHISHOU! WHAT ARE YOU BURNING THIS TIME?!
EH?
CRASH
BANG
THE STEW... AAAAH, YOU EVEN RUINED THE FISH!
Ah.
SINCE TOHRU-SAN'S COME ALL THIS WAY, I THOUGHT IT WOULD BE NICE IF I COOKED FOR HER.
CLATTER
Um...
CLATTER
STOP READING BOOKS WHILE YOU'RE COOKING! HOW MANY TIMES DO I--FIRE!!
GRASH
Are you ...
Put out the fire!
CLATTER
...all right?
pant
pant
pant
SORRY, SORRY.
THE BOOK WAS SO INTERESTING, I COULDN'T PUT IT DOWN.
fwip
IT'S SHIGURE-KUN'S NEW BOOK.
BURN IT!
*Book Title: In the Moonlight

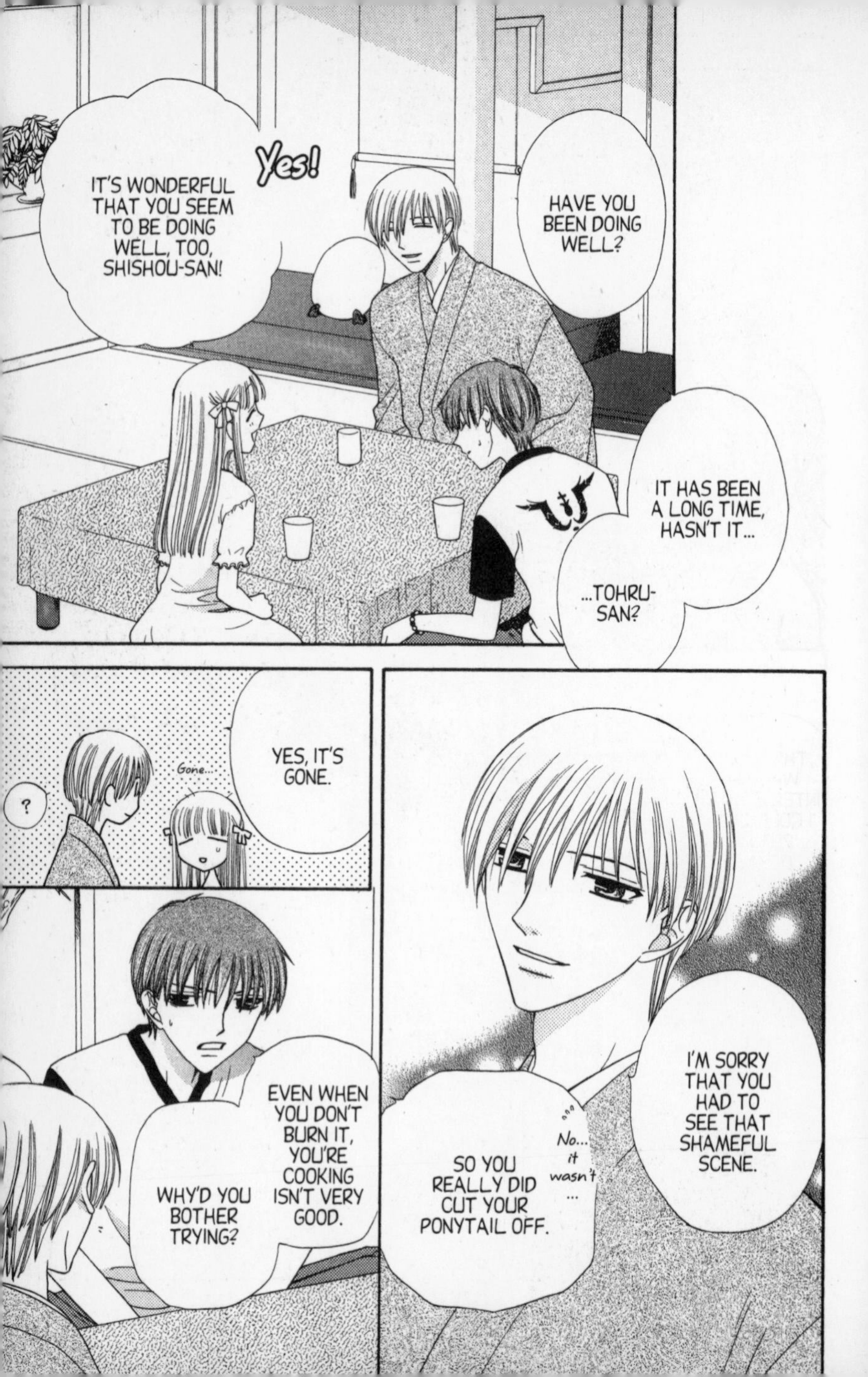
HAVE YOU BEEN DOING WELL?
Yes!
IT'S WONDERFUL THAT YOU SEEM TO BE DOING WELL, TOO, SHISHOU-SAN!
IT HAS BEEN A LONG TIME, HASN'T IT...
...TOHRU-SAN?
I'M SORRY THAT YOU HAD TO SEE THAT SHAMEFUL SCENE.
No... it wasn't ...
SO YOU REALLY DID CUT YOUR PONYTAIL OFF.
YES, IT'S GONE.
Gone...
?
EVEN WHEN YOU DON'T BURN IT, YOU'RE COOKING ISN'T VERY GOOD.
WHY'D YOU BOTHER TRYING?

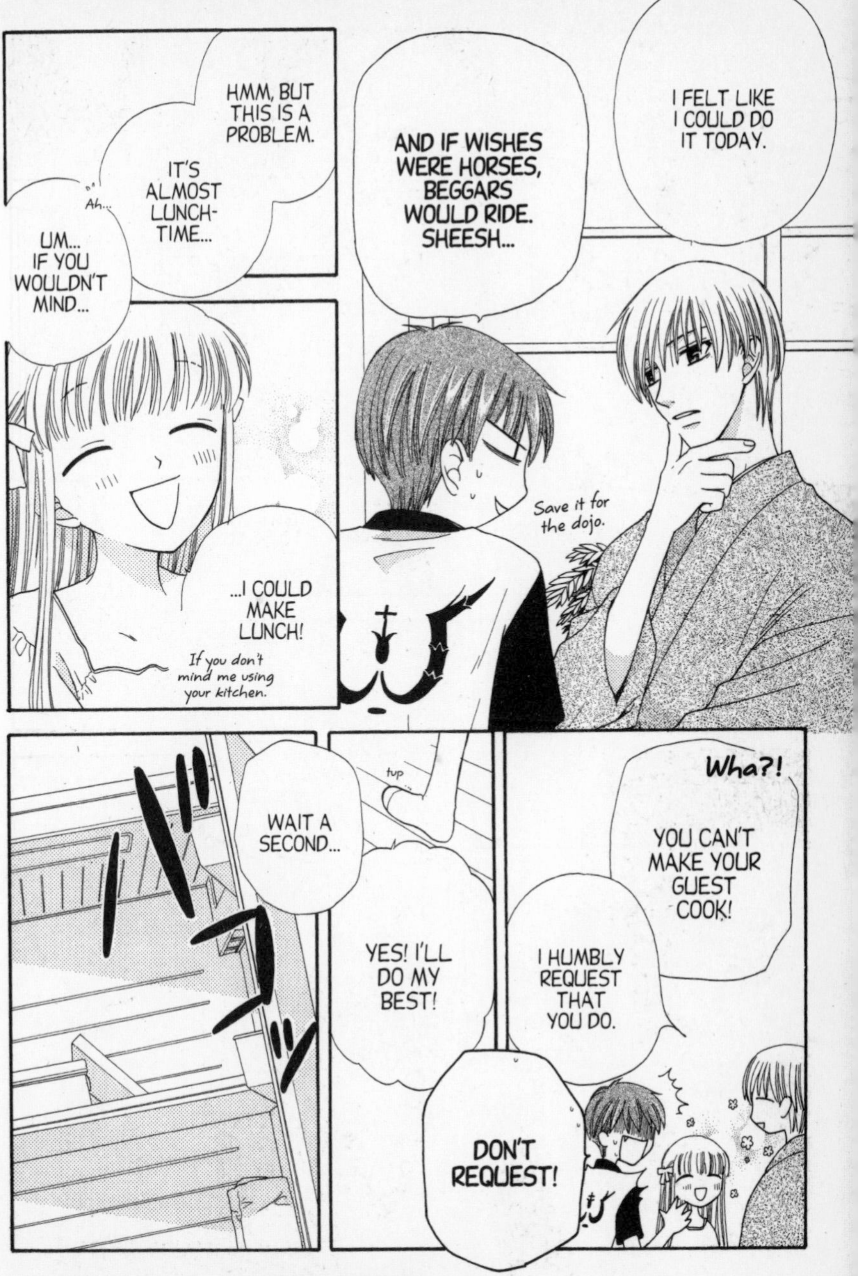
I FELT LIKE I COULD DO IT TODAY.
AND IF WISHES WERE HORSES, BEGGARS WOULD RIDE. SHEESH...
Save it for the dojo.
HMM, BUT THIS IS A PROBLEM.
IT'S ALMOST LUNCH-TIME...
Ah...
UM... IF YOU WOULDN'T MIND...
...I COULD MAKE LUNCH!
If you don't mind me using your kitchen.
Wha?!
YOU CAN'T MAKE YOUR GUEST COOK!
I HUMBLY REQUEST THAT YOU DO.
DON'T REQUEST!
tup
WAIT A SECOND...
YES! I'LL DO MY BEST!

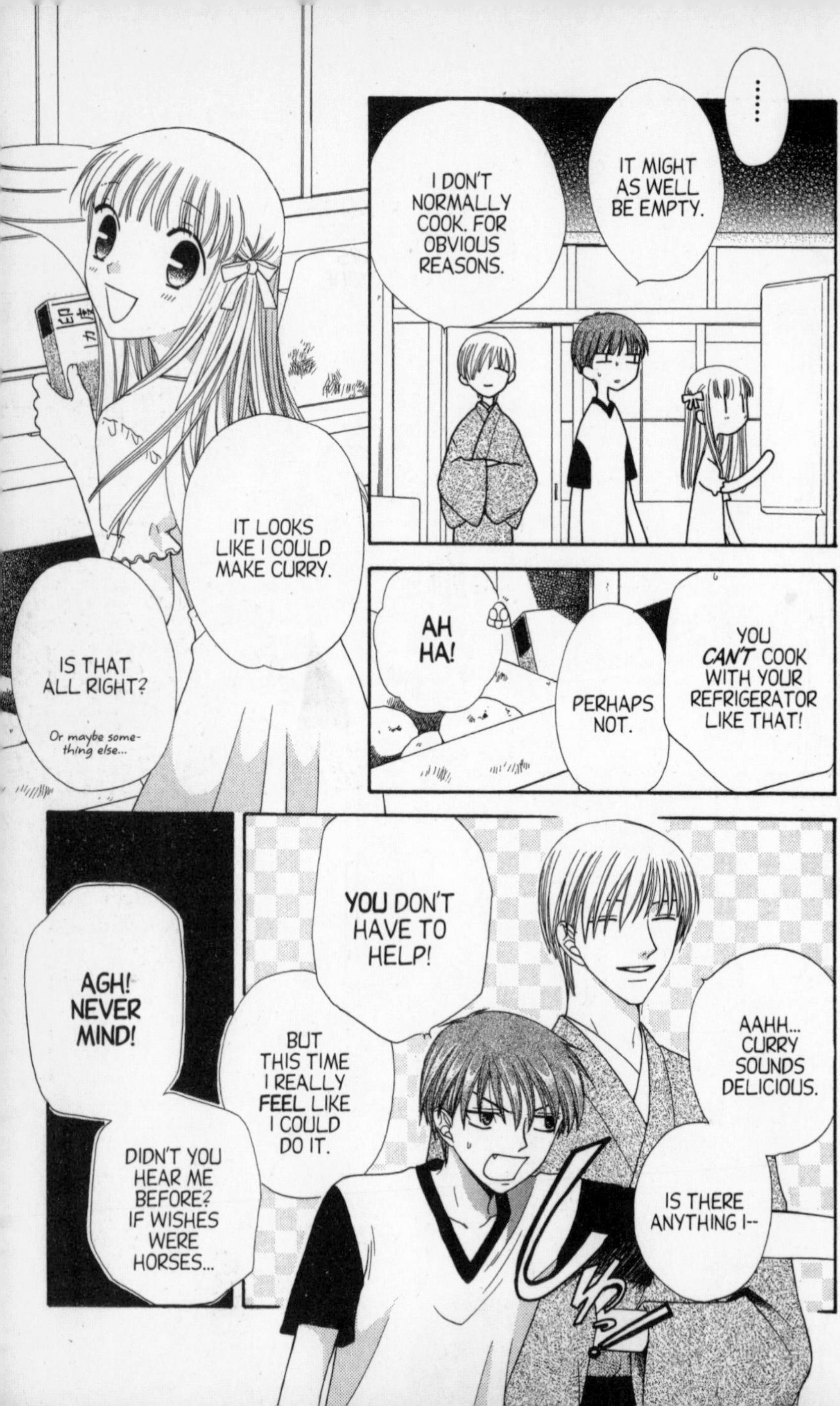
......
IT MIGHT AS WELL BE EMPTY.
I DON'T NORMALLY COOK. FOR OBVIOUS REASONS.
YOU CAN'T COOK WITH YOUR REFRIGERATOR LIKE THAT!
PERHAPS NOT.
AH HA!
IT LOOKS LIKE I COULD MAKE CURRY.
IS THAT ALL RIGHT?
Or maybe something else...
AAHH... CURRY SOUNDS DELICIOUS.
IS THERE ANYTHING I--
YOU DON'T HAVE TO HELP!
BUT THIS TIME I REALLY FEEL LIKE I COULD DO IT.
AGH! NEVER MIND!
DIDN'T YOU HEAR ME BEFORE? IF WISHES WERE HORSES...

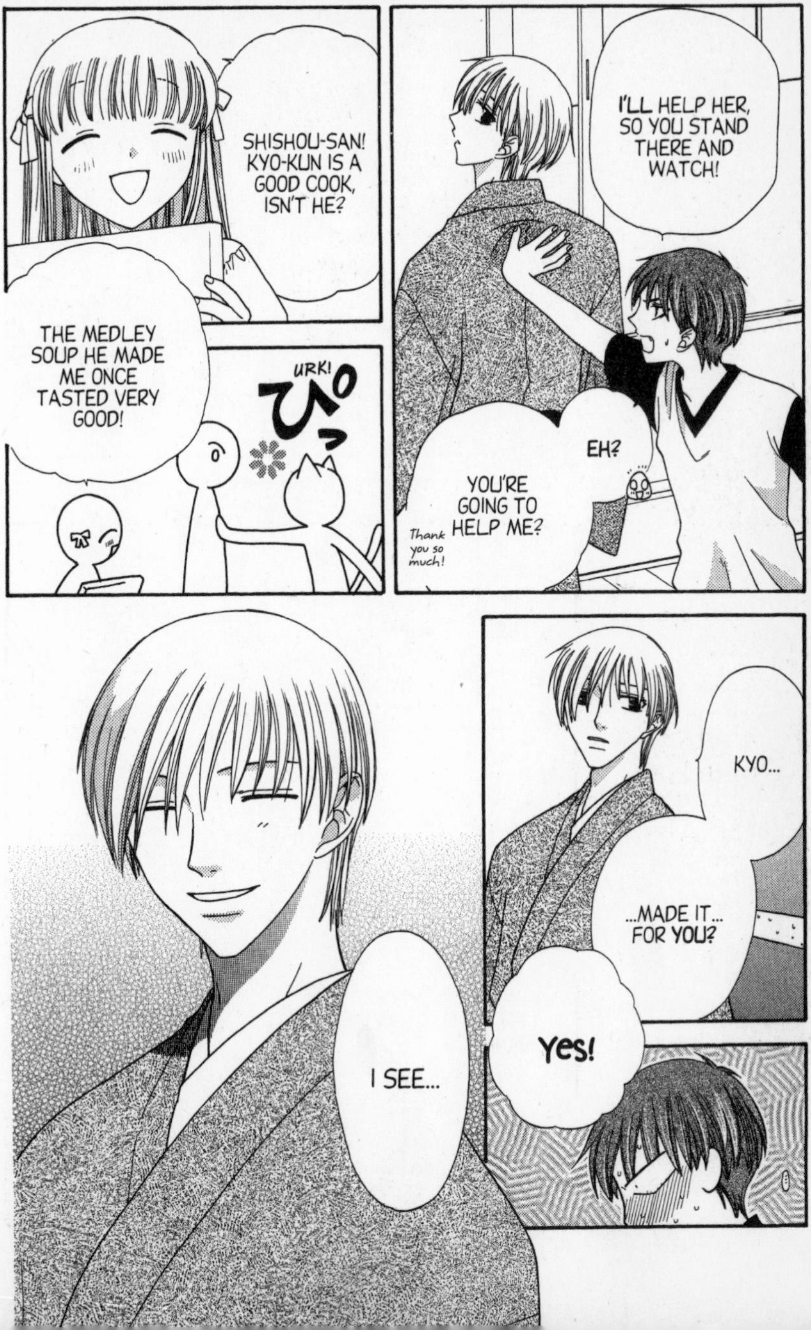
I'LL HELP HER, SO YOU STAND THERE AND WATCH!
EH?
YOU'RE GOING TO HELP ME?
Thank you so much!
SHISHOU-SAN! KYO-KUN IS A GOOD COOK, ISN'T HE?
THE MEDLEY SOUP HE MADE ME ONCE TASTED VERY GOOD!
URK!
ぴっ
KYO...
...MADE IT... FOR YOU?
Yes!
I SEE...

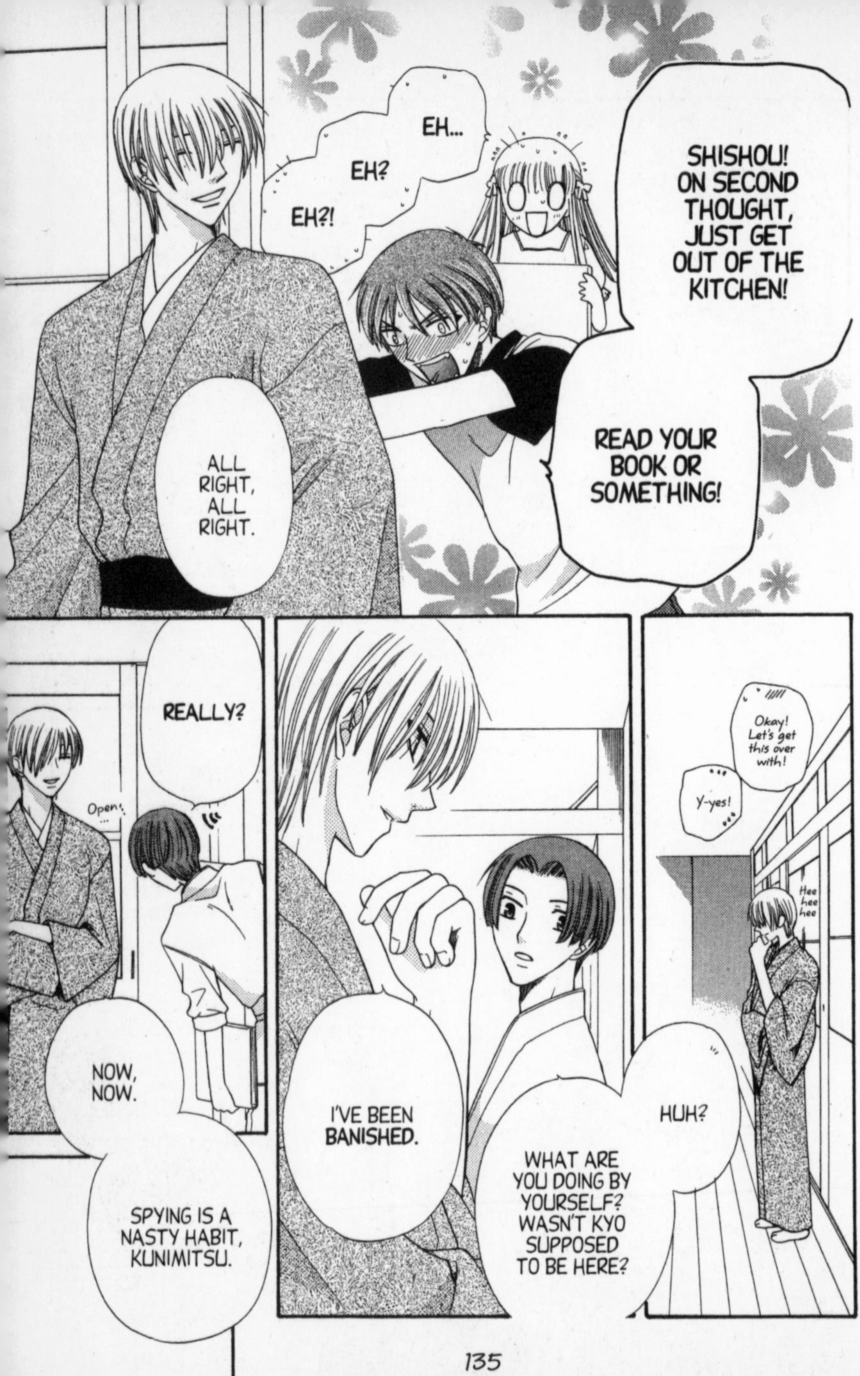
SHISHOU! ON SECOND THOUGHT, JUST GET OUT OF THE KITCHEN!
READ YOUR BOOK OR SOMETHING!
EH...
EH?
EH?!
ALL RIGHT, ALL RIGHT.
Okay! Let's get this over with!
Y-yes!
Hee hee hee
HUH?
WHAT ARE YOU DOING BY YOURSELF? WASN'T KYO SUPPOSED TO BE HERE?
I'VE BEEN BANISHED.
REALLY?
Open
NOW, NOW.
SPYING IS A NASTY HABIT, KUNIMITSU.

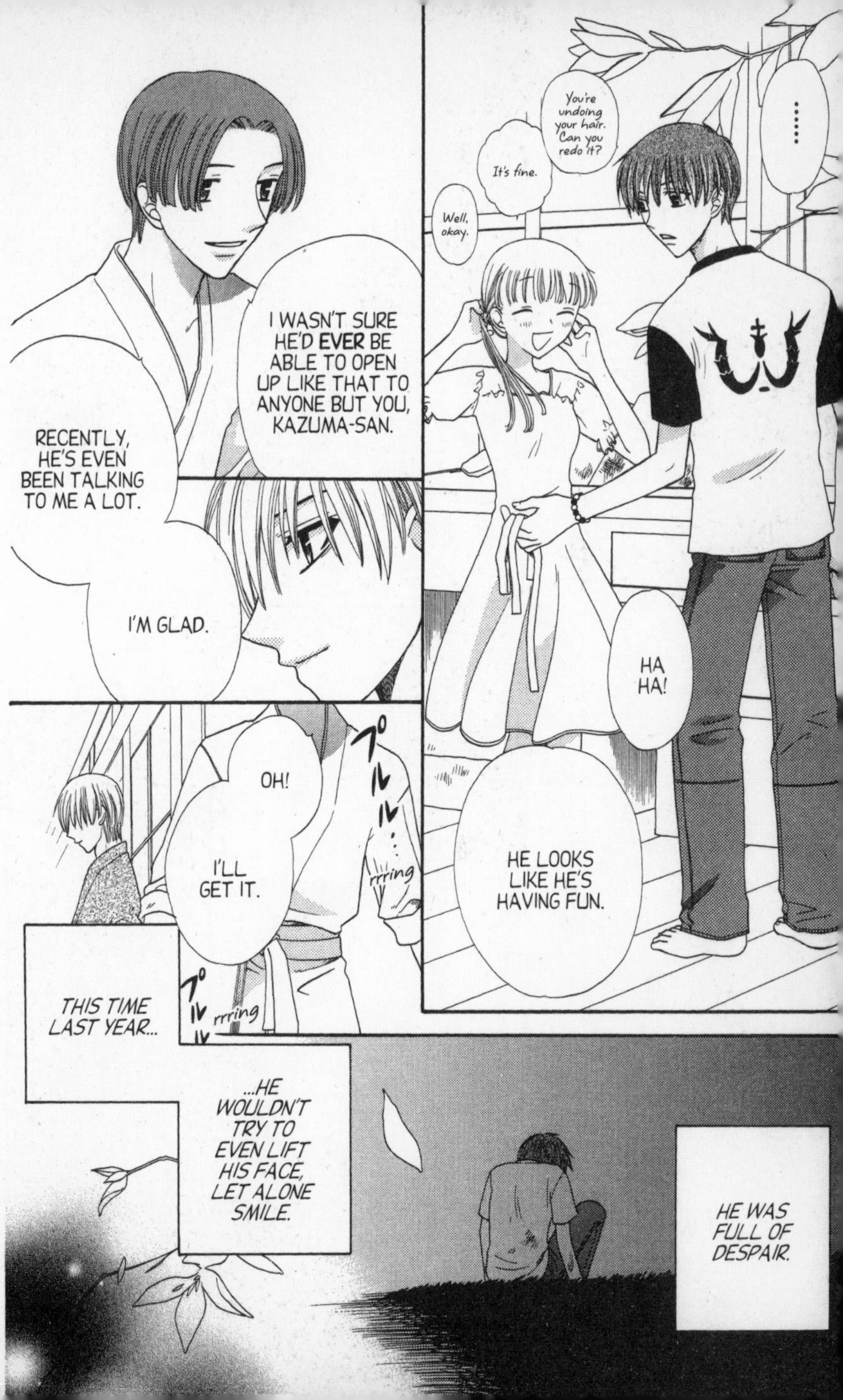
......
You're undoing your hair. Can you redo it?
It's fine.
Well, okay.
HA HA!
HE LOOKS LIKE HE'S HAVING FUN.
I WASN'T SURE HE'D EVER BE ABLE TO OPEN UP LIKE THAT TO ANYONE BUT YOU, KAZUMA-SAN.
RECENTLY, HE'S EVEN BEEN TALKING TO ME A LOT.
I'M GLAD.
プルル… rrring
OH!
I'LL GET IT.
プルル rrring
THIS TIME LAST YEAR...
...HE WOULDN'T TRY TO EVEN LIFT HIS FACE, LET ALONE SMILE.
HE WAS FULL OF DESPAIR.

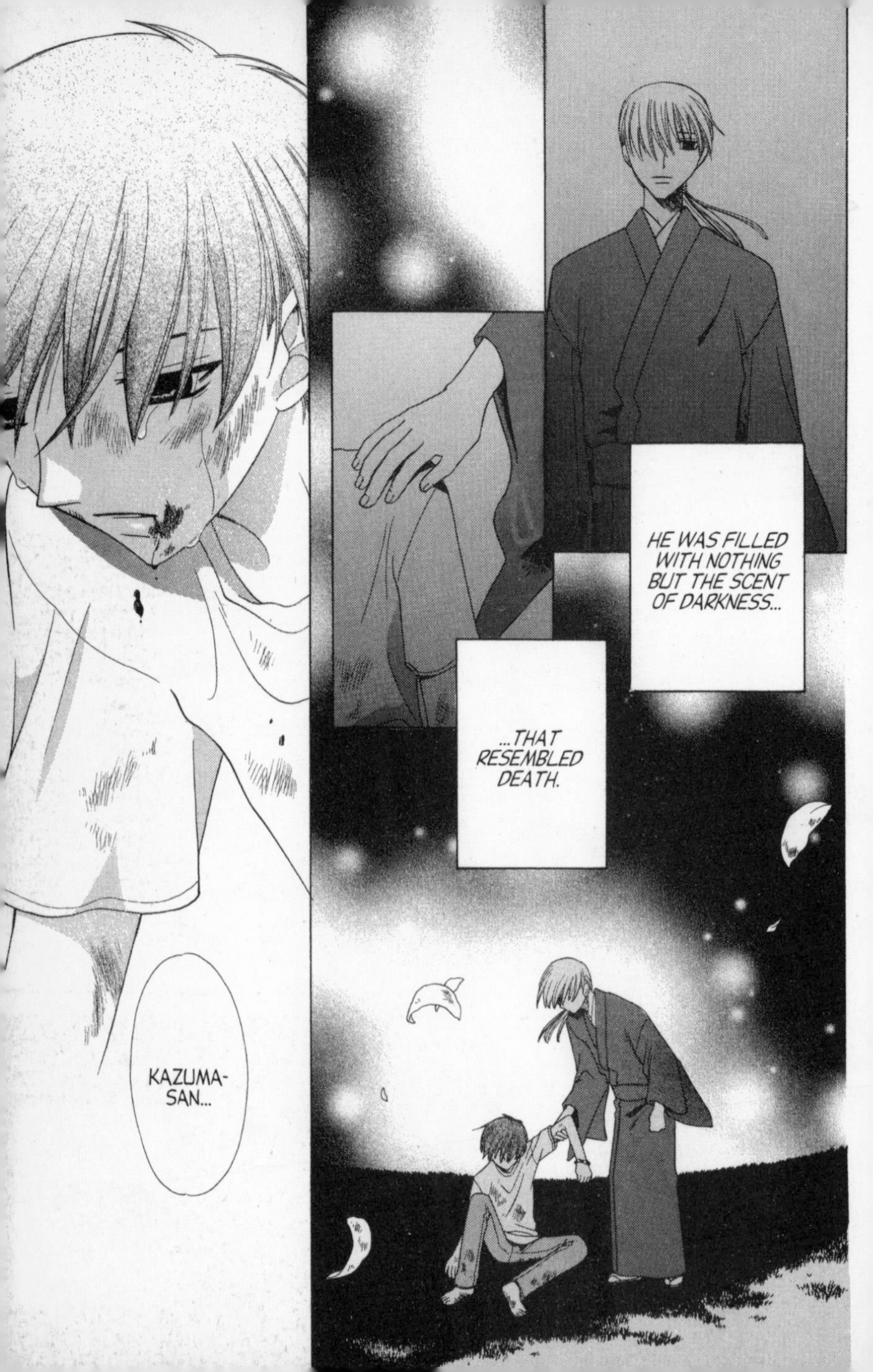
HE WAS FILLED WITH NOTHING BUT THE SCENT OF DARKNESS...
...THAT RESEMBLED DEATH.
KAZUMA-SAN...

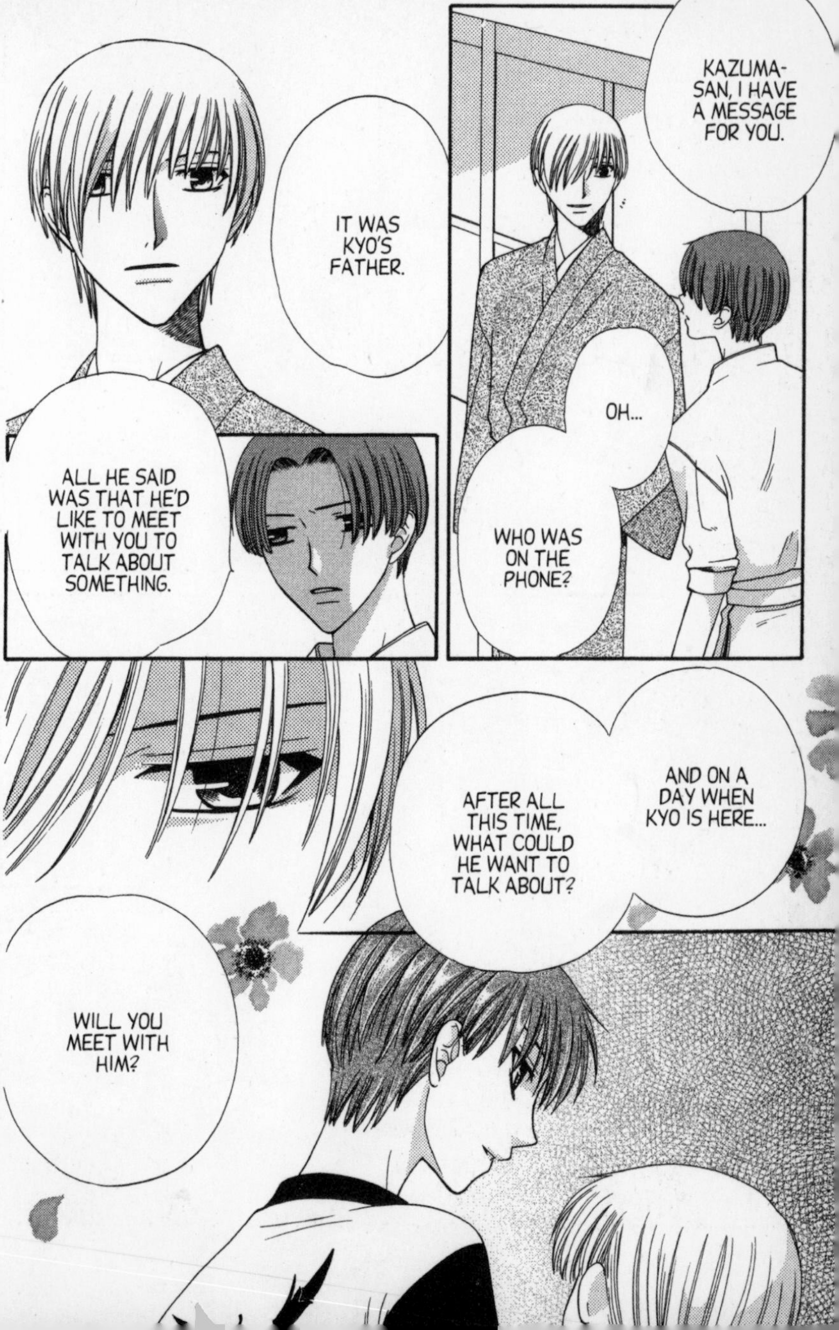
KAZUMA-SAN, I HAVE A MESSAGE FOR YOU.
OH...
WHO WAS ON THE PHONE?
IT WAS KYO'S FATHER.
ALL HE SAID WAS THAT HE'D LIKE TO MEET WITH YOU TO TALK ABOUT SOMETHING.
AND ON A DAY WHEN KYO IS HERE...
AFTER ALL THIS TIME, WHAT COULD HE WANT TO TALK ABOUT?
WILL YOU MEET WITH HIM?

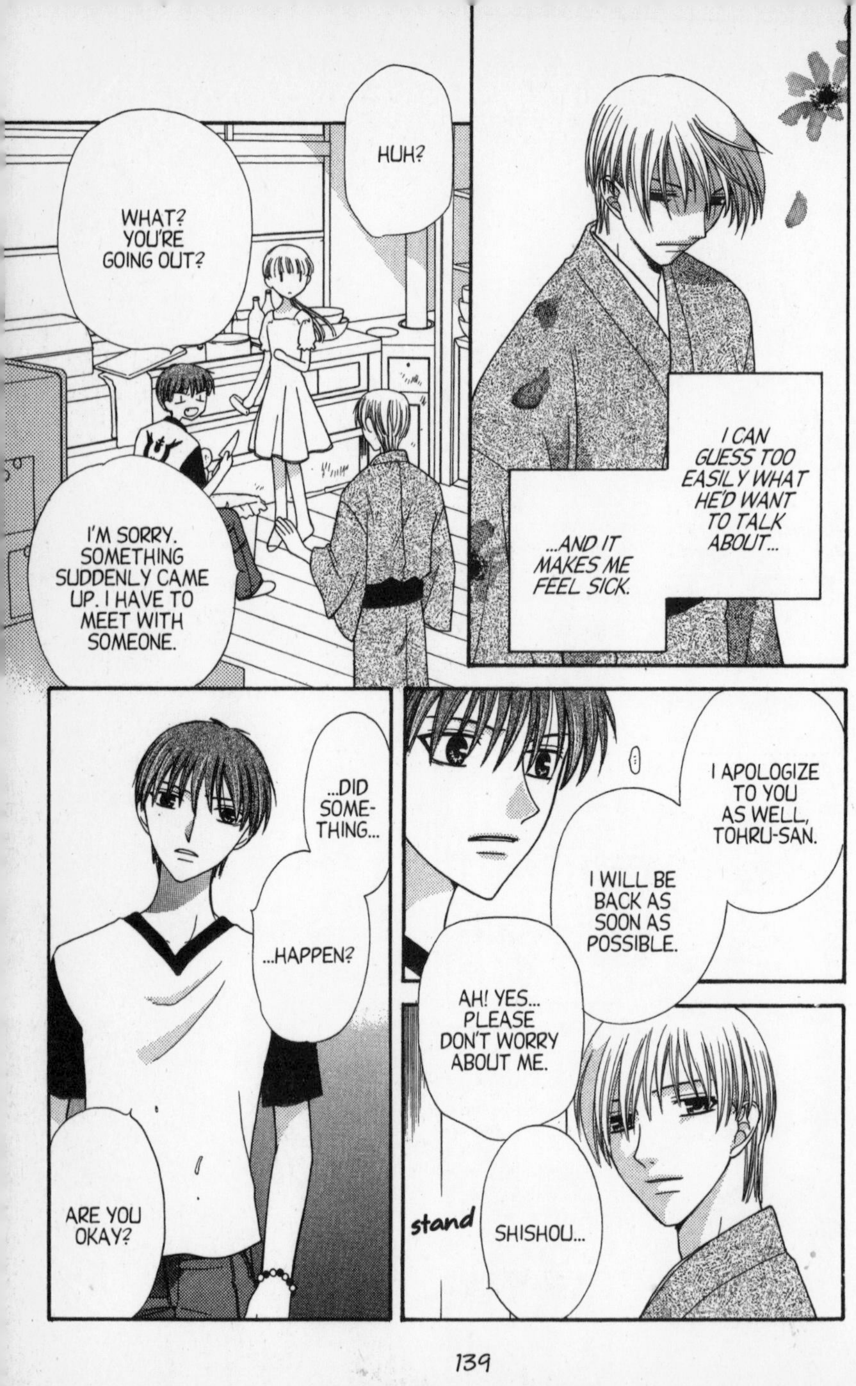
I CAN GUESS TOO EASILY WHAT HE'D WANT TO TALK ABOUT...
...AND IT MAKES ME FEEL SICK.
HUH?
WHAT? YOU'RE GOING OUT?
I'M SORRY. SOMETHING SUDDENLY CAME UP. I HAVE TO MEET WITH SOMEONE.
I APOLOGIZE TO YOU AS WELL, TOHRU-SAN.
I WILL BE BACK AS SOON AS POSSIBLE.
AH! YES... PLEASE DON'T WORRY ABOUT ME.
SHISHOU...
stand
...DID SOMETHING...
...HAPPEN?
ARE YOU OKAY?

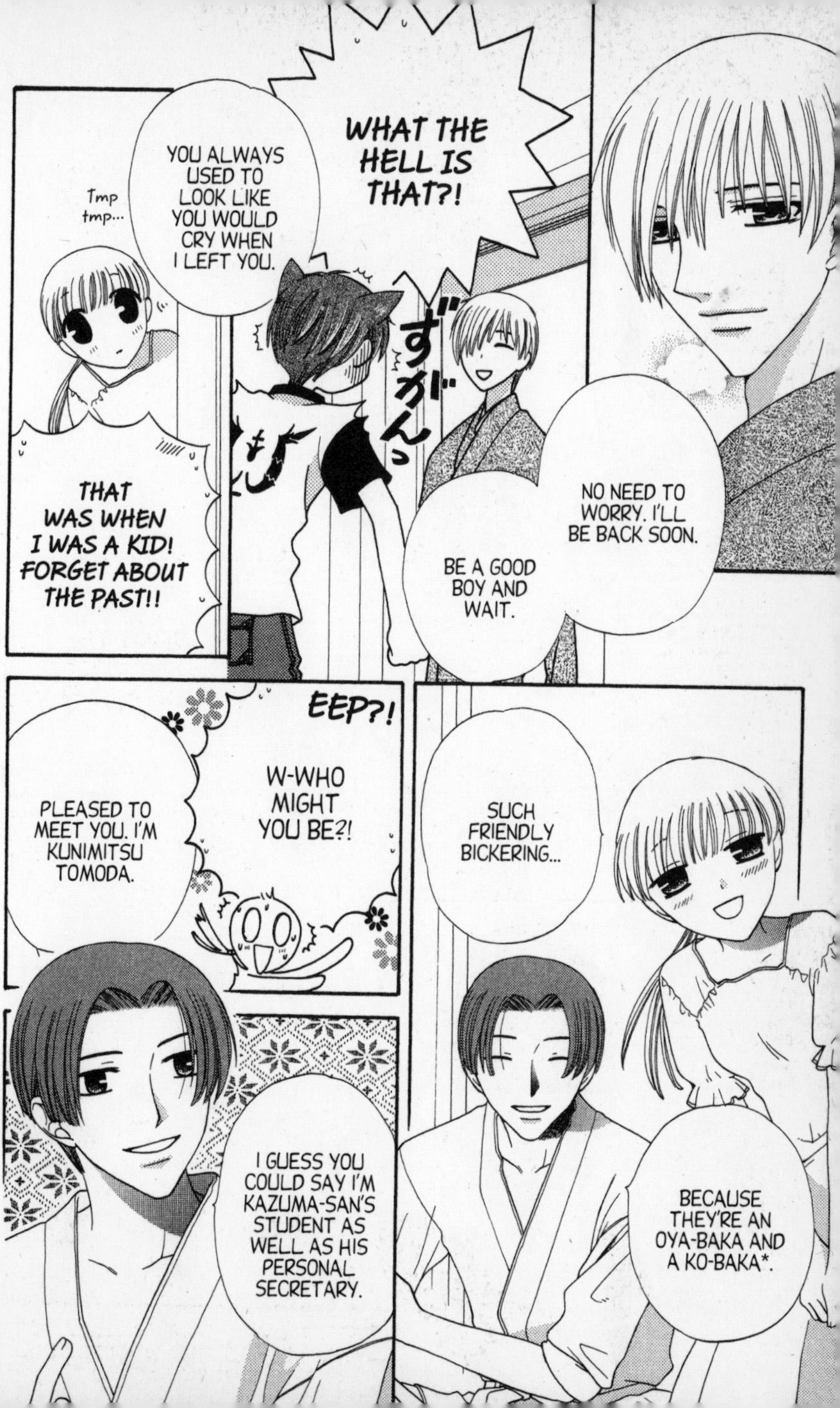
NO NEED TO WORRY. I'LL BE BACK SOON.
BE A GOOD BOY AND WAIT.
WHAT THE HELL IS THAT?!
ずがんっ
YOU ALWAYS USED TO LOOK LIKE YOU WOULD CRY WHEN I LEFT YOU.
Tmp tmp...
THAT WAS WHEN I WAS A KID! FORGET ABOUT THE PAST!!
SUCH FRIENDLY BICKERING...
BECAUSE THEY'RE AN OYA-BAKA AND A KO-BAKA*.
EEP?!
W-WHO MIGHT YOU BE?!
PLEASED TO MEET YOU. I'M KUNIMITSU TOMODA.
I GUESS YOU COULD SAY I'M KAZUMA-SAN'S STUDENT AS WELL AS HIS PERSONAL SECRETARY.

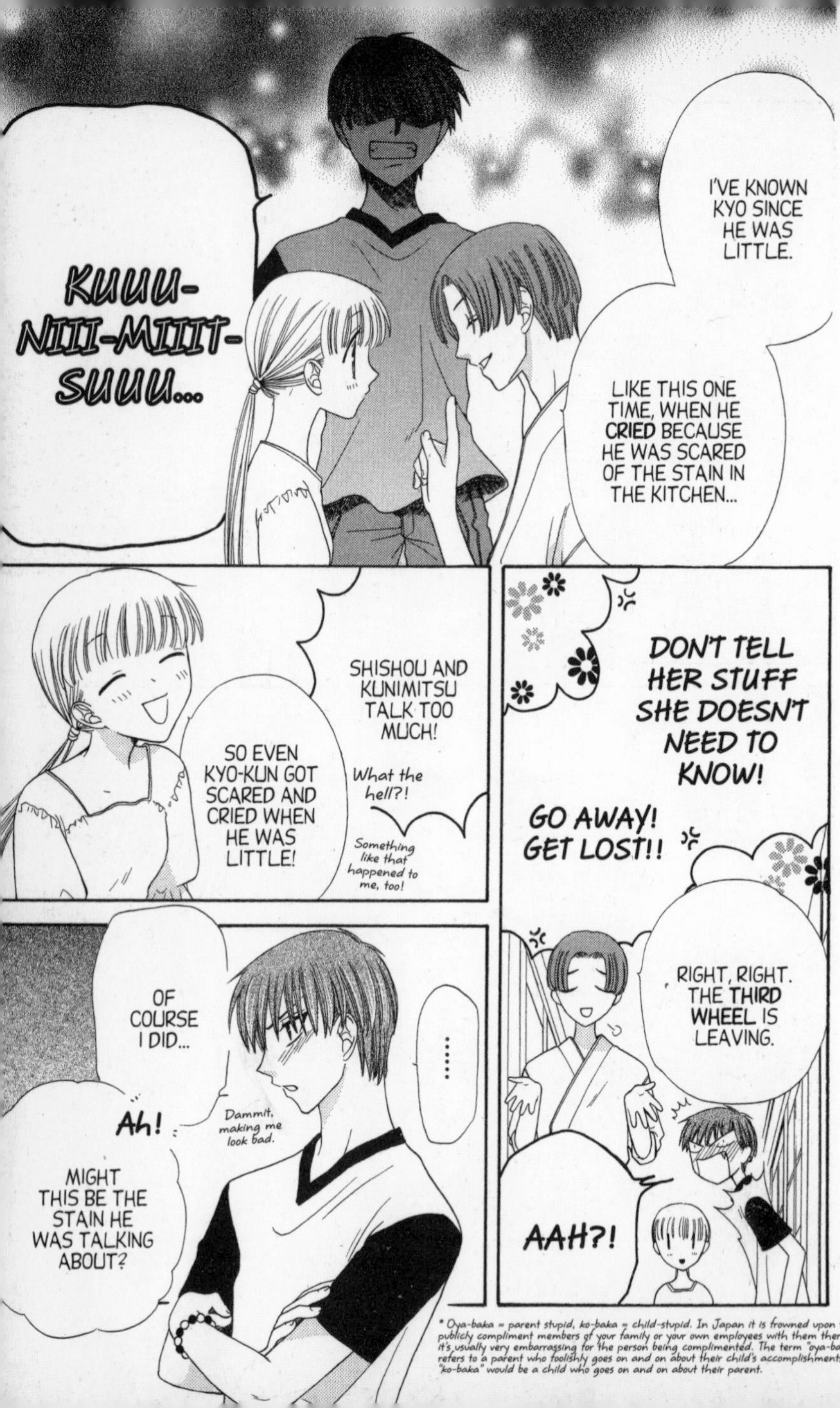
I'VE KNOWN KYO SINCE HE WAS LITTLE.
LIKE THIS ONE TIME, WHEN HE CRIED BECAUSE HE WAS SCARED OF THE STAIN IN THE KITCHEN...
KUUU-NIII-MIIIT-SUUU...
DON'T TELL HER STUFF SHE DOESN'T NEED TO KNOW!
GO AWAY! GET LOST!!
SHISHOU AND KUNIMITSU TALK TOO MUCH!
What the hell?!
SO EVEN KYO-KUN GOT SCARED AND CRIED WHEN HE WAS LITTLE!
Something like that happened to me, too!
RIGHT, RIGHT. THE THIRD WHEEL IS LEAVING.
AAH?!
......
OF COURSE I DID...
Dammit, making me look bad.
Ah!
MIGHT THIS BE THE STAIN HE WAS TALKING ABOUT?

* Oya-baka = parent stupid, ko-baka = child-stupid. In Japan it is frowned upon to publicly compliment members of your family or your own employees with them there, and it's usually very embarrassing for the person being complimented. The term "oya-baka" refers to a parent who foolishly goes on and on about their child's accomplishments, and "ko-baka" would be a child who goes on and on about their parent.

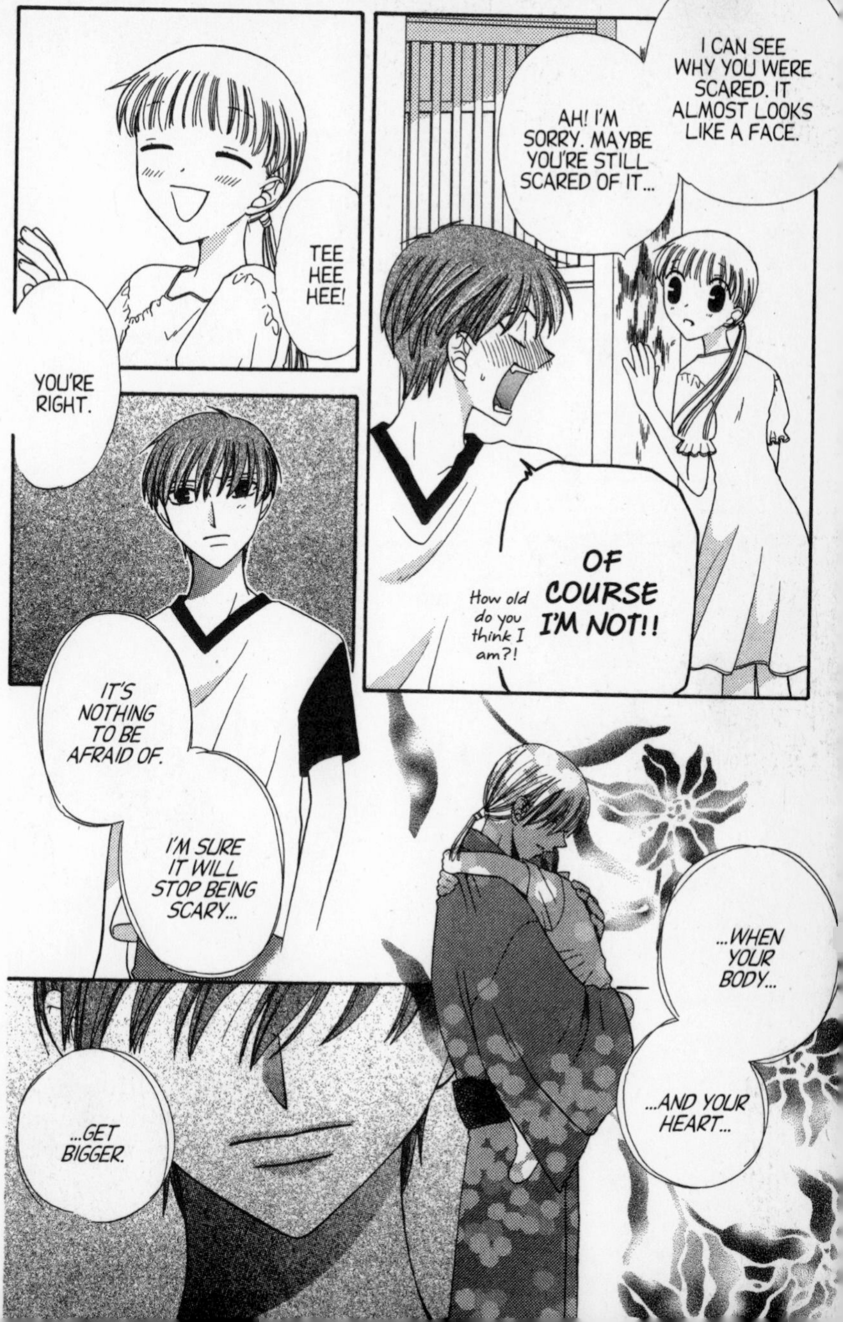
I CAN SEE WHY YOU WERE SCARED. IT ALMOST LOOKS LIKE A FACE.
AH! I'M SORRY. MAYBE YOU'RE STILL SCARED OF IT...
OF COURSE I'M NOT!!
How old do you think I am?!
TEE HEE HEE!
YOU'RE RIGHT.
IT'S NOTHING TO BE AFRAID OF.
I'M SURE IT WILL STOP BEING SCARY...
...WHEN YOUR BODY...
...AND YOUR HEART...
...GET BIGGER.

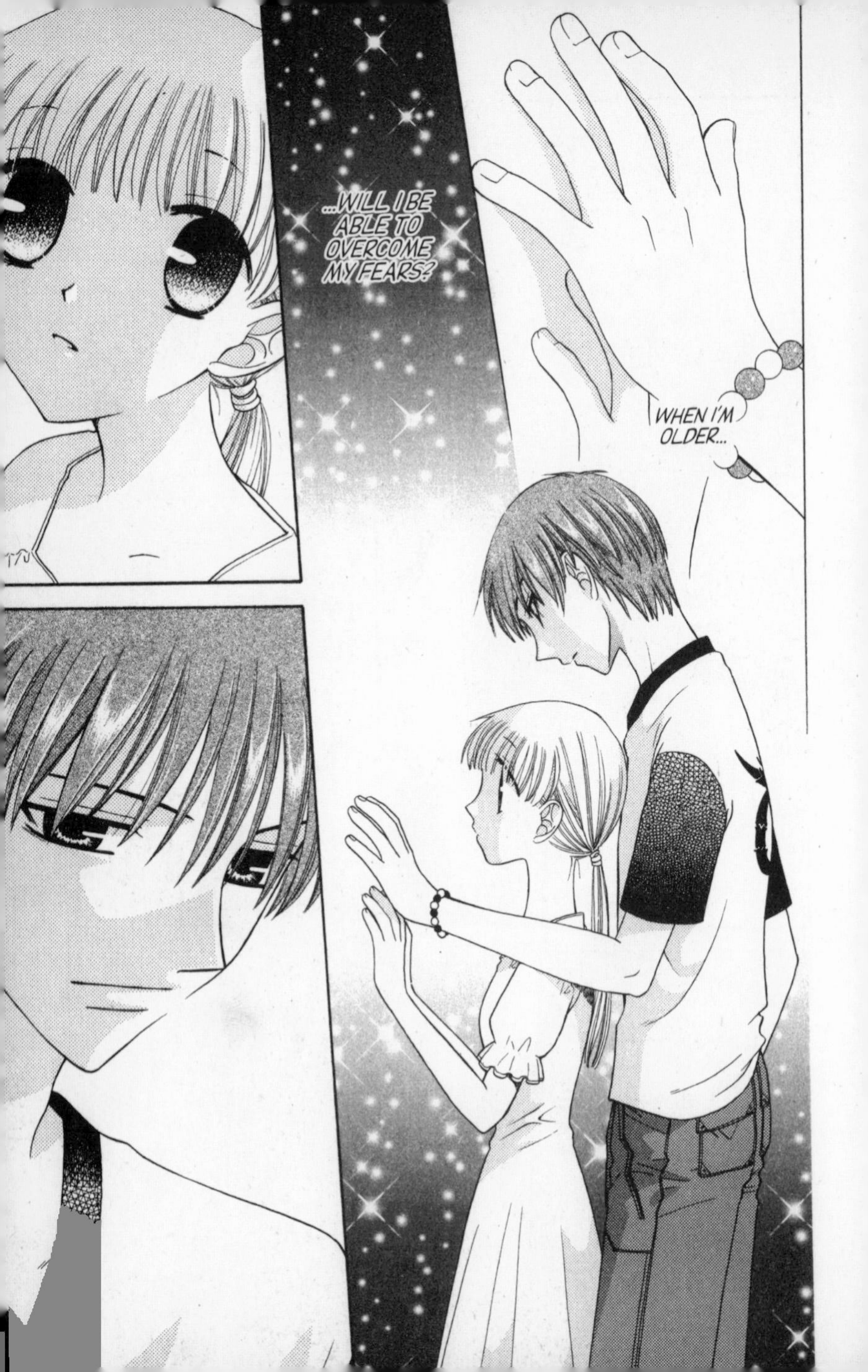
WHEN I'M OLDER...
...WILL I BE ABLE TO OVERCOME MY FEARS?

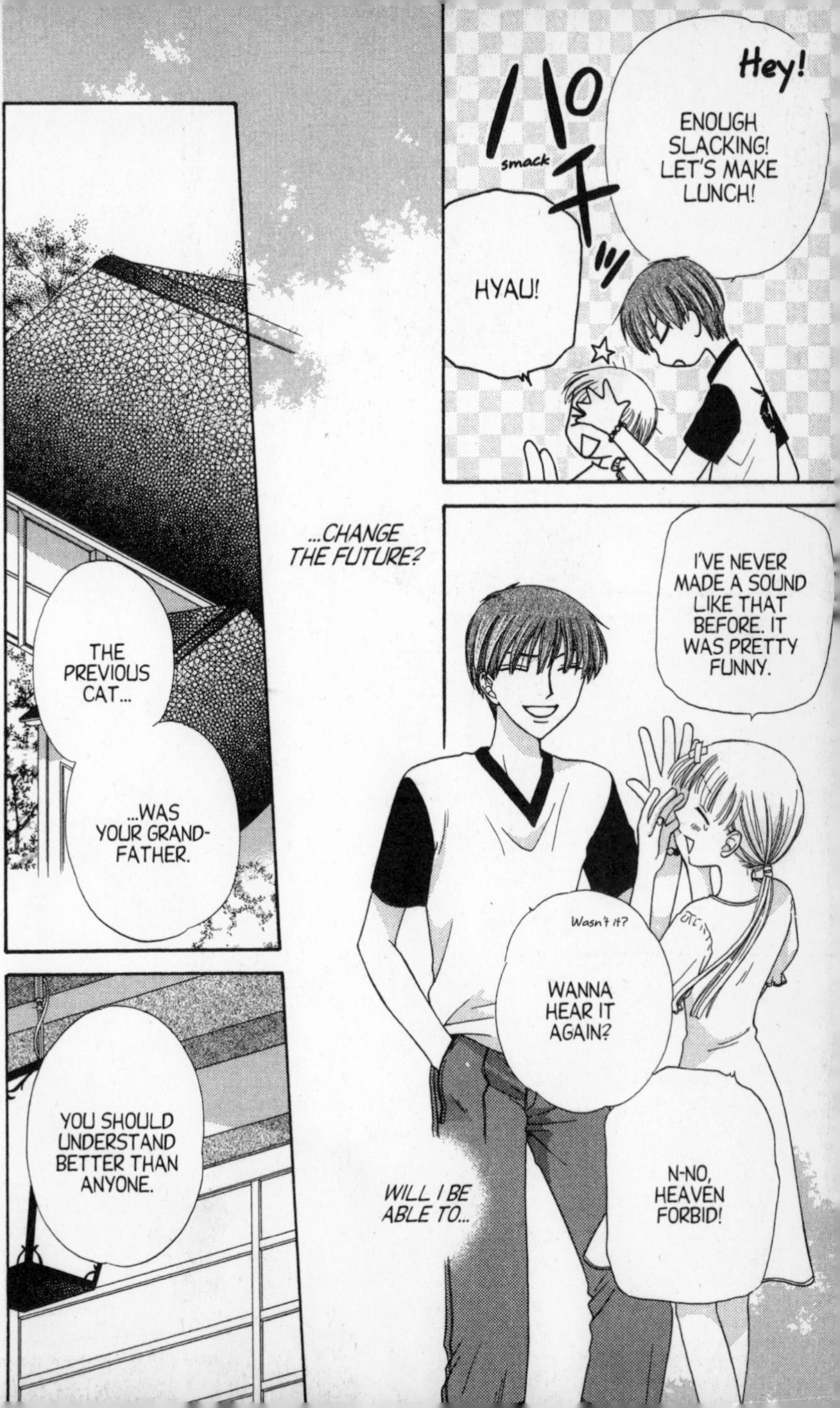
Hey!
ENOUGH SLACKING! LET'S MAKE LUNCH!
smack
HYAU!
I'VE NEVER MADE A SOUND LIKE THAT BEFORE. IT WAS PRETTY FUNNY.
Wasn't it?
WANNA HEAR IT AGAIN?
N-NO, HEAVEN FORBID!
...CHANGE THE FUTURE?
WILL I BE ABLE TO...
THE PREVIOUS CAT...
...WAS YOUR GRAND-FATHER.
YOU SHOULD UNDERSTAND BETTER THAN ANYONE.

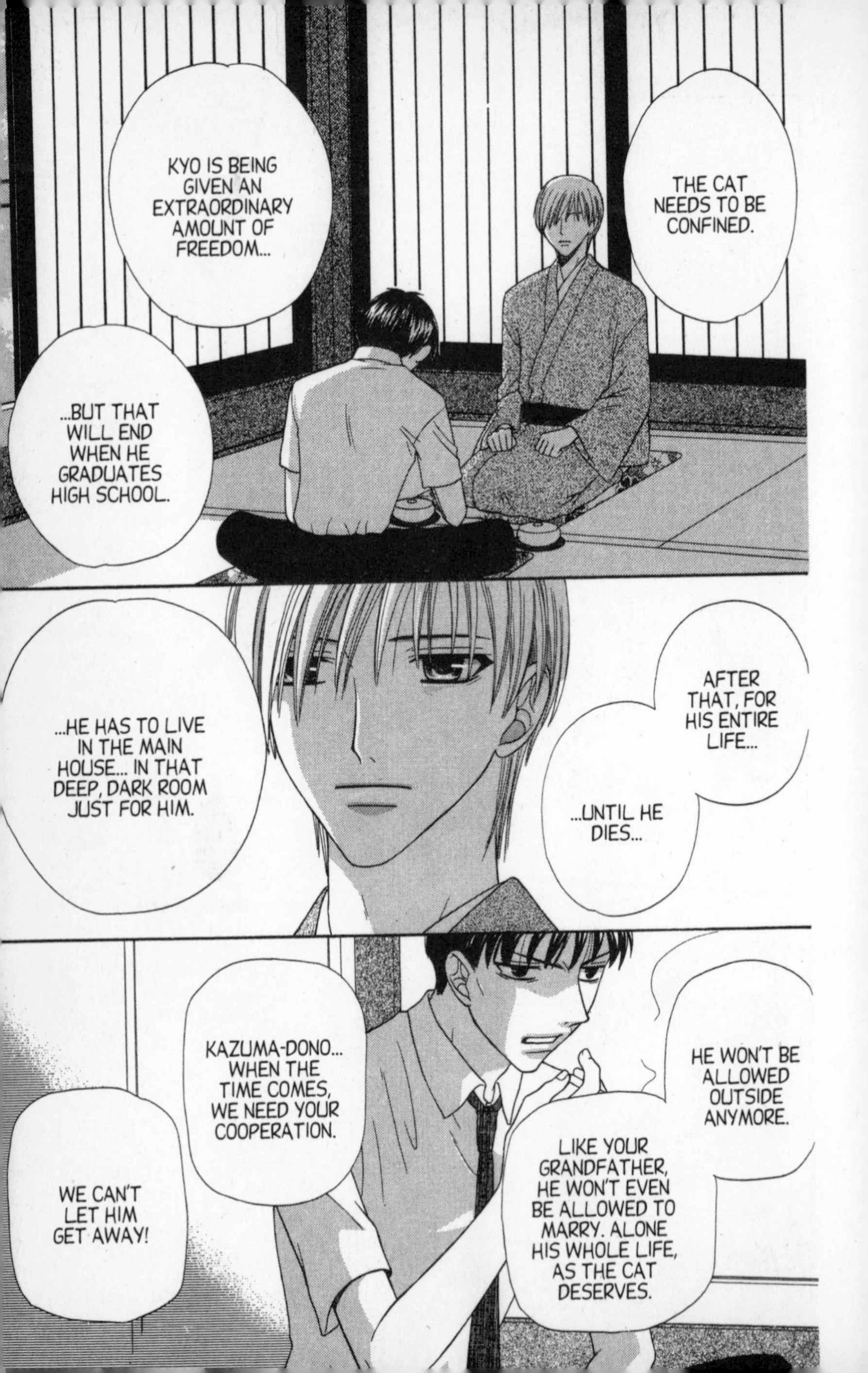
THE CAT NEEDS TO BE CONFINED.
KYO IS BEING GIVEN AN EXTRAORDINARY AMOUNT OF FREEDOM...
...BUT THAT WILL END WHEN HE GRADUATES HIGH SCHOOL.
AFTER THAT, FOR HIS ENTIRE LIFE...
...UNTIL HE DIES...
...HE HAS TO LIVE IN THE MAIN HOUSE... IN THAT DEEP, DARK ROOM JUST FOR HIM.
HE WON'T BE ALLOWED OUTSIDE ANYMORE.
LIKE YOUR GRANDFATHER, HE WON'T EVEN BE ALLOWED TO MARRY. ALONE HIS WHOLE LIFE, AS THE CAT DESERVES.
KAZUMA-DONO... WHEN THE TIME COMES, WE NEED YOUR COOPERATION.
WE CAN'T LET HIM GET AWAY!

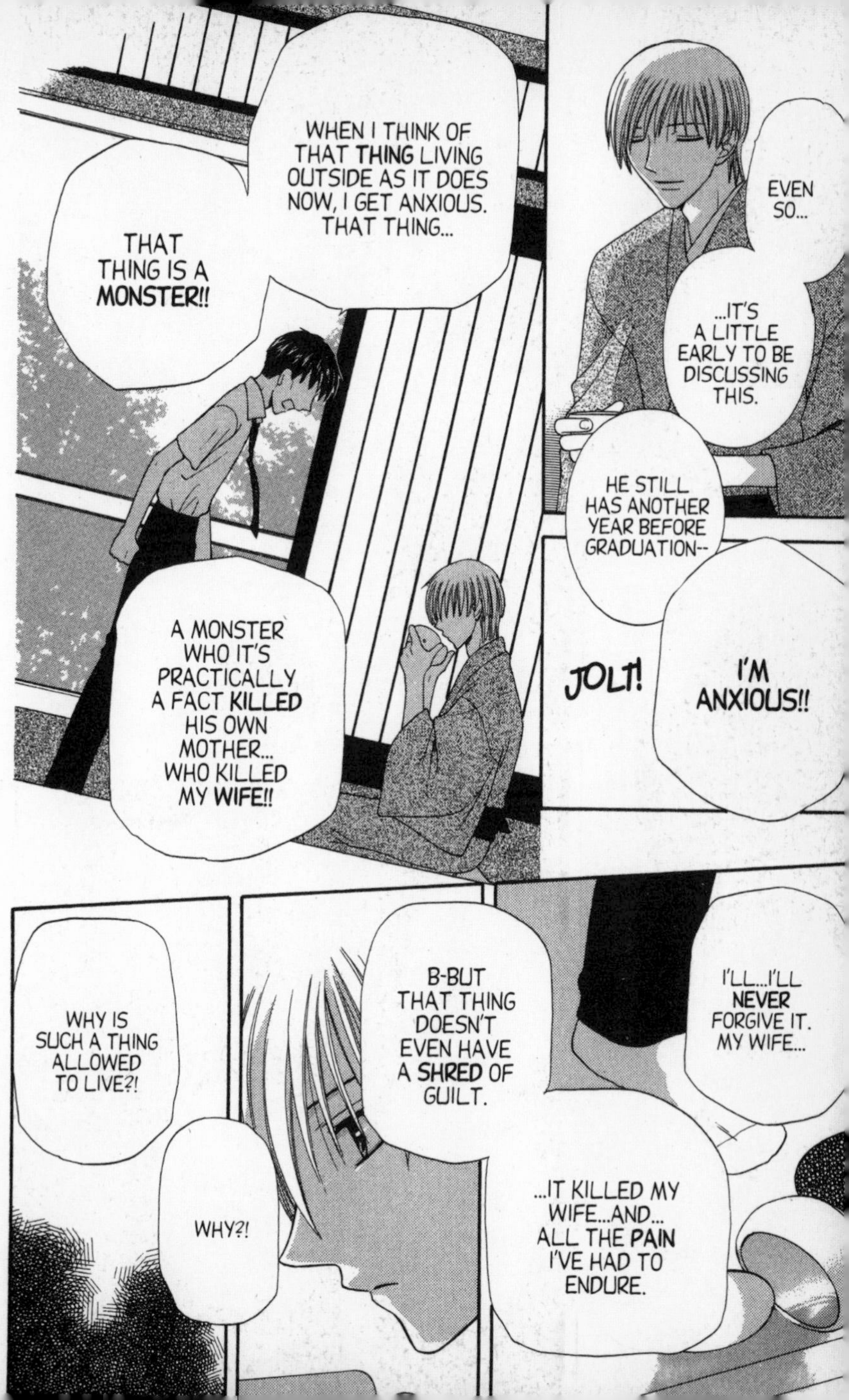
EVEN SO...
...IT'S A LITTLE EARLY TO BE DISCUSSING THIS.
HE STILL HAS ANOTHER YEAR BEFORE GRADUATION--
I'M ANXIOUS!!
JOLT!
WHEN I THINK OF THAT THING LIVING OUTSIDE AS IT DOES NOW, I GET ANXIOUS. THAT THING...
THAT THING IS A MONSTER!!
A MONSTER WHO IT'S PRACTICALLY A FACT KILLED HIS OWN MOTHER... WHO KILLED MY WIFE!!
I'LL...I'LL NEVER FORGIVE IT. MY WIFE...
B-BUT THAT THING DOESN'T EVEN HAVE A SHRED OF GUILT.
...IT KILLED MY WIFE...AND... ALL THE PAIN I'VE HAD TO ENDURE.
WHY IS SUCH A THING ALLOWED TO LIVE?!
WHY?!

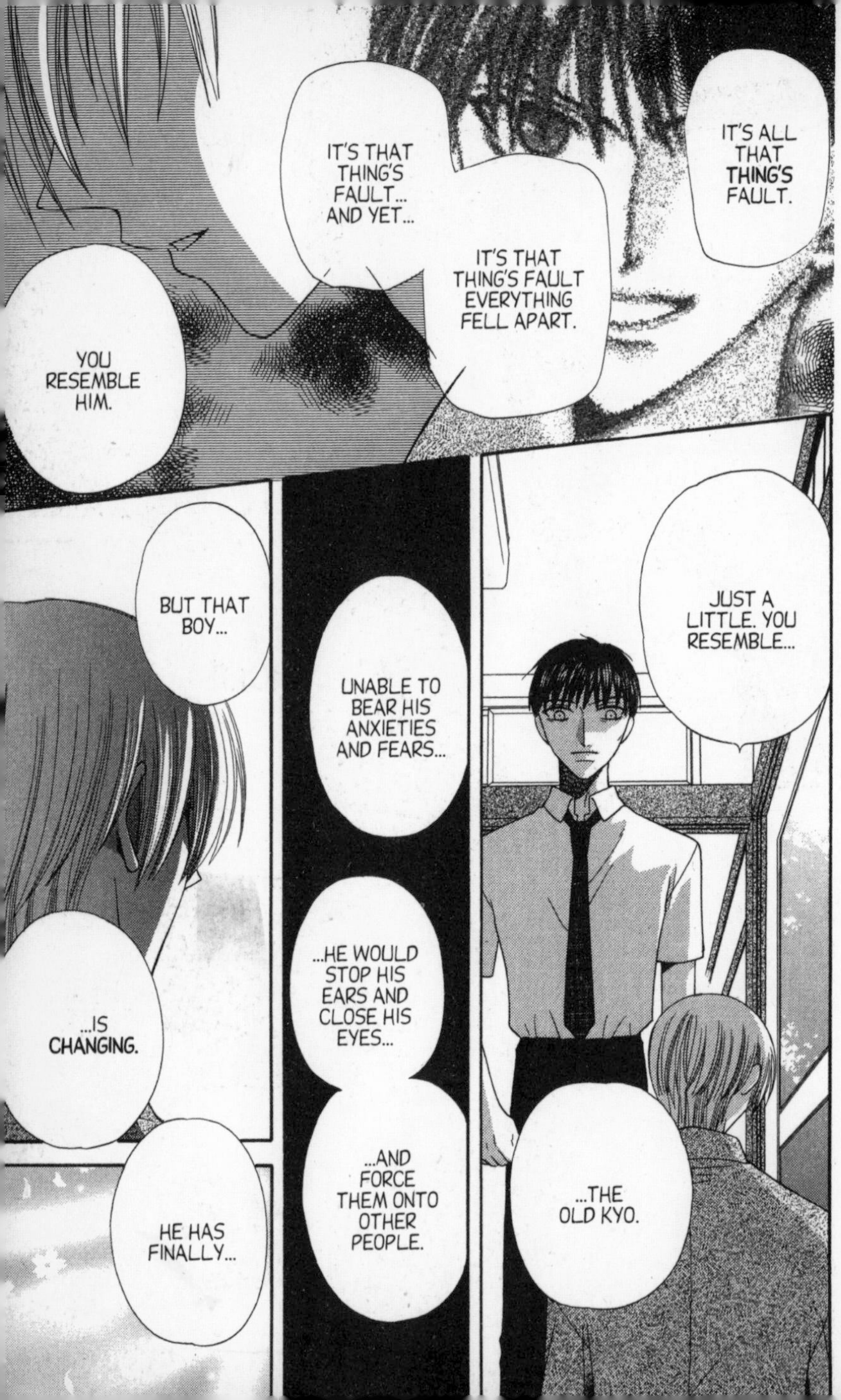
IT'S ALL THAT THING'S FAULT.
IT'S THAT THING'S FAULT EVERYTHING FELL APART.
IT'S THAT THING'S FAULT... AND YET...
YOU RESEMBLE HIM.
JUST A LITTLE. YOU RESEMBLE...
...THE OLD KYO.
UNABLE TO BEAR HIS ANXIETIES AND FEARS...
...HE WOULD STOP HIS EARS AND CLOSE HIS EYES...
...AND FORCE THEM ONTO OTHER PEOPLE.
BUT THAT BOY...
...IS CHANGING.
HE HAS FINALLY...

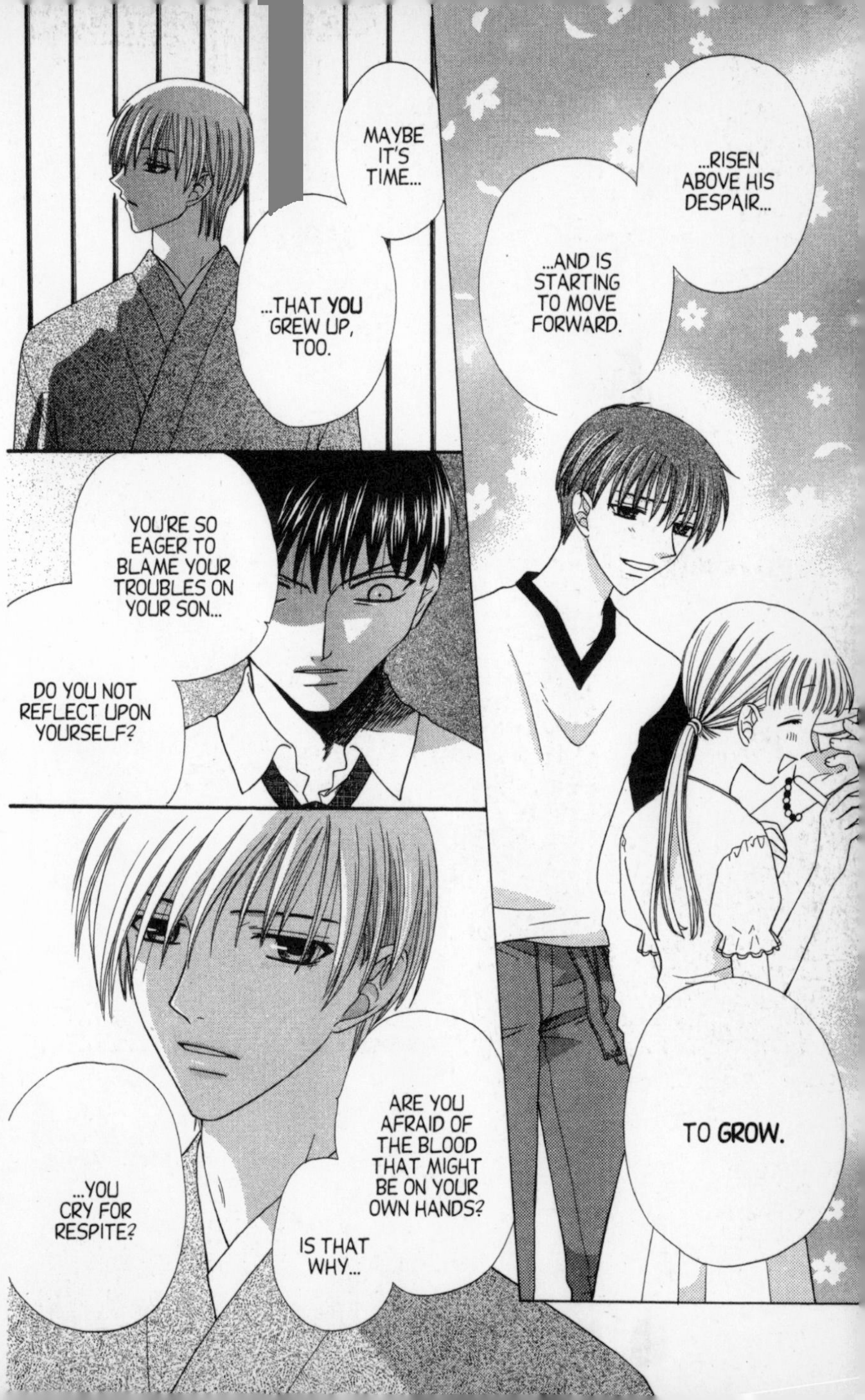
...RISEN ABOVE HIS DESPAIR...
...AND IS STARTING TO MOVE FORWARD.
TO **GROW.**
MAYBE IT'S TIME...
...THAT **YOU** GREW UP, TOO.
YOU'RE SO EAGER TO BLAME YOUR TROUBLES ON YOUR SON...
DO YOU NOT REFLECT UPON YOURSELF?
ARE YOU AFRAID OF THE BLOOD THAT MIGHT BE ON YOUR OWN HANDS?
IS THAT WHY...
...YOU CRY FOR RESPITE?

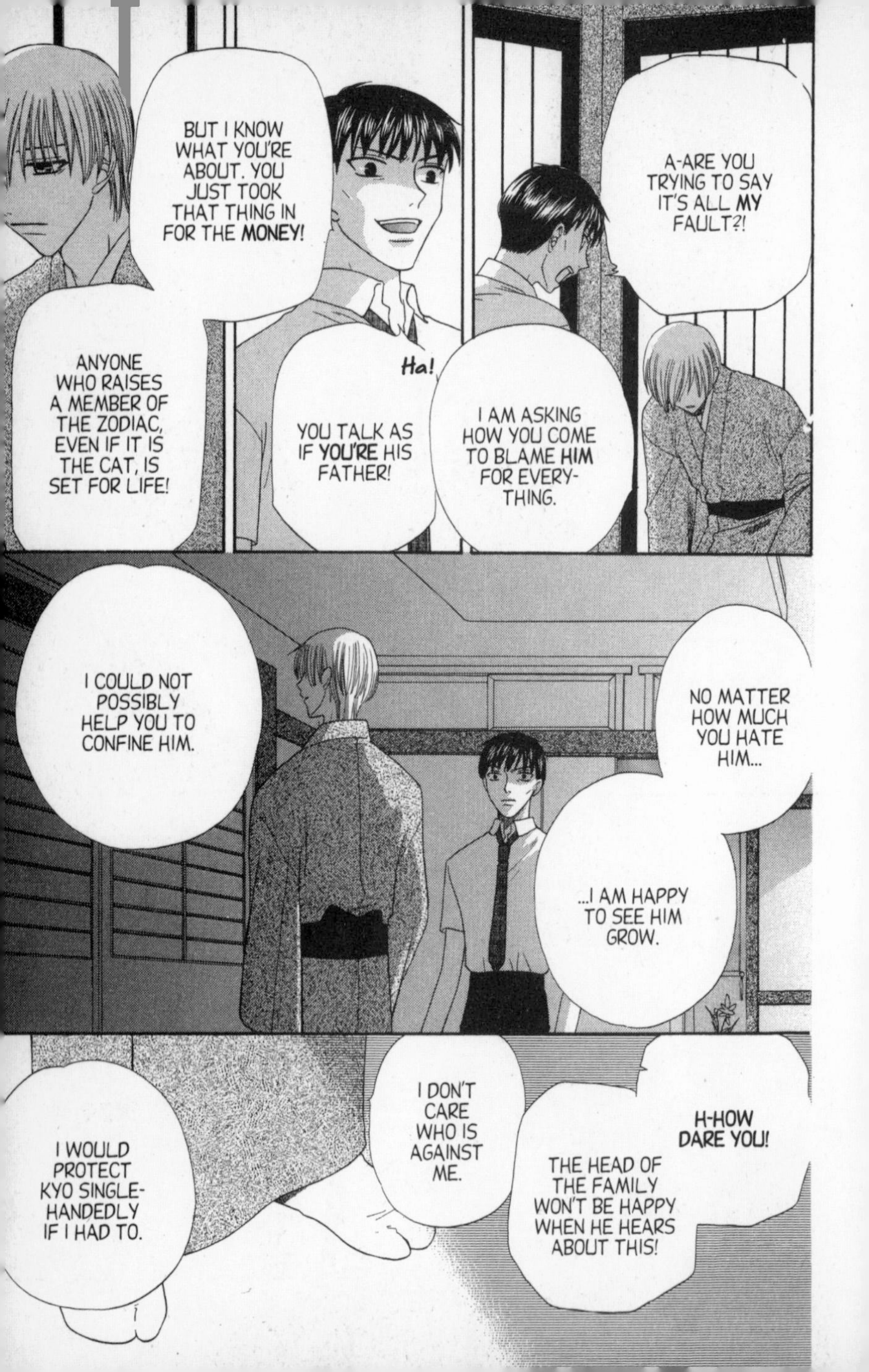
A-ARE YOU TRYING TO SAY IT'S ALL **MY** FAULT?!
I AM ASKING HOW YOU COME TO BLAME **HIM** FOR EVERY-THING.
Ha!
YOU TALK AS IF **YOU'RE** HIS FATHER!
BUT I KNOW WHAT YOU'RE ABOUT. YOU JUST TOOK THAT THING IN FOR THE **MONEY**!
ANYONE WHO RAISES A MEMBER OF THE ZODIAC, EVEN IF IT IS THE CAT, IS SET FOR LIFE!
NO MATTER HOW MUCH YOU HATE HIM...
...I AM HAPPY TO SEE HIM GROW.
I COULD NOT POSSIBLY HELP YOU TO CONFINE HIM.
H-HOW DARE YOU!
THE HEAD OF THE FAMILY WON'T BE HAPPY WHEN HE HEARS ABOUT THIS!
I DON'T CARE WHO IS AGAINST ME.
I WOULD PROTECT KYO SINGLE-HANDEDLY IF I HAD TO.

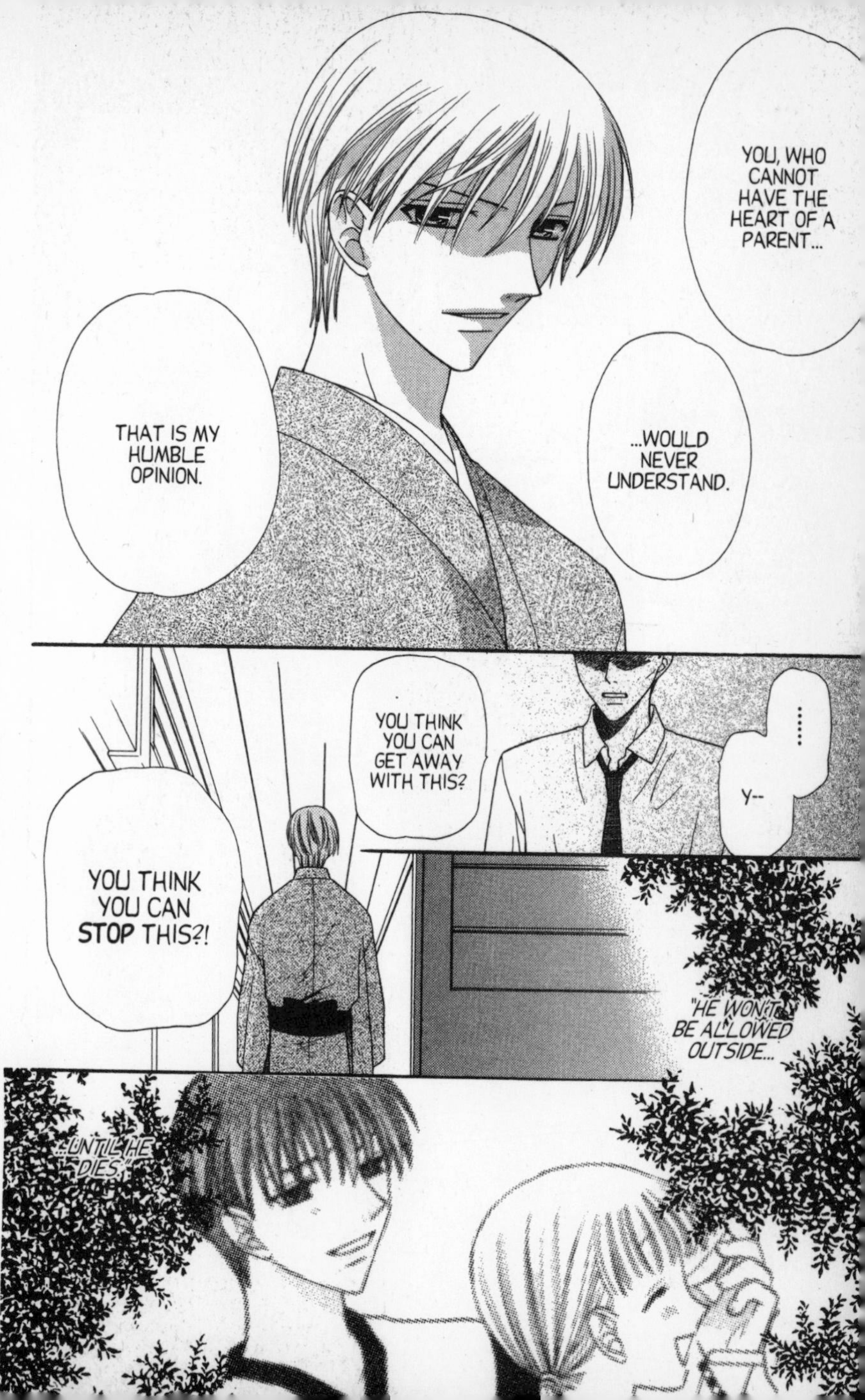
YOU, WHO CANNOT HAVE THE HEART OF A PARENT...
...WOULD NEVER UNDERSTAND.
THAT IS MY HUMBLE OPINION.
......
Y--
YOU THINK YOU CAN GET AWAY WITH THIS?
"HE WON'T BE ALLOWED OUTSIDE...
YOU THINK YOU CAN STOP THIS?!
...UNTIL HE DIES."

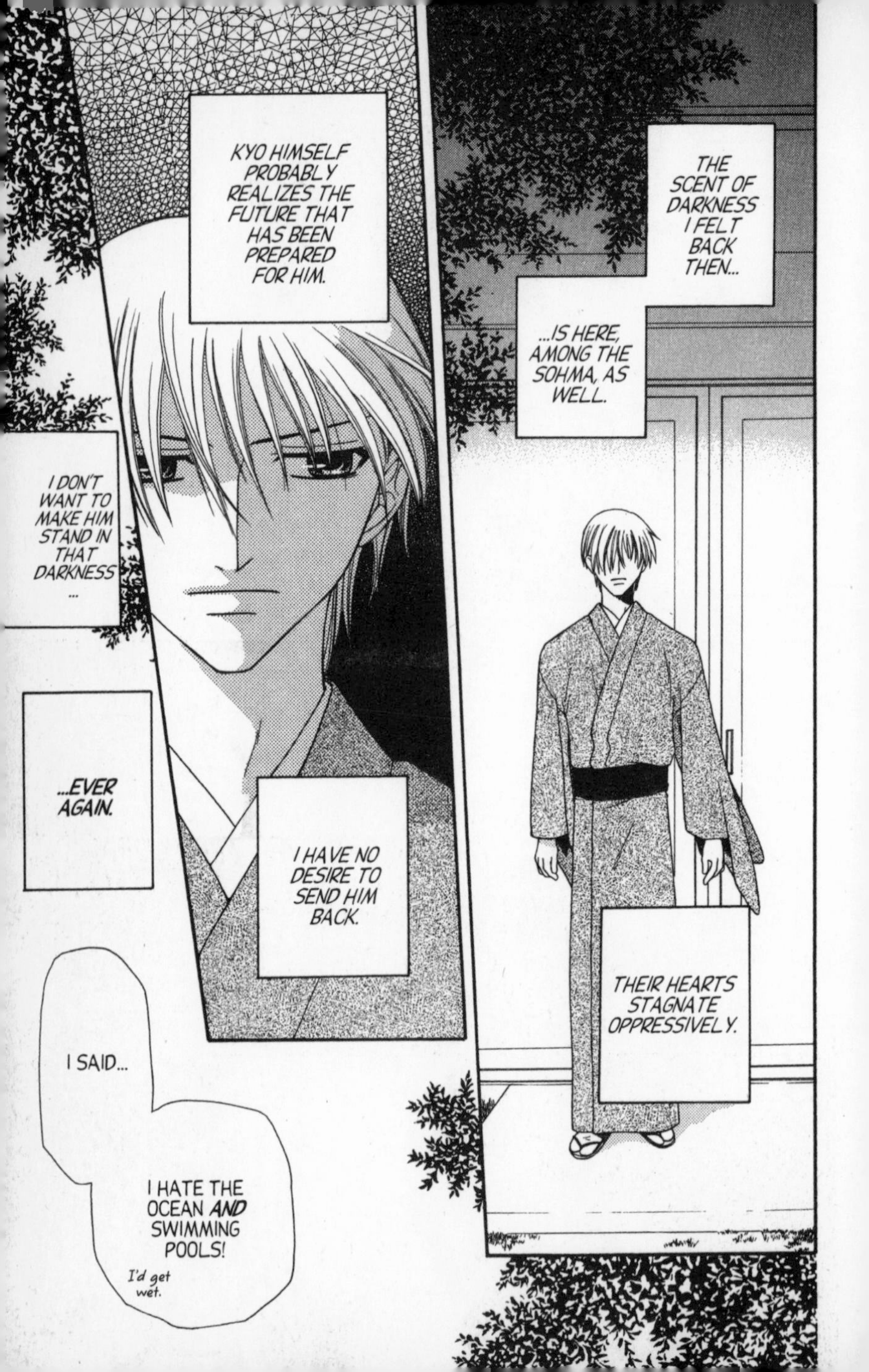
THE SCENT OF DARKNESS I FELT BACK THEN...
...IS HERE, AMONG THE SOHMA, AS WELL.
THEIR HEARTS STAGNATE OPPRESSIVELY.
KYO HIMSELF PROBABLY REALIZES THE FUTURE THAT HAS BEEN PREPARED FOR HIM.
I HAVE NO DESIRE TO SEND HIM BACK.
I DON'T WANT TO MAKE HIM STAND IN THAT DARKNESS...
...EVER AGAIN.
I SAID... I HATE THE OCEAN *AND* SWIMMING POOLS!
I'd get wet.

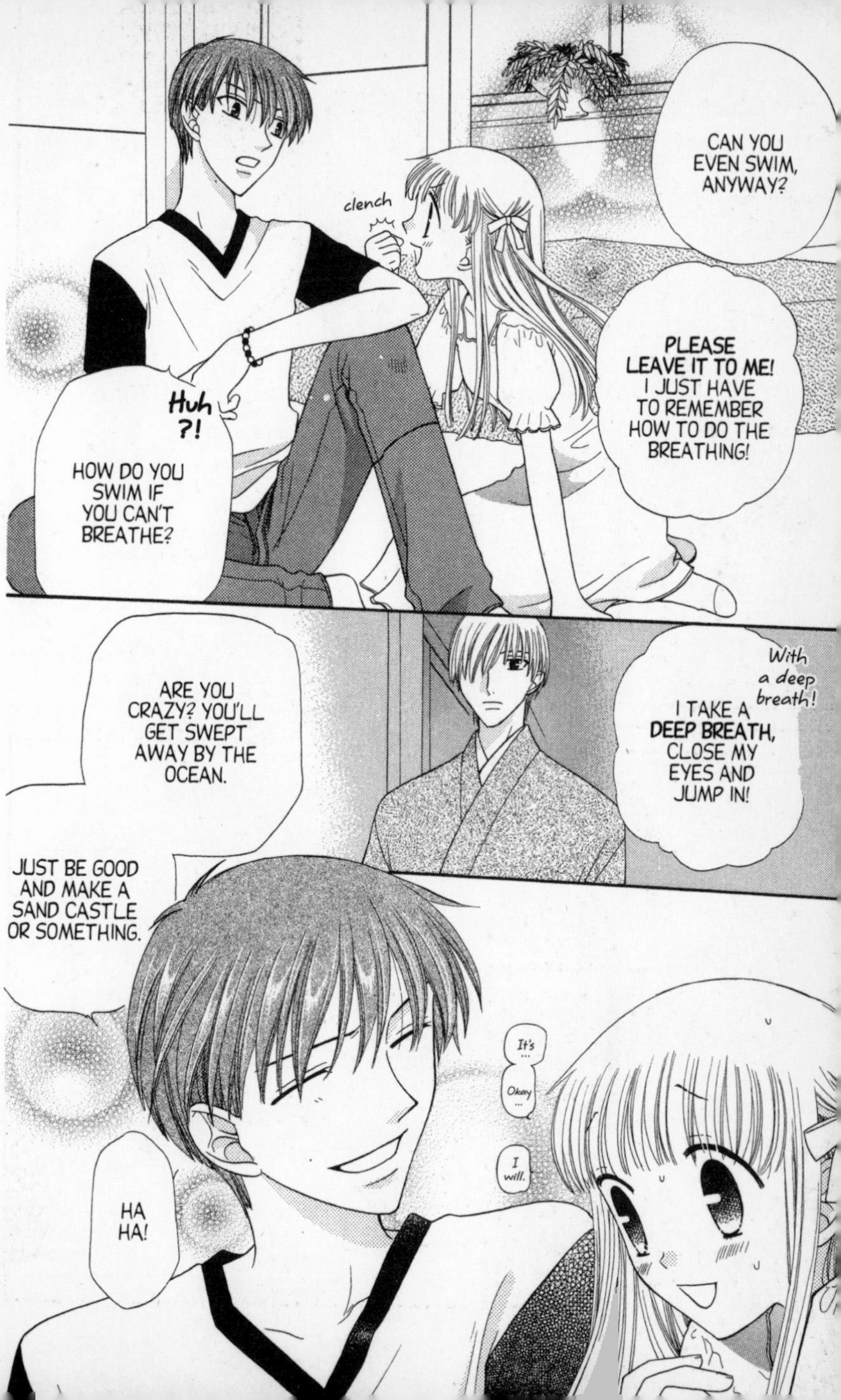

CAN YOU EVEN SWIM, ANYWAY?
clench
PLEASE LEAVE IT TO ME! I JUST HAVE TO REMEMBER HOW TO DO THE BREATHING!
Huh ?!
HOW DO YOU SWIM IF YOU CAN'T BREATHE?
With a deep breath!
I TAKE A DEEP BREATH, CLOSE MY EYES AND JUMP IN!
ARE YOU CRAZY? YOU'LL GET SWEPT AWAY BY THE OCEAN.
JUST BE GOOD AND MAKE A SAND CASTLE OR SOMETHING.
It's ...
Okay ...
I will.
HA HA!

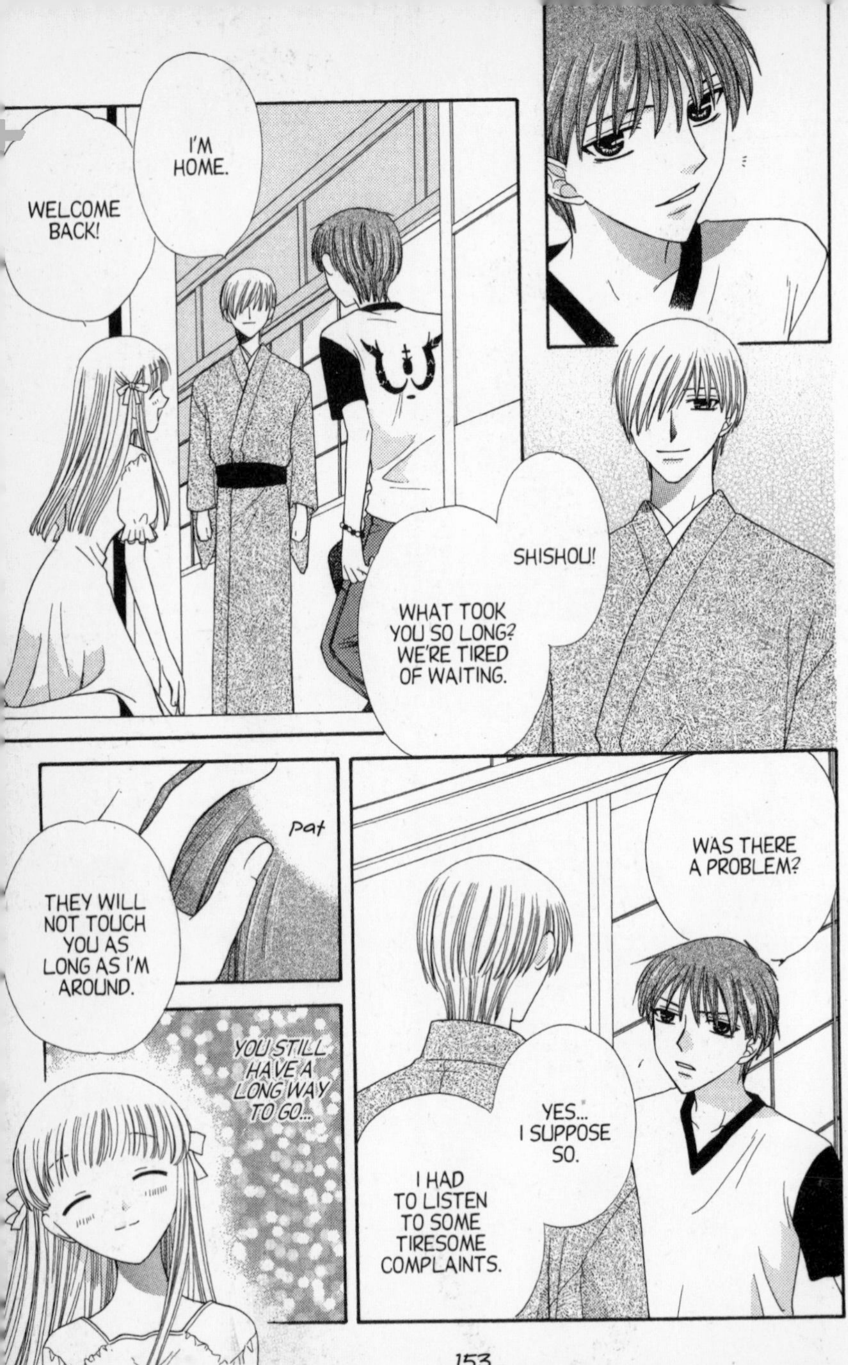

SHISHOU!
WHAT TOOK YOU SO LONG? WE'RE TIRED OF WAITING.
I'M HOME.
WELCOME BACK!
WAS THERE A PROBLEM?
YES... I SUPPOSE SO.
I HAD TO LISTEN TO SOME TIRESOME COMPLAINTS.
pat
THEY WILL NOT TOUCH YOU AS LONG AS I'M AROUND.
YOU STILL HAVE A LONG WAY TO GO...

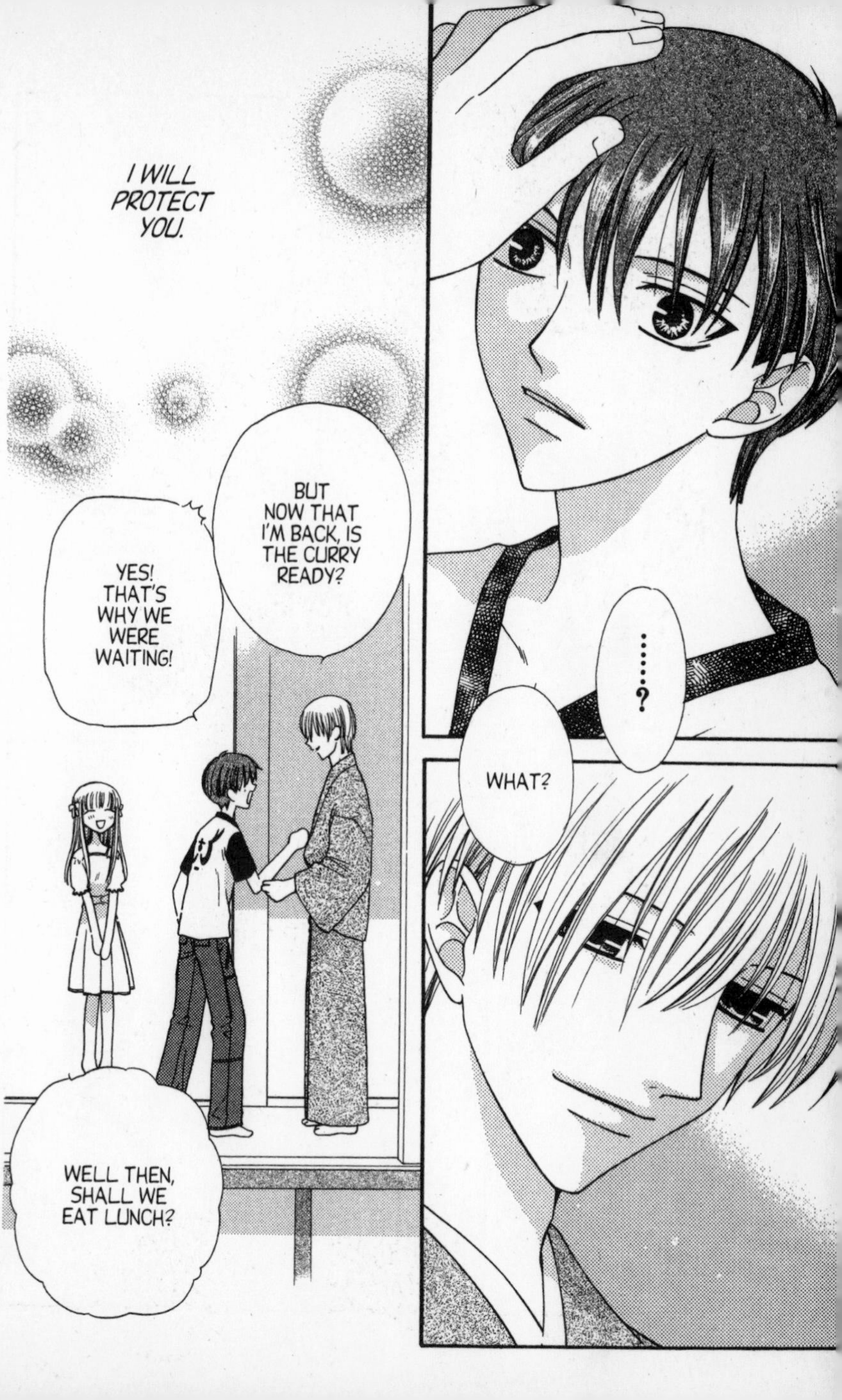
……?
WHAT?
I WILL PROTECT YOU.
BUT NOW THAT I'M BACK, IS THE CURRY READY?
YES! THAT'S WHY WE WERE WAITING!
WELL THEN, SHALL WE EAT LUNCH?

Chapter 53

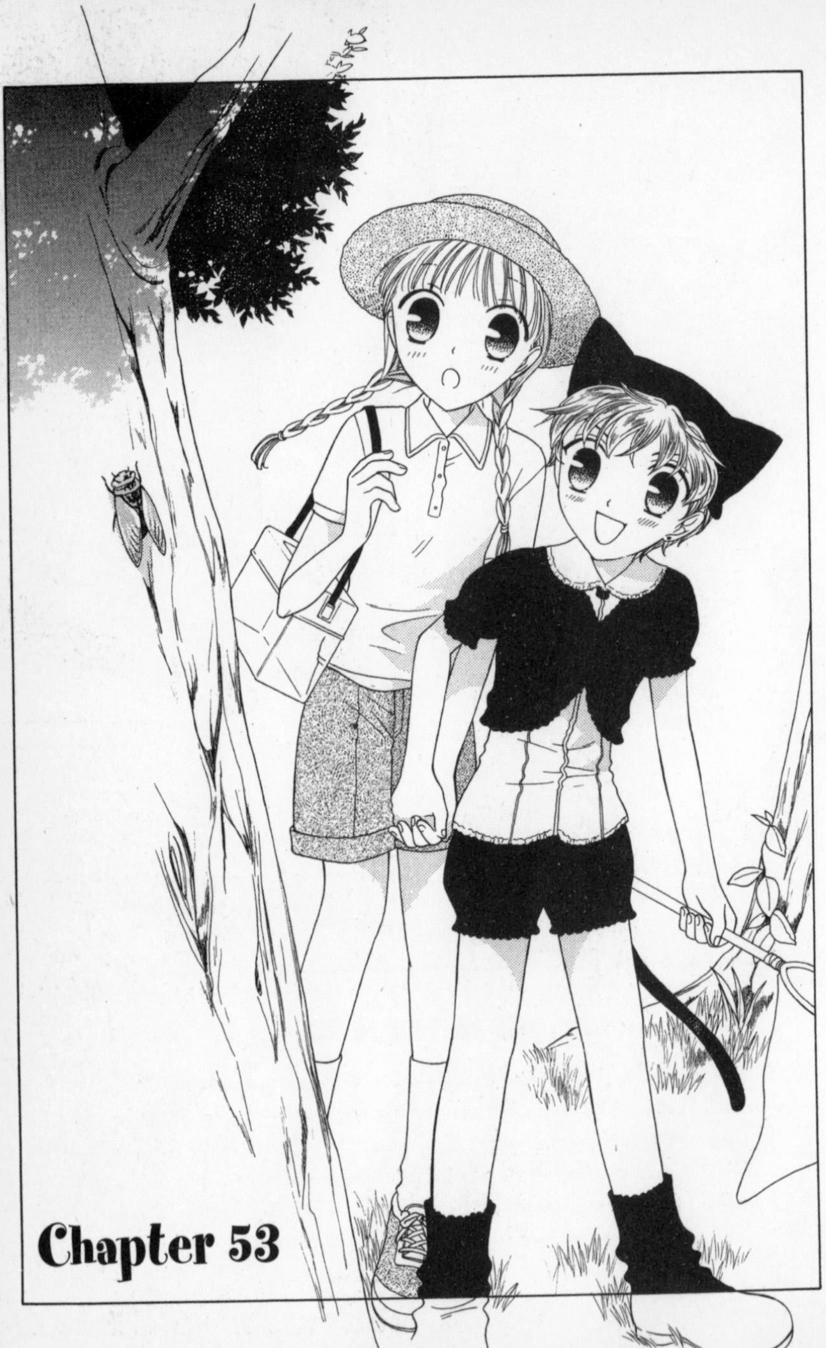

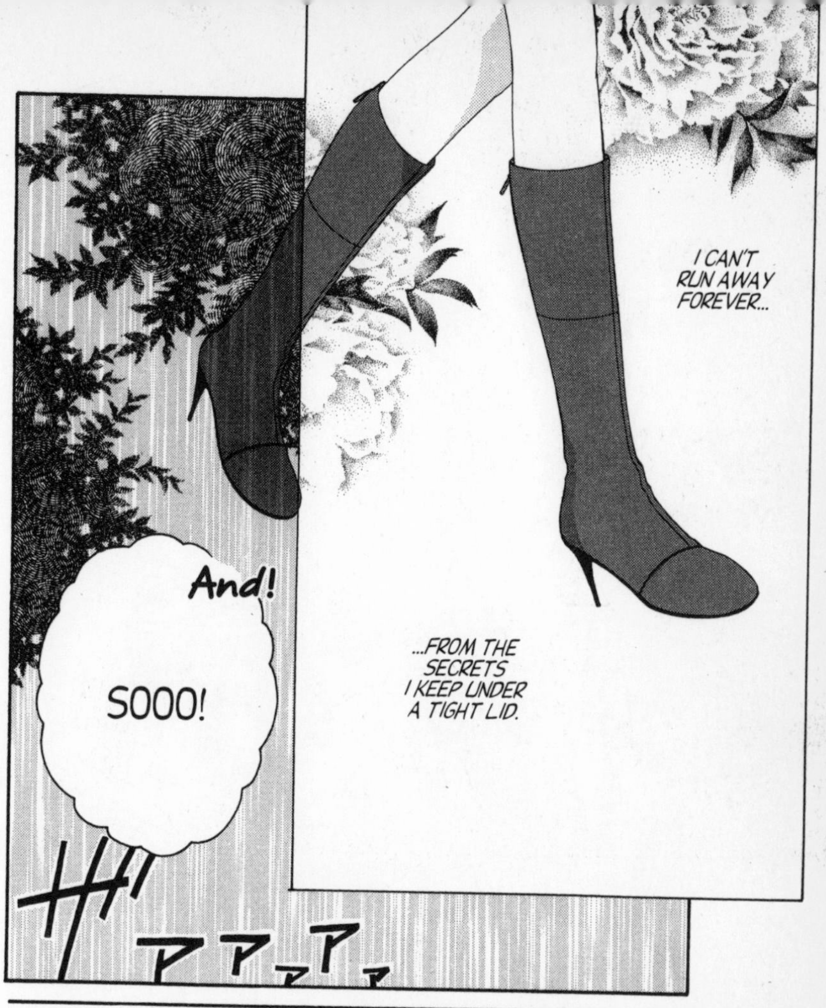
I CAN'T RUN AWAY FOREVER...
...FROM THE SECRETS I KEEP UNDER A TIGHT LID.
And!
SOOO!

NOT BLAH, BLAH, BLAH 5

The clothes Momitchi wears starting on the next page were designed by Mari Hidaka*-sensei. She sent me a fax that she drew of Momitchi that was **sooo cute** that I melted, so I got permission to let him actually wear the clothes in the manga. The original fax is actually **much** cuter. Long sleeves and boots... I'm sorry... It's the best I could do! Anyway, very many thanks, Hidaka-sensei.

*manga-ka of the series VB Rose.

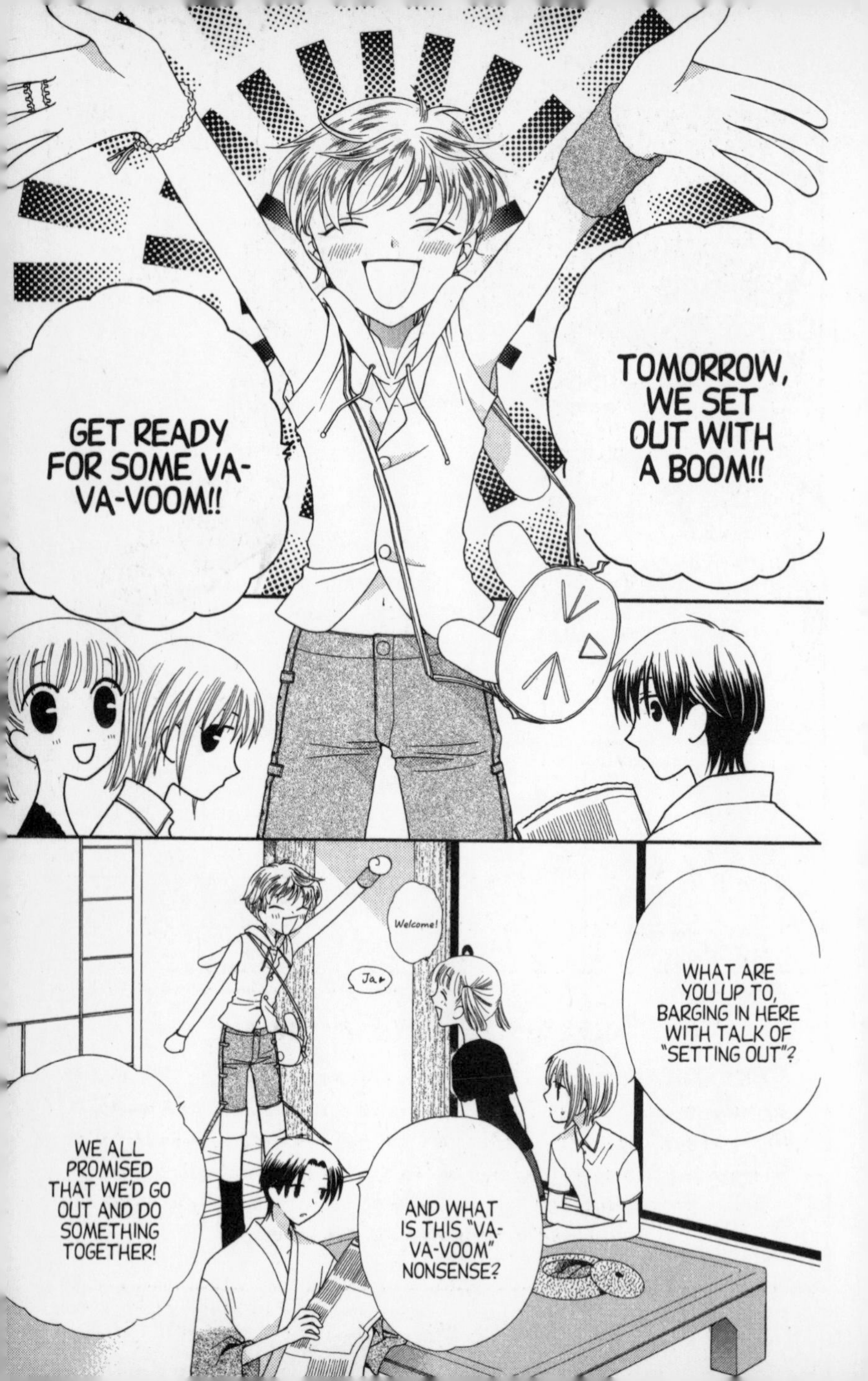
TOMORROW, WE SET OUT WITH A BOOM!!
GET READY FOR SOME VA-VA-VOOM!!
WHAT ARE YOU UP TO, BARGING IN HERE WITH TALK OF "SETTING OUT"?
Welcome!
Ja
AND WHAT IS THIS "VA-VA-VOOM" NONSENSE?
WE ALL PROMISED THAT WE'D GO OUT AND DO SOMETHING TOGETHER!

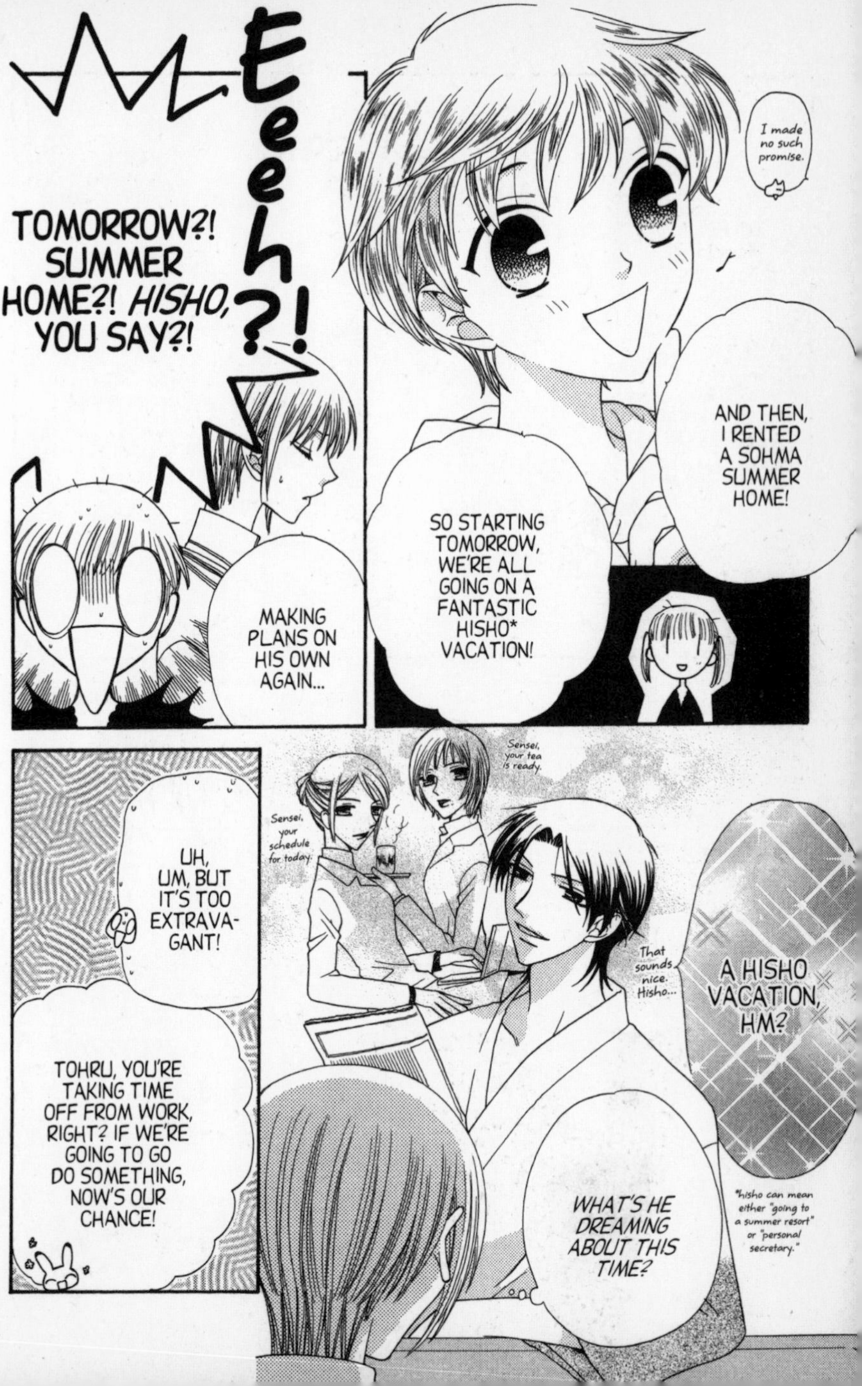
I made no such promise.
AND THEN, I RENTED A SOHMA SUMMER HOME!
SO STARTING TOMORROW, WE'RE ALL GOING ON A FANTASTIC HISHO* VACATION!
Eeeh?!
TOMORROW?! SUMMER HOME?! HISHO, YOU SAY?!
MAKING PLANS ON HIS OWN AGAIN...
A HISHO VACATION, HM?
That sounds nice. Hisho...
Sensei, your tea is ready.
Sensei, your schedule for today.
WHAT'S HE DREAMING ABOUT THIS TIME?
*hisho can mean either "going to a summer resort" or "personal secretary."
UH, UM, BUT IT'S TOO EXTRAVA-GANT!
TOHRU, YOU'RE TAKING TIME OFF FROM WORK, RIGHT? IF WE'RE GOING TO GO DO SOMETHING, NOW'S OUR CHANCE!

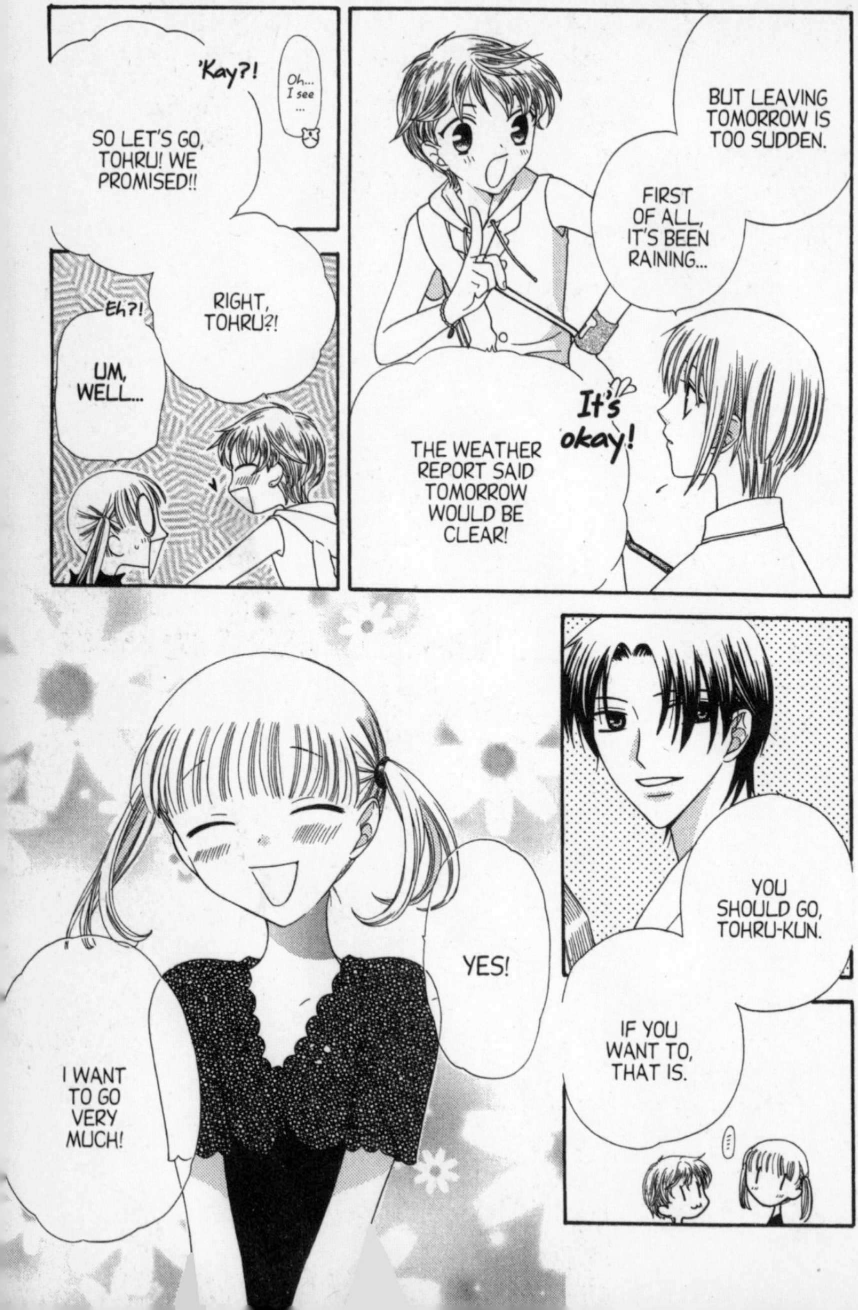
BUT LEAVING TOMORROW IS TOO SUDDEN.
FIRST OF ALL, IT'S BEEN RAINING...
It's okay!
THE WEATHER REPORT SAID TOMORROW WOULD BE CLEAR!
SO LET'S GO, TOHRU! WE PROMISED!!
'Kay?!
Oh... I see ...
RIGHT, TOHRU?!
Eh?!
UM, WELL...
YOU SHOULD GO, TOHRU-KUN.
IF YOU WANT TO, THAT IS.
YES!
I WANT TO GO VERY MUCH!

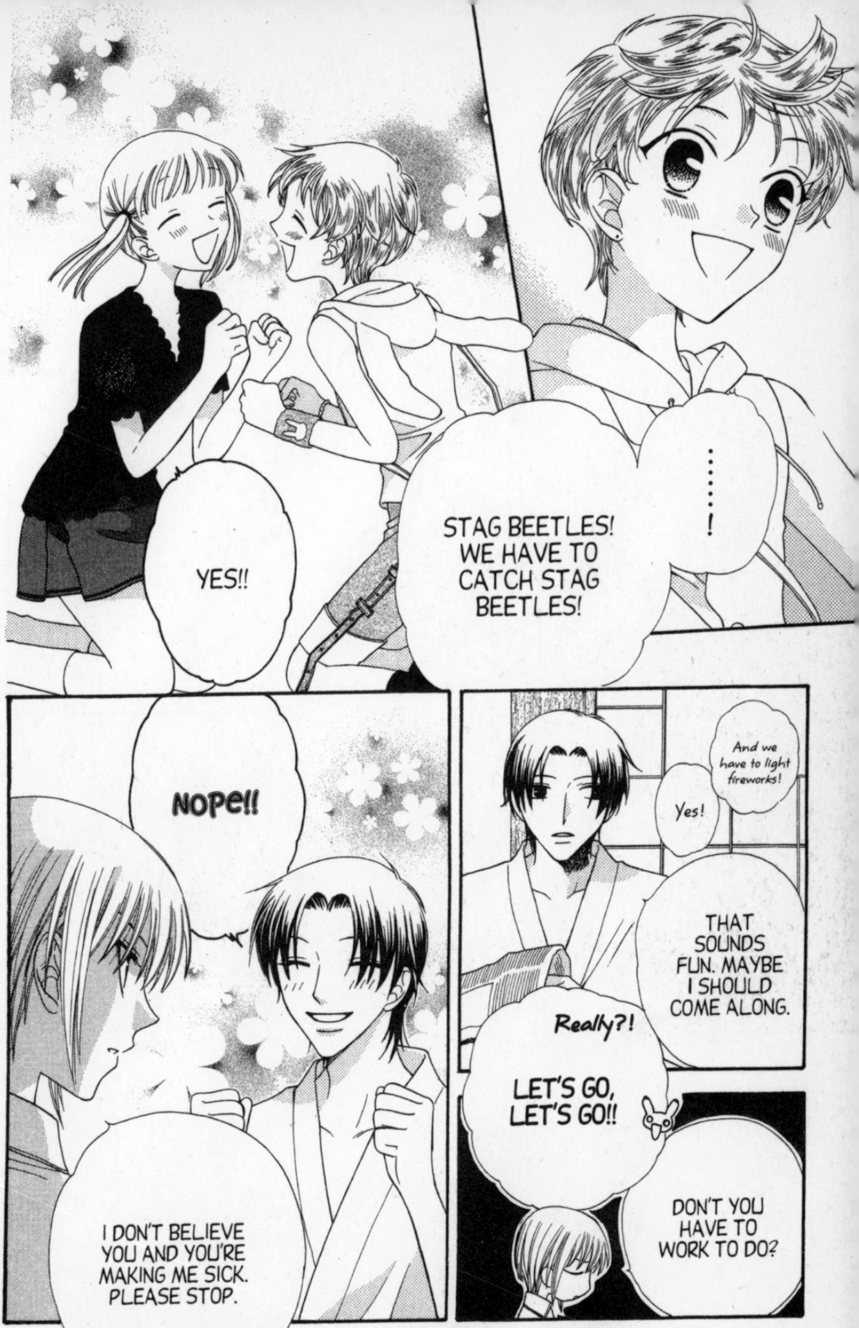
......!
STAG BEETLES! WE HAVE TO CATCH STAG BEETLES!
YES!!
And we have to light fireworks!
Yes!
THAT SOUNDS FUN. MAYBE I SHOULD COME ALONG.
Really?!
LET'S GO, LET'S GO!!
DON'T YOU HAVE TO WORK TO DO?
NOPE!!
I DON'T BELIEVE YOU AND YOU'RE MAKING ME SICK. PLEASE STOP.

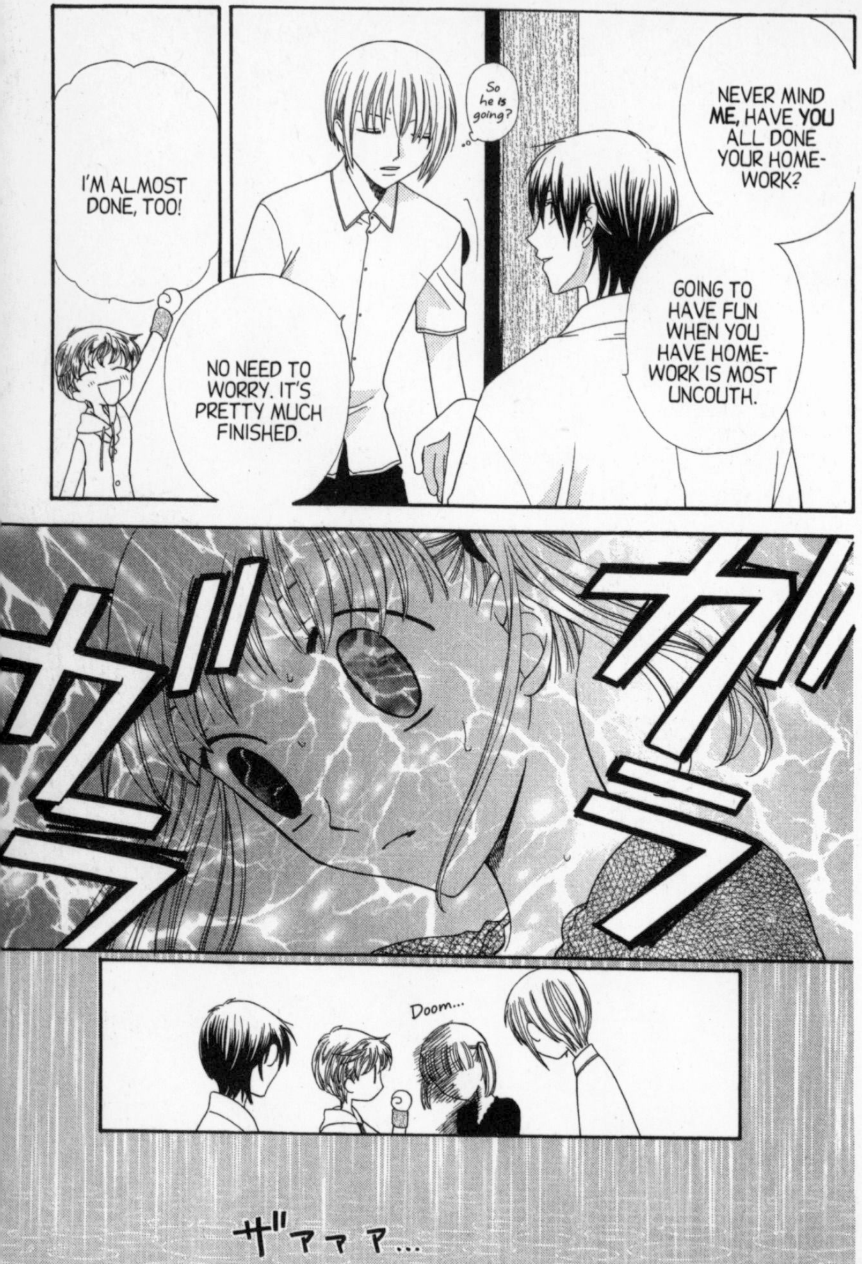
NEVER MIND ME, HAVE YOU ALL DONE YOUR HOME-WORK?
GOING TO HAVE FUN WHEN YOU HAVE HOME-WORK IS MOST UNCOUTH.
So he is going?
NO NEED TO WORRY. IT'S PRETTY MUCH FINISHED.
I'M ALMOST DONE, TOO!
Doom...
ザァァァ...

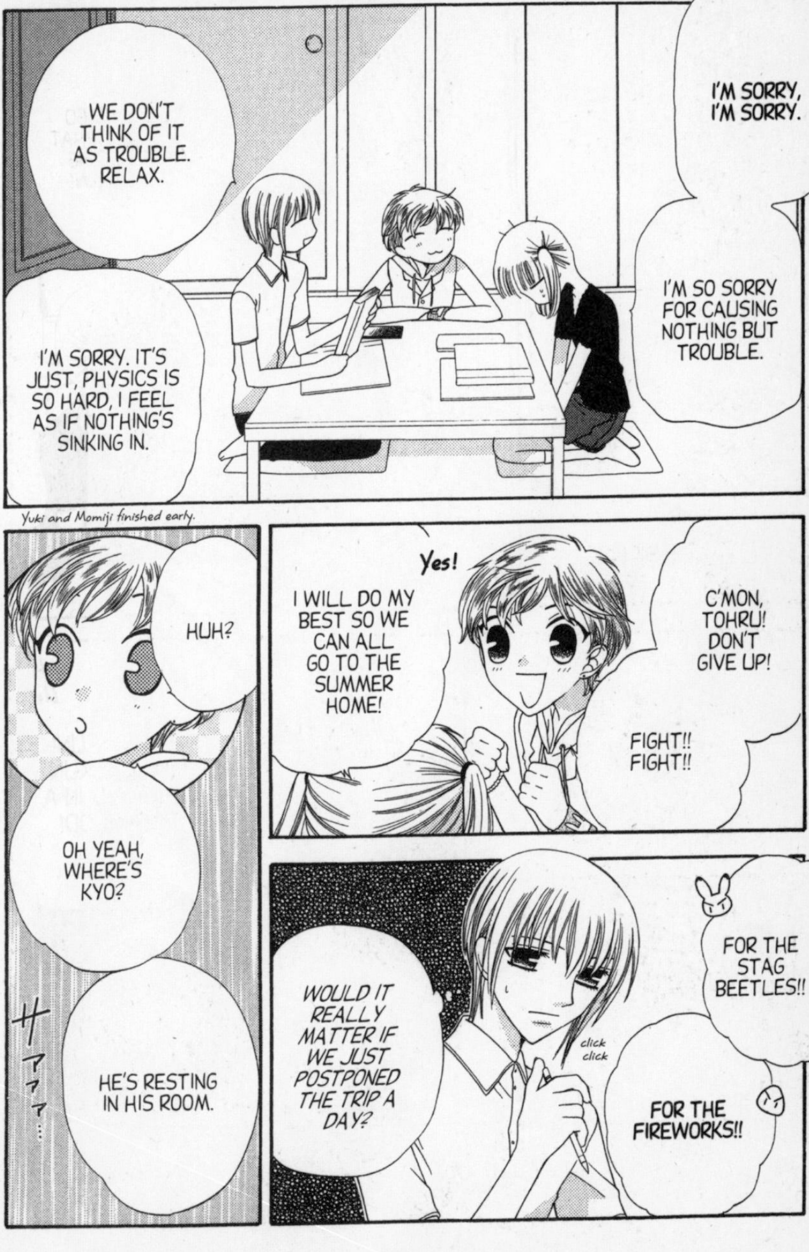

I'M SORRY, I'M SORRY.
I'M SO SORRY FOR CAUSING NOTHING BUT TROUBLE.
WE DON'T THINK OF IT AS TROUBLE. RELAX.
I'M SORRY. IT'S JUST, PHYSICS IS SO HARD, I FEEL AS IF NOTHING'S SINKING IN.
Yuki and Momiji finished early.
C'MON, TOHRU! DON'T GIVE UP!
FIGHT!! FIGHT!!
Yes!
I WILL DO MY BEST SO WE CAN ALL GO TO THE SUMMER HOME!
FOR THE STAG BEETLES!!
FOR THE FIREWORKS!!
click click
WOULD IT REALLY MATTER IF WE JUST POSTPONED THE TRIP A DAY?
HUH?
OH YEAH, WHERE'S KYO?
HE'S RESTING IN HIS ROOM.
サァァ…

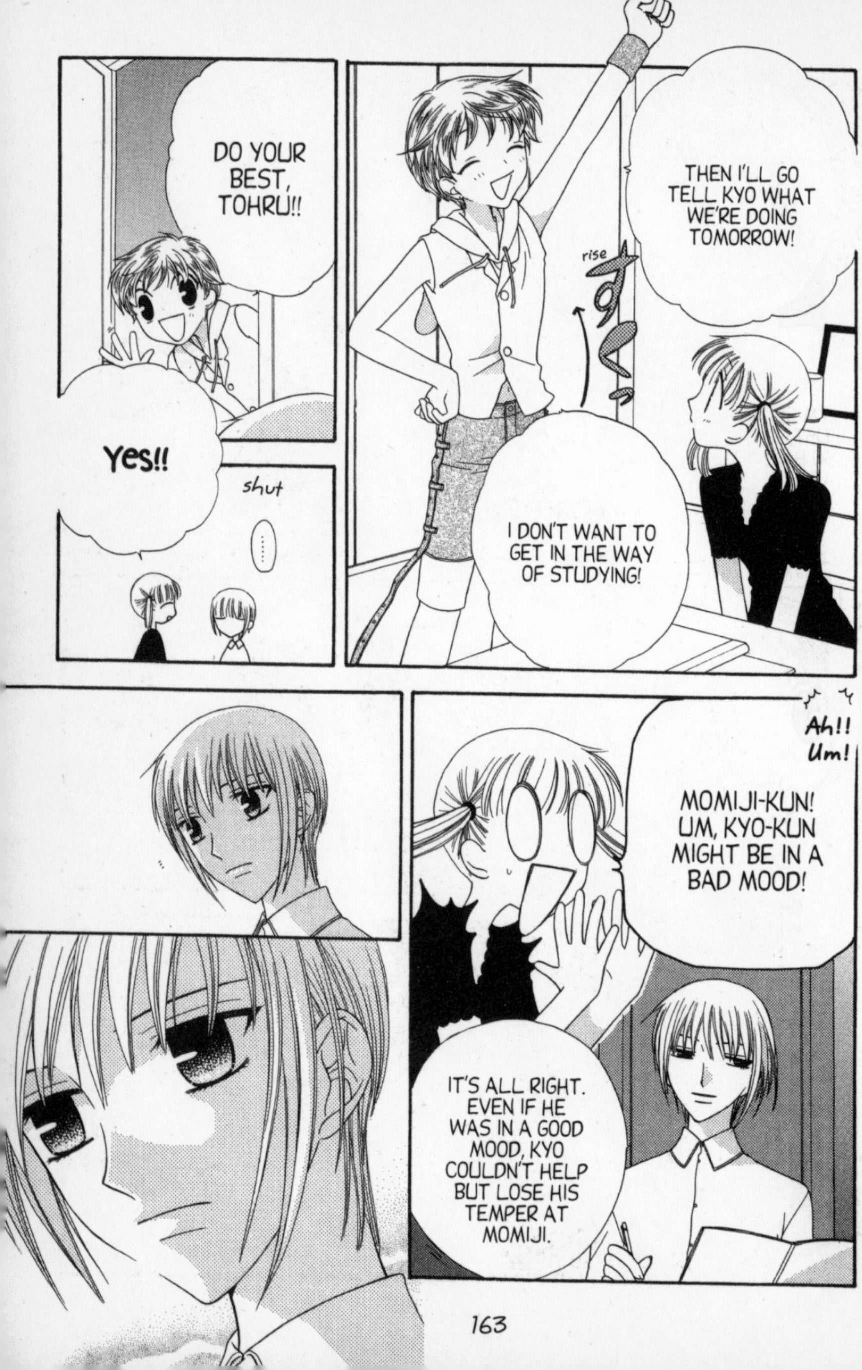
THEN I'LL GO TELL KYO WHAT WE'RE DOING TOMORROW!
rise
I DON'T WANT TO GET IN THE WAY OF STUDYING!
DO YOUR BEST, TOHRU!!
Yes!!
shut
......
Ah!! Um!
MOMIJI-KUN! UM, KYO-KUN MIGHT BE IN A BAD MOOD!
IT'S ALL RIGHT. EVEN IF HE WAS IN A GOOD MOOD, KYO COULDN'T HELP BUT LOSE HIS TEMPER AT MOMIJI.

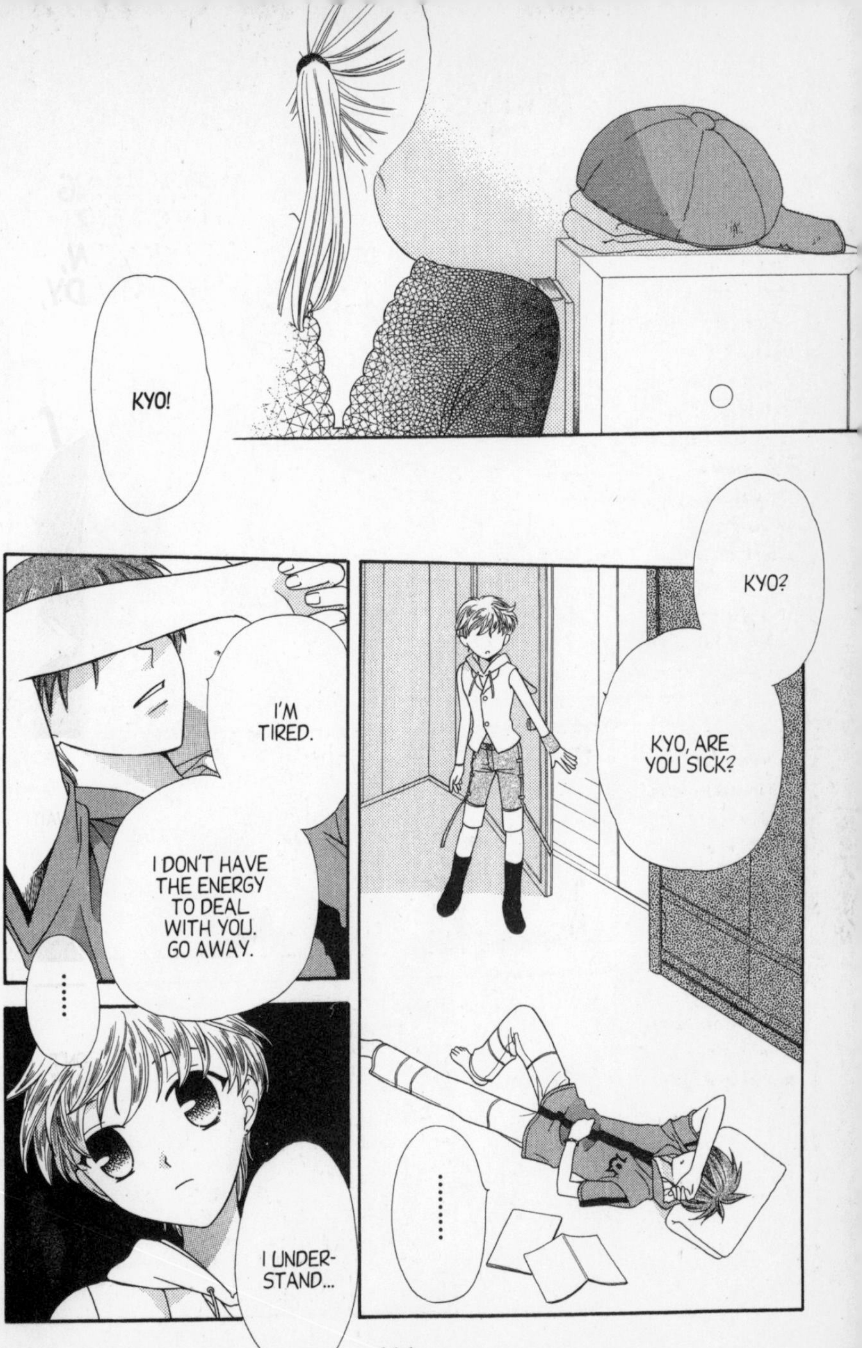
KYO!
KYO?
KYO, ARE YOU SICK?
....
I'M TIRED.
I DON'T HAVE THE ENERGY TO DEAL WITH YOU. GO AWAY.
......
I UNDER-STAND...

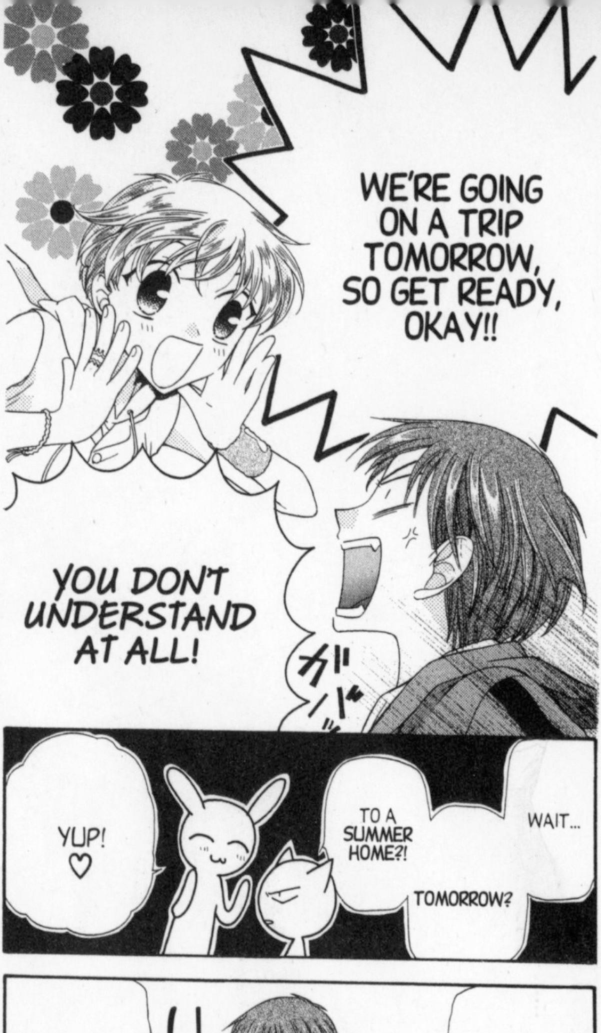
WE'RE GOING ON A TRIP TOMORROW, SO GET READY, OKAY!!
YOU DON'T UNDERSTAND AT ALL!
WAIT...
TOMORROW?
TO A SUMMER HOME?!
YUP! ♡
DON'T "YUP" ME!
THERE YOU GO, JUST MAKING UP PLANS WITHOUT ASKING ANYONE AGAIN!
UWAAAAAH!
KYO HIT ME!

Fruits Basket 9 Part 6

The "Rain Shelter of Terror" that starts on page 181 is something I drew for the **Fruits Basket Special Edition Magazine.** It was a wonderful publication that even had interviews with the anime voice actors! (By the way, they're not selling it anymore.) The drawings were the first I'd done in a year after my recovery, so you can see in them how happy I was to be able to draw. That's how I see them.

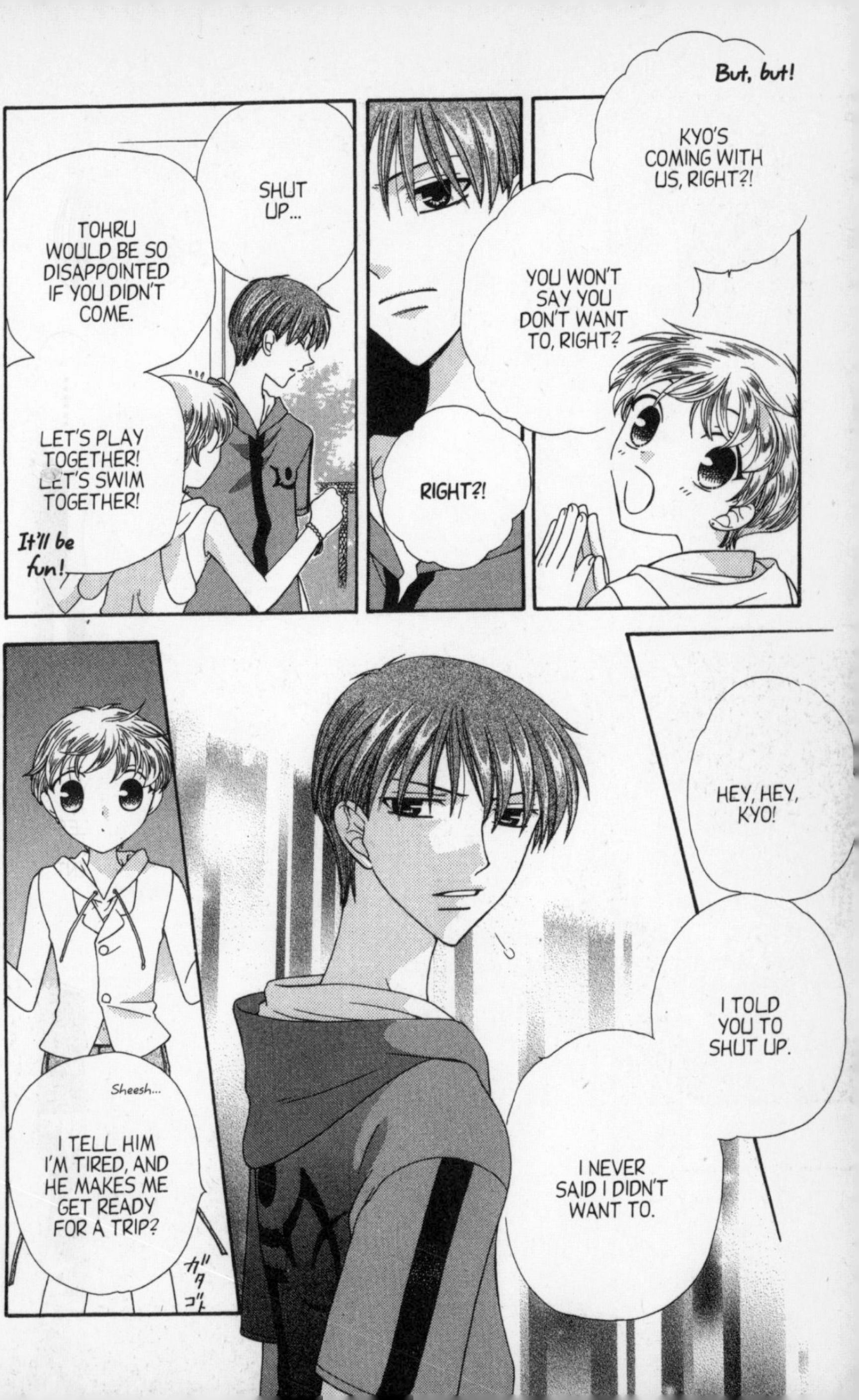
But, but!
KYO'S COMING WITH US, RIGHT?!
YOU WON'T SAY YOU DON'T WANT TO, RIGHT?
RIGHT?!
SHUT UP...
TOHRU WOULD BE SO DISAPPOINTED IF YOU DIDN'T COME.
LET'S PLAY TOGETHER! LET'S SWIM TOGETHER!
It'll be fun!
HEY, HEY, KYO!
I TOLD YOU TO SHUT UP.
I NEVER SAID I DIDN'T WANT TO.
Sheesh...
I TELL HIM I'M TIRED, AND HE MAKES ME GET READY FOR A TRIP?
ガタゴト

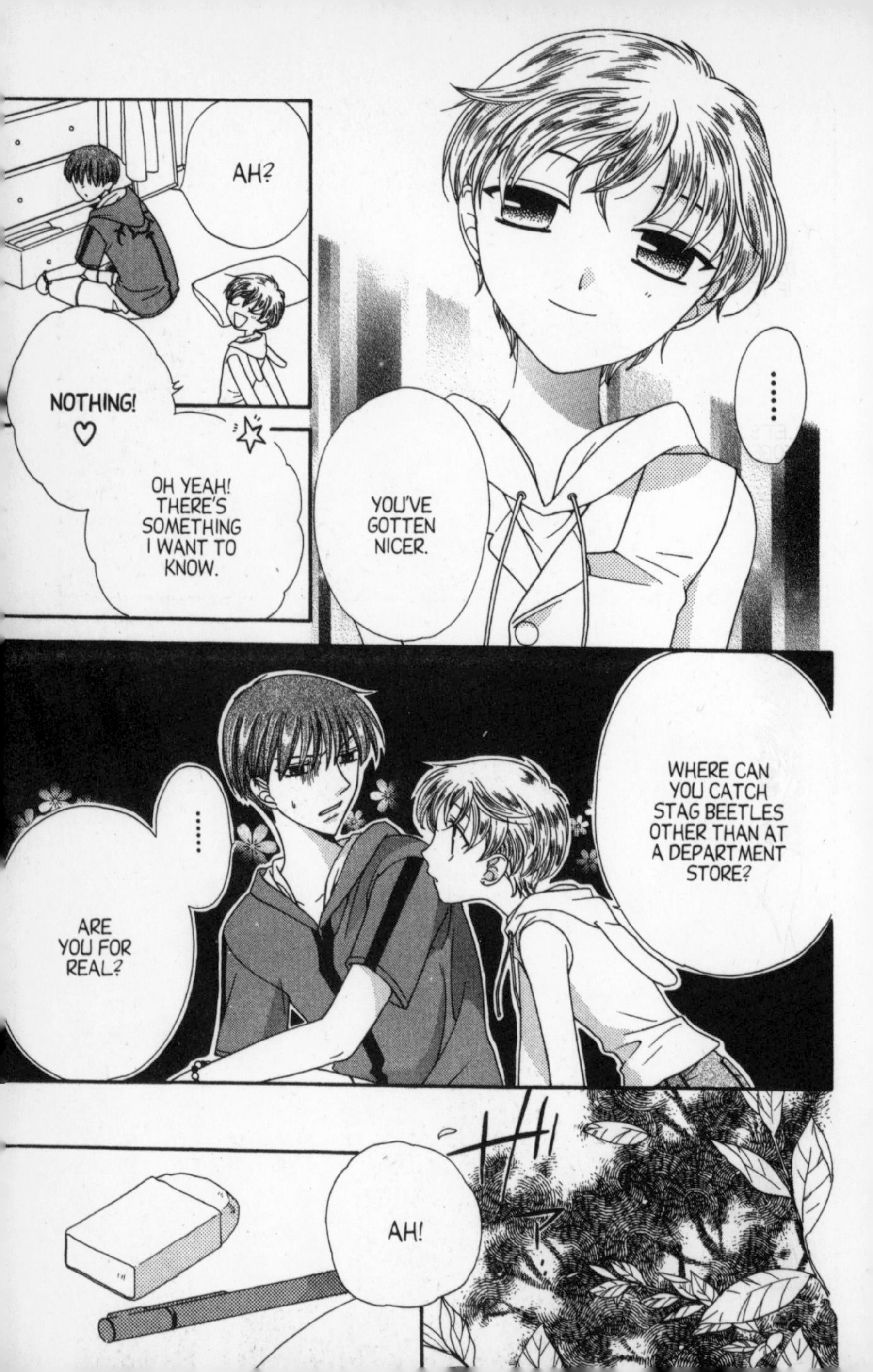
......
YOU'VE GOTTEN NICER.
AH?
NOTHING! ♡
OH YEAH! THERE'S SOMETHING I WANT TO KNOW.
WHERE CAN YOU CATCH STAG BEETLES OTHER THAN AT A DEPARTMENT STORE?
......
ARE YOU FOR REAL?
AH!

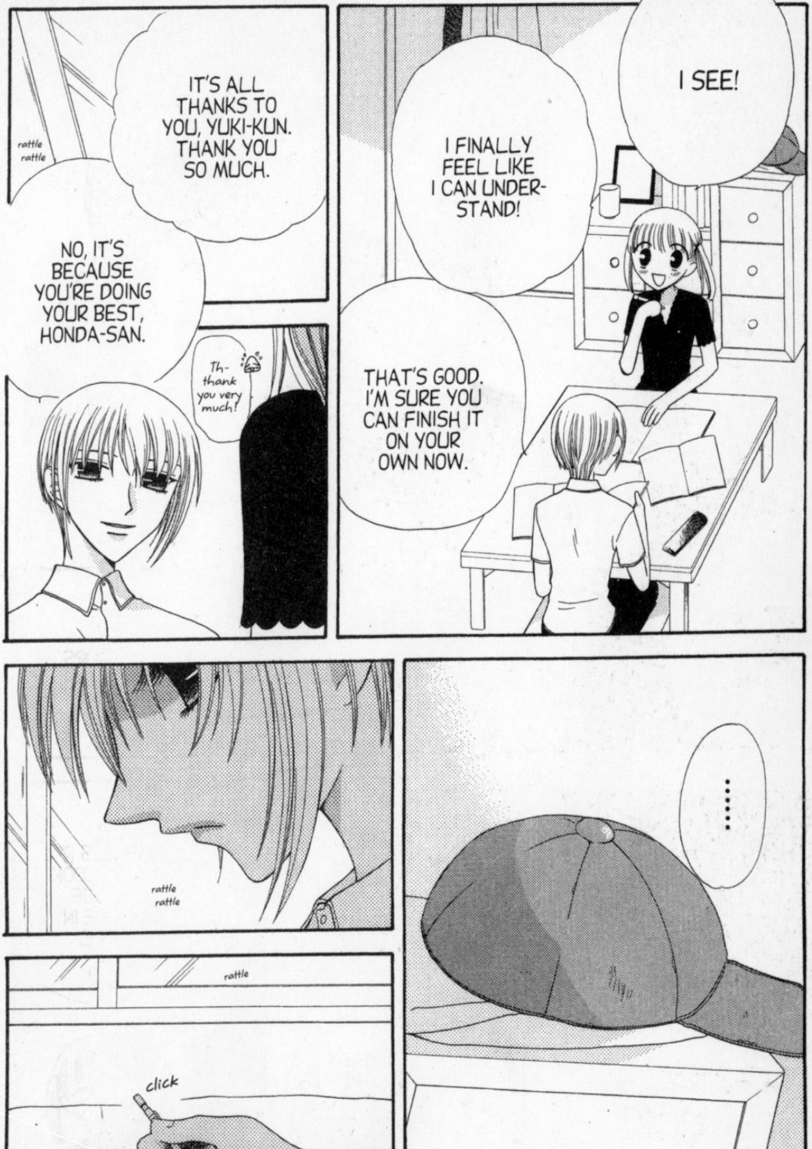
I SEE!
I FINALLY FEEL LIKE I CAN UNDER-STAND!
THAT'S GOOD. I'M SURE YOU CAN FINISH IT ON YOUR OWN NOW.
rattle rattle
IT'S ALL THANKS TO YOU, YUKI-KUN. THANK YOU SO MUCH.
NO, IT'S BECAUSE YOU'RE DOING YOUR BEST, HONDA-SAN.
Th-thank you very much!
......
rattle rattle
rattle
click

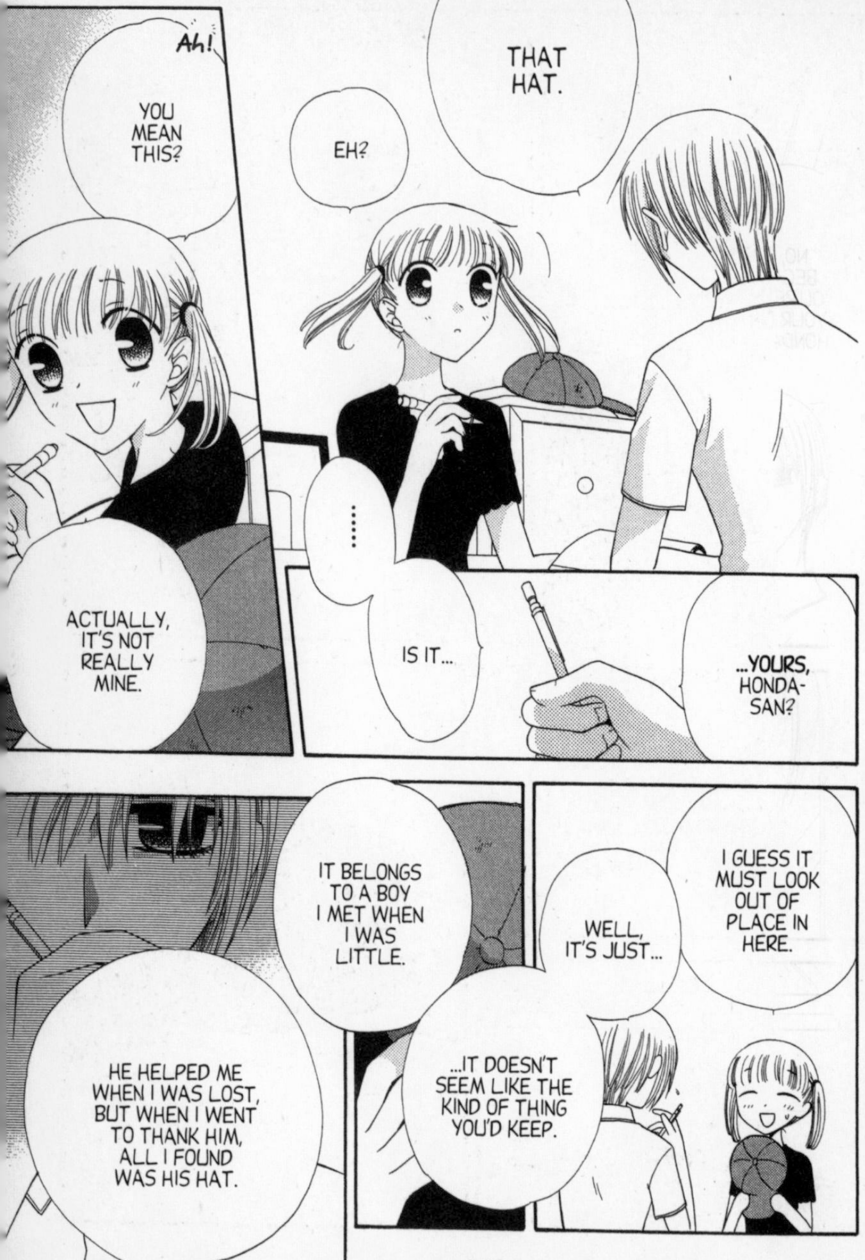
THAT HAT.
EH?
......
IS IT...
...**YOURS,** HONDA-SAN?
Ah!
YOU MEAN THIS?
ACTUALLY, IT'S NOT REALLY MINE.
I GUESS IT MUST LOOK OUT OF PLACE IN HERE.
WELL, IT'S JUST...
...IT DOESN'T SEEM LIKE THE KIND OF THING YOU'D KEEP.
IT BELONGS TO A BOY I MET WHEN I WAS LITTLE.
HE HELPED ME WHEN I WAS LOST, BUT WHEN I WENT TO THANK HIM, ALL I FOUND WAS HIS HAT.

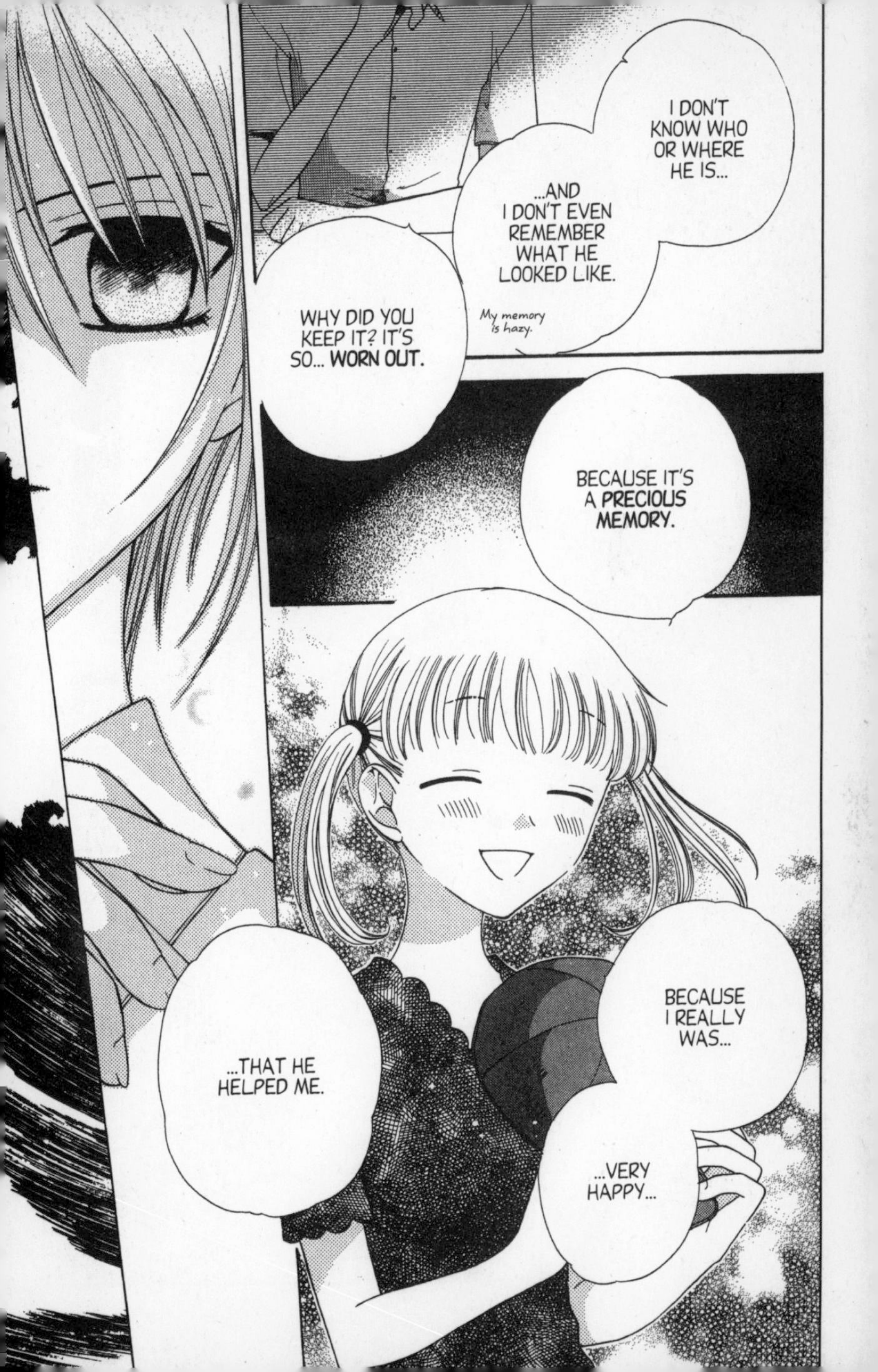
I DON'T KNOW WHO OR WHERE HE IS...
...AND I DON'T EVEN REMEMBER WHAT HE LOOKED LIKE.
My memory is hazy.
WHY DID YOU KEEP IT? IT'S SO... **WORN OUT**.
BECAUSE IT'S A **PRECIOUS MEMORY**.
BECAUSE I REALLY WAS...
...VERY HAPPY...
...THAT HE HELPED ME.

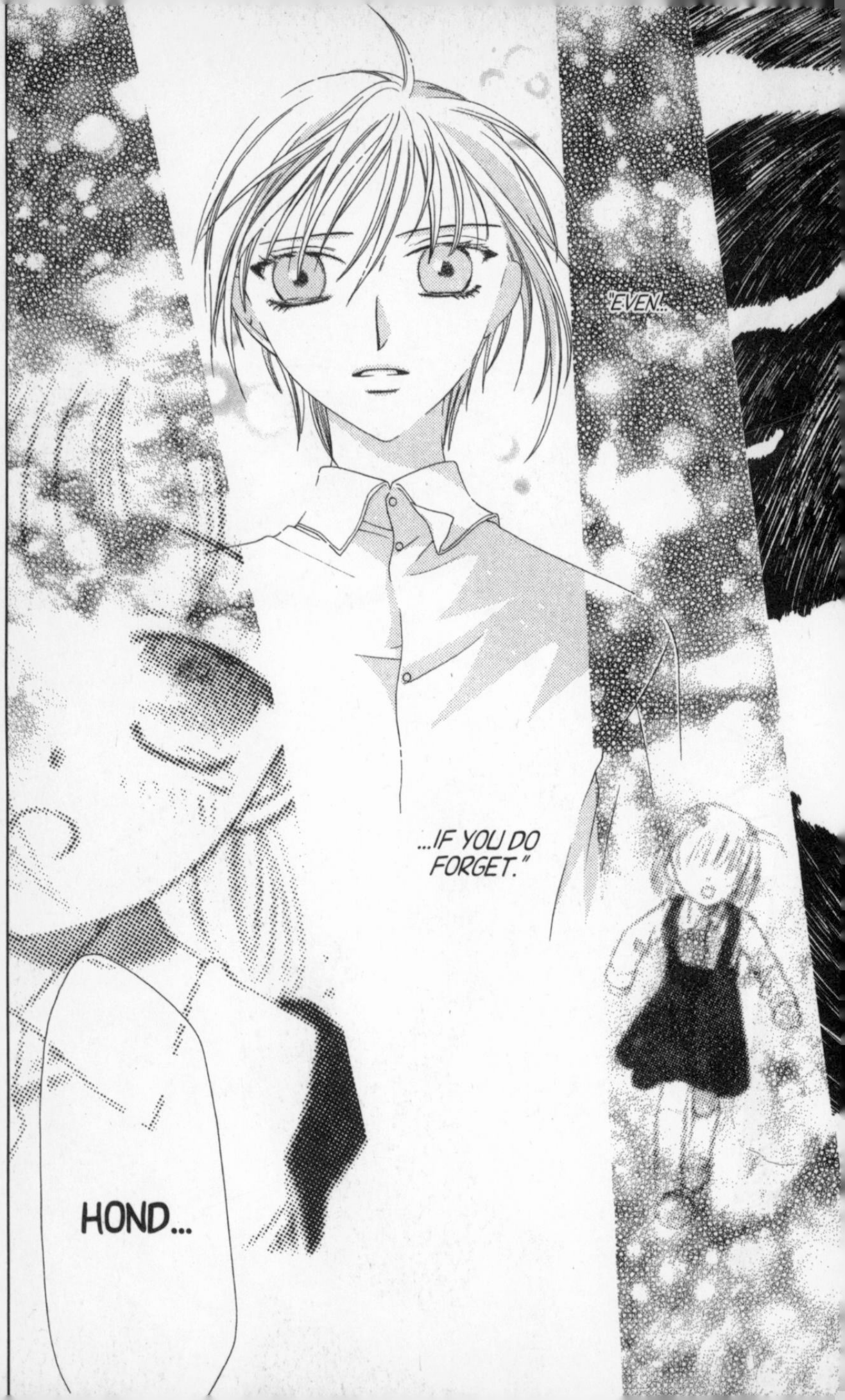
"EVEN...
...IF YOU DO FORGET."
HOND...

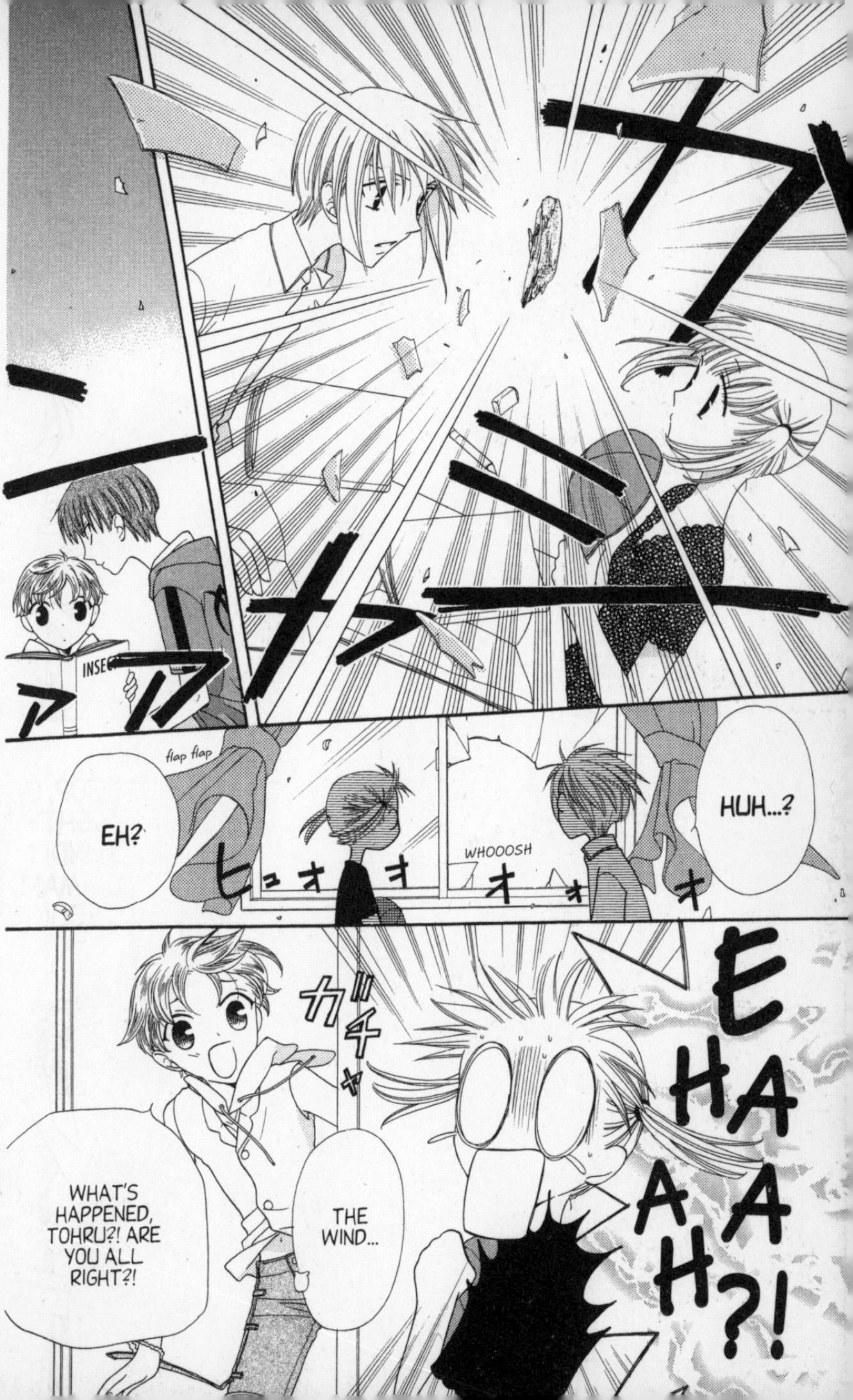
HUH...?
WHOOOSH
ヒュオオオオオ
flap flap
EH?
EHHAAAAH?!
ガチャ
THE WIND...
WHAT'S HAPPENED, TOHRU?! ARE YOU ALL RIGHT?!

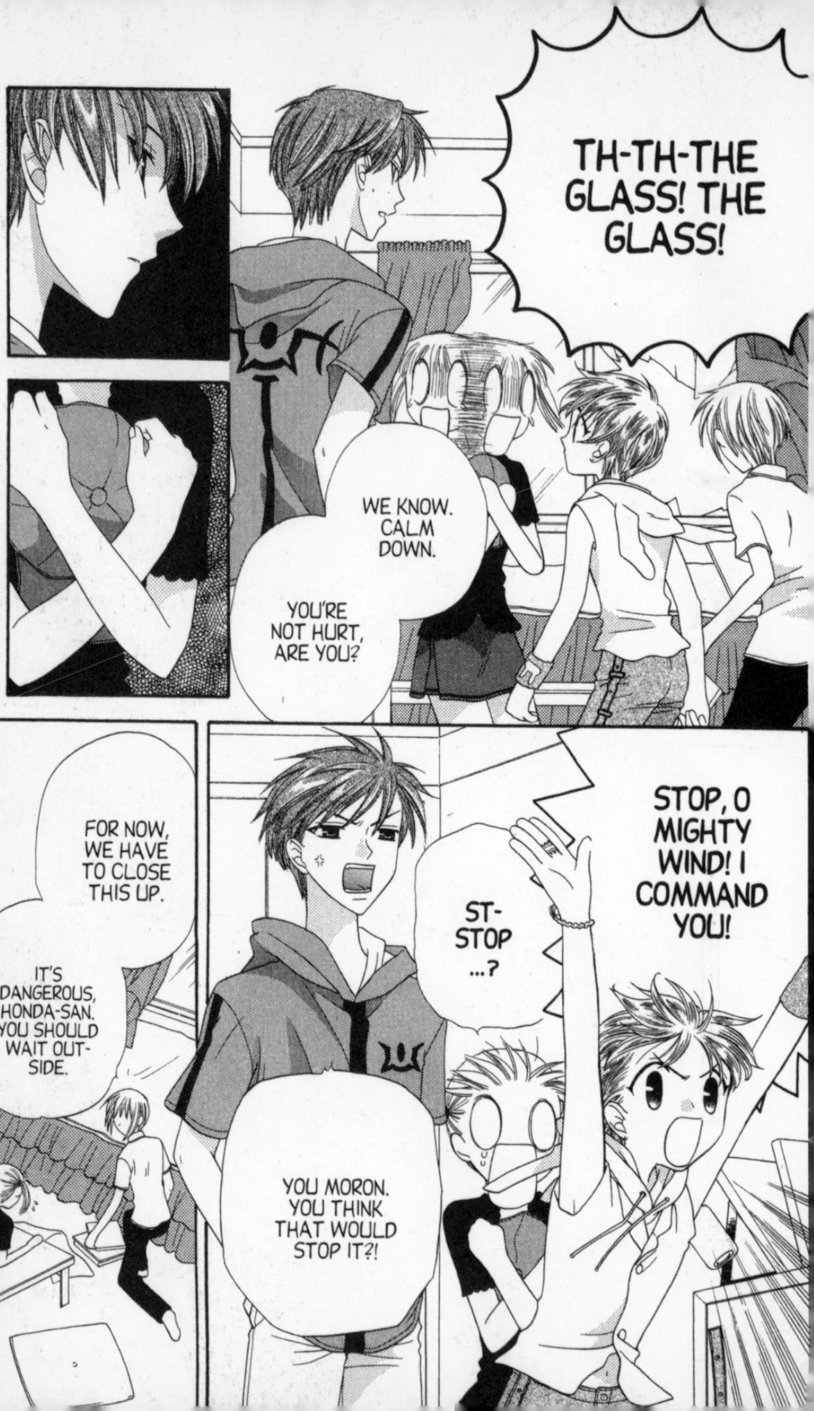
TH-TH-THE GLASS! THE GLASS!
WE KNOW. CALM DOWN.
YOU'RE NOT HURT, ARE YOU?
STOP, O MIGHTY WIND! I COMMAND YOU!
ST-STOP ...?
YOU MORON. YOU THINK THAT WOULD STOP IT?!
FOR NOW, WE HAVE TO CLOSE THIS UP.
IT'S DANGEROUS, HONDA-SAN. YOU SHOULD WAIT OUT-SIDE.
I-I-I'm all right! I'll help!

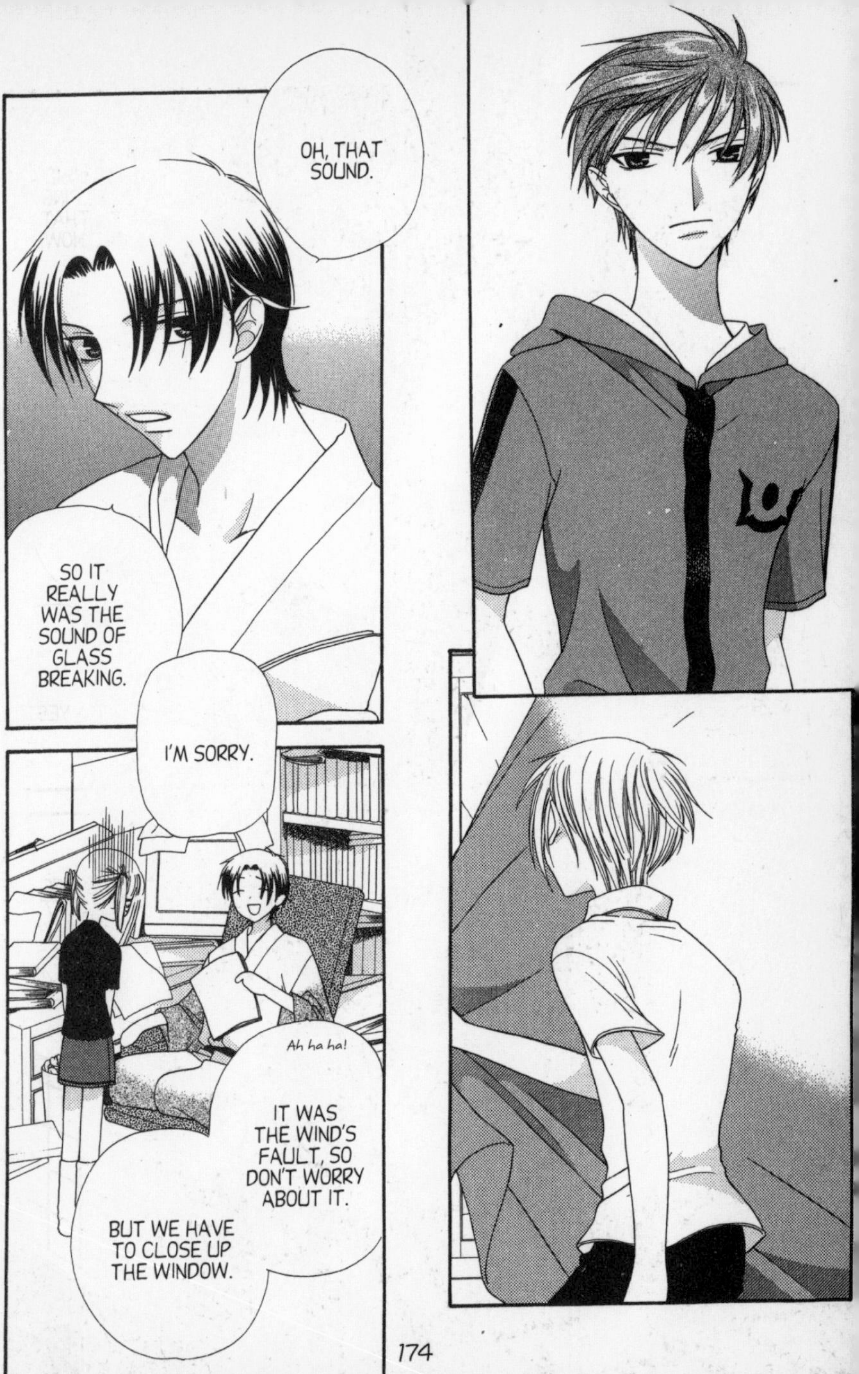
OH, THAT SOUND.
SO IT REALLY WAS THE SOUND OF GLASS BREAKING.
I'M SORRY.
Ah ha ha!
IT WAS THE WIND'S FAULT, SO DON'T WORRY ABOUT IT.
BUT WE HAVE TO CLOSE UP THE WINDOW.

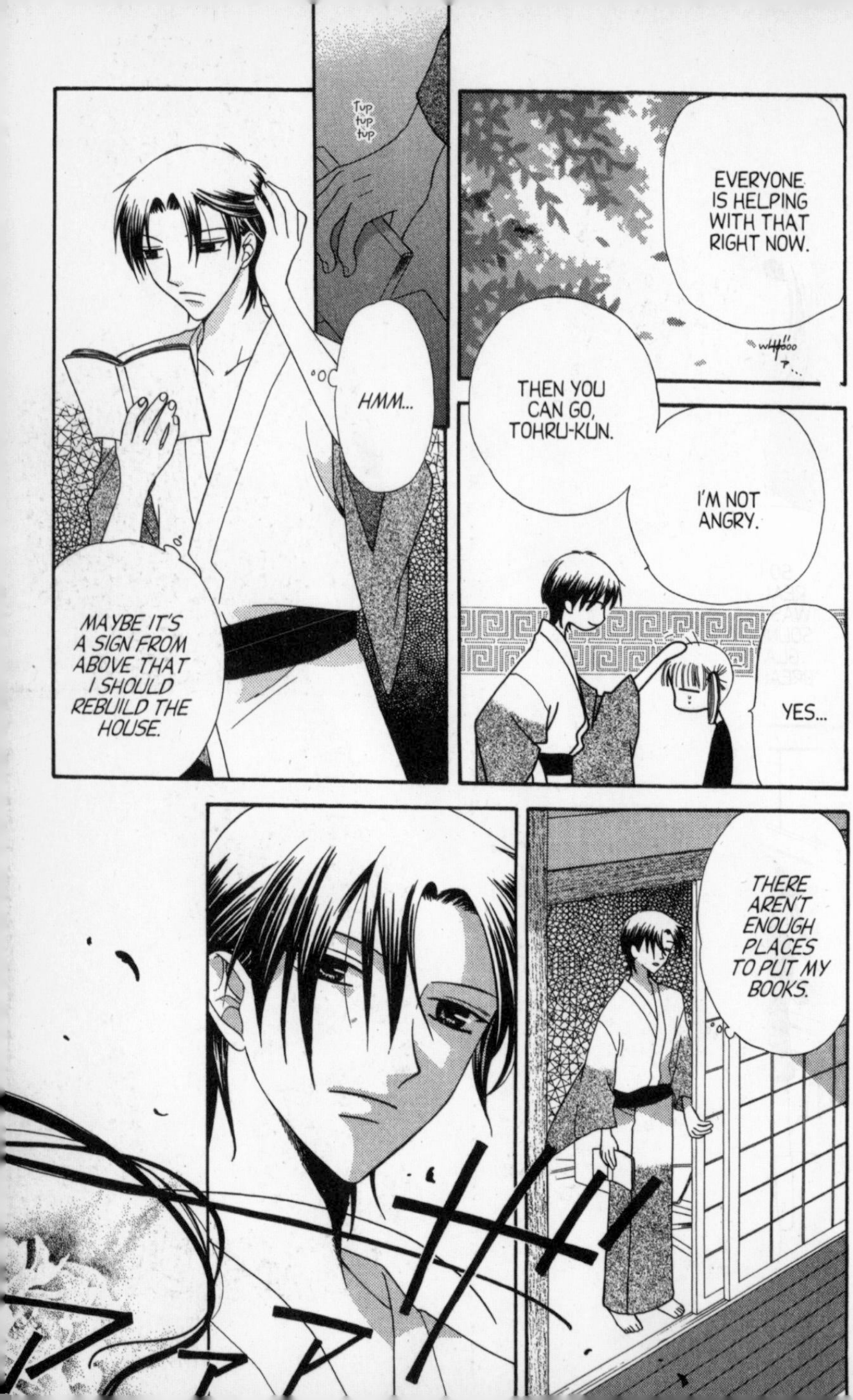
EVERYONE IS HELPING WITH THAT RIGHT NOW.
THEN YOU CAN GO, TOHRU-KUN.
I'M NOT ANGRY.
YES...
Tup tup tup
HMM...
MAYBE IT'S A SIGN FROM ABOVE THAT I SHOULD REBUILD THE HOUSE.
THERE AREN'T ENOUGH PLACES TO PUT MY BOOKS.

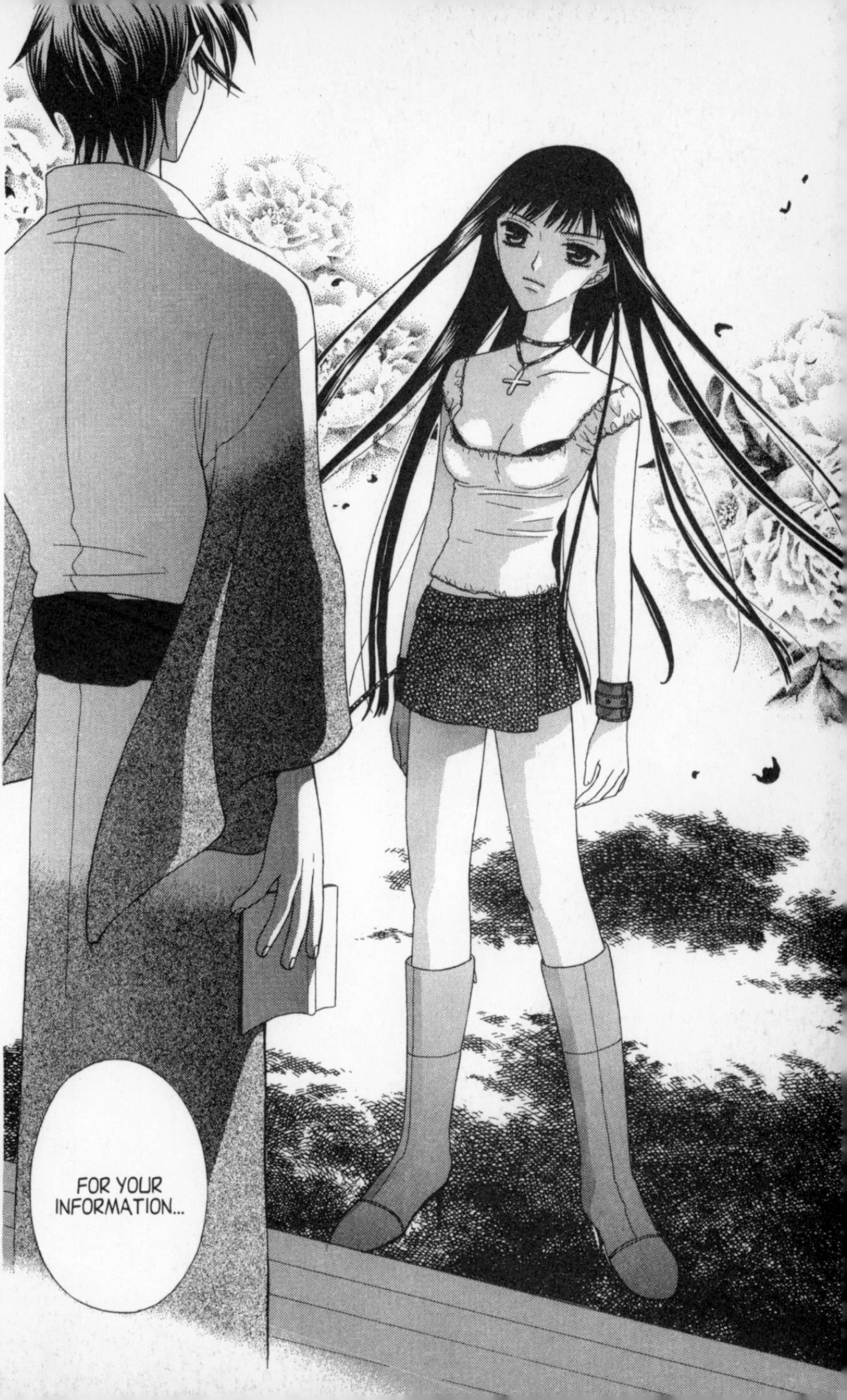
FOR YOUR INFORMATION...

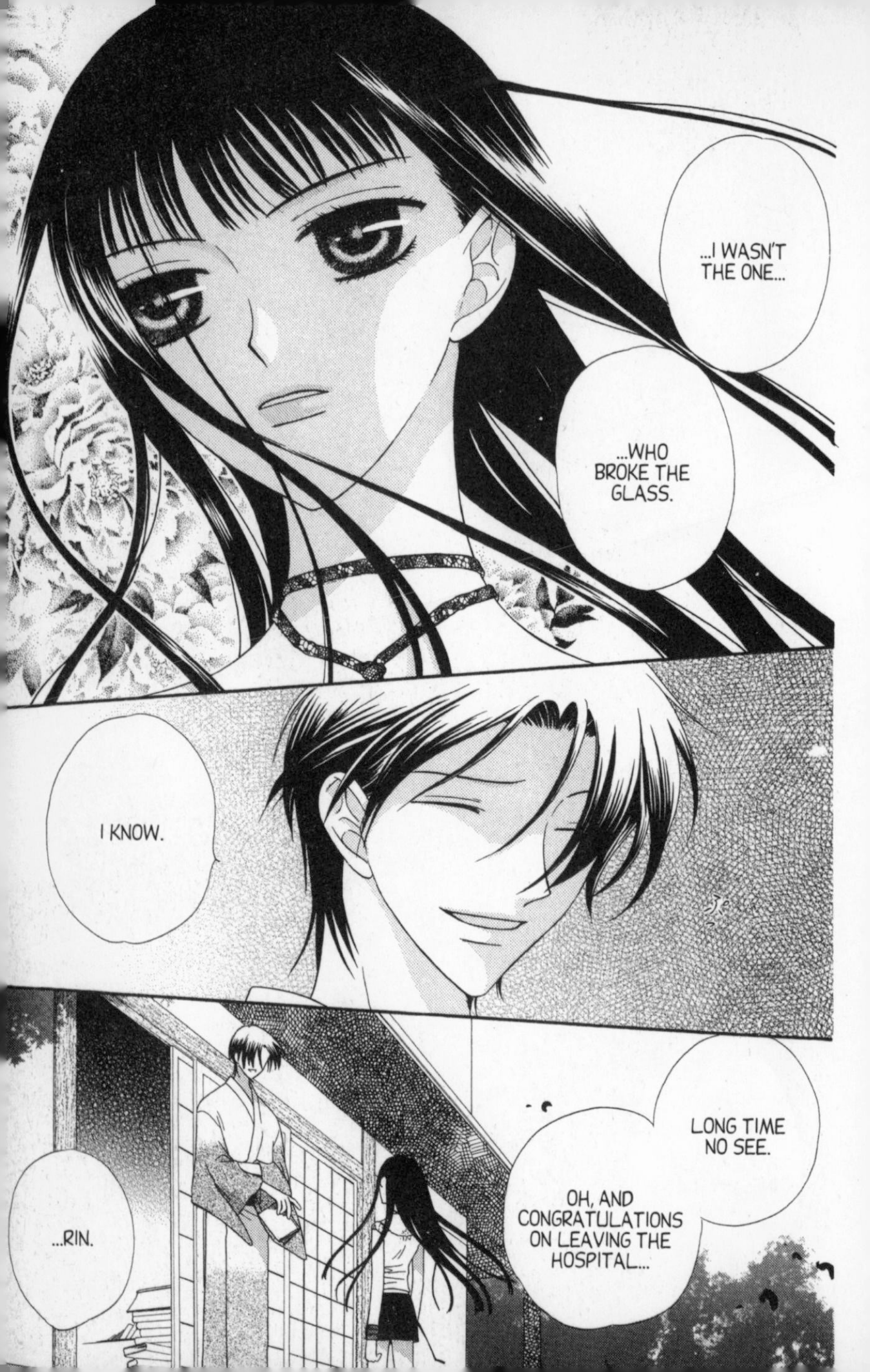
...I WASN'T THE ONE...
...WHO BROKE THE GLASS.
I KNOW.
LONG TIME NO SEE.
OH, AND CONGRATULATIONS ON LEAVING THE HOSPITAL...
...RIN.

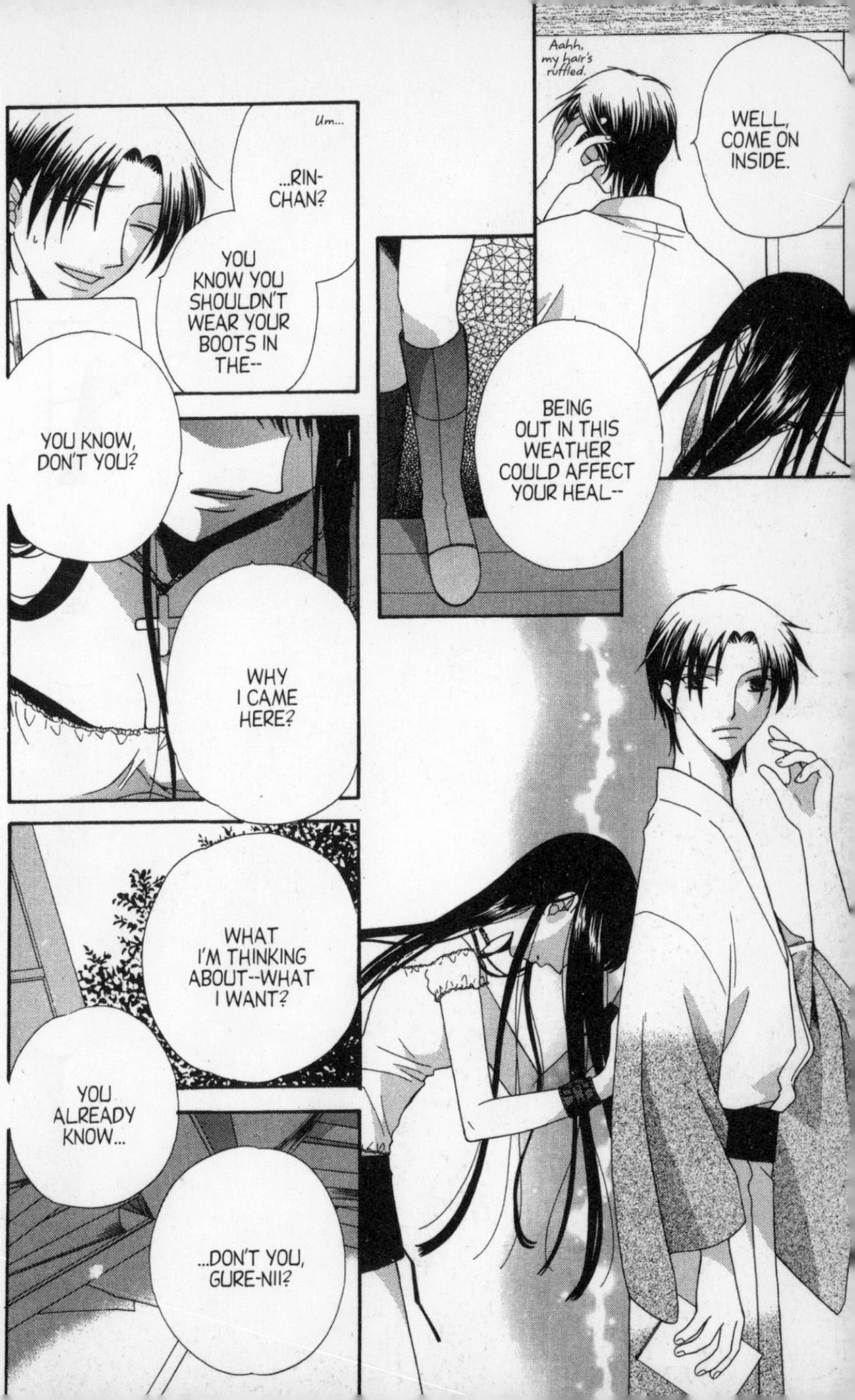
Aahh, my hair's ruffled.
WELL, COME ON INSIDE.
BEING OUT IN THIS WEATHER COULD AFFECT YOUR HEAL--
Um...
...RIN-CHAN?
YOU KNOW YOU SHOULDN'T WEAR YOUR BOOTS IN THE--
YOU KNOW, DON'T YOU?
WHY I CAME HERE?
WHAT I'M THINKING ABOUT--WHAT I WANT?
YOU ALREADY KNOW...
...DON'T YOU, GURE-NII?

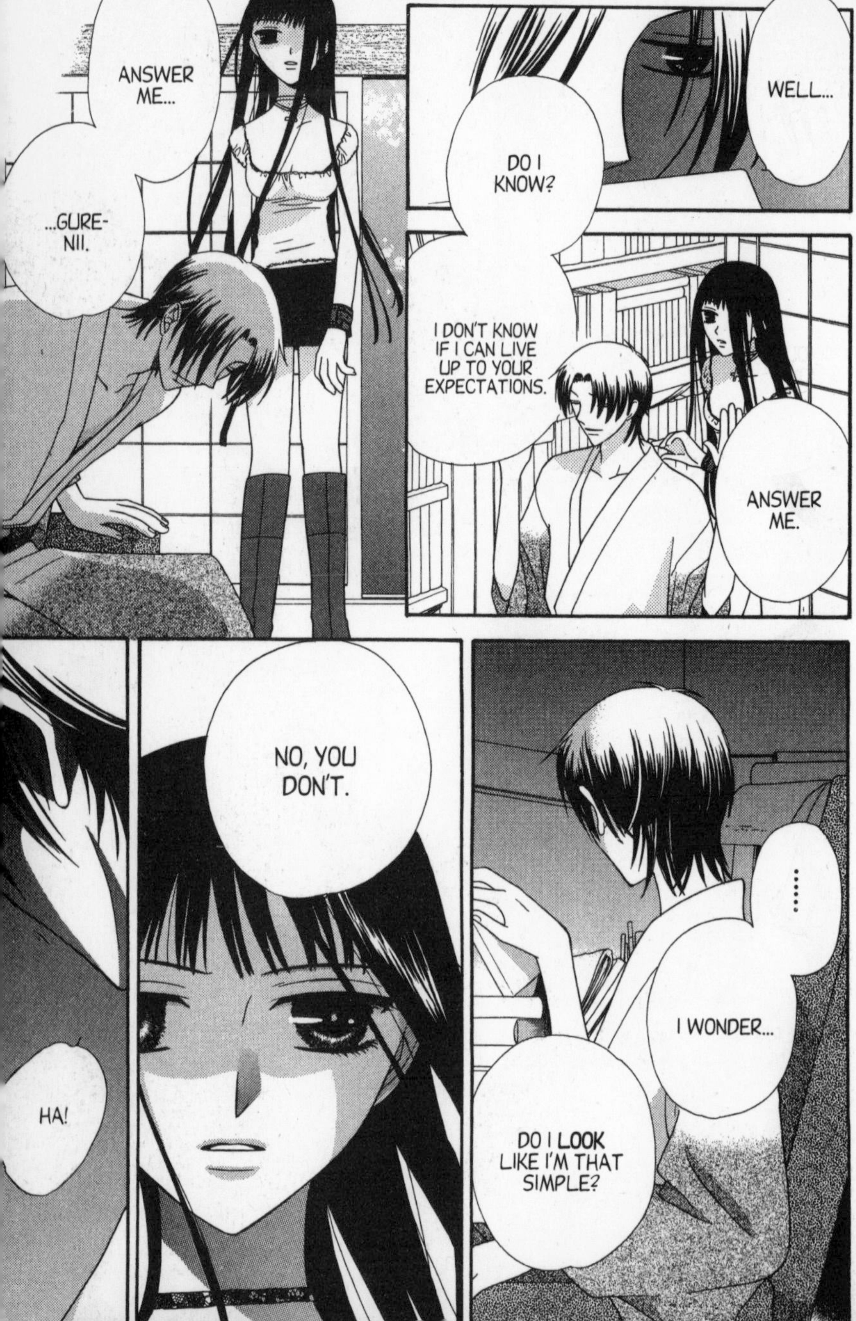
WELL...
DO I KNOW?
I DON'T KNOW IF I CAN LIVE UP TO YOUR EXPECTATIONS.
ANSWER ME.
ANSWER ME...
...GURE-NII.
......
I WONDER...
DO I LOOK LIKE I'M THAT SIMPLE?
NO, YOU DON'T.
HA!

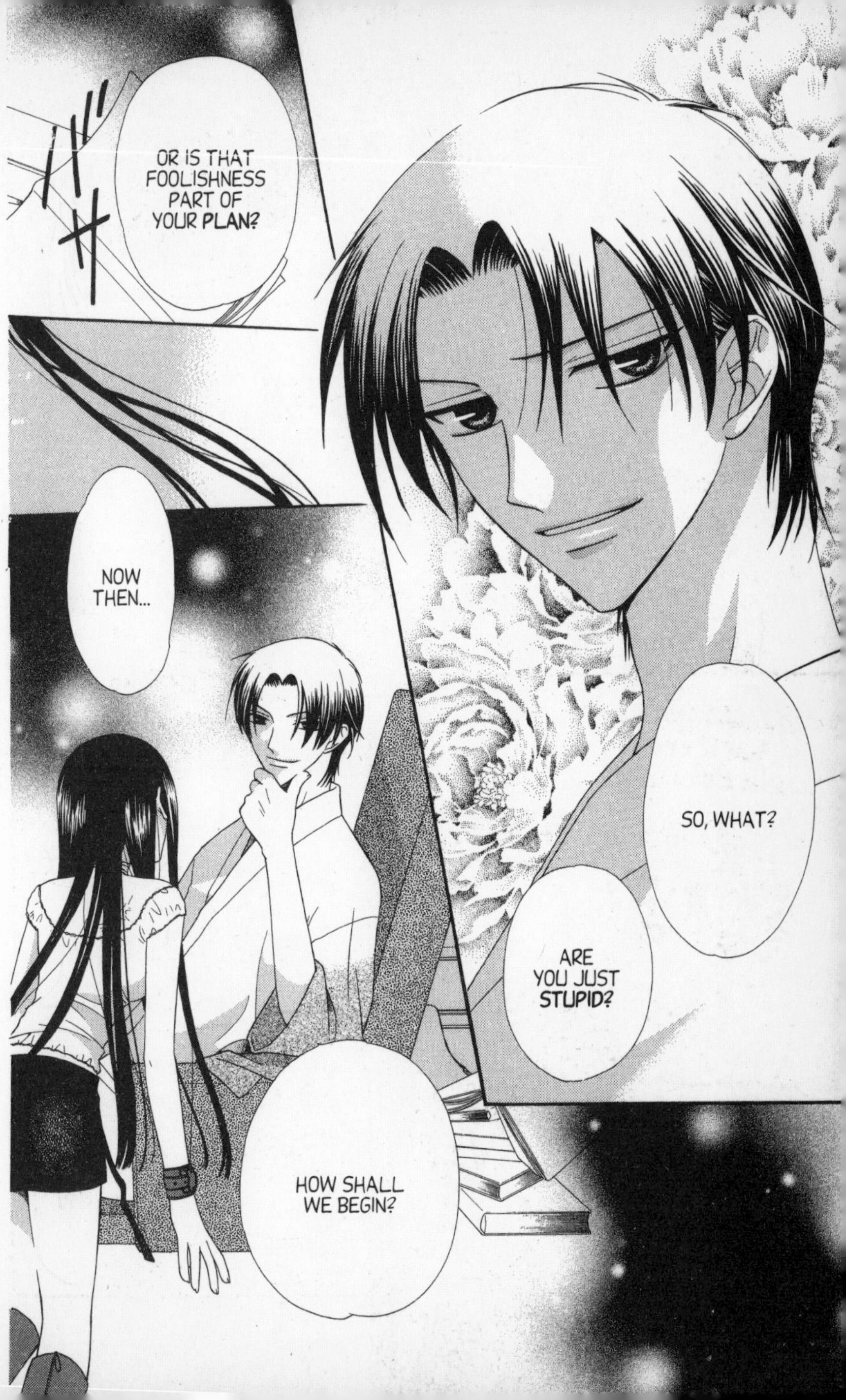
SO, WHAT?
ARE YOU JUST STUPID?
OR IS THAT FOOLISHNESS PART OF YOUR PLAN?
NOW THEN...
HOW SHALL WE BEGIN?

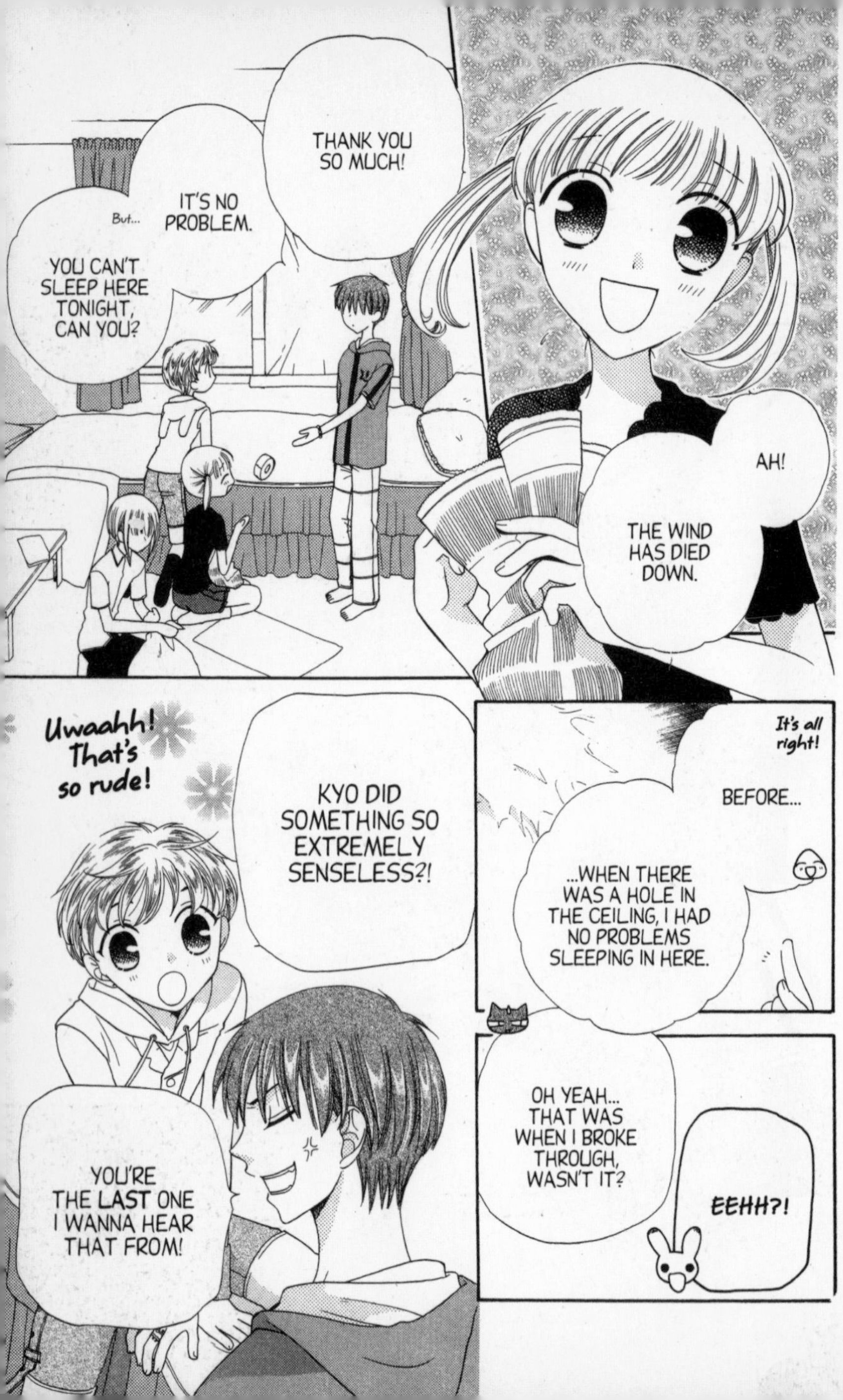
AH!
THE WIND HAS DIED DOWN.
THANK YOU SO MUCH!
IT'S NO PROBLEM.
But...
YOU CAN'T SLEEP HERE TONIGHT, CAN YOU?
It's all right!
BEFORE...
...WHEN THERE WAS A HOLE IN THE CEILING, I HAD NO PROBLEMS SLEEPING IN HERE.
OH YEAH... THAT WAS WHEN I BROKE THROUGH, WASN'T IT?
EEHH?!
Uwaahh! That's so rude!
KYO DID SOMETHING SO EXTREMELY SENSELESS?!
YOU'RE THE LAST ONE I WANNA HEAR THAT FROM!

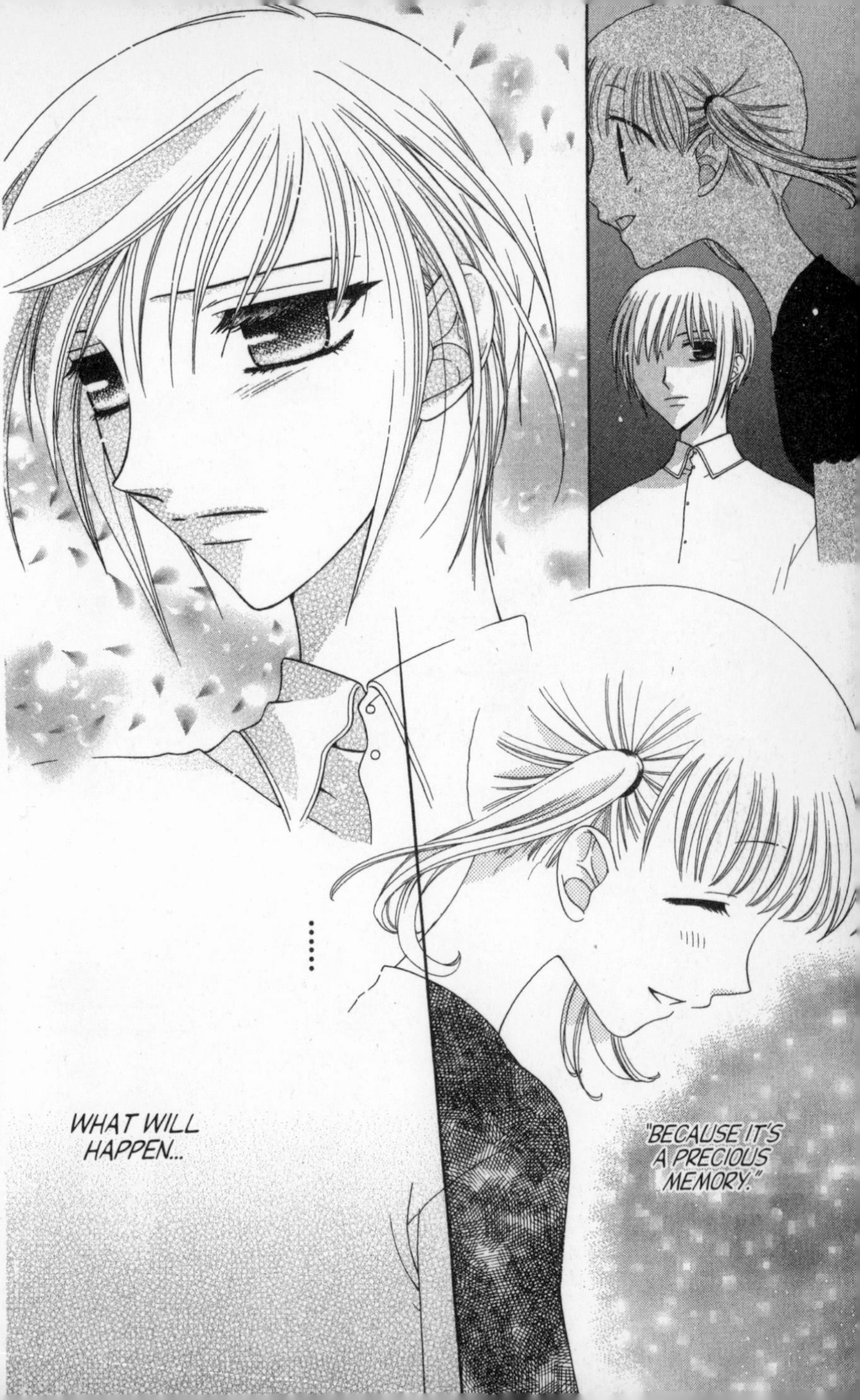
"BECAUSE IT'S A PRECIOUS MEMORY."
......
WHAT WILL HAPPEN...

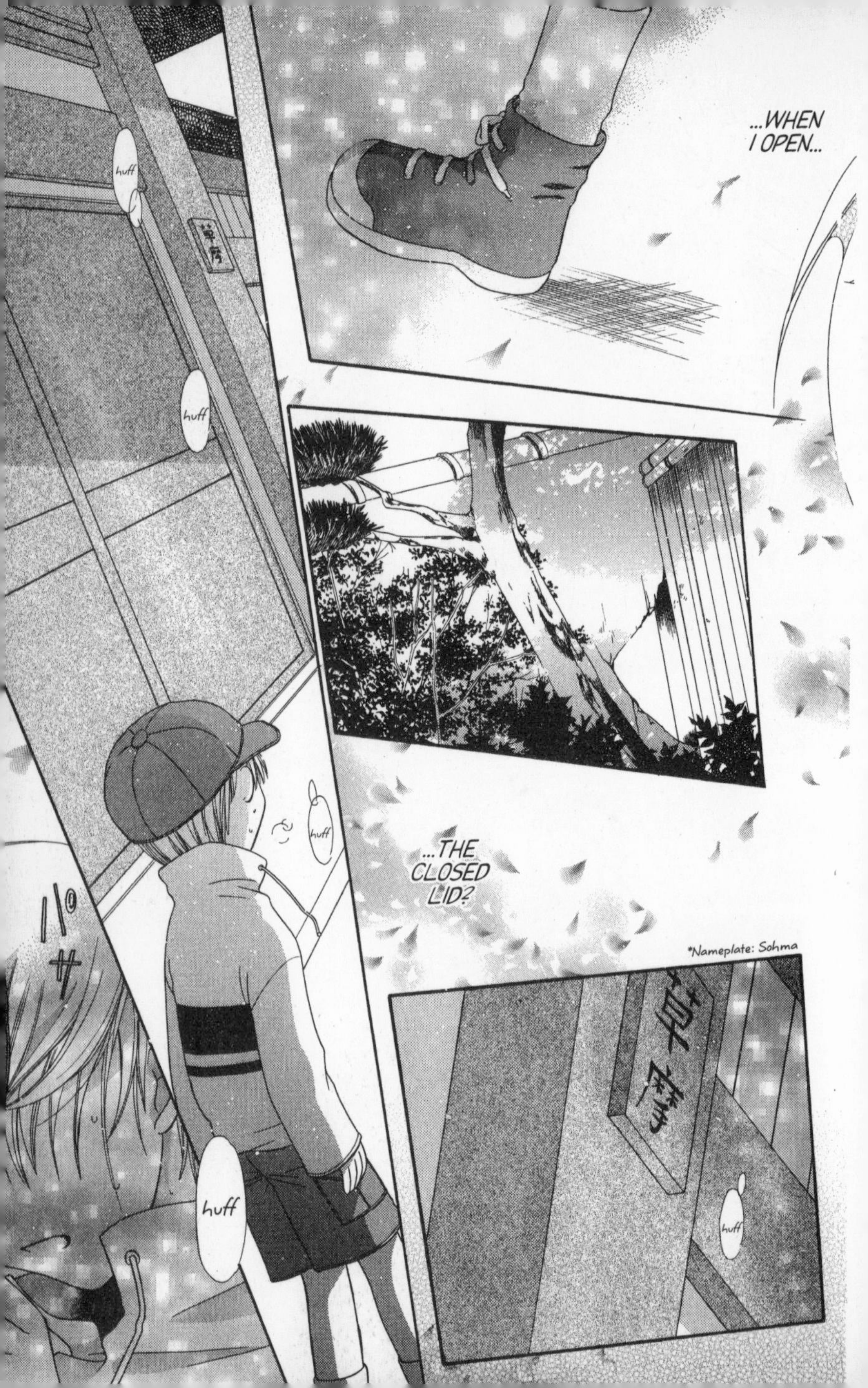
...WHEN I OPEN...
...THE CLOSED LID?
*Nameplate: Sohma
草摩
huff
huff
huff
草摩
huff
ハッ
huff

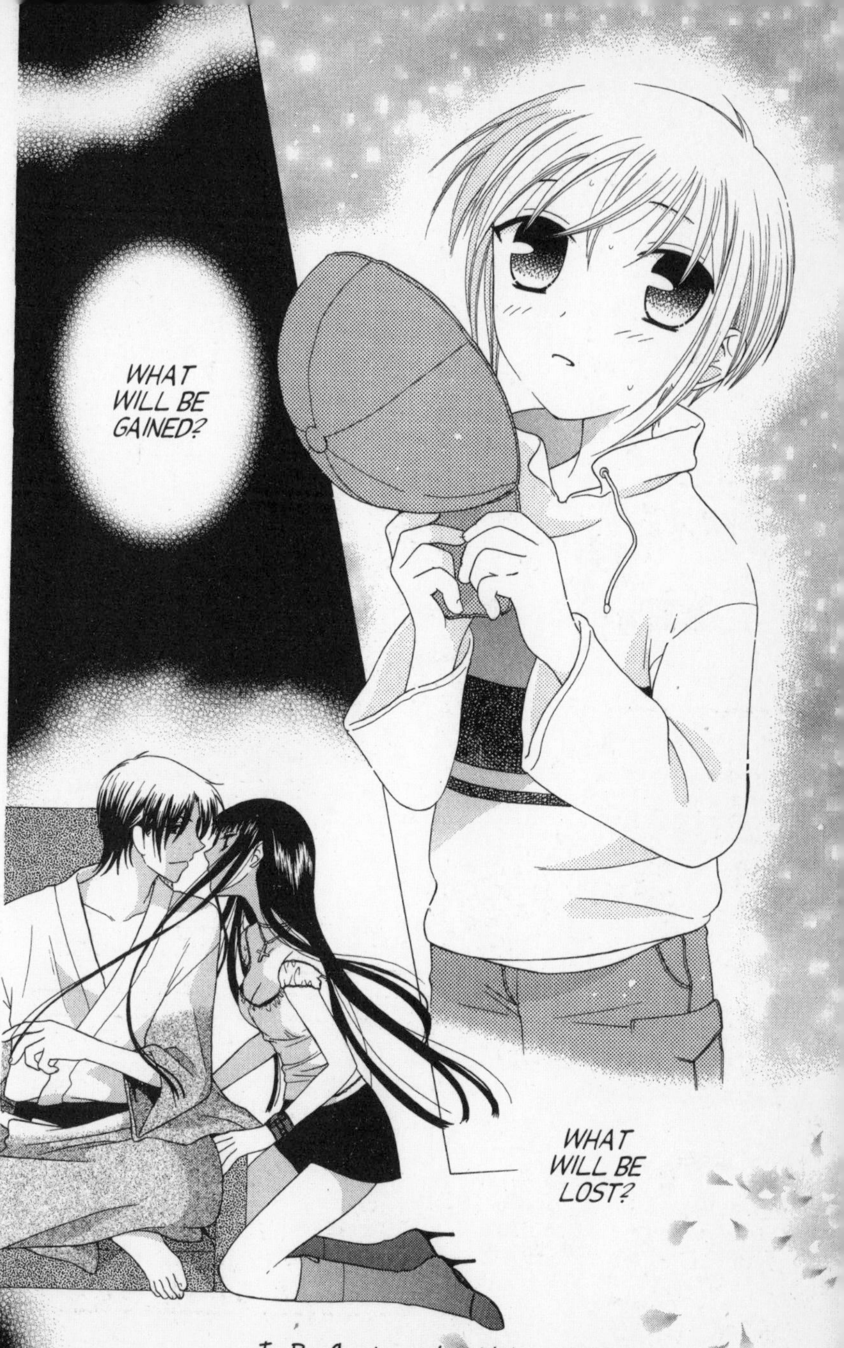
WHAT WILL BE GAINED?
WHAT WILL BE LOST?

To Be Continued in Volume 10...

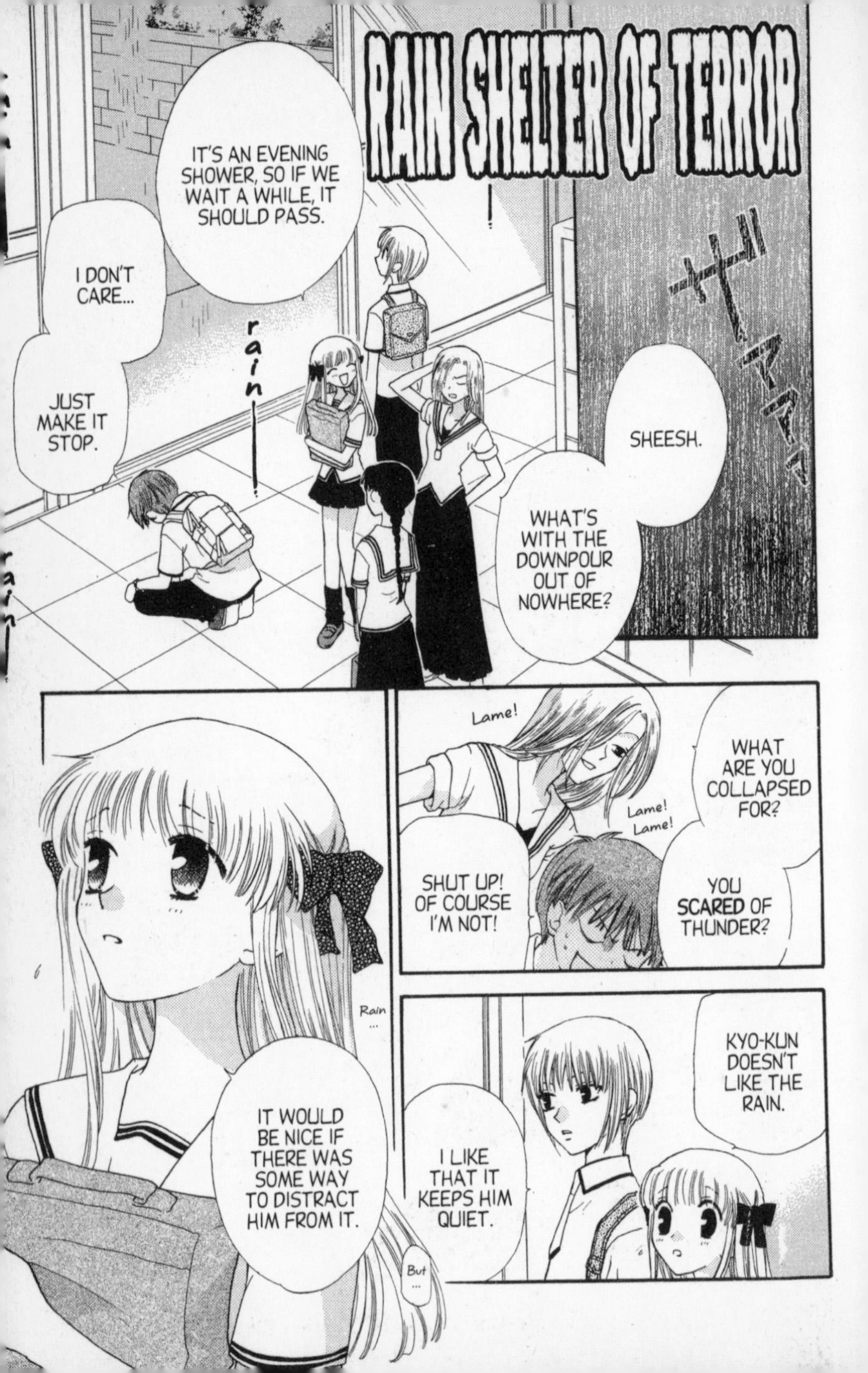
RAIN SHELTER OF TERROR
!
SHEESH.
WHAT'S WITH THE DOWNPOUR OUT OF NOWHERE?
IT'S AN EVENING SHOWER, SO IF WE WAIT A WHILE, IT SHOULD PASS.
I DON'T CARE...
JUST MAKE IT STOP.
rain
rain
WHAT ARE YOU COLLAPSED FOR?
YOU SCARED OF THUNDER?
Lame!
Lame! Lame!
SHUT UP! OF COURSE I'M NOT!
KYO-KUN DOESN'T LIKE THE RAIN.
I LIKE THAT IT KEEPS HIM QUIET.
Rain...
IT WOULD BE NICE IF THERE WAS SOME WAY TO DISTRACT HIM FROM IT.
But...

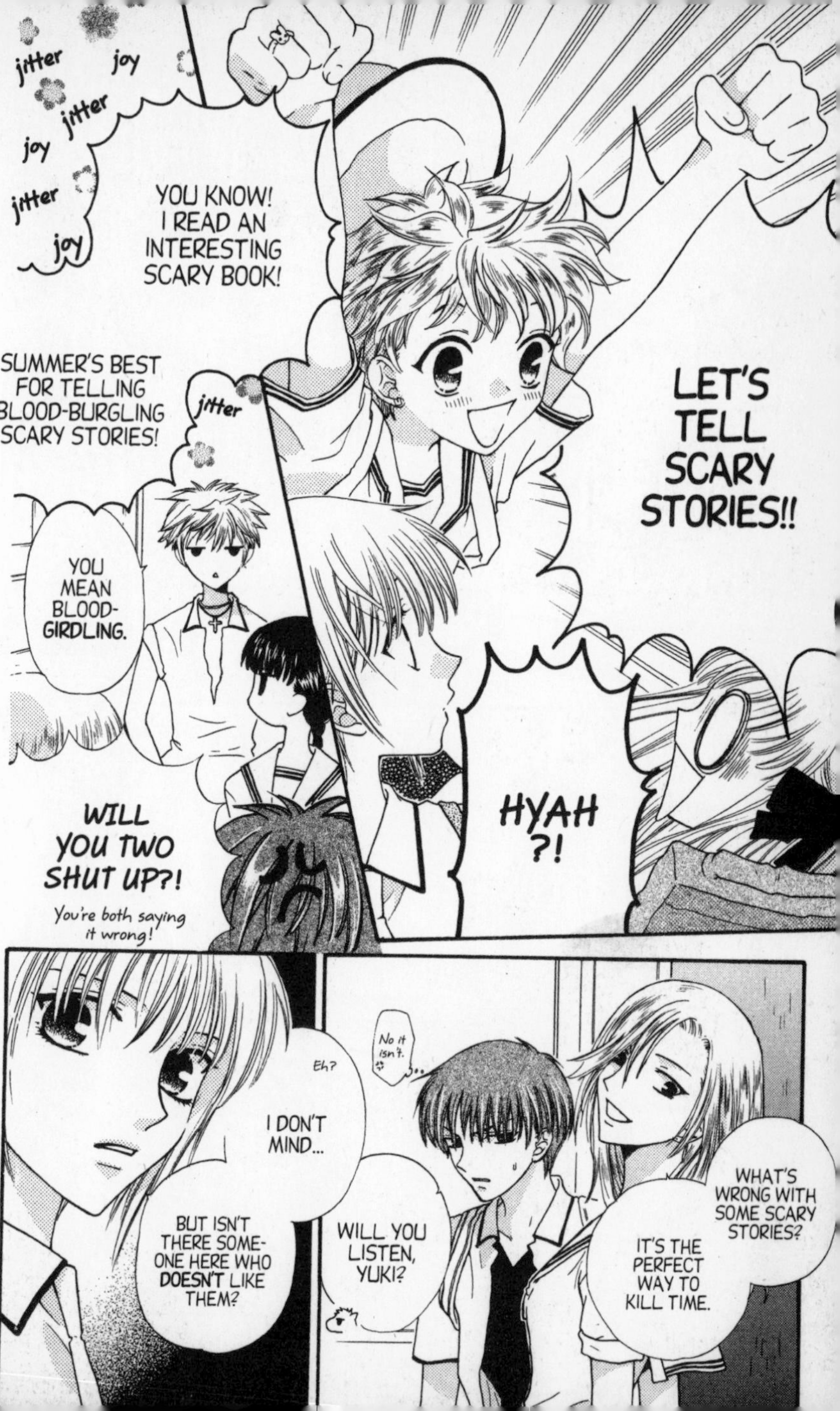
LET'S TELL SCARY STORIES!!
YOU KNOW! I READ AN INTERESTING SCARY BOOK!
jitter joy jitter joy jitter joy
SUMMER'S BEST FOR TELLING BLOOD-BURGLING SCARY STORIES!
jitter
YOU MEAN BLOOD-GIRDLING.
HYAH?!
WILL YOU TWO SHUT UP?!
You're both saying it wrong!
WHAT'S WRONG WITH SOME SCARY STORIES?
IT'S THE PERFECT WAY TO KILL TIME.
WILL YOU LISTEN, YUKI?
No it isn't...
Eh?
I DON'T MIND...
BUT ISN'T THERE SOME-ONE HERE WHO **DOESN'T** LIKE THEM?

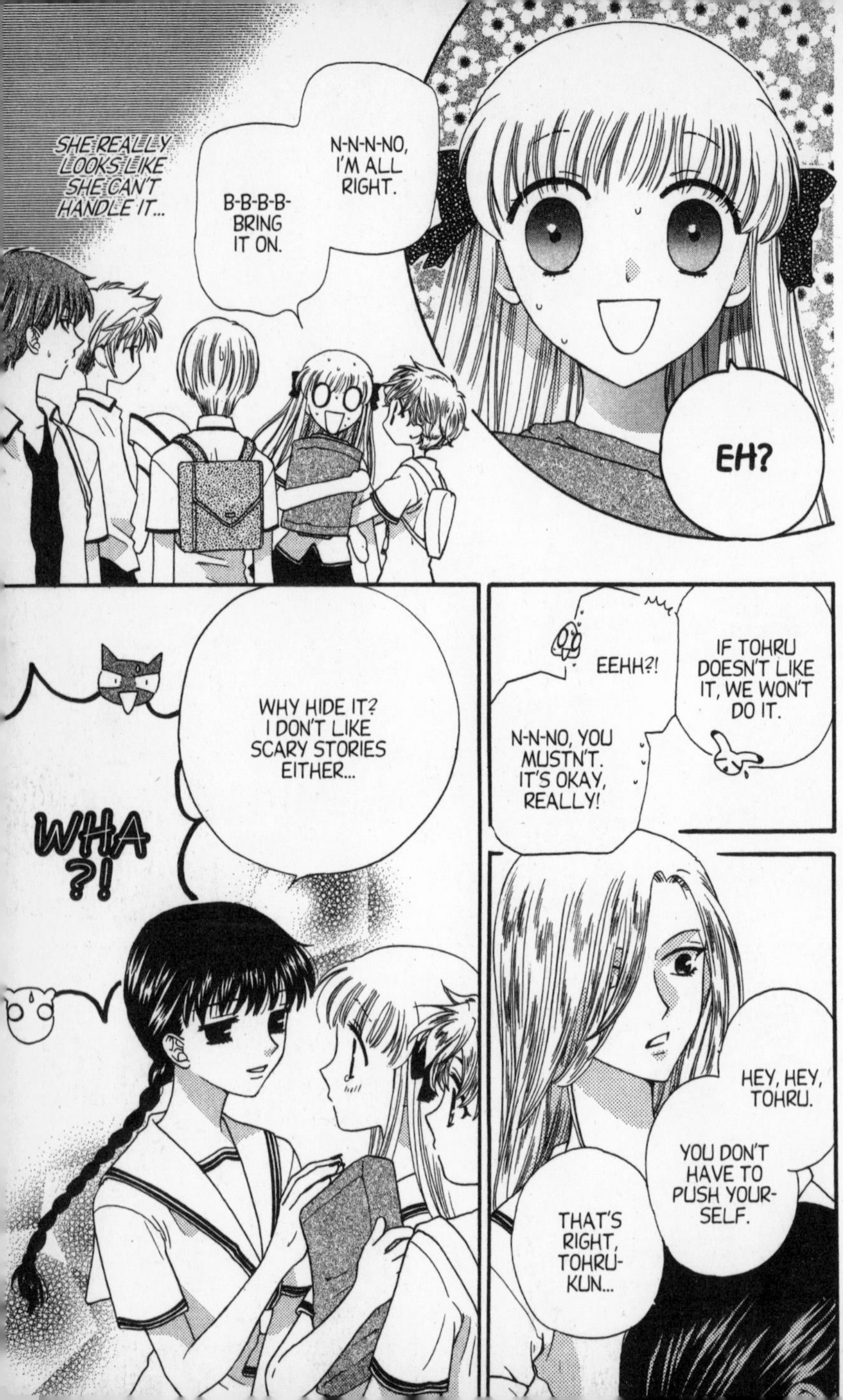
EH?
N-N-N-NO, I'M ALL RIGHT.
B-B-B-B-BRING IT ON.
SHE REALLY LOOKS LIKE SHE CAN'T HANDLE IT...
IF TOHRU DOESN'T LIKE IT, WE WON'T DO IT.
EEHH?!
N-N-NO, YOU MUSTN'T. IT'S OKAY, REALLY!
HEY, HEY, TOHRU.
YOU DON'T HAVE TO PUSH YOUR-SELF.
THAT'S RIGHT, TOHRU-KUN...
WHY HIDE IT? I DON'T LIKE SCARY STORIES EITHER...
WHA ?!

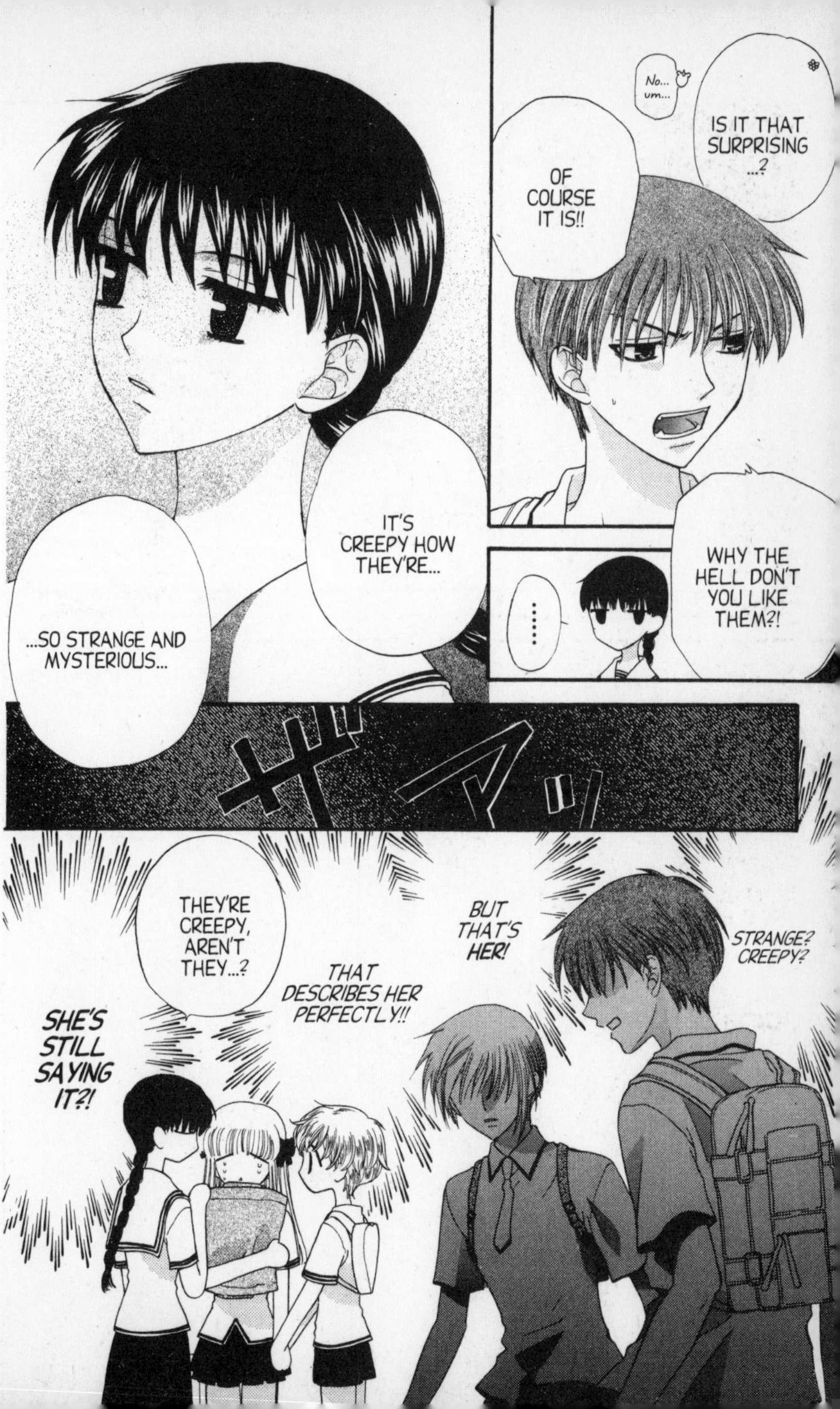
IS IT THAT SURPRISING ...?
No... um...
OF COURSE IT IS!!
WHY THE HELL DON'T YOU LIKE THEM?!
......
IT'S CREEPY HOW THEY'RE...
...SO STRANGE AND MYSTERIOUS...
STRANGE? CREEPY?
BUT THAT'S HER!
THAT DESCRIBES HER PERFECTLY!!
THEY'RE CREEPY, AREN'T THEY...?
SHE'S STILL SAYING IT?!

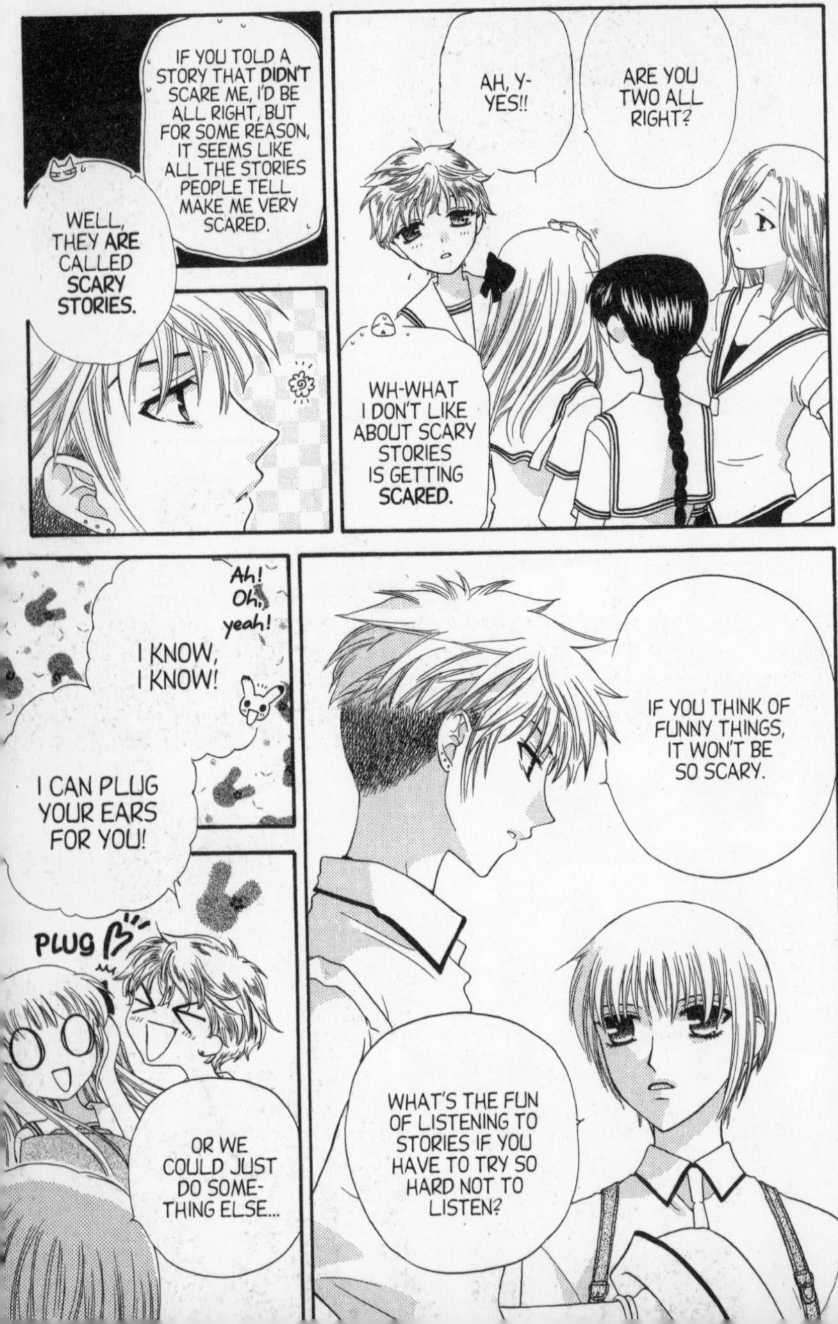
ARE YOU TWO ALL RIGHT?
AH, Y-YES!!
WH-WHAT I DON'T LIKE ABOUT SCARY STORIES IS GETTING **SCARED.**
IF YOU TOLD A STORY THAT **DIDN'T** SCARE ME, I'D BE ALL RIGHT, BUT FOR SOME REASON, IT SEEMS LIKE ALL THE STORIES PEOPLE TELL MAKE ME VERY SCARED.
WELL, THEY **ARE** CALLED **SCARY STORIES.**
IF YOU THINK OF FUNNY THINGS, IT WON'T BE SO SCARY.
WHAT'S THE FUN OF LISTENING TO STORIES IF YOU HAVE TO TRY SO HARD NOT TO LISTEN?
Ah! Oh, yeah!
I KNOW, I KNOW!
I CAN PLUG YOUR EARS FOR YOU!
PLUG
OR WE COULD JUST DO SOME-THING ELSE...

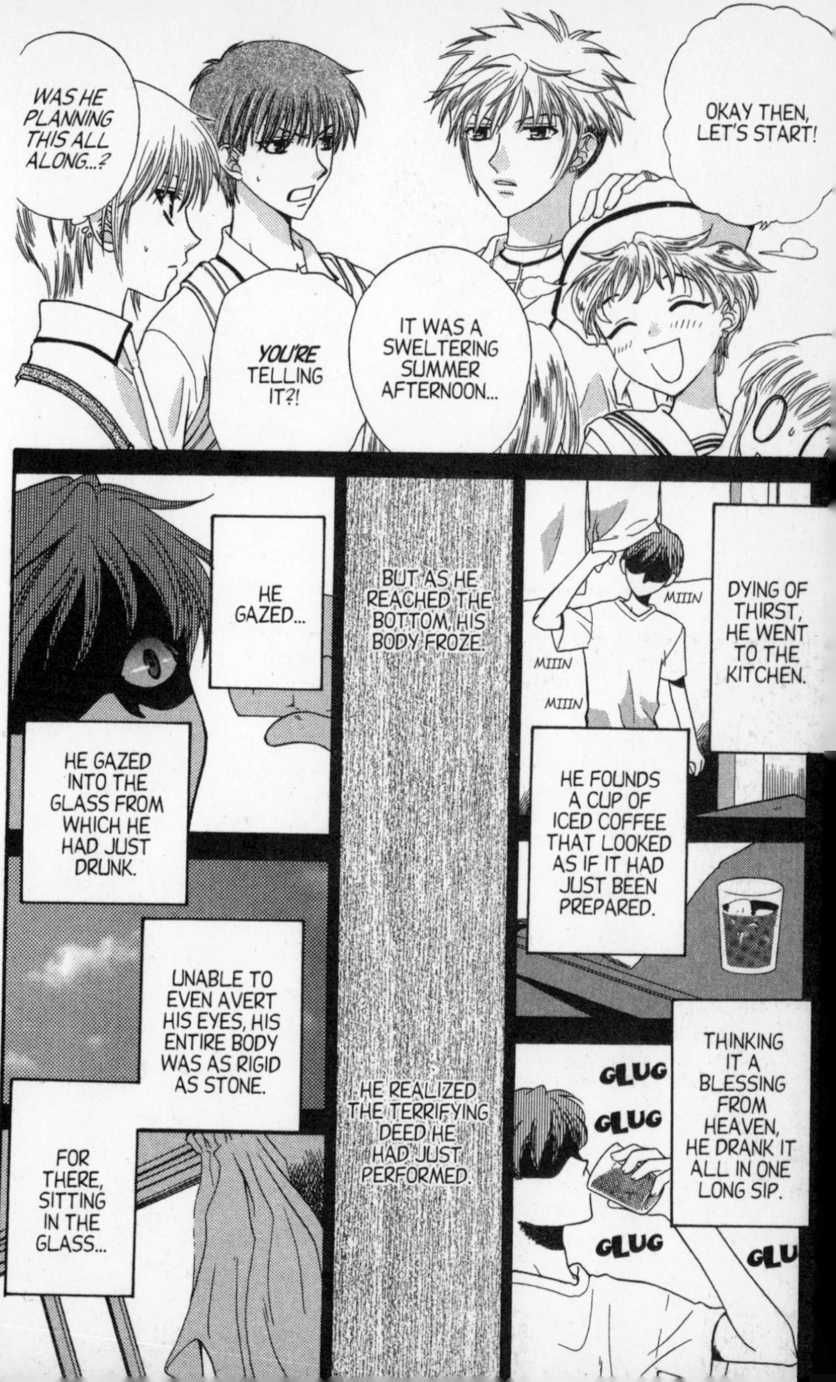

OKAY THEN, LET'S START!
IT WAS A SWELTERING SUMMER AFTERNOON...
YOU'RE TELLING IT?!
WAS HE PLANNING THIS ALL ALONG...?
DYING OF THIRST, HE WENT TO THE KITCHEN.
MIIIN
MIIIN
MIIIN
HE FOUNDS A CUP OF ICED COFFEE THAT LOOKED AS IF IT HAD JUST BEEN PREPARED.
THINKING IT A BLESSING FROM HEAVEN, HE DRANK IT ALL IN ONE LONG SIP.
GLUG
GLUG
GLU
GLUG
BUT AS HE REACHED THE BOTTOM, HIS BODY FROZE.
HE REALIZED THE TERRIFYING DEED HE HAD JUST PERFORMED.
HE GAZED...
HE GAZED INTO THE GLASS FROM WHICH HE HAD JUST DRUNK.
UNABLE TO EVEN AVERT HIS EYES, HIS ENTIRE BODY WAS AS RIGID AS STONE.
FOR THERE, SITTING IN THE GLASS...

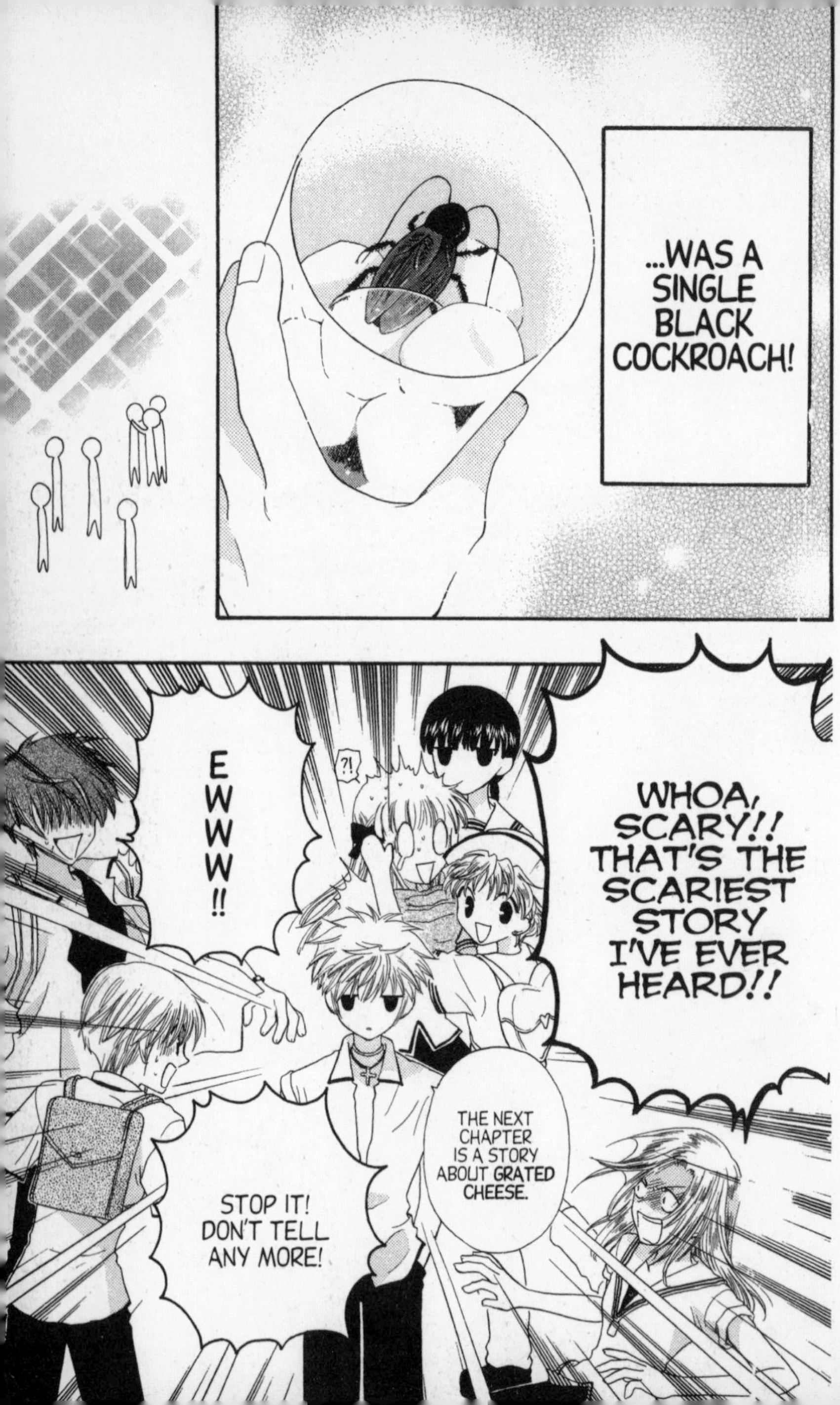
...WAS A SINGLE BLACK COCKROACH!
WHOA, SCARY!! THAT'S THE SCARIEST STORY I'VE EVER HEARD!!
?!
EWWWW!!
THE NEXT CHAPTER IS A STORY ABOUT GRATED CHEESE.
STOP IT! DON'T TELL ANY MORE!

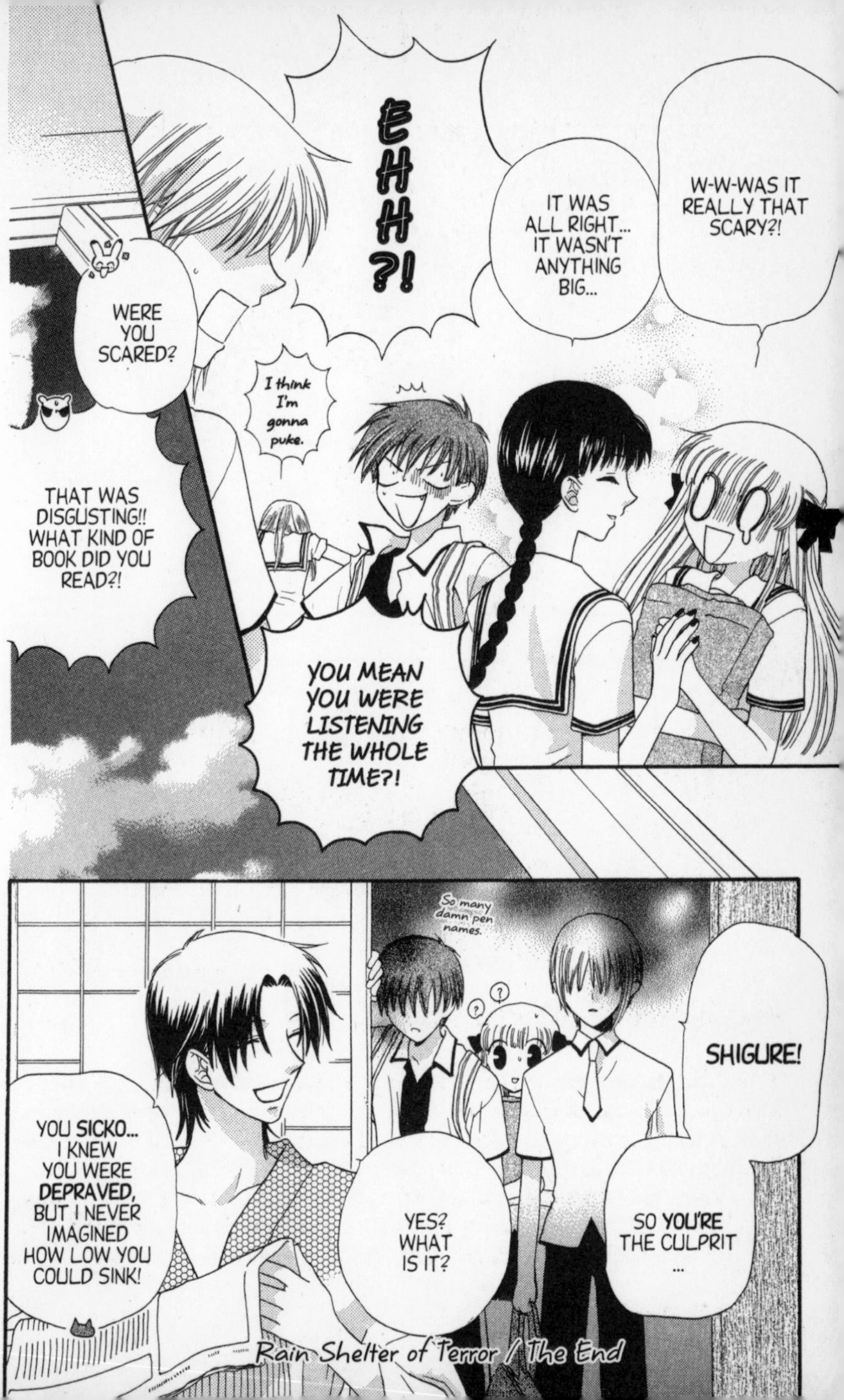
W-W-WAS IT REALLY THAT SCARY?!
IT WAS ALL RIGHT... IT WASN'T ANYTHING BIG...
EHHH?!
WERE YOU SCARED?
I think I'm gonna puke.
THAT WAS DISGUSTING!! WHAT KIND OF BOOK DID YOU READ?!
YOU MEAN YOU WERE LISTENING THE WHOLE TIME?!
SHIGURE!
So many damn pen names.
SO YOU'RE THE CULPRIT ...
YES? WHAT IS IT?
YOU SICKO... I KNEW YOU WERE DEPRAVED, BUT I NEVER IMAGINED HOW LOW YOU COULD SINK!
Rain Shelter of Terror / The End

Next time in...

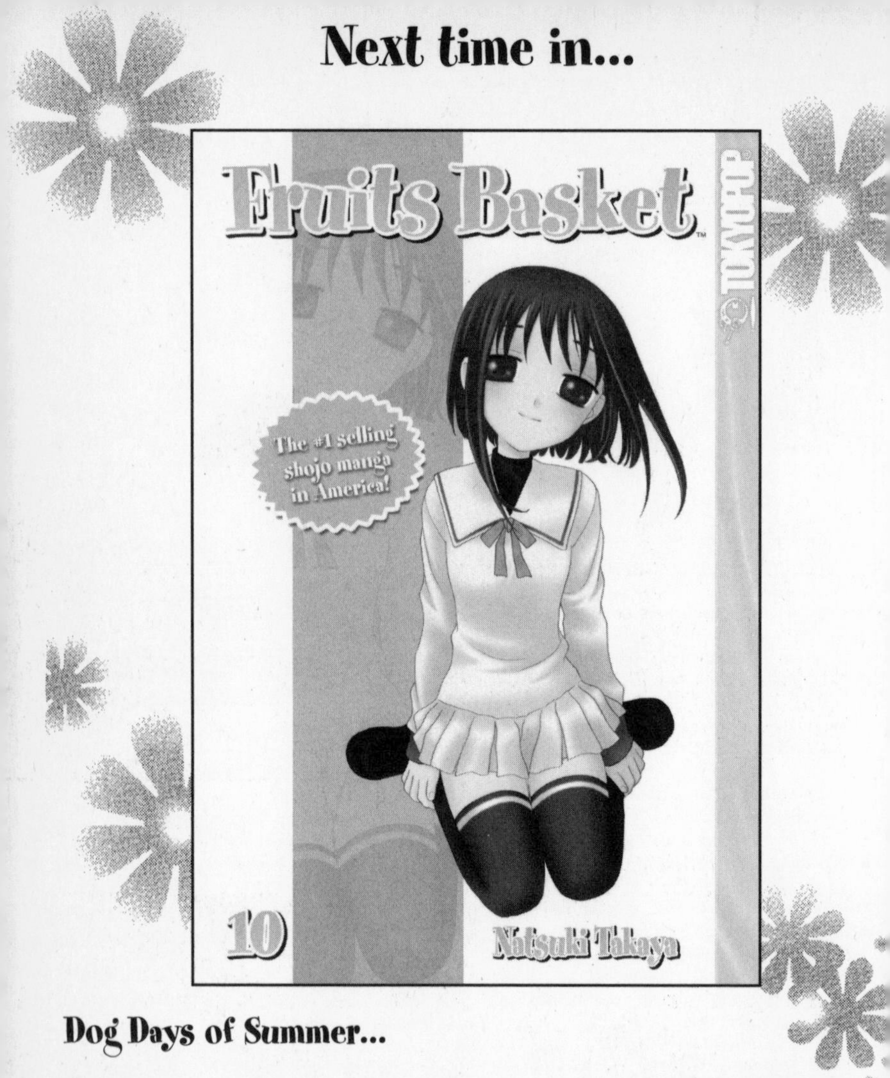
Fruits Basket
TOKYOPOP
The #1 selling shojo manga in America!
10
Natsuki Takaya

Dog Days of Summer...

Tohru and the Sohmas are spending time at the Sohma family's summerhouse, but it's not all fun in the sun on this little trip. Akito pays a surprise visit, causing a commotion for the rest of the family. At the summer house. Shigure takes a trip down memory lane with an old friend, remembering the days when Hatori wasn't so aloof. Meanwhile, Tohru starts thinking--what must life be like for the parents and lovers of a cursed member of the Sohma family? Can life with this family truly be happy while bearing such a burden?

Fruits Basket Volume 10
Available July 2005

Year of the Snake: Slithery Narcissism

Snake

Years*: 1941, 1953, 1965, 1977, 1989, 2001, 2013, 2025, 2037
Qualities: Romantic, Clever, Discreet, Refined, Intelligent
Grievances: Vain, Procrastinator, Hot-Tempered
Suitable Jobs: Teacher, Philosopher, Writer, Psychiatrist, Fortune Teller
Compatible With: Ox, Rooster
Must Avoid: Boar
Ruling Hours: 9 AM to 11 AM
Season: Spring
Ruling Month: May
Sign Direction: South-Southwest
Fixed Element: Fire
Corresponding Western Sign: Taurus

Throughout the ages, Snakes have gotten the short end of the stick and made out to be villains like the Great Kaa in The Jungle Book or the fabled serpent in the Garden of Eden. However, the Chinese Zodiac sees any negative traits in the Snake as it would any of the other animal's dual natures--as yin and yang.

A person born in the Year of the Snake is endowed with great wisdom and even greater beauty. Like Ayame Sohma, fellow Snakes are very sure of themselves, but also incredibly vain and they like to flaunt what they have. Money comes easily for a Snake, but try to get a Snake to loan a friend a few bucks and their stingy nature rears its ugly head. The key to getting Snakes to crack open their wallet is to catch their sympathy. If they see someone that is in need or less fortunate than they are, then they collapse like a house of cards.

Snakes tend to overdo it when it comes to their jobs and prefer to control rather than lead. This is mainly due to Snakes always striving for the limelight. Though heartless at times, Snakes choose their words very carefully and speak them in a listless, yet cautious manner. Depending on the situation and the amount of pressure placed upon them, Snakes will either try to lighten up an atmosphere with jokes or emit an icy exterior to stare down the grim tidings.

Women born under this sign are very quiet and serene individuals, but mainly because they prefer to let their appearance do the talking. Female Snakes prefer to dress to impress and only wear the finest in clothing and jewelry. Friends are also chosen with a Snake's own self as the key frame of reference as they prefer to gravitate towards those who are like-minded and trustworthy. Best of all, relationships with Snakes are always filled with passion and romance.

Celebrity Snakes:
James Van Der Beek
Kim Basinger
Björk
Sarah Michelle Gellar
Ludacris
Chris Martin
John Mayer
Tom Welling

* Note: It is important to know what day Chinese New Year's was held on as that changes what Zodiac animal you are. Example: 1989 actually began on February 6 and anyone born before that date is actually a Dragon.

Fans Basket

This is your friendly, fuzzy-headed Fruits Basket editor, Paul Morrissey, once again presenting amazing fan art from our cadre of addicted readers! Enjoy--I know I do!

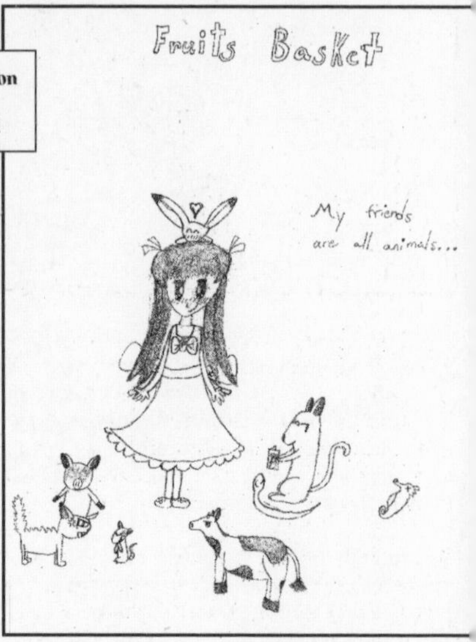
Fruits Basket
My friends are all animals...

Kelly Davidson
Age 9
Salem, OR

Not many kids as young as Kelly send fan art, so I was thrilled to include her sketch. By the way, Kelly, Momiji is my favorite character, too! Keep drawing, Kelly, and keep reading *Fruits Basket!*

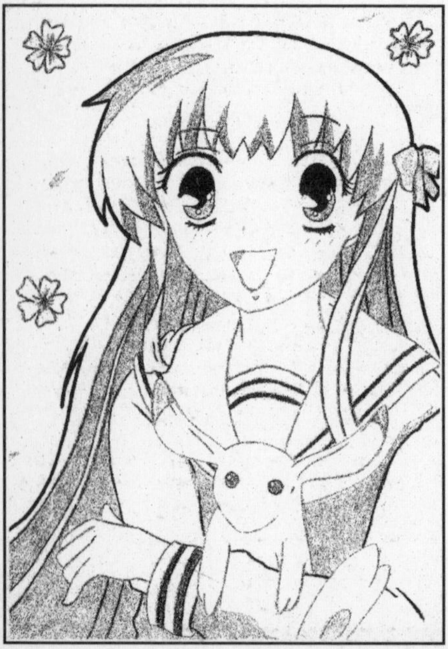

Ciara C.
Age 13
Galway, Ireland

Ciara sent this all the way from the Emerald Isle, and I think her drawing of Tohru and Momiji is a true gem!

Kate Sherron
Age 21
St. Louis, MO

Kate's illustration is so stunningly intricate! It's bold, it's original, and it's way cool!

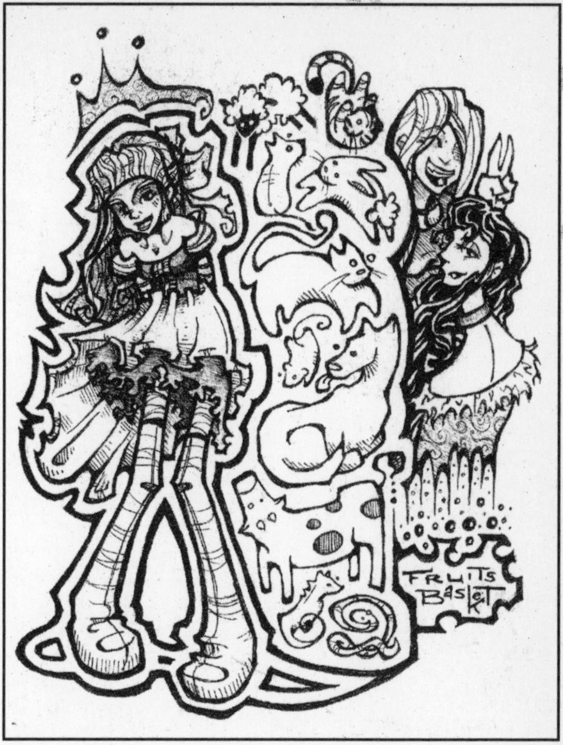
FRUITS BASKET
K

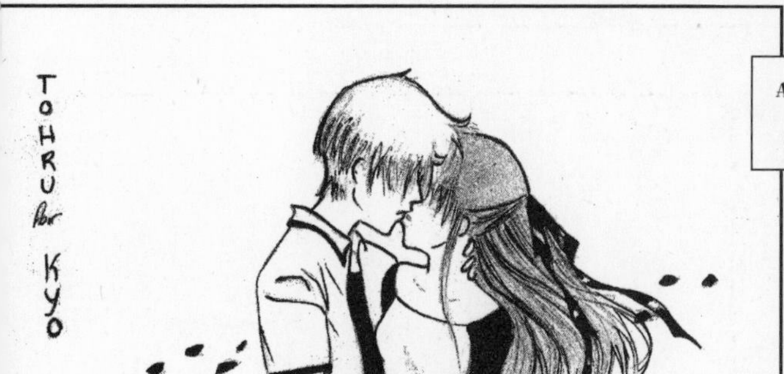
TOHRU por KYO

Ambar Quintero
Age 13
Somerton, AZ

Here's a lovely piece of wish fulfillment! What a wonderful kiss. Just don't hug him, Tohru, or you'll get cat scratch fever!

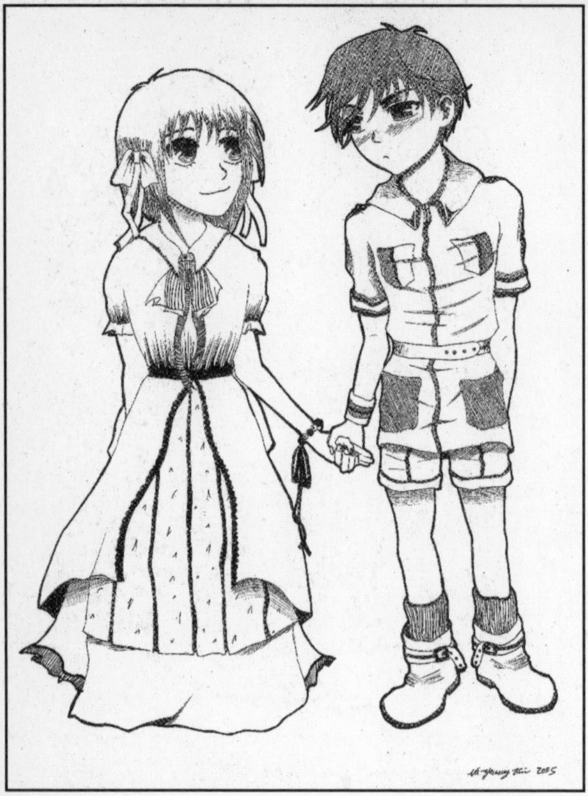

Na-young Kim
Age 16
Spout Spring, VA

I love it when readers submit fan art in their own, unique style. Thanks for the fabulous drawing, Na-young!

Meredith Bray
Age 13
Madison, WI

Kyo looks soooo adorable in this picture, Meredith. He's all squirmy and squirrelly, but I bet deep down, he's really enjoying being force-cuddled! Oh--and Meredith is from my hometown!!

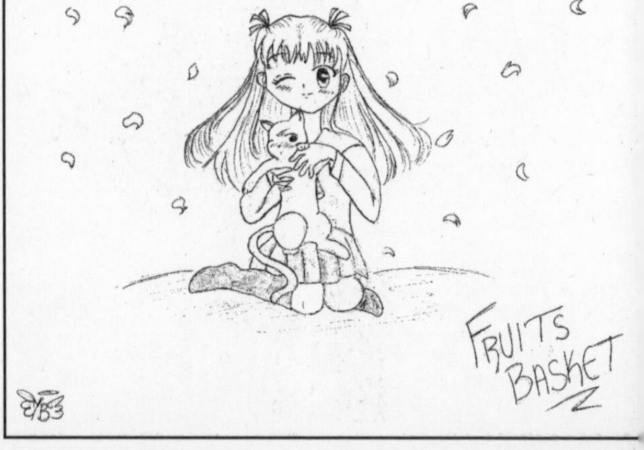
FRUITS BASKET

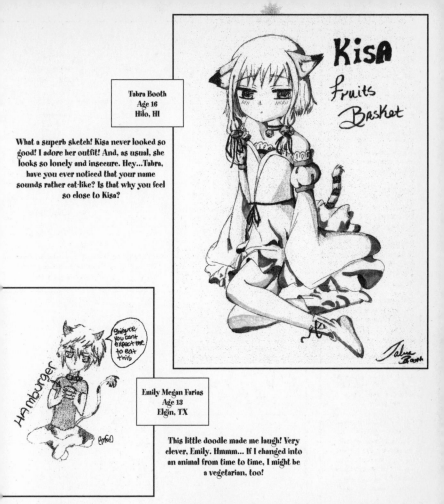

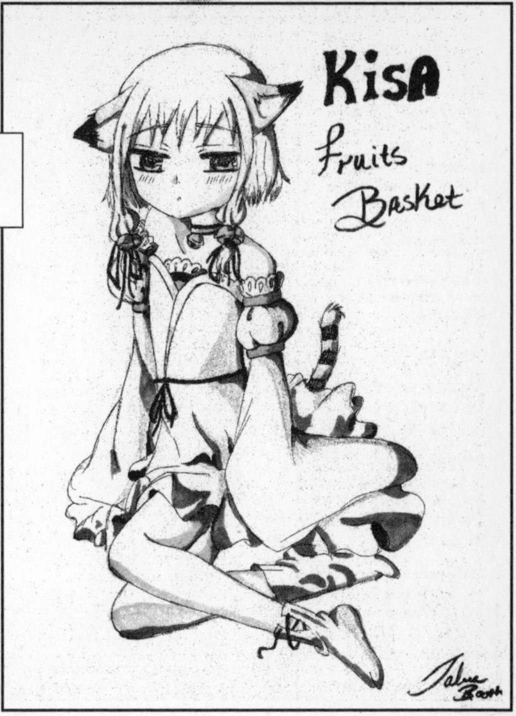
Kisa
Fruits Basket

Tabra Booth
Age 16
Hilo, HI

What a superb sketch! Kisa never looked so good! I adore her outfit! And, as usual, she looks so lonely and insecure. Hey...Tabra, have you ever noticed that your name sounds rather cat-like? Is that why you feel so close to Kisa?

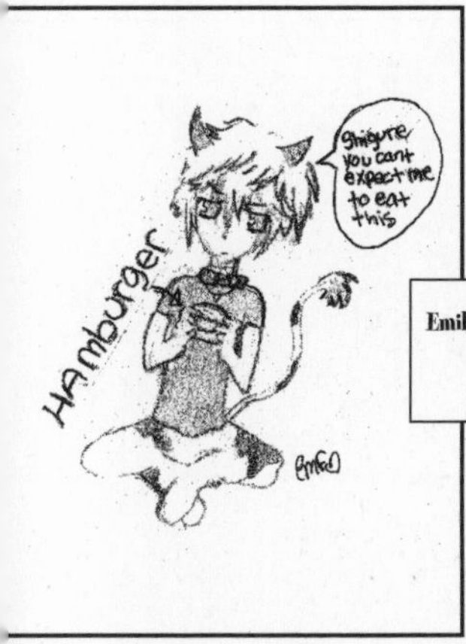
Shigure you can't expect me to eat this
HAmburger

Emily Megan Farias
Age 13
Elgin, TX

This little doodle made me laugh! Very clever, Emily. Hmmm... If I changed into an animal from time to time, I might be a vegetarian, too!

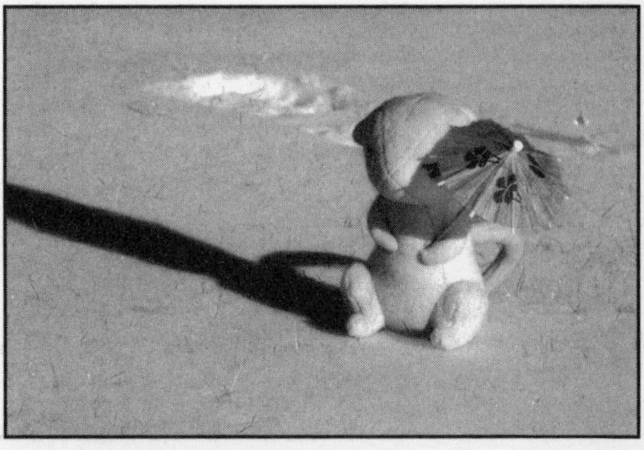

Karen Herrmann
Age 14
Commerce, CA

Wow! What can I say? This is probably my favorite piece of fan art ever! Ingeniously creative! By the way, Karen entitled this photograph "Yuki and Snow."

Do you want to share your love for *Fruits Basket* with fans around the world? "Fans Basket" is taking submissions of fan art, poetry, cosplay photos, or any other Furuba fun you'd like to share!

How to submit:

1) Send your work via regular mail (NOT e-mail) to:

"Fans Basket"
c/o TOKYOPOP
5900 Wilshire Blvd.
Suite 2000
Los Angeles, CA 90036

2) All work should be in black-and-white and no larger than 8.5" x 11". (And try not to fold it too many times!)

3) Anything you send will not be returned. If you want to keep your original, it's fine to send us a copy.

4) Please include your full name, age, city and state for us to print with your work. If you'd rather us use a pen name, please include that, too.

5) IMPORTANT: If you're under the age of 18, you must have your parent's permission in order for us to print your work. Any submissions without a signed note of parental consent cannot be used.

6) For full details, please check out our web-site: http://www.tokyopop.com/aboutus/fanart.php

Disclaimer: Anything you send to us becomes the exclusive property of TOKYOPOP Inc. and, as we said before, will not be returned to you. We will have the right to print, reproduce, distribute, or modify the artwork for use in future volumes of Fruits Basket or on the web royalty-free.

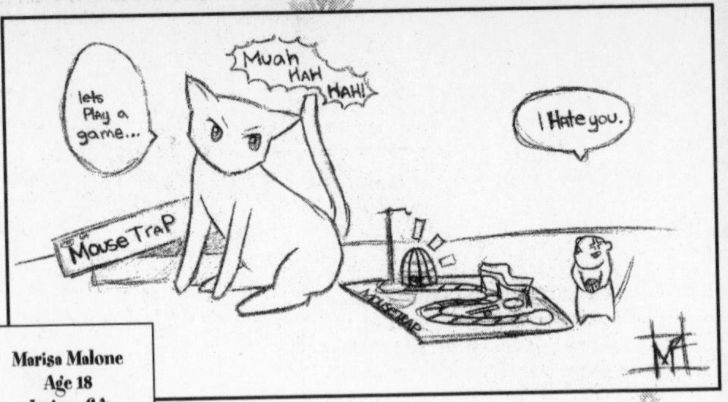

lets Play a game...
Muah HAH HAH!
I Hate you.
Mouse TraP
MOUSETRAP

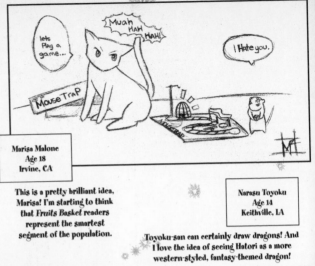

Marisa Malone
Age 18
Irvine, CA

This is a pretty brilliant idea, Marisa! I'm starting to think that *Fruits Basket* readers represent the smartest segment of the population.

Narasu Toyoku
Age 14
Keithville, LA

Toyoku-san can certainly draw dragons! And I love the idea of seeing Hatori as a more western-styled, fantasy-themed dragon!

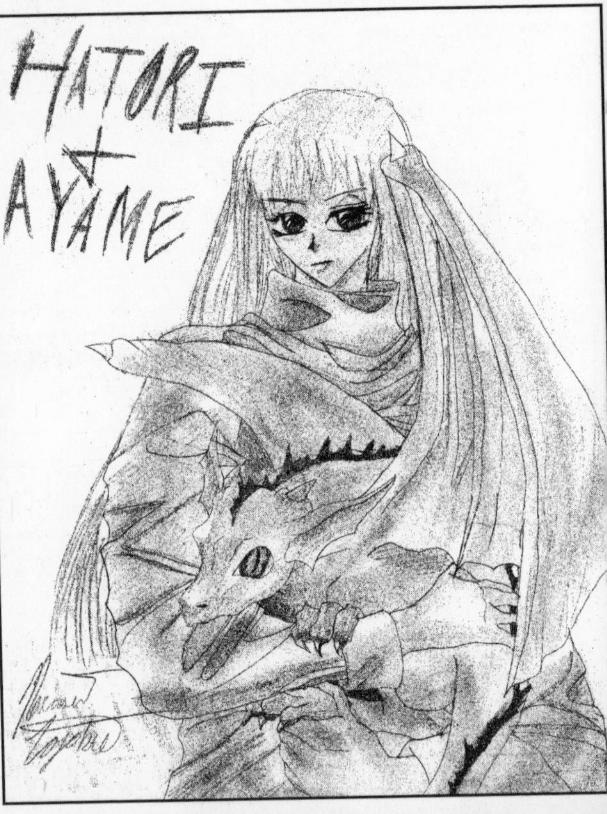

HATORI + AYAME

TOKYOPOP SHOP

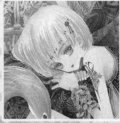
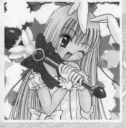

BECK: MONGOLIAN CHOP SQUAD

OT
OLDER TEEN
AGE 16+

ROCK IN MANGA!

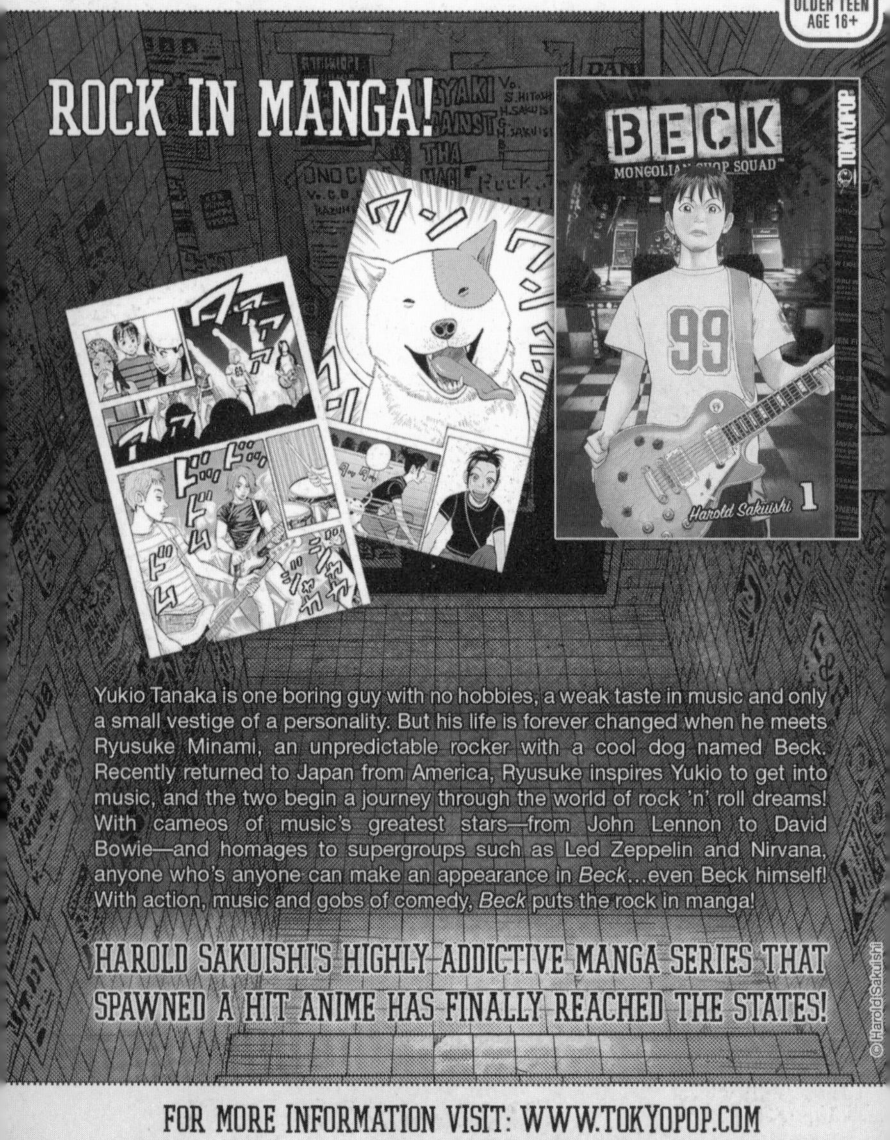
BECK
MONGOLIAN CHOP SQUAD
TOKYOPOP
Harold Sakuishi
1

Yukio Tanaka is one boring guy with no hobbies, a weak taste in music and only a small vestige of a personality. But his life is forever changed when he meets Ryusuke Minami, an unpredictable rocker with a cool dog named Beck. Recently returned to Japan from America, Ryusuke inspires Yukio to get into music, and the two begin a journey through the world of rock 'n' roll dreams! With cameos of music's greatest stars—from John Lennon to David Bowie—and homages to supergroups such as Led Zeppelin and Nirvana, anyone who's anyone can make an appearance in *Beck*...even Beck himself! With action, music and gobs of comedy, *Beck* puts the rock in manga!

HAROLD SAKUISHI'S HIGHLY ADDICTIVE MANGA SERIES THAT SPAWNED A HIT ANIME HAS FINALLY REACHED THE STATES!

FOR MORE INFORMATION VISIT: WWW.TOKYOPOP.COM

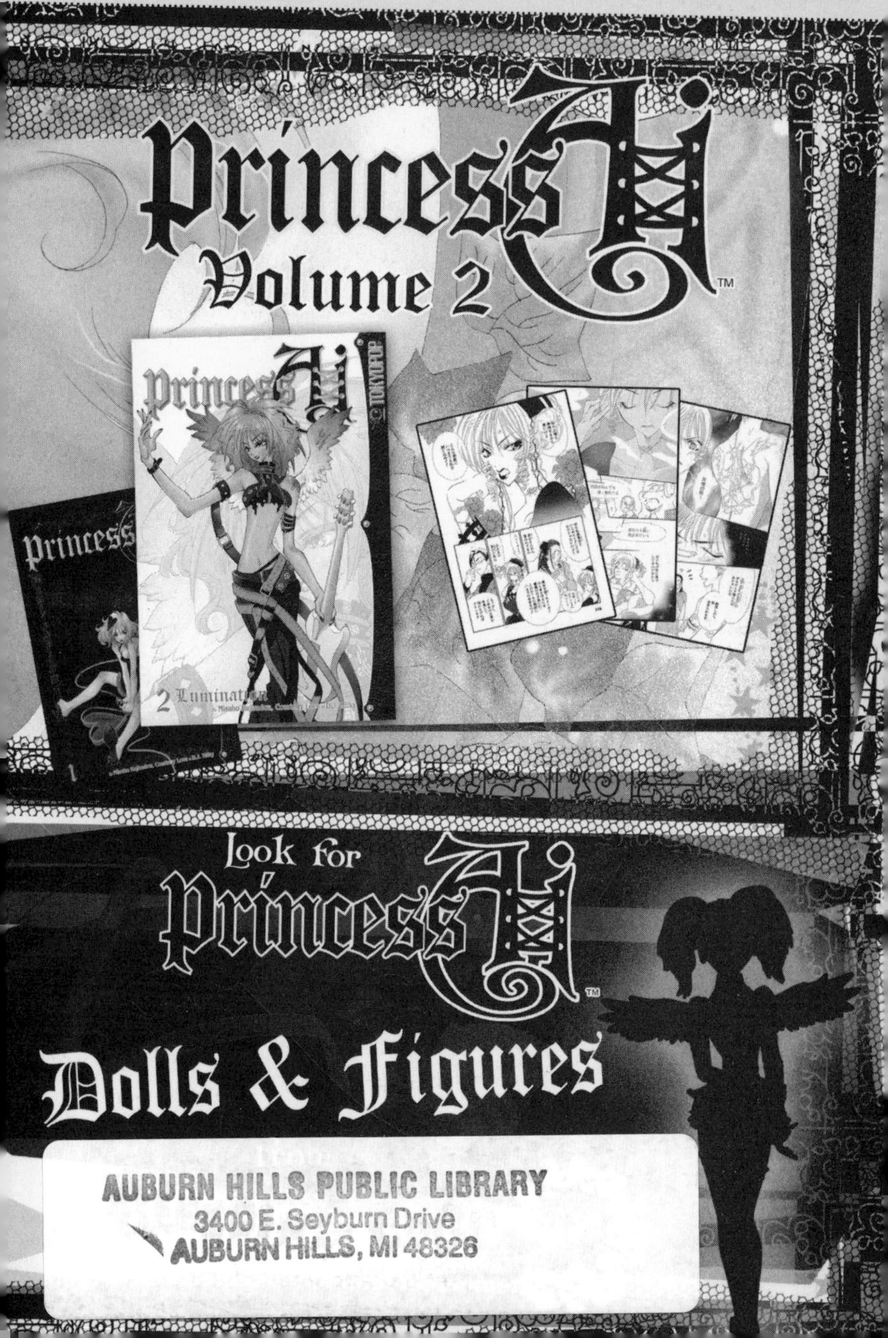
Princess Ai™
Volume 2
Look for Princess Ai™
Dolls & Figures

A Diva Torn from Chaos
A Savior Doomed to Love

Volume 2
Lumination

Ai continues to search for her place in our world on the streets of Tokyo. Using her talent to support herself, Ai signs a contract with a top record label and begins her rise to stardom. But fame is unpredictable—as her talent blooms, all eyes are on Ai. When scandal surfaces, will she burn out in the spotlight of celebrity?

T
TEEN
AGE 13+

Preview the manga at:
www.TOKYOPOP.com/princessai

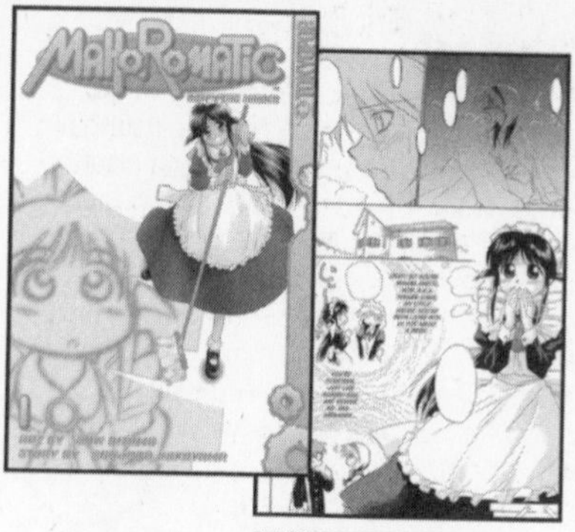
MAHOROMATIC

BY BUNJURO NAKAYAMA AND BOW DITAMA

MAHOROMATIC: AUTOMATIC MAIDEN

Mahoro is a sweet, cute, female battle android who decides to go from mopping up alien invaders to mopping up after Suguru Misato, a teenaged orphan boy... and hilarity most definitely ensues. This series has great art and a slick story that easily switches from truly funny to downright heartwarming...but always with a large shadow looming over it. You see, only Mahoro knows that her days are quite literally numbered, and the end of each chapter lets you know exactly how much—or how little—time she has left!

~Rob Tokar, Sr. Editor

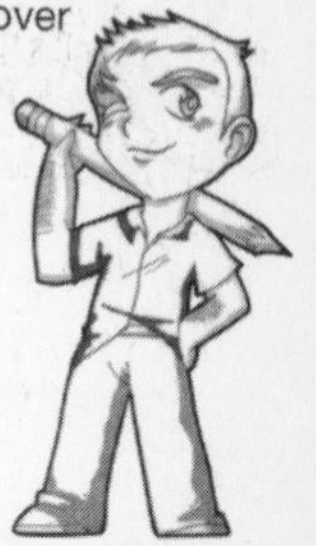

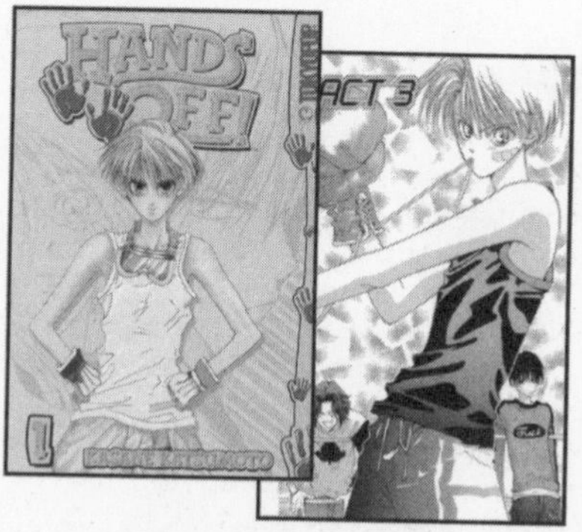
HANDS OFF!
ACT 3

BY KASANE KATSUMOTO

HANDS OFF!

Cute boys with ESP who share a special bond... If you think this is familiar (e.g. *Legal Drug*), well, you're wrong. *Hands Off!* totally stands alone as a unique and thoroughly enjoyable series. Kotarou and Tatsuki's (platonic!) relationship is complex, fascinating and heart-wrenching. Throw in Yuuto, the playboy who can read auras, and you've got a fantastic setup for drama and comedy, with incredible themes of friendship running throughout. Don't be put off by Kotarou's danger-magnet status, either. The episodic stuff gradually changes, and the full arc of the characters' development is well worth waiting for.

~Lillian Diaz-Przybyl, Jr. Editor

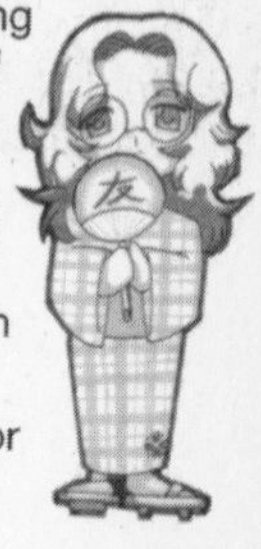

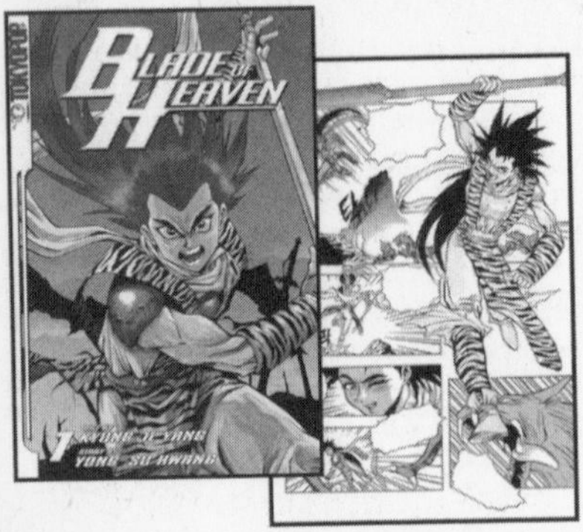
Blade of Heaven
TOKYOPOP

BY YONG-SU HWANG AND KYUNG-IL YANG

BLADE OF HEAVEN

Wildly popular in its homeland of Korea, *Blade of Heaven* enjoys the rare distinction of not only being a hit in its own country, but in Japan and several other countries, as well. On the surface, Yong-Su Hwang and Kyung-Il Yang's fantasy-adventure may look like yet another "Heaven vs. Demons" sword opera, but the story of the mischievous Soma, a pawn caught in a struggle of mythic proportions, is filled with so much humor, pathos, imagination—and yes, action, that it's easy to see why *Blade of Heaven* has been so popular worldwide.

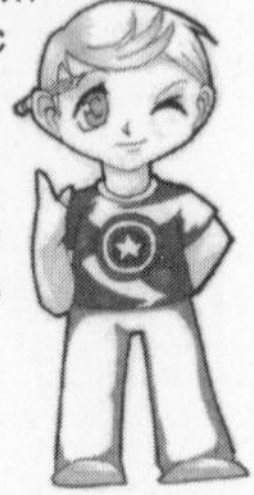

~Bryce P. Coleman, Editor

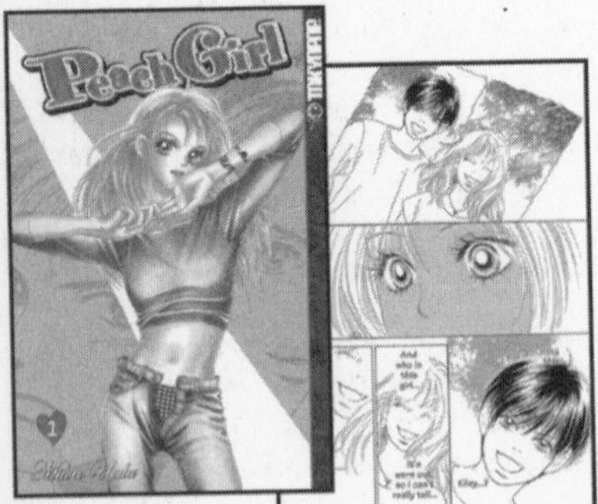
Peach Girl
1

BY MIWA UEDA

PEACH GIRL

Am I the only person who thinks that *Peach Girl* is just like *The O.C.*? Just imagine Ryan as Toji, Seth as Kiley, Marissa as Momo and Summer as Sae. (The similarities are almost spooky!) Plus, Seth is way into comics and manga—and I'm sure he'd love *Peach Girl*. It has everything that my favorite TV show has and then some—drama, intrigue, romance and lots of will-they-or-won't-they suspense. I love it! *Peach Girl* rules, seriously. If you haven't read it, do so. Now.

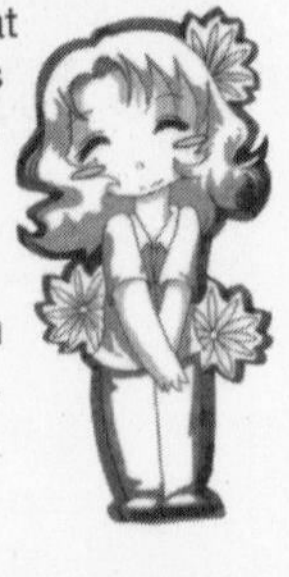

~Julie Taylor, Sr. Editor

ARCANA
BY SO-YOUNG LEE

Inez is a young orphan girl with the ability to communicate with living creatures of all kinds. She is the chosen one, and a great destiny awaits her! Inez must bring back the guardian dragon to protect her country's fragile peace from the onslaught of a destructive demon race.

From the creator of TOKYOPOP's *Model* comes an epic fantasy quest filled with wizards, dragons, deception and adventure beyond your wildest imagination.

© SO-YOUNG LEE, DAIWON C.I. Inc.

DEAD END
BY SHOHEI MANABE

When Shirou's memory is suddenly erased and his friends are brutally murdered, he is forced to piece together clues to solve a shocking and spectacular puzzle. As we follow Shirou's journey, paranoia assumes an air of calm rationality and the line between tormenter and prey is often blurred.

© Shohei Manabe

TOKYO MEW MEW A LA MODE
BY MIA IKUMI AND REIKO TOSHIDA

The cats are back, and a new Mew emerges—the first Mew Mew with *two* sets of animal genes. Half cat, half rabbit, Berry joins the Mew Mew team just in time: a new gang is about to appear, and its leader loves wild game like rabbit—well done and served for dinner!

The highly anticipated sequel to *Tokyo Mew Mew* (*Mew Mew Power* as seen on TV)!

© Mia Ikumi and Kodansha

STOP!

This is the back of the book. You wouldn't want to spoil a great ending!

This book is printed "manga-style," in the authentic Japanese right-to-left format. Since none of the artwork has been flipped or altered, readers get to experience the story just as the creator intended. You've been asking for it, so TOKYOPOP® delivered: authentic, hot-off-the-press, and far more fun!

DIRECTIONS

If this is your first time reading manga-style, here's a quick guide to help you understand how it works.

It's easy... just start in the top right panel and follow the numbers. Have fun, and look for more 100% authentic manga from TOKYOPOP®!

50